EVOLUTION AND CONSCIOUSNESS:

The Role of Speech in the Origin and Development of Human Nature

EVOLUTION AND CONSCIOUSNESS:

The Role of Speech in the Origin and Development of Human Nature

Leslie Dewart

UNIVERSITY OF TORONTO PRESS

Toronto Buffalo London

© University of Toronto Press 1989
Toronto Buffalo London
Printed in Canada

ISBN 0-8020-2690-7

Printed on acid free paper

Canadian Cataloguing in Publication Data

Dewart, Leslie, 1922–
Evolution and consciousness

Includes index.
ISBN 0-8020-2690-7

1. Man. 2. Human evolution – Philosophy.
3. Speech. 4. Consciousness. I. Title.

B818.D48 1989   128   c88-094885-x

For
Doreen Brennan Dewart

Carior carissimae

Contents

Prefatory Note

Very few of the observations and concepts I have used in this investigation are original; indeed, most are not even new. What I have tried to accomplish here – the sort of task that philosophy had always deemed among its chief responsibilities, though in the anglophone world as I gather no longer – is mainly to arrange a large number of tesserae that, if taken one by one, are very familiar, into the single mosaic of a fairly comprehensive and unconventional philosophical synthesis. I would have liked, therefore, to acknowledge all the sources of stimulation on which I have depended, and to explain how I have turned the contributions of many to my own recusant purposes. To have done so, however, would have raised a cloud of minor distractions; for instance, I would have had to discuss the difference between the original and my own version of the ideas I have borrowed. And in a book as long as this one it would have been unwise to take even a modest amount of additional space to do so. I will nevertheless temper my single-mindedness, if only to the niggardly extent of barely mentioning that Marshall McLuhan was among those whose work I have mined. I remain, of course, solely responsible for my conclusions, just as I distinguish between the metal of McLuhan's thought and what I consider to be dross; but I would like to think that in my central hypothesis he might have recognized a possible application of his valuable insight into the relation between the form of human communications and their content.

A research grant from the Canada Council enabled me to conduct field-research in Java on the relationship between Indonesian speech and world- and self-perception. This work is, in considerable part, an outgrowth of that project. Grants-in-aid from the Humanities and Social Science Committee of the Research Board of the University of Toronto and from the Faculty of Arts of the same university assisted me in the preparation of the manuscript. My association with the University of Toronto Press, whose staff I have invariably found most helpful, understanding, and accommodating, has been an extraordinarily happy one. This book has been published with the help of a grant from the Canadian Federation for the Humanities, using funds provided by the Social Sciences and Humanities Research Council of Canada. I wish to acknowledge my debt and express my gratitude to all of these.

PART ONE

Prologue

The creativity and pathology of the human mind are, after all, two sides of the same medal coined in the evolutionary mint. The first is responsible for the splendour of our cathedrals, the second for the gargoyles that decorate them to remind us that the world is full of monsters, devils and succubi. They reflect the streak of insanity which runs through the history of our species, and which indicates that somewhere along the line of its ascent to prominence something has gone wrong.

Arthur Koestler

CHAPTER ONE

The philosophic question
of the origin and development
# of human nature

The purpose of this inquiry is to develop a philosophic theory of the origin and the subsequent prehistoric development of the specifically human characteristics of human beings. No justification need be offered for pursuing this objective. Not only would it respond to a seemingly innate curiosity about our beginnings – part of our natural desire to establish our identity – but it should be useful in other respects as well. If we understood sufficiently well how human nature came into being, we would have mastered why the conditions of human life today are such as they are – which would, of course, facilitate our improving them. Undertaking to investigate the matter anew, however, and under philosophic auspices, implies what is much less obvious: that the explanations of human evolution devised so far by science are neither as satisfactory nor as useful as they might be, and that philosophy might help remedy those defects. It also assumes that the few attempts of philosophy to exercise its jurisdiction on the subject have likewise been wanting; but the latter issue bears much less discussion than the former and will be summarily disposed of.

Philosophic explanations of human evolution have usually depended on the postulation of some sort of evolutionary force that either fuelled the development of life from within, as it were, or else attracted it from ahead or directed it from above. Such assumptions, however, have rendered these theories incompatible with the concept of *natural selection*, the enduring contribution of Charles Darwin's[1] *The Origin of Species*,

---

1 Darwin's own conception of natural selection was 'crude': George Gaylord Simpson, *The Meaning of Evolution* (New Haven, CT, 1949), p. 223. Here I attribute to him refinements made by others later. This historical inaccuracy is not important in the present context, and is justified for the sake of brevity.

published in 1859. Most scientists have therefore dismissed them – justifiably, because the essential aspect of natural selection rests on empirically firm ground. Many details of its operation remain obscure or are moot, but its solid basis is the observation that the characteristics transmitted to offspring differ in the degree to which, given the conditions prevailing in the environment, they enable the organism to survive until it reaches reproductive age. But this means that those characteristics that enhance the organism's chances of survival are, for that very reason, likely to continue to be transmitted from generation to generation. As they accumulate, then, the species changes; a new form of life appears, embodying a particular way in which organisms can be adaptively related to their world. The unfavourable characteristics, in contrast, tend to be self-eliminating, since they render the organism less likely to survive until it reproduces itself. Natural selection is thus nothing but the effect of the interaction between the adaptive and the reproductive functions of organisms.

If this, however, is how evolution comes about – if this interrelation is the *cause* of the transformation of species – then the supposition of evolutionary forces is superfluous. This is true of even purely natural forces inhering in living organisms, such as Hans Driesch's 'entelechy' and Henri Bergson's '*élan vital*,' let alone extraneous, supernatural ones. Indeed, the opinion may be ventured that one of the most significant and original aspects of the concept of natural selection – Darwin himself does not seem to have realized it, and even today few have remarked upon it – was that for the first time in the history of Western thought a causal explanation had been advanced that required the presumption of no force whatever. It was, therefore, the kind of theory that responded to the concerns raised by David Hume and others in the mid-eighteenth century, when they noted the difficulties that plagued the conception of causality as a necessitating force (I will elaborate this point later). At any rate, these philosophic theories of human evolution have also failed to meet the standards of those philosophers for whom only empirically established concepts can support a theoretical construct. For instance, one need not be a scientist to find fault with Pierre Teilhard de Chardin. His key postulate – that the evolution of life tends, as to a predetermined goal, towards reunion with the ultimate reality – goes well beyond what is justified by experience alone.

The question whether the biological theories of human evolution should be deemed defective cannot be quite as peremptorily dismissed; I will discuss it fully at the appropriate time. But a preliminary critique of the approach to the subject favoured by most biologists would be useful, since it would help us define the question that this inquiry seeks to answer and formulate the plan of investigation it will adopt. I should make clear from the outset, however, that I do not intend to impugn the theory of evolution through natural selection in general; on the contrary, I will assume it. Moreover, since it is above reasonable doubt that the functional structures of the human organism are genetically determined, it is beyond all sensible debate that natural selection was at work in the emergence of the human species in particular. I question only the simple extension of the theory to human evolution without sufficient allowance having been made for the peculiarities of human nature; I shall propose instead that the concept of natural selection may be applied to human evolution only if it is first transposed into a human key. But it is too early to discuss any alternative; the prior question is why some sort of alternative should be sought.

Stated concisely before I explain it, my objection to transferring the usual theory to man without qualification is that the natural selection of genes does not actually explain the origin of the specifically human mode of life – not, at least, if by *human life* we mean more than the genetically conditioned physiology of the human organism. If most biologists have been satisfied with such application, the reason is that – sometimes wittingly, sometimes not – they have usually reduced the human mode of life to the biochemical processes that, in fact, are only its *cause*. To understand why they have traditionally taken this approach, and why it is inadequate, we must go back to the origin of some of their assumptions about the nature of *causality*.

Scientists, to their disadvantage, frequently ignore an elementary historical fact: that the 'new philosophy,' as science was long referred to, received many of its fundamental concepts from the 'old' philosophy, medieval Scholasticism; causality was one of these. And the Scholastic idea of causality harked back, in part, to the Old Testament doctrine of creation. Now, in the original metaphorical and mythological categories of Scripture, man and world were envisaged as the 'child' and the 'handiwork' of the heavenly 'Father' and 'Maker' of all things. Centuries before the Middle Ages, however, Christian theologians had reformulated that biblical teaching by resorting to the Greek philosophical concept of 'causality' (*aitia*). According to the Greeks, a cause was a source of 'necessity' (*anankē*), that is, the exertion of a compelling force that brought about change, and without which no change could take place.[2]

---

2 There were, of course, wide differences among the various Greek philosophers in respect of both their assumptions and their interpretations, if any, of the nature of causality. My generalization about Greek thinking concerning causality is nevertheless valid, because a common element – the idea that all worldly events come

For a thousand years before Scholasticism the world had accordingly appeared to Christians as a system of natural forces – a hierarchy of 'causes' and 'effects' – which had itself been caused by the all-necessitating power of a transcendent First Cause. But a further reinterpretation of God's creative causality, developed in the thirteenth century principally by Thomas Aquinas, introduced a novelty that stated with precision what had been, at best, confusedly implicit in earlier Christian thought: God's creativity consisted not only in the causation of *what* creatures were – or of their 'essences' – but above all of their *being* whatever they were – or of their 'existing,' as we would more commonly say today. This revision of the nature of God's causality held important consequences for Scholasticism's – and therefore science's – understanding of the nature of causal processes in the world; it will repay us to take a moment to follow the reasoning that led to them.

In the theology of Aquinas, God creates by exercising his efficient causality so as to bring into being out of nothing, and to continue to maintain in being, an entity's act of existing; the entity's characteristics, including the way in which it operates and causes effects, are in turn the effect of its act of existing.[3] Thus, a creature is indebted to God for

---

about only in obedience to a certain decreed *anankē* – pervades the history of Greek philosophy from its very origins, being rooted as it was in the pre-philosophical common sense of Greek culture that 'fate' (*moira*, literally an 'apportioning') determined all things; see F.M. Cornford, *From Religion to Philosophy: A Study in the Origins of Western Speculation* (London, 1913), and William Chase Greene, *Moira: Fate, Good, and Evil in Greek Thought* (Cambridge, MA, 1944). It is true that Greek philosophers before Aristotle had debated whether events that happen by 'chance' or 'luck' (*tychē*) must not be said to escape causality altogether – or in the alternative, whether nothing could be properly said to happen 'by chance.' According to Aristotle, however, chance can be subsumed under causality, and there is no contradiction between causal determinism and 'fortuitous' events simply because the latter are unpredictable; see his *Physics*, II, 4–6, especially II, 6 (198a5–13). It should not be deemed strange that these views were retained, in modified form, by Christian thought, to which they were so congenial; for instance, according to St Thomas Aquinas the fact that absolutely nothing happens except as an effect of the irresistible Will of God is as clearly manifested by fortuitous, unpredictable events as it is by predictable events subject to natural causality; see, for example, *De Veritate*, especially 2, 14, ad 3; 5, 2; and 8, 12. Determinism of one or else another stripe – but increasingly the kind of determinism that excluded not only the Will of God, but even the possibility of chance events as a result of natural causes – eventually became altogether unquestioned in the Western tradition. It so remained until fairly recent times, and even today it is the most common assumption of philosophers and scientists.

3 More technically formulated, the Thomistic interpretation was that a creature's 'actual existence ... is the efficient cause by which essence in its turn is the formal cause which makes an actual existence to be "such an existence" ': Étienne Gilson,

all its other characteristics, properties, and powers, only because it first owes its existence to him; for unless a thing should have existence it would be nothing at all, and its actually existing is the effect of God's causality. According to Thomas, then, every entity in the world was literally *nothing*, a non-being, *but* for the fact that God had caused it to come into existence and continued to cause it to exist; and since every creature's characteristics, including its causality, were conditioned by its dependent existence, then all its causal powers were likewise nothing but for the fact that it actually existed, which it owed to God. The consequence, however, was that creaturely effects must in turn be deemed to be nothing but what their creaturely causes had determined them to be. Christians must therefore say not only, as of old, that creaturely effects were compelled by their creaturely causes, but also that they were *reducible* to such causes.

The logic is irreproachable. From the premise that 'no cause can produce existence properly so called save only God,'[4] it follows that although the causal power of created beings is enough to effect changes in the world – in the sense that it can bring about a new configuration *of what already exists* – creaturely causes cannot bring about any novelty more radical than such change. Since only God can create existence, only God can be a creative cause. Conversely, there can be nothing in an effect that has not been in some way prescribed by the cause (though the cause may well, of course, contain more than the effect). This implication of St Thomas's reinterpretation of creation was not drawn immediately; but in time it would become clear that a world so conceived was not simply a deterministic system, but a *closed* one.[5]

Eventually the 'new philosophy' bracketed the causality of God on the ground that it was empirically inevident and accessible only to faith. But as science emancipated itself from theology it retained, in addition to the Greek idea that causes compelled their effects, the further supposition that had come to reign in the intellectual tradition – and to a large extent even in the common sense – of Western culture: that effects

---

Being and Some Philosophers (Toronto, 1949), p. 172; see also Étienne Gilson, *Elements of Christian Philosophy* (New York, 1960), chapter 8, 'Being and Causality.'

4 Gilson, *Elements*, p. 188.

5 That is, the world system may be described as a hierarchy of causes and effects not simply in the sense 'that every higher being can act upon every lower one. The sense of the [Thomistic] doctrine is a deeper one. This universe of ours is a hierarchical structure of superiors and inferiors in which efficient causality proceeds by gradation, in the precise sense that the higher beings not only can, but must, act upon the lower ones ... [and that] inferiors are bound to obey their superiors': Gilson, *Elements*, pp. 194–5.

can be 'nothing but' what their causes have compelled them to be. Indeed, this relatively novel idea was to become one of the pillars of the 'new philosophy.' Predictability, for instance, whose importance for science is well known, depends upon it; reducibility alone is what makes effects totally predictable, in principle, from a knowledge of their causes. Thus, to understand man and world as the effects brought into being and maintained in existence by God's causality had been, for the Scholastics, the same as to understand what they *really* were; just so, when a scientist succeeded in interpreting changes in the existing world as the effect of natural causes, he understood what such phenomena *really* were.

Science's retention of the reducibility of effects to their causes, however, was inconsistent with its empiricism. In the absence of the premiss that everything in the world would sink into nothingness but for God's causing it to exist, there can be no reason for supposing that things are reducible to their origin or that effects are necessarily limited to manifesting what had been precontained, as in a principle, in their cause. For nothing we observe in the world leads to the conclusion that the emergence of novelties in worldly causal processes is impossible. Why, then, did the reductionistic concept of causality survive in science? In considerable part for the same reason it was also preserved, albeit confusedly, in our secular culture's common sense: because, although ideas have no measurable mass, they exhibit cultural inertia and acquire historical momentum. In the evolution of human knowledge, the force of logic is not the only form of energy at work.

Contrary to vulgar opinion, the founding fathers of modern science were for the most part faithful Christian believers; assuming the compatibility of scientific reason and Christian revelation they nevertheless promoted the separation of the two – often enough prompted to do so indeed by religious motives. For instance, injudicious (from their viewpoint) though it may now seem to us with the benefit of hindsight, 'the Christians [among scientists] helped the cause of modern rationalism by their jealous determination to sweep out of the world all miracles and magic except their own ... [They reasoned] that Christian miracles themselves could not be vindicated unless it could be assumed that the normal workings of the universe were regular and subject to law. [Thus, when in the seventeenth century] the idea of a complete mechanistic interpretation of the universe came out into the open ... its chief exponents were the most religious men ... They were anxious to prove the adequacy and the perfection of Creation – anxious to vindicate God's rationality.'[6]

6 Herbert Butterfield, *The Origins of Modern Science* (London, 1958), p. 73.

My point, however, is that the early scientists did not always succeed in segregating faith and reason as strictly as they thought they did; for they did not always realize the religious origin of some of the concepts they took for granted as part of the conventional wisdom of their age. The necessitarianism of the idea of causality inherited by scientists went back to Greece, but its reductionism had been devised by Christian thought and inspired by the wish to reconcile reason and faith. Having been thus imported from theology into science through the back door of common sense, the Scholastic concept of causality was preserved even during later stages in the evolution of our culture, when the mere separation of science and religion had become the rift between the two, and when their incompatibility was widely assumed. Reductionistic causality today seems self-evident even to many scientists who profess no religious belief, because all they need do is to repeat uncritically, and without awareness of its historical derivation, what the scientific tradition has transmitted to them. But there are yet other reasons, which have to do with the way in which the human mind works; later we shall touch on some of them.

But the more important question than how scientific reductionism came about is whether it is justified. Is it true that things and events are 'nothing but' the effect of their causes? Does critical reflection support the view that when one ascertains the causes of a certain phenomenon one determines what the phenomenon 'really' is? An affirmative answer should be objectionable to anyone who was committed to abiding by what experience reveals; it would discount the fact that an empirically given reality must be said to be, in the first place, *really* itself. To be sure, we may well judge that it is the effect of certain causes, but this rational construction must be subject to the empirical fact, not the other way about. And overlooking the unqualified reality of whatever is immediately given in experience has an unfortunate consequence: that the burden to be put on its explanation is thereby lightened. Consider this analogy, oversimple though it may be. Let us suppose that Shakespeare wrote *Hamlet* motivated by a compulsion deriving from unresolved Oedipal feelings. If one were to say, however, that *Hamlet* was nothing but a neurotic symptom, one would have discounted a great deal that also needed to be explained – say, those aspects of the play that only the socio-economic and cultural conditions of Elizabethan England can help us understand. Above all, one would have spirited away the literary reality itself. The psychoanalytic interpretation itself might be all the more adequate if it did not reduce *Hamlet* to grist for the Freudian mill.[7]

---

7 But it does not follow that reductions are never justified; if the evidence should warrant it, we should deny Shakespeare's authorship of *Hamlet* altogether and say

The procedure that a strict and consistent empiricism prescribes is thus the opposite of what many scientists continue to assume. One should not expect to discover what a thing really is by ascertaining its causes; on the contrary, one should first ascertain what it really is, so that one can then reliably recognize the causes that explain it. This resolve to accept whatever is given immediately in experience as the fixed starting-point of all investigation – in other words, the attempt to subordinate the explanation to the *explicandum* more rigorously than our intellectual tradition has hitherto managed – is the heart of the procedure that the jargon calls *phenomenology*. Having originated with philosophy, a phenomenological disposition has been cultivated so far mostly by philosophers, though nothing in its nature restricts its usefulness to this field. Phenomenology is at bottom no more – and no less – than a radical empiricism.

We are interested, however, in one particular reduction. To suppose that human life is 'not really' what we directly experience in ourselves, but actually something else – for instance, its causes – is methodologically unsound. Nor does it matter precisely what the human reality should be reduced to. To put it coarsely, there is little to choose from between the propositions that 'Man is nothing but twenty dollars' worth of chemicals' and 'Man is nothing but a creature of God'; both are invitations to the listener to disconfirm his own immediately perceptible reality. Both must be deemed false, therefore, by anyone who apprehends that he really is himself – at least, if he does so trusting his own experience of himself. But *there* is the rub. Are we human beings truly what we experience ourselves to be, or are we not? Some of us, apparently, are not quite sure; by implication, if not forethought, we seem ready to assume that we cannot be quite what we *think* we are. Every disconfirmation of our experience of ourselves points therefore to its underlying tacit premiss: the uncertainty whether our experience of ourselves is fully credible. The reduction of the humanity of human beings – to anything – results from a sort of self-doubt or self-suspicion that is no more justified when it operates under scientific than under theological sanction; behaviourism is a modern form of an ancient prejudice that some human beings seem to have against themselves. Later we shall encounter other manifestations of the curious difficulty that some of us experience in accepting our own perceptible reality. And being con-

---

it was really Bacon's. A reduction is invalid only to the extent that it disconfirms the reality of what in fact is real. But if that which is given *immediately* in experience – as contrasted with that which reason construes – is not to be taken as unqualifiedly real, what is?

cerned with the origins of human nature, we shall be interested in learning also whence it may have come.

A reductionism not much more polished than that of my two homely examples was in vogue at one time among evolutionary scientists: man was 'really' an animal, albeit an unusually complex one; his origins must therefore be explicable by identically the same process that accounted for the evolution of infrahuman life. Nowadays, however, relatively few would take this extreme position. The most common scientific opinion is that differences 'in kind' separate human and infrahuman life; the irreducibility of the former to the latter is frequently acknowledged in those very terms. Acknowledging it, however, has had remarkably little effect upon the theory of human evolution through natural selection; it has not been reflected in modifications to the theory so that it should account *both* for the common aspects and for the qualitative differences between human and animal life. But should a theory of human evolution not be deemed deficient if it explained the origin of everything else in man, but not the origin of his humanity?

Biologists do not generally think so.[8] Most of them feel, apparently, that a theory of human evolution need explain only the origin of the kind of organism that supports the human specificity – whatever it might be – because such an organism is evidently the kind that, in fact, supports the human mode of life. But this is not unlike receiving a gift in the mail and leaving it unopened when the seal proves too strong to break, on the ground that to appreciate the giver's kindness it is unnecessary to ascertain the nature of the gift. Now, it is true that before one opens it one may have faith in the donor's good intentions; but to *know* that such faith is not misplaced one must determine whether the box brings something one could conceivably welcome rather than, say, an explosive device. The biological faith in natural selection amounts thus to an unacknowledged and even unintended reductionism; it is no longer said that man is 'nothing but' a complex animal, but it is assumed that evolution by natural selection need be demonstrated in respect of nothing but the commonalities of animal and man. This is, of course, a practical

8 Some scientists have attempted in recent times to make special provision for human evolution by adapting the theory of natural selection so as to explain – as they hope – the emergence of specifically human characteristics; I refer to the sociobiological hypothesis of 'gene-culture coevolution,' which states that in man the selection of genes may take place through cultural choices as well as through natural selection. I will return to this below. But since this theory also supposes that human culture resulted from nothing but the natural selection of genes, and that in the final analysis human evolution continues to be governed by nothing but the selection of genes, I shall conclude that it suffers from reductionism just the same.

self-contradiction; its passing unnoticed is a good measure of the extent to which the medieval idea of causality maintains its hold on scientific thought even today. Like many another bias, reductionism may be consciously denied yet remain effective just the same.

Philosophical dissatisfaction with the classical concept of causality goes back to the time of George Berkeley and David Hume; but Immanuel Kant's answer to Hume gave it a new, long-term lease on life. It is often said that in the late nineteenth and the early twentieth centuries a scientific revolution finally dethroned deterministic causality. This, however, is an exaggeration. It is true that one branch of science, theoretical physics, found it inadequate, whereupon it was 'replaced by a redefined concept purged of the inconsistencies and absurdities of the old one ... [According to the new concept of causality] every present event is undoubtedly caused, though not necessitated by its own past ... [Thus understood, causality is] entirely compatible with the emergence of novelties in the genuinely growing world.'[9] Unfortunately, however, 'emergent causality,' as it is usually called, has not been consistently applied outside theoretical physics. Even within the physical sciences it has been operative only in certain areas. This is understandable: in the physical world irreducible emergent effects are measurably different from necessary and reducible ones only at the intra-atomic and cosmic-scale extremes of the spectrum of observable phenomena; in respect of ordinary physical events the assumption of reductionistic causality yields the same results as that of emergent causality. However, qualitative differences between effects and causes are easily detectable in the evolution of life; emergent causality should have revolutionized its study. But ironically, it has not – doubly ironically in the case of human evolution. Most biologists agree that evolution is an emergent process, but nevertheless frequently assume – to take a critical instance – that since genetically determined biochemical processes are the causes of consciousness, natural selection is enough to account for its origin. I have no wish to contest the former proposition; the latter would follow, however, only if effects were reducible to their causes, and consciousness were therefore properly describable as nothing but a biochemical event.

What logic allows this inconsistency? Why do so many biologists fail to realize that, if evolution is an emergent process, then either the theory of natural genetic selection must explain specifically the human peculiarities or else its application to man is little more than an act of faith? Part of the explanation may be habituation of thought. Since natural

9 Milič Čapek, *The Philosophical Impact of Contemporary Physics* (Princeton, NJ, 1961), p. 340.

selection does not include what scientists are culturally conditioned to think of as 'causality' – the pre-Humean necessitation of effects by a natural force – perhaps they do not keep in mind at all times that natural selection is a *causal* explanation. If so, they would feel free to think simultaneously in terms of both natural selection and the reduction of effects to their causes – emergent and deterministic causality – mutually exclusive though these are. But there is, in any event, a decisive reason.

What sustains the faith of these biologists is their willingness to discount, usually without much prior deliberation, the human characteristics whose origin must be accounted for. Their willingness is in no small measure the result of inattention to philosophical issues; their customary neglect of epistemology and their consequent adoption of the common-sense position usually called 'naïve realism' are especially unfortunate. By default, their approach to determining the specific difference of human life must rely largely on unsophisticated, casual observations, and on no more disciplined procedures than intuition and good sense. Not infrequently, therefore, they are satisfied with ingenuous conceptions of what makes human life human. I refer in particular to the ideas of consciousness and human selfhood echoed upon occasion by science, such as the conception of thought that has enabled some scientists to believe that computers can think, and the conception of selfhood that has enabled others to conclude that chimpanzees have a self-concept comparable to that of human beings.[10] Somewhat like the Scholastics in their time, then, though in very different respects, too many evolutionary scientists have become over-confident; they admit differences in kind between man and animal, yet do not feel bound to determine critically and systematically the nature of the differences *before* the origin of such differences is theoretically explained. In effect, they *trust* that natural selection explains it just the same.

If one is not quite clear about one's objective, the hope of attaining it is blind; one's theory of the origin of anything could hardly be more adequate than one's prior understanding of precisely *what* the theory is supposed to explain. The first advantage to be expected from a philosophical study of human evolution is that, being more conscious than science, generally speaking, of the shortcomings of the traditional ideas of causality, philosophy would be more scrupulously mindful than science of the need to tailor the explanation to the *explicandum*. Philosophy would therefore appreciate that the initial step of a theory of human evolution must be to determine critically and systematically the nature of the humanity of man. And philosophy could do so with the help of

10 More detailed comments on these two views will be added later.

a stricter empiricism than that of biology; for the scientific method makes no provision for reflecting upon what human beings experience themselves to be, whereas philosophy has had some success in developing techniques for observing, describing, and systematizing what human nature reveals to itself, empirically, about itself.

We shall therefore begin to study human evolution by inquiring into the nature of the human specificity. Our first conclusion, in the next chapter, will be that the essence of human life lies in its having conscious quality; for being conscious is what we immediately experience ourselves to be. Not only thought and understanding, but our behaviour, our feelings, and our immediate sense contact with reality have the quality without which human life would be inconceivable and which we ordinarily call consciousness. Every other specifically human characteristic flows from it. Since conscious experience is the sort that enables the experiencer to become aware of the otherness of the world around him, human beings do not merely perceive things that are real but perceive them as such. This perception in turn makes it possible for them to experience their own otherness to the world; their grasping that things are real empowers them to learn that they themselves are so. It is, therefore, only because their experience is conscious that human beings have selfhood, or that they enjoy conscious identity; to be a self is to be capable of experiencing one's reality as a conscious experiencer and as the conscious agent of one's behaviour. The ability to experience reality as such and oneself as real is the essence of human, conscious life.

We shall then proceed to determine in what consciousness consists. For the moment, however, I need only remark that this quality is not reducible to a function of the organism. I have granted that biochemical processes in the brain (and elsewhere in the organism) are the indispensable and sole causes of consciousness. But it is one thing to say that consciousness is the effect of a biochemical process; it is quite another to suggest that it is a biochemical process. Our observation of our own consciousness shows that consciousness does not look, or otherwise seem, remotely like the latter sort of phenomenon. Indeed, few of us have ever had the opportunity to gain direct acquaintance with any of the cerebral and other physiological events that are essential to being conscious, whereas no one who is conscious can fail altogether to perceive the fact. (Whether he also interprets correctly the nature of consciousness is a different matter.) Thus, not even those who say that consciousness is 'really' a biochemical event lack altogether the ability to perceive the difference between the two; their handicap is rather that they are inwardly compelled to dismiss it, because their assumption –

that effects are reducible to their causes – commits them in advance to treating the difference as non-existent. Of course, we shall have to examine how consciousness can be caused by nothing but organic processes yet be irreducible to an organic process. In this respect, too – understanding the relationship between consciousness and the human organism – the inadequacies of the biological theories can be traced in part to assumptions that have not been subjected to sufficiently thorough philosophical critique.

We shall be interested next in pursuing the consequences of consciousness for human life. It is a defining characteristic of all life that it tends to preserve itself by adjusting to its environment; and it is typical of animal life that its adjustment is mediated by sensory abilities that furnish the organism with experience of itself and its world. Since the conscious quality of human experience is irreducible to an organic function, however, the concept of *adjustment* cannot be simply and univocally transferred from animal to human organisms, but must be suitably adapted to take account of the human peculiarities. Human adjustment differs from the animal kind in that man's relations to his environment are mediated by a special kind of experience: the sort, as we have seen, that endows him with a sense of selfhood and a sense of reality. Unlike an animal, a human being adjusts by relating himself (a) to a world that he perceives as real; (b) to himself, whom he perceives as a self; and (c) to other selves, whom he perceives as beings who perceive themselves as selves and him as a self. Human society and culture, therefore, depend upon, and are manifestations of, the specifically human form of adjustive experience.[11] Conversely, since human adjustment is irreducible to organic adjustment, because it involves conscious processes, human society and culture are qualitatively different from their counterparts in animal life. It also follows that if a theory of evolution could account for the emergence of consciousness, it should explain satisfactorily the origin of human society and culture as well. Indeed, a theory of human evolution would be grossly deficient if it did not explain the social and cultural peculiarities of human life by means of the same theory that it used to account for the individual ones.

The burden of chapter II will thus be merely to explain and to adduce some evidence for the propositions (a) that to be human is to have conscious life and selfhood, (b) that the entirety of the typically human mode of life, including human culture and society, is a consequence of

11 Much the same thesis has been developed at greater length than I am able to do here by Willem H. Vanderburg, *The Growth of Minds and Cultures: A Unified Theory of the Structure of Human Experience* (Toronto, 1985).

consciousness and its adjustive properties, and (c) that consciousness is so related to the human organism that it can be caused by none but organic functions yet be irreducible to them. This examination of the nature of consciousness, however, will alert us to two possibilities we would otherwise not have suspected, since they run directly against the firm convictions of our common sense. In the course of studying the human specificity we shall discover that there is some reason to wonder (a) whether the capacity for experiencing consciously and for becoming a self may not be acquired rather than inborn, and (b) whether the acquisition of consciousness and selfhood by the human individual may not be a consequence of his prior acquisition of the ability to speak. To these possibilities should be contrasted the usual assumptions of most scientists and many philosophers: that the ability to experience consciously develops through the maturation of the genetically determined structures of the human organism, and that consciousness appears in the individual prior to speech.

A distinction, however, should be made. The ability merely to experience is undoubtedly inborn. But as we have known for some time, not all human experience is conscious. Therefore, *conscious* experience cannot be equated with mere experience, but is a special, qualitatively different kind of the latter. Precisely how they differ is a question we shall have to investigate; but whatever the answer, if it is true that some experience is non-conscious, the fact that the individual's ability to experience is inborn and appears through the maturation of the organism does not imply that the same must be true of his ability to experience consciously; the conscious quality of conscious experience may well be acquired. The possibility bears exploring that, whereas the human organism determines *that* human beings are able to experience, while reality determines in all essential respects *what* they experience, their ability to speak determines *how* they typically experience – namely, consciously. It may be that an individual's learning to communicate his experience in the specifically human way has, in addition to its conspicuous advantage of enabling him to produce a communicative effect upon a communicand, a much less obvious but profound effect upon the communicator himself: that it teaches him to render conscious the experience he communicates. But I have referred specifically to speech, the human form of communication; I know of no reason to think that every kind of communication has such effect.

This investigation will thus be guided by the hypothesis that, through speaking, the individual human organism converts its inborn ability to experience into the acquired ability to experience consciously – though once the latter has been developed it is no longer necessary actually to speak in order to experience consciously. Or briefly formulated: consciousness is generated by speech. This expression is not to be understood simply as a metaphor describing the heightening and shaping of consciousness by speech (though that is true also), but literally: consciousness comes into being as a direct effect of speech. But if this should be true, the acquisition by the human species of the ability to speak must have been the origin of its ability to experience consciously and, therefore, to lead a human type of life. Thus a theory of human evolution based on the hypothesis that speech generates consciousness would have to explain essentially three things: how speech may have originated out of infrahuman communication, how this development would have brought about the emergence of a species characterized by conscious life, and how consciousness would have thereafter continued to evolve in accordance with the evolution of the properties of speech, until human nature became what it is today. To do so is the goal that this work aims to achieve.

The study of consciousness alone will but hint that speech is the source of the individual's ability to lead a conscious life; to develop the mere conjecture into a plausible hypothesis it would be necessary to examine the nature of speech. This task will be taken up in chapter III, where we shall ascertain the difference between animal communication and speech, and discover how this difference explains the consciousness-generating properties of the latter. The crucial difference does not have to do with the characteristics of the systems of communicative signs, the *languages*, that humans use, or with the ability to use such systems – also called *language*, or linguistic ability – but with the nature of *speech*, the communicative activity itself. For when human beings speak they do not merely communicate or use vocal signals of a certain type: they do so assertively. By this I mean that they communicate intending to communicate and experiencing the communicative efficacy of their signal-making. Speech is not reducible to mere communication, but is definable as communication of the *assertive* kind.

Nor should we allow ourselves to be distracted by the complexity, the 'symbolic' character, or the other earmarks of human linguistic signs and of the ability to use them; these are no more to the point than the vocal, audible nature of the signs. Human languages *do* exhibit certain peculiarities, in keeping with the emergent quality of the communicative activity that makes use of them; but the same sort of assertive communication that is the essence of speech can be performed using any other signs – vocal or otherwise, linguistic or not – including the simplest, such as even animals use. Conversely, if animals communicate, but do not speak, it is not simply because they lack the ability to process sufficiently elaborate signs or because they cannot make the right kind – true though this may be. It is above all because they cannot learn to experience that signs – any signs – can be used to communicate.[12]

Why assertive communication renders experience conscious, whereas mere communication does not, will too be made clear. We should then also understand why, although the mere ability to communicate is inborn, the ability to speak is acquired socio-culturally; it is not transmitted simply by teaching children how to use a system of communicative signs, but by conveying to them at the same time the idea that signs can be used *in order to* communicate. In other words, not only the skill required to use a given language, but the ability to use any language and indeed any signs *assertively*, be they linguistic or not, is acquired through sociocultural transmission. To this view should be contrasted the usual scientific assumption: that the ability to speak is quite as genetically determined as the ability to experience consciously, with but the difference that the ability to speak cannot mature unless the child be taught a language wherewith to speak. This assumption is plausible, however, only as long as the assertiveness of speech is ignored and the ability to speak is reduced to the ability to communicate using a system of linguistic signs – as long, therefore, as the defining features of human communication are assumed to reside in the characteristics of human linguistic systems and in the ability to use them, and as long as the only question to be entertained concerns precisely what such characteristics are.

Chapters II and III will constitute, then, the preparatory part of this investigation. The remainder of the plan is as follows. In chapter IV the theory of human evolution to which the study of consciousness and speech leads will be outlined. The theory will then be presented more fully and supported in chapters V, VI, VII, and VIII, by showing how it enables us to reconstruct not only the origin of consciousness, but also the continued evolution of the specifically human characteristics of individuals, societies, and cultures up to that point in prehistory when human nature was essentially the same as it is today. Some concluding reflections will be offered in chapter IX.

To explain the theory in much detail at this juncture, before we have thoroughly studied the concepts of consciousness and speech it pre-

---

12 The reason they cannot learn it, moreover, cannot be only that they lack the requisite genetically determined organic equipment; even human beings, who *have* such equipment, do not learn to speak unless they are taught. Assertive communication requires not only certain organic capacities in the individual, but also cultural causes of a specific sort.

supposes, would be premature. Nevertheless, it may be useful if I fore-shadow the possibility we shall explore: that through the operation of nothing but natural selection, a specifically human evolutionary mech-anism that was not reducible to the natural selection of genes may have emerged. The reason was that when animal communication evolved into speech through natural selection – a process I shall try to reconstruct here from an analysis of the differences between animal communication and speech – what emerged was more than a new and higher form of communication: it was also a new form of *reproduction*. For speech, which generates consciousness in the speaker, is not innate, but acquired through learning from those who already know how to speak, whose speech has generated their conscious level of life. The hypothesis that speech *gen-erates* consciousness should be understood, therefore, not only in the sense previously noted – that a human organism's actual exercise of its ability to speak enables it to learn to experience consciously – but also in the yet more fundamental sense that when an infant is taught to speak it is being endowed by its forbears with the distinctive and es-sential aspect of human nature, namely the potential to experience in the conscious mode. The transmission of the ability to speak is the inheritance mechanism whereby conscious life reproduces itself in suc-cessive generations. When I say, then, that speech has a reproductive as well as a communicative function, I intend no metaphor. The ma-chinery through which the human specificity is perpetuated is not re-ducible to the sexual reproduction of the human organism – though, obviously, the self-reproduction of conscious life requires the prior cre-ation, through sexual reproduction, of an organism genetically endowed with the requisite organic capacity for its communicative behaviour to become speech and for its experience to develop the quality of consciousness.

Let us recall, however, how infrahuman evolution operates: the nat-ural selection of genes is the effect entailed by the interaction of the adaptive and the reproductive functions of organisms. In respect of infrahuman characteristics the selective effect is, of course, necessarily a *genetic* selective effect; the reason is that the adjustive abilities of in-frahumans are determined genetically, since these are reducible to or-ganic functions reproduced in offspring through the transmission of genes. In other words, as long as the reproduction of the adjustive abilities of organisms should depend on the transmission of genes, nat-ural selection can select nothing but genes. However, the essential prop-erties of the selective process do not have to do, of themselves, with the *genetic* nature of the reproductive functions or with the *genetic* de-termination of the adaptive characteristics of organisms. If, as in human organisms, the adaptive abilities should have ceased to be reducible to what genes alone can determine – because reproduction had ceased to be reducible to the transmission of genes – the evolutionary mechanism would have ceased to be reducible to the natural selection of genes. How would it have operated instead?

The mechanism through which the specifically human characteristics evolve is the selective effect entailed by the interaction between the specifically human adjustive and reproductive functions – that is, the interaction between experience and speech. Although natural selection alone produced speech, the emergence of consciousness was not the result of natural selection; consciousness appeared when the interaction between mere experience and speech transformed the plain, animal ability to experience into the human ability to experience consciously. As noted earlier, however, the emergence of consciousness entailed a transformation in the nature of adjustment. This meant that the 'rules' of natural selection, as it were, had changed. The appearance of the human type of adjustment implied that the interaction between adjustive characteristics and reproduction was no longer screened by the criterion of mere organic survival; evolution now selected for characteristics that contributed to the value that the conscious life of human beings had for them; evolution protected, in ways that we shall investigate, the satisfaction of the individual and collective needs of human organisms insofar as they were selves.

The subsequent evolution of human nature followed in accordance with the same mechanism; it depended on the interaction between the peculiarly human form of adjustive experience (namely, consciousness) and the peculiarly human way in which the ability to experience consciously reproduces itself (i.e., through the socio-cultural transmission of the ability to speak). The human organism continues to be, of course, subject to natural genetic selection; but this fact is negligible, because the evolution of the humanity of human beings – the evolution of consciousness – does not depend upon it. In capsule form, then, the answer that will be proposed here in reply to the question of human evolution is: human nature originated through the interaction between the functions of experiencing and speaking, which created consciousness, and thereafter it continued to evolve – as it has to the present – as a result of the interaction between the properties of conscious experience and the properties of speech.

Note well that according to this theory what is transmitted to human offspring with consciousness-generating and -developing effects is not any particular message or set of messages but the ability to speak. The *content* of speech is not what matters – at least not primarily – but rather the assertive *form* of speech. Therefore, although the origin and evolution of consciousness depend, as the theory proposes, on the generation and development of consciousness through a socio-cultural process, this process should not be confused with the 'cultural evolution' that the current biological theories make allowance for as an adjunct to 'organic evolution.' Such 'cultural evolution' is deemed to affect the conditions of human life and the contents of human experience through the transmission of messages having specific contents, but does not result in changes in the nature of conscious experience or in the way it operates; for the characteristics of consciousness are inherited, supposedly, exclusively through the transmission of genetic information from parent to offspring. In my suggestion, however, what evolves through the human variant of natural selection is not only the contents of human cultures, but the nature of the experiential functions of individual human organisms – though the evolution of the latter entails the evolution of culture as well. Cultures do evolve, and their evolution is part of the evolution of human nature; but they evolve in accordance with, and subject to, the evolution of the properties of consciousness, which depends upon the evolution of the properties of speech. Cultural evolution through the evolution of the contents of speech is thus an important but secondary and dependent process, which ultimately relies for its effectiveness on the evolution of the nature of speech. (The differences between the theory developed here and those biological theories that propose twin organic and cultural human evolutionary processes will be more fully examined in chapter IV.)

If society, culture, and our entire mode of life are the consequences of consciousness, then the theory should account for all that human beings are today, and how they typically behave, by reference to the origin, nature, and evolution of speech. It should explain why the kind of society and culture has emerged where art, law, politics, morality, and economic, social, and other conventions, but above all religion and philosophy – though more recently also science – have traditionally institutionalized the means to satisfy the requirements of the specifically human form of adjustment. As I have underlined, human beings need to adjust to themselves and each other insofar as they are selves, and to the world insofar as it is real. This demand of their nature – for it is created in them by their consciousness – can be met only through their devising some sort of self- and world-interpretation that should render meaningful the reality of the world, of themselves, and of the human situation. And to help them so to meet it is precisely what societies and cultures try to do.

If the theory is to explain, however, *all* that human beings have come to be, then it must account not only for the normal but also for the abnormal manifestations of conscious life. For when evolution brought forth consciousness, it evidently produced not only the sort of organism that individually and in groups could achieve a life-promoting adjustment to self and world, but also the kind that could become dangerous to itself; this turn of events may not be unrelated to the extraordinarily high degree of specialization that consciousness amounts to. But since evolution is, so to speak, the reward of adjustment, the emergence of a self-imperilling form of life is almost a paradox. Nevertheless, it has happened. The kind of organism that lacked not only the intelligence and the manual dexterity to build cathedrals, but in the first place the inclination to do so, became the sort that likes to cast its dreams in shapes of mortar and stone, and is, moreover, apt to embellish them with the lovingly sculptured projections of its worst nightmares. A theory of human evolution would be incomplete unless it explained the origin of some of the unhealthy, neurotic forms that human life has observably taken in the past, and continues to take, down to our own day.

Finally, I touch upon a methodological question that might give pause to some. In historical times, speech, thought, and consciousness began to 'fossilize,' to leave tangible traces of *what* human beings said, thought, and experienced, from which we might infer *how* they did so. But how could philosophical analysis, in the absence of almost all palaeontological evidence about human speech and consciousness, reconstruct their prehistoric origin and development? In this respect, however, the situation of philosophy is not very different from that of biology. Explaining the nature of evolution and tracing its course are not the same thing; palaeontological evidence is most valuable for biology, especially because it confirms and illustrates in detail what the theory explains comprehensively and in principle, but the biological theories of evolution have not been built piecemeal out of dry bones. When Darwin first proposed the concept of natural selection and applied it to man, hardly any prehistoric hominid fossils had been found; it was, indeed, partly his theory that spurred the search for the 'missing link,' as it was described in contemporary terminology. The theory of natural selection was rather an attempt to explain the *outcome* of the evolutionary process – the variety, characteristics, and distribution of the innumerable forms of life that exist today. For though a process may leave traces in its wake, the essential clues to its interpretation are rather the indications that it brings along with it, as it were, in the form of the final effect; through an analysis of the result one may determine the only conditions under which it could have been reached from a certain starting-point. This technique is used, for instance, by astrophysicists to theorize about the origin and evolution of the universe on the basis of the constitution and distribution of matter at present. Thus, from an analysis of human nature as we can observe it in ourselves, we should find it possible to determine the conditions that alone can explain how, given its infrahuman point of departure, it could have become what it now is.

These remarks underscore again the importance of establishing at the very beginning of an investigation of human evolution exactly what the outcome of such process has been. The extraordinarily ambitious project on which we have embarked requires a correspondingly painstaking preparation; but simple prudence is not the whole reason why I shall devote an unusually large proportion of my available space to the preliminary task of ascertaining the nature of man. Yet more important are the demands of a strict empiricism. For we should have learned enough from the deficiencies of the biological theories of evolution to avoid, if no other, the strategic mistake that under the influence of the traditional concept of causality they have commonly made: attempting to explain how humanity may have originated and evolved to its present condition, without having first determined – methodically, critically, and very carefully – precisely what human beings have become.

PART TWO

The Nature of Man

CHAPTER TWO

The nature of consciousness

In accordance with the proposed agenda, in this chapter we shall be concerned, first, with whether consciousness properly describes the human specificity, and next, with the nature and principal characteristics of conscious life. I shall then raise the question how consciousness, which scarcely comprises the totality of a human being, is related to the human organism. Out of the discussion of these problems the hypothesis that speech generates consciousness will begin to emerge.

I have said, however, not only that the biological approach to the subject (at least as ordinarily conceived in the past) is insufficient, but also that phenomenology – a procedure that philosophy has long used but which has been especially developed in the twentieth century – is essential to understanding human evolution. What peculiar advantage does this mode of inquiry bring to the study of the humanity of human beings, and therefore to any attempt to understand human origins? It is its willingness to take into account the presence of the observer to the observed. But this, too, requires explanation. Let us therefore begin by examining briefly the difference between the methodological predispositions that science and a phenomenological philosophy, respectively, bring to the study of man.

1. The ontological and the phenomenological approaches to the study of human nature

In the Western scientific (and in the older philosophical) tradition it has long been taken for granted that an adequate investigation of the nature of anything, including man, requires the kind of procedure that may be described as *ontological*. This is its most proper name, since its aim is to determine the nature of entities (*ta onta*) as such – that is, as they are in themselves. But *objectivity* is a more familiar tag for the same methodological orientation. An investigator who adopts this approach observes an object supposing that his observation, to be correct, must reveal the object not in relation to the observer, but absolutely or in itself. At first glance this approach seems to make good sense; but reflection should demonstrate that it involves an assumption contrary to fact. To try to observe anything as it is in itself requires pretending that one can observe it as if it were not being observed. But this is much like pretending that one does not exist: one can so pretend, and under certain circumstances there might be good reason for doing so; but the pretence itself is conclusive evidence that the fact is otherwise. And when the fact is relevant, the pretence is wrong.

The fact is not always relevant. In many ways, and in the investigation of many objects, it makes little or no difference whether one takes into account the relationship of the observed to the observer that necessarily results from observation; four centuries of spectacular progress in Western science demonstrate that it may be ignored. For the ontological approach is predicated upon some false suppositions, but also involves some that are true. To the extent that it is only approximately correct, however, it has limitations. These have become increasingly apparent and troublesome in a few areas of science; to account for certain observations at the extreme ends of the spectrum of physical phenomena, theoretical physicists such as Albert Einstein and Werner Heisenberg found it necessary to reckon with the relativity of the observed to the observer. But for most purposes of physics and many other sciences, these refinements can be omitted without any appreciable distortion in our construction of reality. However, when the object of investigation is human nature, the unrealism of the ontological perspective warps the results to a much less tolerable degree; for it now affects the investigation not at the periphery, but at the focal point.

Objectivity is often defended by science on the grounds that it would surely make no sense knowingly to allow one's subjective dispositions so to influence one's perceptions and reasoning as to distort one's representation of reality; the observer should, therefore, subtract himself from his observation and prescind from all that he, as an observer, brings to his observing activity. Besides, the argument continues, objectivity is required not only to ascertain the objective truth, but also for the sake of practicality and human values; only the understanding of reality as it actually is can serve as a sound foundation for both useful and ethically valid decisions. Unfortunately, the fact that superficial critics of objectivity often proclaim the irrationality of values and the subjectivity of truth – as if the mere negation of the false necessarily yielded the true

– lays a veneer of plausibility upon science's defence of objectivity. If the question were merely whether empirical observation and rational argumentation were more reliable bases of inquiry than empirically groundless convictions and appeal to authority, the matter would not bear much discussion. The issue is, however, whether mere objectivity is sufficiently rigorous, sufficiently consistent with its own resolve to abide by the empirical facts. Perhaps the ontological mode of inquiry was the best that our intellectual tradition could have mustered at one time, but through the very practice of objectivity we have learned that objectivity is less than fully adequate to its own ends. It is deficient in at least two respects.

Less important of the two is the naïvety of supposing that prejudice can be avoided through scrupulous observance of the canons of objectivity. We should have amassed enough collective experience in the human ways of self-deception to realize that few tricks are more easily accomplished than rationalizing one's prejudices. Quite apart from self-deception, moreover, it is impossible for anyone to experience being mistaken or prejudiced *now*; one can, at best, experience *having been* in error or biased. To overcome one's prejudices demands, therefore, the opposite of what objectivity recommends: for one must first admit that one's prejudices are such, and this requires that one confront one's subjective dispositions. Objectivity can thus be achieved only to the degree to which it is not needed; what sound scientific observation calls for is rather honesty and truthfulness. The investigator, then, need not pretend that he does not exist; on the contrary, he would be well advised to take into account the fact that he does.

Much more important is the second deficiency. The truly formidable stumbling-block in the pursuit of truth is not the bias created by wishes and values, but predispositions inherent in human nature; these include the characteristics that the mind itself has come to possess as it has evolved. For even if it were possible to check one's prejudices at the door to the laboratory, one cannot very well leave one's mind behind; the observer must bring his observational activity to the observing task. If this proposition is true – and it seems to state an empirically verifiable fact – then no one's understanding of reality can be more secure than his grasp of, or more reliable than his assumptions about, his own ability to understand. This is not to say that the mind's very process of *understanding* necessarily interferes with its experience of reality; that, too, would be incorrect and self-contradictory, the product of a shallow criticism of objectivity. The point is rather that the mind's *self-interpretation* may do so. Intelligence officers say that a field-agent's report is only as good as his controller's assessment of its reliability; likewise, one's experience of reality is profoundly affected by one's assumed or explicit assessment of precisely what one has accomplished when one has experienced it.

Moreover, not only must one venture into every inquiry bringing along one's own mind, but one must do so accompanied by numberless other minds that one has interiorized and that now make up the foundation and background of one's own; in other words, one brings along one's culture and its history. For every effort to understand occurs at a specific time and place; being but the latest episode in the biography of the individual and in the evolution of a tradition, it can never take place except within a given cultural and historical context. Thus, when an individual tries to understand man and world, it is too late for him to do what his ancestors did when they first became human: to begin at the beginning. For he has already been taught to think and inquire by a developing tradition that he did not create, but that on the contrary created him. The scientific ideal of objectivity and the notion of objective truth are themselves typical instances of culturally conditioned ways of thinking; they are not eternal, immutable truths. But since scientists tend to neglect the cultural and historical context of science,[1] they sometimes mistake as self-evident and deem to be unquestionable what in reality is not a little problematic and open to criticism.

The historical, socio-cultural nature of human understanding is thus both a help and a hindrance. Without their intellectual traditions human beings would have many fewer prejudices than they usually do – but also little to be either prejudiced or unprejudiced about. It is for this reason that it would be misguided (even if it were feasible) to attempt to understand reality by trying to wipe clean the slate of one's mind – as René Descartes thought he had managed to do. If anyone were to succeed in this endeavour, he would have squandered his intellectual patrimony; and having returned to the impoverished state of his primitive forebears he could expect to make no more progress in his own short lifetime than they in theirs; man's intellectual history can be written only one page at a time. This hardly means, however, that human beings are doomed to endless repetition of their individual and collective pasts. Intellectually, as in other respects, to the very extent to which they become conscious of the conditioning of every here and now by a former

1 Their reasoning seems to be that, although the scientific discovery of truth has of course a history and occurs in given cultural contexts, the truth itself cannot be historically and culturally conditioned, since it is determined exclusively by what reality objectively is. Therefore, understanding the historical and cultural process whereby any scientific truth has been discovered can be interesting and otherwise useful, but cannot contribute to the discovery of truth.

time, they can review, and if need be revise, their inherited presuppositions. This is what philosophy calls, in the precise and technical sense of the term, *criticism*. To be sure, no individual and even no generation can reasonably expect to have more than limited success in criticizing the fundamental concepts with which they are equipped almost from birth. But the deficiency of the ontological approach – its unrealistic neglect of the crucial empirical fact that the experienced reality is, as such, relative to the experiencing mind – can be compensated for, at least to some extent, by taking into account such relativity. And to do so is, in effect, to adopt a phenomenological approach.

The phenomenological method, then, is not the diametric opposite of the ontological; it is a more comprehensive one than the latter, whose merits it preserves and whose inadequacies it tries to remedy. It does not remotely mean the canard that everyone is entitled to take as true whatever he may imagine, or that he is free to affirm as valid whatever he might wish were so; criticism of scientific objectivity does not force upon us, as an alternative, the absurdities of subjectivity and scepticism. For human experience reveals to itself the fact that it has *content*, which is 'given' to experience neither by the properties of experience nor by the nature of the mind but by the experienced reality; this is the one true aspect of the matter that the ontological approach one-track-mindedly and myopically pursues. In other words, the ontological procedure still favoured by science is not dead wrong; but since it is, after all, only a human device, a technique, it is subject to improvement. In this case, however, improvement demands a fairly radical revision, a restructuring of ideas we have lived by for many generations. Science and our culture in general will take a long time to make the required readjustment – if they make it at all.

In what concerns the study of human nature, the deficiency of the ontological perspective is that – quite the opposite of the optical – it foreshortens what is near the observer and magnifies what is remote; it tends to flatten out the peculiarities of man. Anyone who should be disposed to study human nature as if it were alien to him, abstracting from the privileged information that he can as an insider obtain immediately about himself, would have in effect prejudicially assumed the reducibility of the human to the non-human; for he would have presupposed that the non-human, being what was first and best understood by him, provided the standard against which he could measure himself. The ontological bias is betrayed thus by the attempt to define man by establishing the difference between man and animal, since this approach presupposes that human nature is intelligible only in relation to animal life; this is what biology, following the ancient tradition, has always done. The biological theories of evolution in particular do not question the adequacy of this procedure.

A phenomenological procedure would be guided by the opposite consideration: since we have direct access to ourselves, our self-understanding need not be mediated by our prior understanding of anything else. This is not to deny that man can usefully compare himself to infrahumans; to determine what is essential to man is, in effect, to determine also what makes him both like and unlike all other beings. But we can be in a position to *infer* how animal life differs from ours only after we have ascertained what defines human nature, only after we have determined the feature *in man* by reference to which his entire reality can alone be understood. And I say to *infer*, not to perceive it directly, because animal nature, not our own, is the truly alien one: we shall forever remain limited to understanding it only as outsiders can. Therefore, the terms human *specificity* and man's *specific difference*, coined by the ontological tradition in accordance with its own assumptions, should be used by philosophy today only in a sense very different from that which they have long conveyed. To determine the human specificity, which will be our next task, shall mean here only coincidentally the same as to determine what differentiates the human from the infrahuman. Principally and most properly it shall mean: to ascertain that which most basically makes human nature immediately intelligible to itself.

But this procedure should be yet more precisely delimited. Recognition of the human specificity must be derived from observing what human beings reveal about themselves directly to themselves – but recognition of the humanity of *other* human beings begins in each one of us with recognition of his own. It is true that we can learn about human nature in general by observing others as well as ourselves; but in the last analysis, by *human being* no one can possibly mean anything but the kind of being who in every essential respect is the same as *he* is. And his understanding of his own humanity will depend on his ability to perceive and interpret what he himself exhibits directly to himself about himself. In the study of human nature, thus, renouncing introspection is more than an unnecessary, self-decreed hobble: it is an impossibility. The only choice open to us is whether introspection will be unacknowledged – and therefore unsystematically and unintelligently resorted to – or critically and methodically used.

Among the reasons why the necessity of this procedure does not always seem obvious is the fact that, after we gain even a little familiarity with our own humanity from immediate experience of ourselves, the same human quality that we apprehend in us can be detected in others through indirect though highly reliable outward signs; it is easy thereafter to confuse the indicia of humanity with humanity itself. For instance, bodily appearance being a patent mark of human quality, I look around me at passers-by and I need no further inquiry or interaction with them before I can be certain who is a fellow human and who is an ape in mufti. But though I am unlikely to be mistaken when I assume that anyone who looks like me is human, this hardly means that human nature is definable by the appearance that all human beings share. We may likewise correctly predict, judging by its origins, that a conceptus from human parents will eventually become a human being; but whether it is *already* a human being is a different question – and for reasons not altogether unconnected with this inquiry, a most controversial one. It is also one, however, that we can spare ourselves; for what concerns us here is rather that, regardless of whether a fetus is correctly deemed to be human, the question whether a given organism is actually human can be reasonably answered only from prior knowledge of what sort of feature it must exhibit before it can be properly so called. And in the final analysis this knowledge can only refer to whatever we judge truly human in ourselves, through our immediate experience of ourselves. Well, then, what does our immediate experience of ourselves tell us about ourselves?

2. The human specificity

The immediately observable fact about human nature and indispensable starting-point of every critical inquiry into the subject should be clear to anyone who reflects upon his own experience of himself: the characteristic that makes human beings human is the conscious quality of their experiential processes. All that makes our life to be what it is, without exception, either is conscious experience or else affects – or is capable of affecting – our consciousness. Our experience also reveals, of course, that conscious experience is never found in a disembodied state; the human organism is an essential part of human nature. But it is so only because of its bearing on conscious experience (and on the selfhood that goes together with consciousness). For instance, my metabolism is not an experiential function, let alone a conscious one; I must nevertheless count it as an integral part of my nature because, if it breaks down, my conscious life and my experience of myself as a self come to an irrevocable end. If I could function consciously regardless of what happened inside my body's cells, I could rightly judge that my organic functions were no part of me; but since I cannot so function, I cannot so judge.

Likewise, if I were to say that I enjoy 'life,' but thought that what I found enjoyable was 'really' a collection of biochemical events, I would betray utter confusion about myself. Such events may be a necessary cause of my enjoyment, but are hardly what I enjoy; indeed, as I have pointed out, ordinarily I remain unaware of them. What I actually enjoy is, of course, having the *conscious experience* that such events make possible, and in the first place the *conscious experience* of being alive. The 'life' that human beings enjoy is their conscious life. By the same token, most people would agree that human life is of great value; but their thinking would be incoherent if they supposed that the biological processes of the organism had any human value even in the absence of the capacity for all conscious experience. If someone's organism had, through irreversible brain damage, permanently lost the ability to experience consciously, what difference could it make to the injured person whether biochemical processes continued to take place or not? As a human being he would have already died, even if some level of life remained. Man is not definable simply as a consciousness, but he is definable as a conscious organism.

I have also stipulated, however, that being human does not depend on actual consciousness and I should explain why not. Although human beings are sometimes not conscious, their experience of themselves as selves is not discontinuous as long as the organism retains its *ability* to become conscious. The continuous exercise of such ability is not essential, because organic continuity of the capacity for conscious functioning is enough to ensure the continuity that conscious life exhibits to itself. For instance, upon awakening in the morning we experience one and the same conscious life, one and the same selfhood, that we had the night before; the continuity of our experience of ourselves has not been interrupted. Thus, as William James remarked long ago, consciousness is *experientially* or 'sensibly continuous';[2] in consciousness 'there are no breaks or cracks ... there is a felt, experienced continuity.'[3] And this is

2 William James, *Principles of Psychology* (New York, 1891), vol. I, p. 146.
3 Edna Heidbreder, *Seven Psychologies* (New York, 1933), p. 168. This observable fact is not readily evident to most of us; we are likely to rejoin that our consciousness is interrupted during sleep, fainting spells, and like events. The reply is, to begin with, that ordinary sleep and analogous states cannot be equated with absence of consciousness; they only approximate total lack of consciousness. Dreaming, for instance, is usually a conscious experience – a form of imagining – though it typically lacks the intensity of imagining of the ordinary waking state. (Nonconscious dreaming seems to be a possibility as well.) However, the deficiency of consciousness during dream and like states is variable; the dream experience may have greater or lesser 'self-presence' (as I will call the essential characteristic of consciousness in the next section). Sometimes, if the dreaming has enough self-presence, the dreamer is aware that the dream is a dream; at other times the dreaming has just enough self-presence to be a conscious experience, but not enough

the continuity that matters to us for its own sake, not that of the organism's capacity for experiencing consciously. However, the latter being the condition of the former, it follows that, although consciousness is intermittent from the viewpoint of the organism, a human organism's humanity is not intermittent as long as it retains its capacity for consciousness. But reference to actual consciousness, even if only from time to time, is essential; for only the possibility of its ultimately affecting our conscious experience invests any aspect of our organic life with the human quality we experience in ourselves.

That the essence of our humanity lies in our consciousness should be readily agreed to, since our own consciousness provides us with direct evidence of it. Nevertheless, some may cavil at this, and their two most likely objections should be heard. First, does the foregoing not imply that only human beings are conscious? That animals cannot experience consciously at all? Preliminarily and without the niceties, the answer is that, so far as we can tell, such must indeed be the case. If I put it tentatively, however, it is only to stress that this is no more than an inference; since we have no immediate access to animal experience, we cannot answer on the basis of observed fact. Later, when we examine the nature of consciousness, we shall see why we can nevertheless be reasonably certain of it; at this time we need but remark on the precise significance of the matter, which is the more important methodological issue. If it were shown that either some or all animals were or had

---

for the dreamer to be able to appreciate its imaginative nature. Of course, dreamless sleep is also a possibility; but it does not ordinarily amount to total loss of consciousness. A minimal level of it is implied by awareness of 'the passage of time' during sleep, as we usually call this experience; upon awakening the sleeper perceives that he has endured through a more or less well-defined measure of time during which he was not otherwise conscious, though it is only upon awakening that he becomes sufficiently conscious to be able fully to realize that he had been experiencing it.

But these considerations are not important; I have mentioned them only to bring to light some of our common confusions about our own consciousness. For, even if ordinary sleep does not usually exhibit it, temporary yet total absence of consciousness is perfectly possible, though rare; it can result, for instance, from deep anaesthesia under sodium thiopental. But this does not contradict the empirical continuity of consciousness; it is indeed the sort of phenomenon that best illustrates such continuity. For in these cases, when the sleeper awakes he does not feel that any time has elapsed between his becoming non-conscious and the present; it is as if he had not lost consciousness for a time. The experience is very strange, for the very reason that one experiences that no gap or break has interrupted one's *experience* of oneself, despite the fact that, as one *infers* – from clocks and other events – one's organism has lived during a period of time that did not exist at all so far as one's consciousness was concerned.

become conscious, very interesting conclusions would have to be drawn – but about animal, not human, life. For instance, we would have to say that the animals were essentially human despite their differences from us in such non-essentials as outward appearance; but this would not mean that the definition of man as a conscious organism had to be revised. Much ink has been wasted in debates between those whose study of human nature begins with the premiss that there is an essential difference between man and beast and those whose starting-point is that there is none. But the nature of human life must be understood from what it shows to itself about itself. That humans and animals differ in kind – or for that matter, that they do not – is rather a conclusion we may draw, if we can, from comparing what we know immediately about ourselves and what we can infer about animal life.

The logic of the foregoing paragraph may give some trouble to those who assume that a definition is supposed to state the specific difference of that which is being defined. If my earlier arguments against this methodological assumption and its implicit reductionism have not been sufficiently persuasive, perhaps the following analogy will help. When the Spaniards first came in contact with the natives of the New World the issue was raised whether the latter were truly human; it was debated for decades, since it had evangelical, political, and economic overtones. Precisely how the Spaniards proceeded to resolve it is not to the point, except for this: it would have been very strange if any Spanish theologian, for all his ontological predispositions, had begun his inquiry by wondering whether *he* was human, or if he had concluded that though the Indians were human *he* was not. For his question was surely not whether he was of the same nature as the Indians, but whether the Indians were of the same nature as he. In this respect, at least, the Spaniards proceeded correctly. Had they come to a negative conclusion, they would have been mistaken about the Indians, not themselves. And had they first misjudged the Indians and then recognized their mistake, they would have had little reason on that score alone to revise their understanding of themselves. Imagine, then, that evolution had produced other conscious species besides man. How would they differ, except in non-essentials, from human beings? Concluding that they did not, however, would hardly imply that we had misconceived what *we* were.

A different objection is that conscious experience is intangible and insubstantial, being but a quality of certain organic functions. Could it be said that the defining characteristic of humanity is to be found in *how* human beings experience? We naturally tend to think not, because our culture's common sense assumes the reducibility of qualities, states, functions, processes, and like *happenings* to the more solid reality of the subjects to which – as we significantly put it – they 'accrue' or 'grow onto.' Support for this view comes from the fact that events are never encountered by themselves, but only as happening to, or as being made to happen by, a subject; for from this fact we may infer that events are not apt to have any independent reality. This inference is valid; the problem is rather the gratuitous assumption that subjects have such reality. They are deemed, therefore, to be real and intelligible in themselves, whereas processes and other events are thought to have only a lesser, not fully real, reality. And if this assumption is made, it *does* follow that the defining characteristic of man must reside in some substantial reality – and if not in the organism, then in some other substantial principle capable of existing by itself, such as a soul or mind. The observable fact, however, is that subjects are never found except in the state of undergoing the events that happen to them and of activating those events that they make happen. Like subjects, events are abstractions from the single reality that unites both. It follows that, although events can happen only as embodied in subjects, subjects are definable by the events that happen to them and that they make happen to others. It is justifiable, then, to define man by the consciousness that 'accrues' to the experiential functions of his organism, and by the conscious life that he actively leads.

Here, too, theoretical physics has been the most philosophically sophisticated and the most hard-headed among the sciences, the most willing to entertain only concepts that are empirically grounded regardless of how much they may offend common sense. The matter of modern physics has lost 'its character of a substantial entity existing *in* space and enduring *through* time';[4] it is no longer the antecedent subject of events. In the nineteenth century elementary particles were conceived by physicists as independently existing bits of solid stuff whose immutable properties were manifested in variable dependent effects describable as fields of force; they were thought of, in effect, as the submicroscopic analogue of tangibly real things like bar magnets surrounded by a less than fully real, literally ethereal, magnetic field. Today, on the contrary, particles are envisaged as manifestations of fields and definable as events happening in such fields: 'This was the basic idea of modern field theory, which banished forever the old idea that particles and fields

4 Milič Čapek, *The Philosophical Impact of Contemporary Physics* (Princeton, NJ, 1961), p. 287.

were separate entities. Fields [are] the fundamental entities, but they [are] manifested in the world as particles.'[5] The properties of quantum particles are thus 'identical'[6] with the properties of their fields, and the interactions of particles are identical with the interactions of their fields. In short, material entities *are* material events.

No comparable readiness to conceive animal life as a vital event, however – let alone human life as a conscious organic event – can be detected in the other sciences; like most pedestrians, scientists tend to take for granted that consciousness is too wraith-like to define the human reality. Consciousness becomes thus relegated to the category of one among many processes that flow from human nature; or which is the same, it is generally assumed that a human being is human *before* he experiences consciously or leads a human life. We therefore seek for the explanation of consciousness in an antecedent human nature, and it would strike us as highly unusual to proceed the other way about. But the assumptions that so incline us are unwarranted.

Let us agree, then, that nothing should bar our crediting the observation that consciousness defines the human specificity. If so, the next question is: in what does consciousness consist?

3. The self-presence of consciousness

If we examine our conscious experience letting the facts lead us where they may, our very first observation may be that when we are conscious we do more than merely experience an object. This is no self-contradiction; I have not said that a conscious experience is more than a conscious experience, but that it is more than merely experiencing *an object*. Experiencing *an object* is an obviously essential part of being conscious; there can be no conscious experience unless in respect of some particular thing or other (or, of course, several at the same time). But another invariable element of experiencing an object consciously consists in experiencing, moreover, *that* the object is being experienced. We seldom remark upon it, but careful introspection reveals that we can never be consciously aware of anything without being thereby – through the same act and at the same time – aware *that* we are aware of it.

This observation points directly to the essence of consciousness. If we cannot experience anything consciously without simultaneously experiencing also our experiencing of it, then it could be said that, when

5 Heinz R. Pagels, *Perfect Symmetry: The Search for the Beginning of Time* (New York, 1986), p. 175.
6 Ibid., p. 191.

experience is conscious, the experiencing contains itself within itself. To avoid the grossly spatial connotations of this metaphor, however, let us put it literally: in every conscious experience the act of experiencing is present to itself. This implies that if one should experience an object, but the experience lacked *self-presence*, such experience would be non-conscious. Now, non-conscious experience is a difficult notion to grasp; indeed, it is not readily evident whether there actually is any such kind, either in humans or in animals. But whether, and what, non-conscious experience might be does not alter the fact that conscious experience exhibits self-presence. Non-conscious experience is not self-revealing, but conscious experience is.

Self-presence is not peculiar to certain conscious experiences; it is common to all. Nor is it restricted to our experience of ourselves, such as our conscious experience of our own organisms or of our inner states. It is a quality of our ordinary experience of all things: ships and sealing wax, cabbages and kings. In other words, the essence of consciousness is the same regardless of whether the object of the experience is external to the experiencer or an inward part of him. The description of conscious experiences of inner objects, however, is more complex than that of external ones; in this chapter we shall therefore be concerned principally with the latter. Throughout this section in particular a typical instance of conscious experience will be the sort we ordinarily have when we look at, say, an apple, and have the experience we call 'seeing' it. Of course, we are never visually conscious of an apple in isolation from many other objects which, taken all together, make up the field of experience; whenever we see 'apple' we also experience, for instance, 'red,' 'green,' 'round,' 'on the table,' and 'beside the pear.' Thus, what I have proposed as an elementary instance of conscious experience is a simplification, an abstraction out of a more complex reality. Nevertheless, the abstraction is useful – though it might mislead us if we failed to realize that it was an abstraction. Nor does the abstraction necessarily falsify the reality of our experience; for though we never see simply an apple, we *do* see things such as apples as part of the more comprehensive (and flowing) experience we ordinarily have.

But to return to the main point: we have no difficulty in observing that when we have conscious visual experience of an apple, *what* we experience is the apple. We are readily aware of the *content*, though not so readily of the *act* – even if experiencing the act itself is an integral part of every conscious act. How the human organism, especially the brain, functions so as to achieve this self-inclusion is a different question. But to understand the nature of consciousness one need not know how one does it, any more than to understand the mocking nature of cocking a hoop one needs to know – or indeed, is helped by knowing – how the physiology of sensori-motor co-ordination makes it possible to place one's thumb squarely on the tip of one's nose.

The concept of self-presence is a convenient and simple way to sum up the most elementary facts about consciousness, but the same facts may be described in very different terms. Since experiencing an object consciously includes experiencing that it is being experienced, we may say that in conscious experience the object is tagged, so to speak, as 'an [experienced] object.' This 'tagging' of the apple as '[experienced]' gives me no additional object besides the apple; it simply bestows upon the apple the status of being '[experienced].' My purpose in putting the word 'experienced' in brackets is indeed to stress that it refers only to the *status* of the object, not to a second object. And I call it the status of the apple because it is clear that being '[experienced]' is not a constitutive element of the apple itself, but merely the condition that it acquires exclusively in my experience of it and by virtue of nothing but my act of experiencing it. In contrast, the fact that the apple has this status is an intrinsic and cardinal part of my conscious experience; it is what makes it conscious. Everyone can verify this for himself. The proof is that, although we may under certain circumstances wonder whether the apple of which we are conscious is real, it is impossible ever to wonder whether it is being experienced. We can never be in any doubt whether we are experiencing it, in conscious imagination if not through sense contact with it in reality.[7]

Among the factors that needlessly add to the difficulty we experience in understanding the nature of consciousness, one of the most significant is also, in theory at least, one of the most easily remedied: our received vocabulary. We tend to use the terms *experience* and *awareness* as synonyms of *consciousness*, and to assume, therefore, that *conscious experience* and *conscious awareness* are redundancies; naturally, we are then bound to reason that the very concepts of *experience* and *awareness* include *consciousness* as an essential part of their meaning. Conversely, since this terminology implies that there is no experience or awareness but the conscious kind, even those who fully acknowledge the reality of nonconscious experience sometimes find it hard to 'resolve satisfactorily ... the contradiction between the two words.'[8]

7 The questions how the doubt may arise whether an object of experience is real or imaginary, why this doubt does not ordinarily arise, and how it can be resolved when it does arise are not directly relevant to the present topic; the answers, however, should become clear from later remarks.

8 Ronald D. Laing, *Self and Others* (Harmondsworth, England, 1969), p. 30.

We should not, however, allow words to dictate to us what they shall mean. The traditional acceptations are understandable; since in the past we had not realized that we have any but conscious experience, we could hardly have devised a different lexicon. But novel observations demand new ways of speaking. With the discovery of non-conscious experience a distinction between *experience* and *awareness*, on the one hand, and *consciousness*, on the other, has become imperative. The latter is the narrower term and presupposes the former; conscious experience consists of an experiential base, as it were, upon which conscious character is superimposed. This is, of course, a metaphor; consciousness does not rest on its experiential base as a bust rests on a pedestal. Consciousness *qualifies* experience. It is related to experience as 'fast' is to an impala's running, or better yet, as 'superb' is to Karen Kain's dancing – a superbness that does not refer to the role of Scheherazade, but to *how* she performs in it. Well, the conscious quality of conscious experience is describable as self-presence. Without self-presence the experience would remain an experience, and it would have the same contents, but it would not be a conscious one. But what would an experience be like if it were not a conscious one?

The problem in understanding conscious experience is that we are so dazzled by the object present to the act that we can easily fail to perceive the presence of the act to itself as part of the same experience. Our difficulty in understanding non-conscious experience is the opposite; we are not blinded by the obtrusiveness of the object, but are mystified by its seeming absence. In truth, however, it is not the object that is wanting; what the experience lacks is the self-presence of the act. Our self-mystification would be compounded if we thought that to understand non-conscious experience we had to experience consciously a non-conscious experience. But of course, if we did, the experience would have lost its non-conscious quality. We can nevertheless gain a little conscious insight into non-conscious experience, though only by indirection, by deducing that some of our conscious experiences have had their origin in, or have been affected by, prior non-conscious experiences. To do this is, in effect, to raise the non-conscious experience to the level of consciousness. But when we do so, we can observe that the new, conscious experience contains information we had previously processed and that had already affected us, though we had not processed it so that consciousness had resulted.[9]

9 But conscious experience is not always the result of the delayed transformation of non-conscious into conscious experience; a good deal of our conscious experience has conscious quality as soon as the information from the object is received.

The best-studied, though not the most basic, instance of this phenomenon is the Freudian unconscious. Sigmund Freud's explanation of how and why 'repression' causes the unconscious to become such may be disputed, but the fact itself is hard to deny. With but a little sophistication one may discover – always in retrospect, of course – that objects have been present in our mental processes and have created corresponding dispositions in the organism (or in the terminology I will propose later, have *in-formed* it), without there being any consciousness of such presence or of such dispositions in him who has been affected by the objects. Moreover, these objects may have been mentally manipulated and processed by the experiencer without any awareness of his having done so. The experiencer is conscious, however, of the effects of these processes upon his conscious experiences. Emotional disturbances and parapraxes – self-defeating behaviour such as slips of the tongue – are among these effects. If the unconscious becomes conscious, one may recognize in the conscious experience what had already been at work for some time in the experiential processes; now, however, the fact that it is present and at work is itself also present and at work.

The Freudian unconscious cannot be the basic form of non-conscious experience, because the repressed unconscious was originally conscious. There are, however, non-conscious experiences that are so from the outset, and that develop into conscious experience, if at all, only through further processing. This type overlaps with what Freud called the *preconscious*, and is extremely common. But since most of us, as I have said, are prone to identifying consciousness and experience,[10] we explain preconscious experience away by invoking 'inattention.' It would make little difference what we called it, if what we called it were not an excuse for ignoring inconvenient facts. There are countless ways in which stimulation impinges upon the experiential faculties of the human organism, affording it the same information as when the experience becomes conscious, but without consciousness arising: the experience does not include reference to the fact that such information has been conveyed. To explain this by saying that the organism is 'not attending' is not so much incorrect as it is vacuous and misleading, if what we really mean is that the organism has not raised the received information to that level at which experience is present to itself.

What we may not say is that before 'attention' was turned to it there was no experience at all; for information had been acquired through

10 Therefore, we tend simultaneously to suppose that animal experience is, like man's, conscious, which grants too much to animals, and that man has no non-conscious experience, which recognizes too little in man.

sense organs and might well have been used by the organism. Stimulation of the organism, say, by the weight of one's glasses on the bridge of the nose, does not begin when one 'attends' to it. One had been receiving the information for some time, but the experience lacked consciousness; that is, the experiential apparatus had been engaged, but not at the level of functioning that results in conscious experience. Much the same thing is observable when human beings are stimulated lightly during sleep; responses such as brushing away at a tickle leave no doubt that the sleeper has received sensory stimuli, though he makes no conscious motor response and does not later report having had any conscious experience at the time.

Hypnosis also illustrates the difference between conscious and non-conscious experience in humans. The subject is not conscious of the obstacle he has been commanded not to see, yet does not stumble onto it; he does not *see*, though evidently he 'sees.' The hysterically blind and the somnambulist do likewise. Their disability is not faked; there is good reason to infer that they actually 'see,' but that somehow, at the same time, they do not really *see* – consciously. The explanation may be that a sort of self-prohibition produces a purely functional 'blindness'; the conscious quality of the visual experience is either blocked or in some way nullified, though non-conscious visual experience continues. The self-presence of consciousness is what makes this self-prohibition possible; self-coincidence gives the act of experience a hold on itself, as it were, which enables it to manipulate itself.

But these are unusual phenomena. Perfectly homely is another, which is the very opposite of a hysterical symptom since it consists in arranging to receive stimulation while one is not conscious (which one will, therefore, experience non-consciously to begin with), for the very purpose of becoming conscious when the information is processed. We call this 'setting one's alarm clock.' If we did not 'hear' the sound non-consciously before becoming conscious, we would not wake up and become able to *hear* it consciously. Conversely, if there were no non-conscious experience, the attempt to awaken someone through sensory stimulation could never succeed, because he would have to be awake before he could experience it. Note, however, that the quiescence of the brain during sleep is not identical with loss or diminution of consciousness; animals sleep. But sleep affects the experiential faculties of the organism, which in man include the brain's ability to function in the way required for consciousness. Nor can non-conscious experience be equated with sleep, since it can occur in the waking state.

If even human experience can be non-conscious, the possibility that animal experience might be limited to the non-conscious level need not be strained at. It is clear that animals receive information from reality through their senses, and that receiving and processing the information so affects them that their subsequent behaviour is a function of the information; being so affected is what we may otherwise call their *experience* of the object that informs it. But there is no reason to think that the animal enjoys the advantage of having any information about the informational status of its information, or that its experience includes awareness of the experiential nature of the experience. For instance, gratification would satiate it, but would not amount to what we call pleasure because the gratification would not be felt as a [felt] gratification; the experience of pain would energize it, but even when it drove the animal into a frenzy it would fall short of unhappiness or distress, because the painful experience would not include experiencing that the experience was painful. Theirs would be, therefore, an experience that behaviourists would readily recognize, an experiencing reducible to the physiology of the experiential apparatus because it was not present to itself. Thus, when an apple is dangled before Adam and he sees it consciously, part of his experience – the contents – is the same as that which his pet chimpanzee Cheetah would have if she were in his place (or as that which he would have if he did not experience it consciously). Like Cheetah, he has been 'marked' by the apple, in the sense that his subsequent behaviour will be a function of the apple's causal, informing activity upon his senses. The difference is that his experience also includes a characteristic and unmistakable reference to the fact that the apple has informed him about itself.

I have only explained, however, why animal experience does not necessarily imply consciousness; the further question might be raised whether animals in fact exhibit signs of it. The reply would be oblique, but not inaccurate, that whereas children born of human parents always – well, usually – grow up to be human adults, young anthropoids become only monkeys and apes. That infrahumans are not conscious cannot be positively demonstrated; we can only reason from the absence of positive indications. In human beings, however, consciousness has certain consequences for their mode of life that are not observable in animals, even in lesser degree.[11] Only one inference can be reasonably drawn.

---

11 Both science and common sense often assume that the criterion of the difference between human and animal nature, if any, is intelligence; this, too, we have inherited from Greek philosophy through Scholasticism. This view gains plausibility from the fact that human intelligence does have qualitative as well as quantitative advantages over animal intelligence. The reason, however, is that intelligence is transformed once experience develops conscious quality, since it can be used consciously. For instance, both human beings and animals learn to solve problems;

I have said that it is by a single act and at the same time that we are aware of the object and of the act of experiencing it. I insist on this, because it is possible to glimpse the self-presence of consciousness but nevertheless misinterpret it by describing it as if two acts were involved. The result is that consciousness is defined as 'experience of experience' or as 'awareness of awareness.' Some go further still and construe consciousness as if it were the same as self-consciousness, or as if it consisted in the distinctively human awareness of oneself as a self. The absurdity of the latter version should be most readily apparent and will be considered first.

We can, of course, have conscious experience of ourselves. Indeed, the conscious experience of oneself as such – the experience of selfhood – is especially important for human beings; we shall presently study how selfhood necessarily follows from the conscious quality of human experience and how it lies in the background of all consciousness once the organism develops selfhood. However, if to be conscious were the same as to be conscious of oneself, one could never be conscious of anything but oneself. But self-experience is not our only conscious experience; we are also conscious of reality,[12] of things other than ourselves. Behind these misinterpretations, however, is the more fundamental mistake: supposing that conscious experience is awareness of awareness, the *reflexive* perception of prior experience. If this were so, experience could not be conscious whenever we perceived anything other than a prior experience. The matter deserves further exploration, because not a few have stumbled into this pitfall.[13]

Re-flexion – the 'bending back' of experience – consists in taking a

---

human beings, however, also learn that problems can be solved and therefore apply themselves to solving the problem of how to solve problems: they devise methodologies. The same confusion between intelligence and consciousness is manifested in other ways; for instance, some scientists have raised the question whether there is 'intelligent life' on other planets, though what they actually have in mind, as the context reveals, is the kind of life that should be essentially like our own in respect of consciousness and selfhood.

12 In deference to common usage I will ordinarily refer to external objects in general as 'reality,' and by 'a reality' I will mean an external object. But this is a misnomer; an inner object of experience is no less real than an external one. This is not to say that an inner object is the same as an external object, but that there is no warrant for supposing that external objects are the paradigm of reality.

13 The idea that the human mind can be aware of its own experiential activity only by means of a reflexive act goes back to Greek philosophy; see Aristotle, *Metaphysics*, XII, 7 (1072b19–23). But it became a well-developed view only in the Middle Ages; cf. Thomas Aquinas, *Summa Theologiae*, I, 87, 3, ad 2. In simplified form this view was adopted by the British empiricists (see, for example, John Locke, *Essay Concerning Human Understanding*, II, 1, 2–5) whence it descended to more recent times.

prior act of experience as the object of a later one. It is true, of course, that we can reflect upon our prior experience; but of itself this has nothing to do with consciousness. It is not, indeed, even a human prerogative. For instance, many animals exhibit memory; they can retain information and recall it. And to re-experience absent objects is, in effect, to experience them indirectly, through an imaginative experience that has for its direct object the prior experience of the real object. Therefore, animals are able to have reflexive experience. But if an animal is incapable of experiencing consciously, its reflexive experience of its prior experience can only be a non-conscious reflexive experience. A human being, however, being capable of both reflecting and experiencing consciously, can have a *conscious* reflexive experience of a prior *conscious* experience.

But no amount of reflexion can create consciousness out of a non-conscious experience, animal or human. To suppose the contrary is indeed illogical. For either the original experience was conscious from the outset or it was not. But if it was, a subsequent act of reflexion would be unnecessary for making it conscious. And if it was not, a subsequent experience could hardly operate retroactively so as to make the earlier to have been conscious. Moreover, if the second, reflexive act were needed to make the first conscious, what would make the second act conscious? Either the reflexive act is conscious without the need for yet another act, or else an infinite series of reflexive acts would be required before the original act could acquire consciousness. To be conscious, then, the original experience itself must be present to itself; and for the second, reflexive experience to be conscious, it itself must be present to itself.[14]

It is understandable if self-presence is often confused with reflexion;[15]

14 The confusion of some authors between direct conscious experience and reflexive conscious experience is what allows others to reason as follows: 'Some writers ... use the term [consciousness] ... meaning ... "awareness of self" or "awareness of awareness" – so that consciousness would be something which could be attributed mainly to persons. Here, we will use the term more generally to denote just "awareness" or "sentience," leaving open the likelihood that consciousness is a state which we share, at least to some degree, with other animals ... It is distinguished from states of *un*consciousness, like sleep, and from automatic episodes which are performed habitually': Charles Furst, *Origins of the Mind* (Englewood Cliffs, NJ, 1979), p. 3. To be sure, if consciousness is equated with experience, and if only reflexive experience is deemed peculiarly human, it does follow that (a) animals are conscious, since they experience, and that (b) human experience is different from that of animals only in degree. Lack of awareness of the nature of their own conscious experience accounts for the reluctance of many to believe that consciousness might be distinctive of human beings.

15 Henceforth I will adopt this somewhat unusual variant spelling to emphasize that

the latter shows a seeming self-inclusion that is reminiscent of self-presence. However, taking a prior act of experience for the object of a second does not involve *self*-inclusion; it does not bring about the inclusion of an act of experience within *its own* purview. It is rather the inclusion of one act in a second act as the object of the latter. Prior to reflexion, then, we are not aware *of* our being aware: we are aware *of* the object. But at the same time, and through the *same act*, we are also aware *that* we are aware of the object. I use this terminology, distinguishing between *awareness of* and *awareness that*, to codify the observable fact to which all reasoning in the matter must constantly return: when I see an apple consciously, I see a '[seen] apple.' I can of course reflect upon this experience; I then experience 'having seen the apple' – or more exactly, 'having seen the [seen] apple.' But I need not do this later in order to appreciate from the outset the '[seen]' status of the apple; this had been part of my original experience of it.

These affirmations rest on empirical ground. If we attend carefully to our own experience,[16] we may observe that even when we are oblivious of ourselves, so acutely concerned with an external or internal object that we are not conscious of being conscious, our experience is conscious none the less. Let us try an imaginary experiment.[17] Suppose a person who is totally absorbed in a theatrical performance, or else astounded by a sudden catastrophe; if someone speaks to him, he does not hear; if he has been wounded, he feels no pain. He is aware solely of the events unfolding on stage or of the paralysing fear that grips him; he is unaware of his awareness of them. Eventually he comes back to the everyday world and someone asks: 'What were you doing at such-and-such a time?' He replies, 'I was *watching* a play.' Or to the question 'Why has your hair turned white?' he answers without hesitation: 'I had a harrowing *experience*, living through an air-raid.' He recalls not only the play, but that he was watching it; and not only his terror, but the experiential nature of his fear. His certainty is not derived from his deducing it only now, upon reflexion; upon reflexion he recalls that he was watching, or cowering, *then*.

Could someone who reflects upon his prior experience learn only now, as if for the first time, that he has consciously experienced a certain

---

consciousness involves reflecting only in those instances where it takes itself for its own object.

16 The analysis to follow is, therefore, like every other phenomenological analysis of consciousness, a reflexive one; but the analysis describes its object, namely, the prior non-reflexive conscious experience that we subsequently reflect upon.

17 Cf. Jean-Paul Sartre, *L'être et le néant* (Paris, 1943), p. 19; George Herbert Mead, *Mind, Self and Society* (Chicago, 1934), p. 137.

external or internal object in the past? No; if one does not know it consciously from the first moment one never will; the experiential status of the object must have been part of the original experience, or else the experience cannot be recalled as a conscious one. The self-presence of consciousness prior to all reflexion explains why no one who is conscious (of anything) can be uncertain whether he is conscious (of something). Nevertheless, he can be conscious without being conscious of being conscious; indeed, most of our conscious experience is of this sort. This is not to belittle, however, the value of reflexion; scientific, philosophical, and all other intellectual, moral, and personal development, individual and social, depends upon it. But reflexion is of great value to man only because it is conscious; otherwise we would hardly know, literally, what to do with it.

Another illustration of the difference between ordinary and reflexive consciousness is afforded by a curious historical fact. We have few indications of when consciousness emerged in human evolution, but doubtless it was in prehistoric times; for even the earliest historical records reveal the type of human mind whose conscious character we can recognize as such. For instance, our classical Greek ancestors were demonstrably conscious: what they wrote communicates the kind of experience that, when we have it, we call conscious in ourselves. But though they were conscious, and indeed reflected philosophically upon their experience, they did not discover that their experience was conscious; they were not reflexively conscious of their consciousness. At least, nothing that they wrote shows otherwise.[18] It has been only in

---

18 In *The Origin of Consciousness in the Breakdown of the Bicameral Mind* (Toronto, 1976), pp. 67–83, Julian Jaynes has analysed some samples of early Greek authors showing that they did not think of their experience as being conscious. In my estimation, an analysis of the doctrine of even the later Greek writers should lead to the same conclusion, though Jaynes (pp. 255–92) and others hold a different opinion. It would be impractical to debate the matter here; but I mention that perhaps the crucial case is the doctrine of Aristotle, whose *Metaphysics*, xii, 7 (1072b19–23), is not infrequently quoted as evidence of awareness of consciousness. In this text Aristotle explains why the human mind finds it possible to understand itself despite the fact that it cannot experience itself from the outside, as it can external objects. But Aristotle's explanation is that the human mind does indeed understand itself by becoming, in a way, its own object. Since the mind is nothing but the ability to experience, he argues, it is clear that, if it could understand how it experiences objects, it would understand itself. But to determine how we experience objects is perfectly possible; we do it by reflecting upon our experience of objects. Therefore, he concludes, the mind is able to understand itself. To those for whom consciousness is the same as awareness of awareness, this proves of course that Aristotle was aware that human beings are conscious; to me it only shows that Aristotle was

recent centuries – since the Middle Ages – as a result of a long-sustained collective effort of further philosophical reflexion, that we have gradually become conscious of consciousness and that we have attempted to understand not simply the fact that we experienced but also the fact that our experience had the quality we call consciousness. And it has been only yet more recently that we have begun to understand what that quality is.

A brief digression to provide some support for these assertions would be justified; for present purposes it should be enough to consider the etymology of *consciousness*. The Greek word used today to mean the same as *consciousness* – namely, *syneidesis* – is very ancient. Although it does not seem to have been part of the technical vocabulary of the classical Greek philosophers, it is found, for instance, in the *koinē* of the New Testament;[19] its Latin equivalent, *conscientia*, also goes back to the same period. As their roots would lead one to suspect, the original meaning of both *syneidesis* and *conscientia* was not unlike that conveyed by the modern expression 'inside knowledge' – that is, knowledge obtained through consultation with someone who has privileged access to confidential or generally unavailable information, as contrasted with the mere 'beholding' and the 'knowing' (*eidesis, scientia*) for which one depends on no more extraordinary channels than one's own resources. But given their most important connotations – that *syneidesis* and *conscientia* referred to a specially reliable, keen, or vital kind of awareness – the meaning of these words tended to shift. The aspect of reliability gained prominence at the expense of the source. Eventually they came to mean any knowledge obtained through attentive or painstaking consideration; this is their ordinary meaning in the New Testament. The reliability of *syneidesis* no longer depended on consultation with another, but in thinking the matter over carefully. It resulted, so to speak, from consultation *with oneself*.

A further shift in the meaning of the terms obeyed theological causes. Early Christianity, as is well known, placed much importance in the doctrine of the 'abrogation of the Law,' since this was part of the belief that the Old Testament had been superseded by the New. When the questions arose how moral certainty could be had despite the 'abrogation of the Law,' and how uniformity of Christian moral norms could be maintained, the concepts of *syneidesis* and *conscientia* were ready at hand to help solve the problem. In the Christian literature these terms soon

aware that human beings are capable of understanding themselves by reflecting on themselves.

19 2 Corinthians 4:2; Hebrews 10:2.

came to designate the kind of knowledge about moral matters whose reliability depended not on the explicit clarity of 'the letter of the Law,' the moral code promulgated in Sinai which demanded *verbatim* obedience, but on the 'spiritual' nature of the moral law inscribed by God in the human heart, as it were, which could be discerned by the Christian listening inwardly as he would to a privileged source. This meaning is preserved, of course, in our *conscience*.

The next great shift began to occur towards the end of the Middle Ages. As the modern Christian vernaculars emerged, many of them retained a single word (e.g., French *conscience*, Spanish *conciencia*) to signify somewhat ambiguously two meanings that even before Descartes had been growing appreciably dissimilar, but that after him would become unavoidably disparate. In English, however, the separation was codified in the distinction, taken for granted by John Locke and generally well-established by the end of the sixteenth century, between *conscience* and *consciousness*. The bifurcation had begun with the formation of two adjectives, *conscientious* and *conscious*, out of the single word *conscience*; when *consciousness* was then coined through back-formation from *conscious*, the process was complete. The difference between *conscience* and *consciousness* was, of course, that the latter abstracted from the moral connotations of the former. Moreover, *consciousness* (and the equivalent second acceptation in the European languages that continued to use the same word in both the moral and the non-moral senses) now increasingly connoted not 'awareness of self' in particular, but 'awareness' of anything. These shifts reveal a growing recognition of the conscious nature of human experience – I mean, in the contemporary sense of *conscious* – since it grants to awareness in general the intimacy and immediacy that the patristic and mediaeval meaning reserved for self-knowledge, and that the classical term restricted to knowledge obtained through privileged channels. The self-presence of consciousness was beginning to rise to the surface.

For all that, the modern usage sanctioned a perception of our own experience that was very inadequate; it hallowed and institutionalized the difficulty we still experience in recognizing that *awareness* is not the same as *conscious awareness*, and that consciousness includes, but is not reducible to, experience. It also implied that self-experience can be obtained exclusively by reflexion. Nevertheless, it was insightful enough to permit us eventually to face the true issue: whether immediacy was not part of *all* conscious experience rather than peculiar to self-experience or to experience obtained through reflexion or through special channels. For the early-modern usage did not altogether rule out, as *syneidesis* and *conscientia* originally did, the possibility of non-conscious experience (in the modern sense of that term). The classical terms precluded it, because they implied their own distinction between conscious and non-conscious experience (i.e., between *syneidesis* and *eidesis* and between *conscientia* and *scientia*), though this was a distinction that had nothing to do with our present one. (The original meaning of *eidesis* and *scientia* referred, of course, to forms of experience that, in the modern sense, were every whit as conscious as *syneidesis* and *conscientia*.) The original vocabulary embodied thus a deeper level of non-consciousness of consciousness, a yet more confused perception of the conscious nature of human experience, than that which, despite our still inadequate terminology, prevails today.[20]

Quite as the self-presence of consciousness should not be construed as involving two acts of experience, it should not be taken for the simultaneous presence of two objects in experience. Nevertheless, consciousness does involve a true duality; the [experienced] *object* is one thing, whereas the *act* of experiencing [the object] is another. But this does not mean that conscious experience is the mental *repetition* of external objects; the 'content' of experience is not a representation of the object, but is the real object itself. The duality found in consciousness may therefore be likened to a polar field; one pole is the object [of experience], which exists only in reality; the other is the experiencing [of the object], which occurs exclusively in the experiencing organism. In non-conscious experience, to be sure, there are both an act and an object. But the two do not make up a field because only the object is present to the act; the act is not present to itself. Thus, an organism that experiences non-consciously has become related to an object, but its being so related is no part of the experience itself. In conscious experience, however, the organism is simultaneously informed by the object and by the fact that it is so informed. That is why the human organism can react not only to *the* object – that is, conformably to the object's properties, as animals can – but react to it also *as* object, or in relation to its [experienced] status. Let us therefore mark well – because we shall need to use this conclusion later – that only a conscious experiencer can

---

20 It is one thing, however, to claim that the Greeks were not conscious of being conscious, in the sense that they did not think of their experience as being conscious; it is quite another to suppose that they were not conscious, as Jaynes does. What the Greeks said in their interpretations of human nature is only evidence of the former. The evidence that they *were* conscious is that they interpreted human nature at all, and that they communicated their interpretations to posterity in ways that are possible only to those who are conscious.

relate himself to an object experienced precisely *as an object*, or to an *other* that is experienced precisely *as other*; for only this kind of experience informs itself about itself.

Note, finally, one more indication that consciousness is only a quality of the human experiential functions: that consciousness has no particular object of its own. Objects of conscious experience are the same as objects of non-conscious experience, but experienced consciously by those who have the capability; the difference between the two is unlike the difference between two sense powers such as hearing and seeing, which require different organic receptivities in relation to different types of information provided by reality. But seeing and hearing require no new or different object of experience in order to be *conscious* seeing and hearing; they require only additional processing. Thus, we can see consciously and hear consciously, and we not only sense external and internal objects consciously but also imagine and remember them consciously. Our reasoning about them, too, is conscious. Whatever can be experienced non-consciously can also be experienced consciously by any experiencer who has the organic wherewithal and who has acquired the capacity to process information in the appropriate way.

We have established, then, that consciousness is the distinctive quality of human experience, and what this quality consists in. We have so far taken for granted, however, the nature of experience. Before we continue we should, if only briefly, look into the organic function that is apt to acquire conscious quality when performed by a human organism.

4. The experiential base of consciousness

All experiential processes, animal or human, conscious or non-conscious, have a fundamental characteristic in common: they begin with sensation, the reception of information. By *information* I mean the effect wrought on sentient organisms by the efficient causality of objects of experience. Thus, although conscious experience depends for its conscious quality solely on how the information is processed, without the reception of information there could be no consciousness, since there would be nothing to process. And without an object, of course, there can be no information. Therefore, an interpretation of consciousness can be no more adequate than its explanation of the causal process whereby the organism acquires information, with which all experience begins.

The proposition that objects exert efficient causality upon sentient organisms can be valid only if understood in the sense warranted by the observable facts. Ordinarily, however, we are inclined to think of information as something that, albeit insubstantial, intangible, and purely 'formal,' is actually *transmitted* from the informing reality to the informed organism and actually *received* by the organism. But in fact, all we can observe is that sensible objects have certain characteristics, and that sensing organisms behave differently in respect of such characteristics and in proportion to them. This proportion between the object and the organism's behaviour entitles us to speak of the relationship between the two in causal terms; it is scarcely a mere coincidence that when a dog is shown Wow-Bits it salivates, wags its tail, and unerringly proceeds to consume the food, whereas in the presence of masked strangers it barks, snarls, and attacks. And the simplest experiment would show that its responses were mediated by physiological processes that included the operation of its visual and olfactory apparatus. But nowhere do we observe the 'transmission' of anything called 'information' from the object to the experiencer[21] or the latter's 'reception' of it. I will, for the sake of convenience, retain here this familiar terminology as I explain how objects cause information in sentient organisms; but since in reality nothing passes from the one to the other, we should be warned that the traditional vocabulary makes use of a thoroughly inappropriate and grossly misleading metaphor.

We are not wrong when we think that sensation involves a causal process; the problem is that we are likely to mistake the nature of causality in the first place. Most of us assume that it consists in the exercise of a 'power' that resides in causal agents, which they bring to bear upon

---

21 It could be argued that, at least in some forms of sensation, physical continuity between the object and the sense organ appears to be preserved through the transmission of particles – though in the light of modern physics the questions might be raised in what sense this was true of any sense modality and whether it was true of all. The truth of the matter, however, would not be to the point. No philosopher since Gorgias has proposed that information is a substantive entity that travels from the object to the experiencer riding on either particles or waves; and for my part I do not contest that, in at least some forms of sensation if not all, objects can exert physical efficient causality on sentient organisms only through some sort of physical contact. What I deny is merely that when they do so *information* passes from the one to the other. The difference between object and experiencer – the fact that one is not the other – would be bridged through *transmission* of information properly so called only if we were to suppose, as our philosophical tradition long did, that the object contained within itself something of the order of experience (e.g., an 'idea,' a 'form,' an 'essence,' or as we would say today, 'information'), which was somehow replicated in the experiencer as an effect of the object's causality. But my argument is, indeed, that even this purely formal transmission of information would be an empirically unjustified supposition. The fact that the causality of the object upon the sentient organism has an 'informing' effect does need explaining, but it should not be explained through suppositions that lack a foundation in observable facts.

a patient as 'energy' or 'force' so as to compel or 'necessitate' the effects. But as David Hume pointed out, this idea of causality is not supported by observation: no compulsion, no necessary connection, and no force or transfer of force is actually observable. All we can witness is the causal events and the effects, and the proportion (including invariable sequence) between them. Since even science has not yet managed, except in a few isolated respects, to forgo the supposition that causality involves the transformation of energy and the exertion of forces vested in particles or other 'material' substantive entities, it should not come as a surprise that the common-sense notion of causality has survived Hume's criticism unscathed. Nevertheless, it is possible to think in causal terms while adhering to the empirical facts.

To do so we need but take into account the mutual relativity of all things. For instance, if one is resolved – as Einstein was[22] – to abide by experience, motion cannot be ascribed to bodies as their absolute characteristic. Indeed, absolute motion is a contradiction in terms; it would be *absolute* motion *in relation to* absolute space. And since the only reason why anyone should postulate an absolute space – as Newton did – is that it would be required by absolute motion, we must forgo absolute space and motion and affirm that bodies are in motion only in relation to each other. Note that the relativity of motion does not gainsay its reality; for though it means that things do not have motion within themselves as a characteristic in their possession, the change in mutual spatio-temporal *relations* that constitutes motion is utterly real none the less. Now, assuming the relativity of motion and the superfluousness of absolute space, Einstein was able to explain gravitation without resorting to the concept of force: the relative motions of bodies in free fall are affected by their mutual presence in proportion to their respective characteristics; for though they do not exert a force on each other, their mutual presence defines the spatio-temporal environment in which each one operates; changes in their spatio-temporal relations are changes in

22 There was, however, a limit to Einstein's resolve. Despite his empiricism regarding motion he never overcame his *a priori* belief in deterministic causality (which is why he later rejected Werner Heisenberg's uncertainty principle). Evidently, he did not realize the implications of his general theory of relativity for the concept of causality. Curiously, Heisenberg's limitation was the very opposite; he was aware that quantum theory implied a non-deterministic concept of causality (*Physics and Philosophy* [London, 1959], pp. 81–2), but nevertheless retained the concept of force 'in complete analogy to [classical] macroscopic dynamics' (Max Jammer, *Concepts of Force: A Study in the Foundations of Dynamics* [New York, 1962], p. 250). Indeed, he even drew the consequence that energy or causal power is the single ultimate reality out of which all material entities are made (*Physics and Philosophy*, p. 139).

the mutually relative conditions under which the characteristics of each, in fact, operate. Thus, 'gravitation in general relativity has not the character of a force. It is a property of space-time.'[23]

It may be suggested, however, that the same principle of relativity applies to all the other characteristics of things; they are real, but relative to those of other things. For there is no warrant in experience for thinking that the other characteristics of things are their absolute possession any more than their motion is; to say that a thing has certain properties is rather to say that it can make a certain difference to other things. To be sure, a thing affects other things by virtue of its being such as it is; it acts upon others as it does because of characteristics that belong to it. But we can say that it is such as it is, and that it has certain characteristics, only because it affects others as it does. For instance, to identify the chemical properties of a given substance we test its interactions with other substances; to identify those of organisms we observe how they relate themselves adjustively to their environment. In short, the characteristics of things are intelligible only by reference to the characteristics of other things, and their causality is intelligible only by reference to the differences that they make to each other. Among these differences are to be included those which one characteristic of a thing can make to other characteristics of the same thing. For things can act causally upon themselves; that is, things can make a difference to themselves by virtue of the relationships among their properties.

This relativity may be enough to explain the nature of all causality. Deterministic causality is imagined to reside within the causal agent absolutely, under the guise of a gratuitously postulated energy or force; Newtonian gravitational force is an instance of it. But *relativistic causality*, as we may refer to it, requires no force or necessitation, and explains causal processes resorting to the observable relationships among things; relativistic gravitation is only an illustration of it. Consider, say, a seal leaving its mark upon wax. The wax has undergone an effect rightly attributable, in part, to the seal. But since it has been shaped – or given its new form – by the seal, we can say that it has received *in-formation* from the seal by virtue of the properties of the seal. No shape, however, has been trans-mitted, sent across from the informer to the informed.

---

23 Jammer, *Concepts of Force*, p. 260. However, the 'revision of the concept of force ... is far from ... [complete] even at present. In fact, it has been carried out successfully so far only with respect to gravitational forces ... If it were possible to work out a unified field theory that subjects electromagnetic and possibly also nuclear forces to a similar treatment as gravitation, it would lead us to a final stage in the history of the concept of force' (pp. 257, 263–4). As of this writing, the situation to which this statement refers remains unchanged.

For the seal retains *its* shape; and the shape 'acquired' by the wax is likewise its own and never was the seal's. Indeed, to say that it was 'acquired' by the wax does not mean that it existed anywhere before the wax 'acquired' it; it simply describes the fact that the shape of the wax has changed – a change that bears proportion to the shape of the seal. Likewise, when one billiard ball strikes another, no motion, energy, or information has been transferred to the second ball, though the motion of the second has undoubtedly changed by reason of, and in proportion to, the motion of the first. Let us say, then, that the second's motion has been informed by the first's. Physical efficient causality is, therefore, the elementary form of communication, and efficient causality in general may be described as an informational process.

The relativistic explanation of efficient causality is, therefore, (a) that things are constituted by certain properties; (b) that these properties are self-consistent and coherent; (c) that they are, nevertheless, relative to the properties of other things (as well as mutually relative within the same thing); and (d) that when things interact, they are mutually informed by each other's properties and in proportion to them. The mutual relativity of the properties of things means that they make a difference to each other in proportion to their respective properties; it is this proportion that lends itself to the illusion that something has been 'transmitted' by one and 'received' by the other, and that the expeditionary 'force' despatched by the cause has compelled the yielding of the effect. But in reality the events have happened as a matter of fact – quite as a body accelerating in a gravitational field with mathematically predictable regularity does so strictly as a matter of fact. Likewise, the cause of evolution, as we have seen, is no evolutionary force, but the interaction between the mutually relative reproductive and adaptive functions of organisms. By the same token, the concept of an organism's 'environment' refers to no more absolute a reality than does that of space: the environment is constituted as such by the relation that others bear to the organism, quite as the organism's 'adaptability' is constituted by its relation to its environment. To Darwin should go the credit for having been the first in our intellectual tradition, long before Einstein, to have provided a relativistic causal explanation of anything.

The absence of force in causal processes, however, does not mean that the invariable sequence of causal events is inexplicable. A causal explanation has been found when out of information provided by reality a conscious experiencer composes a logically coherent narrative that tells how the invariable properties of things account for the invariable way in which, strictly as a matter of fact, they act and interact. The relativistic concept of causality allows thus for the emergence of effects that, although irreducible to their causes, are intelligible only by virtue of their relationship to them. Conversely, though effects are, in principle, exhaustively explicable *by* their causes, they are not absolutely predictable *from* their causes. Retrospective logic does not imply prospective necessity. Causality has a built-in arrow, to which consciousness gives recognition by means of the category of *time*.

Let us return to sensation. Sense experience begins with the causal activity of an object upon the kind of organism we call sentient – the kind that has the ability to receive information in the peculiar way we shall consider in a moment. But apart from this special receptivity there is no difference between this causal process and one that involves only inanimate providers and recipients of causal information. As in every other instance where causality is at play, the sentient organism is informed – it becomes *marked*, as it were – by the cause, in the senses that, once the cause has acted upon it, its behaviour will be different than it would otherwise have been, and that such behaviour will bear proportion to the cause. Below the level of life, however, things inform each other but can take no initiative in shaping their own reality; they are 'inert,' totally at each other's mercy, so to speak. However, since they lack even the inherent purposiveness of living things (namely, self-preservation), let alone more complex forms of purposiveness, there is no sense in which they could be properly said to take advantage of the effects that their mutually informing activities work on them.

In marked contrast, even the most elementary form of life determines itself in part. For every living organism acts so as to participate in the processes whereby it is related to other beings; its behaviour is 'adaptive.' *Adaptation*, however, does not connote vividly enough the active *self-determination* implied by life. The activity of a living entity contributes to its condition, its 'shape,' at any given time; the events that befall it are not caused exclusively by its environment. For the environment is reacted to by the organism, whose response is determined not only by the nature of the stimulus but also by that of the organism. Correspondingly, a living being *takes advantage*, for its own adaptive purposes, of the properties of other things.

At the most fundamental level of life, an organism does so by incorporating others into itself. Organic life cannot be maintained by any entity except at the expense of foreign substances that it appropriates. At the higher level represented by sentient life, however, the organism's role in determining its life unfolds in a novel, unilateral, *interior* way: sentience benefits the sensing organism, but not at the expense of the sensed. The course of the organism's life continues to depend in part upon the causal activity of others, but its own causal role overshadows that of the other. The difference is that the sentient organism not only maintains its own existence, but shapes it in a new way: it makes use of the informing, causal activities that others bring to bear upon it, but entirely within itself and without affecting the other in any way. That is, it takes advantage of the information that the other provides *in place of itself*. The peculiar 'receptivity' of sentient organisms consists in their ability to receive information specifically in this way. Sentience is the sort of communicative process that depends not only upon the mutual relativity of all things, but specifically upon the *self-relating* ability of certain organisms.

These remarks should explain why I feel entitled to say that, when the object informs the sensing organism, information is no valid sense either transmitted or received. Nor does the information represent the informer, or create a counterpart of it in the informed.[24] It also explains why no experience – conscious or otherwise, animal or human – may be said to have contents of its own that represent the contents of the object. Only the object may be said to have contents – namely, the characteristics that make up the object itself. But the sensing organism is informed by the informing object in accordance with the latter's characteristics. Thus, on the one hand, when the organism thereafter processes the information, it experiences specifically the object that has informed it rather than any other. On the other hand, how the organism processes the information – how it proceeds to experience – is not determined by the information or the informer but only by the nature of the experiencing organism itself.

I have so far treated *sensation* and *sense experience* as synonyms, though a strict terminology would distinguish between them. The difference is that whereas sentience began with the simple 'irritability' of primitive

---

24 It might seem to follow that nothing could ever be properly said to be a representation, duplicate, or counterpart of another thing. But this is surely false; do not photographs, carbon copies, and magnetic tape recordings represent, duplicate, and stand as counterparts of their originals? They do indeed, but what does this mean? We tend to think that a representation performs in relation *to an original*, the function of representing it. In fact, however, a representative represents the original *to an experiencer* who, being conscious and able to experience both the original and the representation, is able to experience also the similarity (or other ground of association) of his experience of one to his experience of the other. Thus, one reality can represent another – to an experiencer – but experience cannot be a representation of reality, since experience is the precondition of the representation. The fact that representations are such only for an experiencer also explains why representations need not depend on similarity to the represented; whatever may serve to relate one experience to the other – even convention – may be a sufficient basis for the representation to represent the original to an experiencer.

animal life, its evolution ultimately brought forth the kind of sentient life that could improve the quality of its adaptive responses through accumulating and processing information received from objects. To adapt had then become: to profit from 'experience' – or as the etymology of the word graphically reminds us, 'from having gone around.' Unlike mere sensation, then, experience includes the ability to inject feedback from earlier into current sentient processes. (We shall have occasion later to verify that the self-presence of consciousness builds specifically upon sense *experience* thus understood, and not merely upon the relatively passive sense 'reception' of information.) Organic life had risen thus to a new level of spontaneity and self-determination. As the characteristic purposiveness of all life became goal-oriented rather than goal-dictated behaviour, a novel 'freedom' from stereotypy of behaviour appeared; the organism now not only found what it needed, but also sought it and selected it from among objects sensed.

Experience virtually contains, then, the lower level of mere sentience, but is not reducible to it. Its evolutionary novelty did not concern so much the ability to receive information or to act upon it as it did its processing. For the organism now enjoyed not only the ability to participate in the events that determined its life, but also the ability to determine *how* to take part in such determination; it was responsible for the *quality* of its adaptive responses. It was able, therefore, not only to adjust as a function of the sense information received, but also adjustively to modify its adjustive behaviour. What mattered at this stage of evolution, in short, was not merely how much and what information was received, but above all *how* the information was experienced. Differences in the quality of experience would be even more important at the next stage; man and anthropoid receive much the same kind and amount of information from objects, but because they process it differently they can put the same information to vastly different use. The difference between experiencing objects non-consciously and experiencing the *same* objects, but consciously, is the difference between the animal and the human modes of life.

5. The consequences of consciousness for the human mode of life

The direct consequences of consciousness for the individual are three; all other manifestations of humanity follow from these. First, the conscious experiencer is able to appreciate the *reality* of the real. This proposition refers in the first instance to the reality of the non-self, or world. But if an experiencer can experience realities as real, then he is capable, second, of experiencing his own reality; he can think of himself as a *self*. Therefore, third, appreciating both his reality and that of the world, he can give himself a positive identity by interpreting himself in relation to an interpreted world; this self-given identity I shall call the *self-definition* of the self. These three consequences for the individual, however, converge upon, and are embodied in, a further consequence for the human group: they generate its *culture*. For the institutionalization of the processes by which individual selves define themselves as they interpret themselves and reality is what defines a society's culture in the strict, human sense of the term. Let us see why all this should be maintained.

In animal experiencers, adjustment depends upon the simple reception of information from the world, whereas the emergent character of conscious experience, as we have seen, depends on the inclusion, within such experience, of the informational status of the information. Therefore, conscious organisms do not merely adapt to objects, but specifically to objects whose objectivity is appreciated. In other words, since the conscious organism does not merely experience an object, but an object that is '[experienced],' the concomitant of the ability to experience an object consciously is the ability to experience it as *other-than* the experiencing of it. I do not say, however, other-than the *experiencer*. We shall see presently that experiencing oneself as an experiencer, and therefore as a self, is indeed a normal consequence of the ability to differentiate between objects and the activity of experiencing them – but it is the outcome, not the pre-condition, of consciousness. Thus, to our previous conclusion (that whereas all experience relates the organism to an object, conscious experience relates it to an object as such) we may now add: whereas at all levels of sentience and experience the object is other than the experience, at the level of consciousness the other is, moreover, *experienced* as other.[25] The difference between experiencing *an* other and experiencing it *as* an other is the difference between experiencing objects

25 If one is not well aware of this distinction, one will inevitably overlook the fact that it is typical of consciousness to *differentiate* itself from its object, and one will therefore mistake consciousness for the *assimilation* of the object by the mind. That is, a philosopher may observe that human beings experience the otherness of objects, but he may conceive the otherness of the other as a pre-condition of experience; he will then explain consciousness as the mind's overcoming of its original alienation from objects. Thus, the alienation of the mind from its objects was explicitly noted by the later Scholastics at least as far back as the seventeenth century, when John of St Thomas said that to know was 'to become the other than self ... as other than self' (*Cursus Philosophiae: De Anima*, IV, 1). But this formula served only to perpetuate the confusion that had generated it. To experience consciously, I underline, is not to *become* the other as other, but to *experience* the other as other.

that in fact are real, but without experiencing that they are real, and experiencing them with awareness of their being real. It is thus that the sense of reality is generated in the human mind.

The necessary counterpart of the sense of reality is the sense of *self*. The reason is that otherness is a relationship. To experience the other as other is to experience it as other-*than* something else, or as other-to-another. And since to experience an object consciously is to be aware of it as other-than the act whereby it is experienced, it follows that to be conscious of an object is the same as to experience it as relative to, or as other-than, the 'something else' that is the act of experience. This 'something else' is what eventually the conscious organism learns to call *me*.

But only eventually: for what we call *I* or *me* – the self that experiences consciously – is originally devoid of all identity; it comes into being bereft of all positive content. We can understand why, if we reflect upon the process I have just described. The conscious organism awakens to its own reality by experiencing itself merely as the 'something else' to which real objects are relative; the self is, to begin with, nothing but other-than-the-object. It is, indeed, if I may awkwardly but exactly put it, nothing but the other-that-the-other-is-other-than; it is, therefore, born to conscious life as a purely negative reality, being merely that which is *not*-the-object. Selfhood begins, then, as a mere capacity for *acquiring* identity; this capacity is grounded on the fact that the organism's experiential activity has included itself (albeit purely negatively, as its *not-being* the object) in the experiencing of the object. Thus, conscious organisms possess their own identity only because they construct it; they are persons only because they develop personhood. Selfhood is the quality that conscious experience earns for itself in consequence of its presence to itself.

What I have just proposed runs counter to our common assumptions, which suppose that the self is an aboriginal substantive reality. According to preference, the I may be identified with the organism (or at least with its immature, genetic potentialities) or with a non-organic soul or mind, or else with the composite of organism plus mind, or body and soul; but, in any case, the human person supposedly pre-exists his development. The *ego* is, therefore, deemed the subject of accidental events and operations; it comes into being first, and after it has human reality and existence it activates its faculties and obtains experience. Among other experiences, so runs the argument, it experiences its own reality and conscious nature, eventually becoming conscious of its consciousness and of the selfhood that it possessed at least in immature form even before it was conscious.

This construction, however, is not justified by experience. It is indeed absurd, if one accepts the fact that one is *really* whom one experiences oneself to be. For the most fundamental empirically given characteristic by which one can identify one's selfhood is: being the experiencer who performs one's conscious acts. To be oneself is above all to be the owner of one's own experience. But the self could perceive itself as the performer of its conscious acts, or as the owner of its own experience, only *after* the organism had performed conscious acts and only *after* there was conscious experience that could be owned. Thus, selfhood is not the antecedent, but the consequent, of conscious experience; the only antecedent required by selfhood is an organism that can function consciously, though it is not yet a person.[26] But consciousness personalizes itself; better yet, the organism creates its personality by means of its ability to function consciously. When experience becomes present to itself as an act that is other-than-the-object, it provides itself with an inner receptacle, so to speak, which in time it can fill with empirical contents about itself. But by creating its identity the human organism eventually *contains* itself and experiences that it *owns* itself. Of course, self-appropriation is achieved by individual human beings to very different degrees; in any event, it is the result of a long process.

The same analysis also shows why the interpretation of consciousness as the inner mental possession of the outer world (for instance, as the 'symbolic' representation of it) is topsy-turvy. To describe non-conscious experience – the mere reception of information – as an 'assimilation' of the object to oneself or as a 'union' of object and experiencer would be incorrect, if taken literally, but would be a tolerable figure of speech. The peculiarity of conscious experience, however, runs in the very opposite direction: it is that conscious experience has an essentially negative relationship to reality. Self-presence enables the experiencer to *differentiate* himself from everything that is other-than-himself; consciousness *separates* itself from the object that informs it. Being informed is, of course, the pre-condition of the self-differentiation of consciousness from the world; but, by experiencing the other precisely *as other*, the conscious experiencer *stands off* from the other; he introduces a di-stance, or interposes a boundary of mutual opposition, between the object and himself. So doing is indeed what enables him to experience the object as real, or *as itself*, and himself *as himself*.

The concept of reality is thus the foundation of the human mode of

26 Its aboriginal lack of selfhood, however, does not prevent its having the inborn, genetically determined dispositions that will later condition the self-identity that it will give itself.

life, first, in the sense that it is essential to the conscious experiencer's organization of his experiences of himself so as to create his self-identity. By means of self-attributions based on experience we can give ourselves a positive identity and construct an elaborate selfhood – but only if we first experience ourselves as real, since only then can we ascribe to ourselves *as our own* what we experience ourselves to be. Animals can, of course, experience what in fact is themselves, but they cannot appropriate it; they cannot own themselves. In other words, perception *of oneself* is hardly the same as perception of oneself *as a self*. If I were not able to think of myself – both my organism and its conscious experience – as being *really* who and what I perceive myself to be, my self-experience would remain a succession of impressions about an object, but not about *me*. I would be, to myself, a bundle of facts, not a *self*. That is, I would organize my perceptions of myself in the same way as I would organize my perceptions of fellow creatures, and I could behave (as even animals can) in the light of perceived differences between self and other; but I would not *experience* that there was a difference. In sum, my own self would be quite as alien to me – quite as objective an object – as would anything other than myself.

The distinction between perception *of oneself* and perception of oneself *as a self* should help us interpret critically the results of a well-known experiment. Chimpanzees can learn to use a mirror to groom themselves and to explore areas of their bodies not otherwise visible to them; and they have been observed searching their faces, by means of a mirror, for marks made by the experimenter which they could have seen for the first time only in the mirror.[27] These results have been widely accepted by scientists as evidence of 'self-awareness' and of a 'self-concept' comparable to the 'sense of self-identity' which 'has been held unique'[28] in human beings. This conclusion, however, seems to me unwarranted. The results indicate that a chimpanzee can learn to recognize a mirror image as a duplicate of a directly perceptible object, and vice versa, including an object that happens to be its own body. But they do not indicate that chimpanzees perceive their bodies as their own, whether directly or by means of a mirror.

The rationale of the experiment was that 'to correctly infer the identity of the reflection must ... presuppose an already existing identity on the part of the organism making the inference. Without an identity of your

27 See Gordon G. Gallup, Jr., 'Self-Recognition in Primates: A Comparative Approach to the Bidirectional Properties of Consciousness,' *American Psychologist*, 32 (1977), pp. 329–38.
28 Ibid., pp. 329, 334.

own it would be impossible to recognize yourself'[29] in a mirror. This reasoning, however, reveals a certain amount of confusion. Recognizing the image of one's body in a mirror as an image of oneself requires not merely a prior 'existing identity,' but a prior *experience* of such identity. And the prior experience requires more than the experience *of* one's organism; it presupposes the experience of one's organism *as one's own*. But the prerequisite of the latter is the experience of *one's experiencing* as one's own – in other words, consciousness. For a self is not simply an organism that can experience itself, but one that can experience itself as the experiencer of its experience. Thus, a dog chasing its tail chases an object that in fact is its own organism (as *we*, who are conscious, are able to appreciate), but this hardly implies that the dog *experiences* its organism as its own, or that it *experiences* selfhood. In short, consciousness is the pre-condition of experiencing selfhood; the experience of selfhood is in turn the antecedent of experiencing one's organism as one's own; and it is only if one has learned to experience one's organism as one's own that one can experience the reflection of one's organism in a mirror as an image of oneself.

The experience of self-identity was, therefore, not detectable by this experiment; all it could have told us was whether the animal could learn to use a mirror – that is, whether it could learn to identify a mirror reflection of an object and the directly perceived object. The experiment demonstrated that it could. This ability may require a great deal of intelligence, but it has nothing to do with selfhood; for if an animal could learn to use a mirror to identify other objects and their images, it would need no additional skill, and certainly no experience of selfhood, to do it when the object happened to be its own body. Under the heading of 'self-recognition' the experimenter confused recognition *of* one's own organism and recognition of one's organism *as* one's own. I underline that his confusion was about the *human* experience of self-identity, not about chimpanzees. Though human beings learn from a fairly early age to perceive themselves as selves, it is evidently less easy for them to understand precisely what they thus learn, and how. A human being might, therefore, have a sense of self-identity, yet have so vague and inaccurate an idea of what self-identity meant that he might devise an experiment as unsuitable as the foregoing for demonstrating anything relevant to the question whether chimpanzees have self-identity in the human sense.

Second, the concept of reality operates in the same way – as the foundation of the human mode of life – when it is used to organize our

29 Ibid., p. 334.

experience of the non-self. It is for this reason that the succession of experiences does not remain for human beings a series of biologically and behaviourally related, but experientially incoherent, events. Under the concept of reality they are organized as *world*. Consciousness does not live merely in what, as a matter of fact, is a world; it lives in and adjusts to the world *as world*, because it experiences objects as objects making up a world. And as the experiential life of consciousness grows, its world expands. Through experience, the conscious experiencer learns to perceive himself as living out his reality in world that, being open to interpretation and reinterpretation, constitutes his *situation*, the environment in which he lives as a self. Even in respect of the physical environment, then, human adaptation is essentially different from its animal counterpart. For instance, when objects are experienced as real, they can be experienced as 'stuff,' 'supplies,' 'furniture,' 'ingredients,' 'ore,' and the like. Things become useful and instrumental, in principle and universally, for the satisfaction of human wants and needs; they become 'property.' They can also be thought of as 'matter' by the simple expedient of abstracting from the differences that characterize them and reducing them to their common denominator – namely, their being available to us, because they are other than us. Some animals may use tools, and a few may even learn to make tools; but for us the world itself – whatever is real – is a tool.

The idiosyncrasies of human adaptation are especially noteworthy, however, in respect of the peculiarly human environment, the non-natural, non-physical world that humans create for themselves in consequence of their being conscious. Since every conscious experiencer experiences his own reality, he must adapt to that reality which is himself; and since he experiences other human beings as selves (or as experiencers who experience themselves as selves and him as a self), he must adapt to them also in the same respect. Of course, the others must, for their part, adapt themselves to themselves as selves, and to him as a self. The outcome of the processes that begin when experience becomes present to itself is thus an artificial, self-perpetuating network of experiential relations constituted by consciousness of oneself and of other selves – in other words, *society* and *culture* in the human sense. This is the world in which conscious experiencers as such willy-nilly live, since they create it automatically, simply by being conscious. The fact that this environment is artificial, and that human beings manufacture it out of nothing more tangible than their experience of themselves and each other, makes it no less real than the natural, physical environment. Indeed, this experiential environment is the yet more important locus of their lives than that which contains rock-hard stuff; for it offers a far more serious challenge to the human adjustive abilities than the one they share with other forms of life.

I have explained how the socio-cultural environment emerges, but not why it challenges the adjustive powers of consciousness. The reason is that experiencers who are conscious of themselves and each other cannot take themselves or each other for granted. Like oneself, the others are real. They are *there*, and they, too, experience one, even as one experiences oneself. Individually and collectively, then, human life is not only lived, but consciously lived; it is a life that is *managed*. It may be barely or closely administered, adequately or inadequately conducted, well- or ill-planned – but in any event it is *led*. For upon becoming conscious of its wants, a self can decide what it *shall* want; it is able not only to select among the objects that can satisfy its wants, but unlike an animal it can also decide whether to want anything that it could select. Once human beings experience themselves and each other thus, as the conscious agents of their behaviour, they conceive expectations of themselves and each other, and their conduct depends on the self-directedness that they more or less adequately develop in themselves and more or less reasonably demand of each other.

Therefore, whereas the behaviour of all living things is mediated by their inherent purposiveness, and that of animals by purposes elicited through experience, human behaviour is mediated by conscious purposiveness – that is, by the kind that is experienced to be such. This is not the only determinant of the course of human life, but it is the one through which all the non-conscious purposes from within, and all the constraints from without, are channelled. Accordingly, the mutual adjustment of human beings in the various dimensions that make up their culture – social, political, legal, economic, familial, and so on – follows no predetermined pattern, such as could be genetically programmed in them at least in outline. Rather, it must be imaginatively invented by them as best they can. Not only individually, but above all socio-culturally, they must create their identity for themselves.

To sum up, the environment that challenges the adjustive abilities of consciousness is created by consciousness itself. This is not to gainsay the genetic and physical imperatives within which human beings exist and which they must willy-nilly take into account as they create themselves; for consciousness and its organism are not two entities but one. In a moment we shall turn to this. Separate mention should first be made, however, of two human socio-cultural peculiarities that follow from the properties of consciousness and its attendant categories of reality, self, and other.

One is *morality*. We have just seen that he who experiences himself as a self will experience responsibility to himself and to others for what he does, and expect others to feel responsible to him for what they do; it is a different question, of course, to what degree he and they allow themselves to accept such responsibility and live up to it. The other peculiarity is the foundation of all those institutions – let us call them *religious* in the widest sense of the term – that embody the response of human beings to their own questions concerning the meaning of human life and death. This is an especially significant index of the bearing of consciousness upon the human mode of life, because it follows directly from man's sense of his reality. Since, as noted, whoever experiences himself as a self will be unable to take his own reality for granted, he will sooner or later have to interpret his own reality to himself in order to find it meaningful – if he can. He will, for the same reason, not only have to adjust to those dangers to the continuation of his existence that may assail him from without, but eventually be hard pressed to confront the menace that his own inherent mortality poses to his selfhood. And he will ultimately have to face the certainty that the threat will be accomplished in the fact. The socio-cultural consequences of this component of self-definition alone would comprise a lengthy catalogue.

6. The relationship between consciousness and the human organism

In the intellectual tradition continuously handed down from ancient Greek times to our own, one of the most intractable problems has been that of the unity of man. We experience ourselves as a single entity, and it is clear that we have an organism. If we say, however, that man is constituted by a single element, and that that element is the organism, we seem bound to deny what experience also reveals about ourselves: that the mental aspects of the single human reality are no more reducible to the organic than the latter are to the former. Thus, the alternative to a reductionistic explanation of human nature has usually been some sort of dualism.

Probably the least-acceptable solution so far as concerns scholars has been the extreme dualism of Plato, a variation of which was that of Descartes. Even during the Middle Ages – unfairly deemed by some to have been the apogee of dualism – very few thinkers actually described man as a non-organic soul inhabiting a body alien to his nature, or constituted by two substances, body and soul, yoked together to function as one. The difficulties with these constructions are insuperable, and I shall not be further concerned with them here, having mentioned them only because a simplified version of dualism – that one's *I* inhabits one's body – remains typical of our common sense. If some sort of *modified* dualism was for many centuries the most common interpretation held in the Western world, the reason was the wish to respect the empirical fact that conscious experience is not reducible to an organic function. For everyone experiences himself as a self which is not identical with the organism, since he perceives his organism as owned by him – it is *his* organism. Nevertheless, every dualism, no matter how tempered, must in the end construe man as a composite of two elements. Even modified dualisms have, therefore, not been generally satisfactory. In the result, as monism has become increasingly acceptable in recent centuries, the irreducibility of man's humanity has had to take the hindmost.

Dilemmas, however, are often of our own making; sometimes our unacknowledged assumptions impose conditions upon the evidence about where it may lead us and where not. If we allow ourselves to be guided by our observations, however, we must agree at the outset that, if a human being is a single being, then a valid explanation of human nature must be monistic. And since the starting-point of all reasoning in this matter must be that no one has ever encountered either consciousness or selfhood in the absence of an experientially functioning organism, there is no option but to maintain also that the single element in man is the human organism. Whether this implies the reducibility of consciousness to a function of the organism, however, is another question – the answer to which depends on how one pictures consciousness in the first place.

The observable fact that consciousness *depends* upon functions of the organism is often taken to imply that consciousness *is* a function of the organism. But this assumption is, at best, a gratuitous one. Indeed, an empirical indication to the contrary was mentioned earlier. Consciousness has no specific object; it can attach to any modality of inner or outer experience: we hear consciously, see consciously, imagine consciously, reason consciously, and so on. This means that we need not search for the organic basis of consciousness in any particular type of sensory function or organic receptivity; we should look instead to the way in which the human organism, unlike the animal, can process whatever information it may receive from objects. The same sort of functional structure that, processing the information in one way, would produce plain non-conscious experience could also produce conscious experience by processing it differently. This is hardly inconsistent with the fact that consciousness is never found except as attaching to some experiential function of the organism. The harmony of the two types of observations is assured by what we have repeatedly noted, but which we should now ponder anew with care: consciousness is a *quality* that may colour the experiential functioning of the human organism.

For if consciousness is such a quality – if it is *how* human beings experience – then it cannot be an experiential function of the organism, although it is nothing but an organic event (or rather part of one) and although it depends upon no other cause than the experiential functioning of the organism. Conversely, consciousness is an organic *event*, though not reducible to an organic *function*, since it is rather the *way* in which the function takes place. The same experiential functions that otherwise would produce non-conscious experience develop consciousness when the functions are exercised in a distinctively human manner, namely, in such a way that the act of experience becomes present to itself. Thus, a monistic interpretation of human nature need not imply reductionism; being an irreducible quality of the experiential functions of the organism, consciousness cannot be equated with a function of the organism.

No peculiar organic structure need be supposed for experience to become present to itself – although the complexity achieved by the human brain, so much greater than that of the highest animals, is presumably a prerequisite for the exercise of experiential functions by humans in such a way that the experiencing becomes present to itself. Now, the physiology of the brain is hardly a philosophical issue. Ordinary observation, however, suffices to suggest that even in animals experience proper is distinguishable from lower orders of sentience by the fact that *past* information is somehow fed back into the processing of current information, making it possible for the organism to learn. In conscious experience, whatever its physiology, the feedback is of a higher order; in addition to past experience, *present* experience is fed back into the present experience itself. The organism can thus behave adjustively not only with the benefit of accumulated information, but also in the light of the fact that it is receiving and has received information and accumulated it.

The phenomenological study of consciousness is, therefore, enough to inspire the guess that the more complex functioning of the human brain may well consist in its taking advantage of feedback loops in neural pathways so as to make it possible for the organism to superimpose, upon the experience of an object, the experience of the experiencing activity itself; the two would then be simultaneous and coincident elements of a single act of experience. And happily, one's speculations receive some unexpected support from scientific opinion: 'There is more than a suspicion [among neuroscientists] that such phenomena [as con-

scious perceptions] result from the [brain's] computation pathways act-
ing in some way on themselves, [though] exactly how this happens is
not known.'[30]

Be that as it may, what matters to philosophy is that it would be false
and misleading to say that consciousness was produced by the human
brain; it is produced rather by the way in which human beings *use* their
brains. But this observation may contain a most important implication,
which for the moment I only mention in passing: that the ability to
experience consciously is not inborn but *acquired*. For if it is not an organic
function, but a quality – I mean, an irreducible quality – of a function,
then it cannot appear through maturation of the genetically determined
functional structures of the organism. The human organism inherits the
potential to become conscious, in the sense that it is genetically endowed
with experiential organic structures suitable for operating in the way
required for consciousness. But to become actually able to function consciously human beings have to acquire the ability by learning to use
their organism in the appropriate way. Though we commonly assume
the contrary, the ability to render experience conscious has to be *generated*
in the already-existing organism. This is to suggest, however, only *that*
consciousness is somehow inherited through a reproductive process that
culminates, but which is distinct from and subsequent to, organic generation. *How* consciousness may conceivably be generated remains to
be seen. I shall of course return to this.

Consciousness, then, is related to the experiential functions of the
organism in the same way in which these functions are related to the
structures; consciousness is, so to speak, a function of a function of the
organism. This interpretation accounts for the seemingly contradictory
indications that consciousness introspectively provides to itself. It appears to be both a determinant of, and determined by, organic events.
Being rooted in the organism and dependent upon it, it may appear to
itself as if it were an organic function, hence contained by the organism;
but being present to itself and irreducible to an organic function, it
appears to itself as other than the organism. In other words, it appears
to itself simultaneously as *having* an organism and as *being had* by it, and

30 F.H. Crick, 'Thinking about the Brain,' *Scientific American*, 241 (1979), 3, p. 221. Cf.
Roger W. Sperry, 'Mental Phenomena as Causal Determinants in Brain Function,'
in G.G. Globus and G. Maxwell, eds., *Consciousness and the Brain* (New York, 1976),
pp. 163–80. If it were confirmed that the physiological cause of consciousness is
some sort of feedback mechanism in the brain, and if such functioning could somehow be monitored, it should be possible to put to scientific test the philosophical
deduction to which I will presently arrive, namely, that the ability to experience
consciously is learned.

it is difficult to imagine how that which possesses the organism can itself be the possession of the organism. Moreover, once consciousness is assumed to be a function rather than a quality of a function, the *interaction* between the mental and the organic becomes inexplicable; this is true even if body and mind are not deemed two distinct entities, but all the more so if 'a second fundamental element and a second form of energy'[31] in addition to the organic are supposed. For this assumption forces even those who suppose only one element and only one form of energy to ask '[h]ow mental activity results from brain activity,'[32] as if two activities or events were involved. This is as prejudicial a way to pose an unanswerable question as if, wondering how Karen Kain manages not only to dance, but to dance superbly, one were to ask how her dancing caused the superbness of her performance; one would have succeeded in creating the insoluble problem of the 'performance-dance' relationship.

Only one element is observable in man: the organic. And only one form of energy, the somatic, is at work in him. But if consciousness is a quality of experience, there can be no question of one organic event (that is, biochemical processes) causing a second event (namely, conscious experience) or vice versa. Every conscious experience is a single organic event – the exercise of the functional capabilities of the experiential structures of the human organism – though it is the kind of complex event that lends itself to being misconstrued as if two different but causally related events were taking place, with causality flowing in either direction. There may be, however, a more adequate way to interpret the relevant facts. The explanation would be facilitated if we should first step back and consider the relationship between structure and function in living organisms.

At the level of inanimate reality, one entity existing independently of another can cause effects upon the other, and vice versa; by virtue of their having a multiplicity of related characteristics, moreover, things can act causally even upon themselves. Likewise, the organic functions and structures of one and the same organism can be causally related. But since they are not mutually independent realities – for an organic function without its corresponding organic structure, and a structure apart from its function, are abstractions which do not correspond to anything actually found in living reality – organic structures and functions are not causally related in the same way as independent inanimate entities are, or in the same sense. The vital activities of living entities are explicable as causal processes in which structure and function interact

31 Wilder Penfield, *The Mystery of the Mind* (Princeton, NJ, 1975), p. 79.
32 John I. Hubbard, *The Biological Basis of Mental Activity* (Reading, PA, 1975), p. 188.

reciprocally; life is, indeed, nothing but the self-involving, circular process called self-preservation, whereby organisms act within and upon themselves so as to remain able to act within and upon themselves. The causality that characterizes vital processes may thus be called *immanent*, as contrasted with the *transitive* causal activity of one self-contained entity upon another.

I do not mean, however, that functionless structural events in organisms cause functional events, any more than that structureless functional events cause structural events. The functioning structure is a single reality, and it *causes* only a single succession of events (or which is the same, *undergoes* only a single succession of events, since in immanent processes the agent and the patient are one). Nevertheless, structure and function do condition each other. For instance, if insufficient protein in the diet affects the muscular structure, the function will be weakened; conversely, exercise can strengthen the muscle, which can then grow in size if enough protein is available to it. Thus, the reciprocal involvement of the mutually related function and structure – let us continue to speak of them as if they were independent but conjoined – means that, although structure and function do not impinge on each other from outside each other, they can nevertheless truly cause changes in each other within the single, continuous series of events which is the ongoing immanent functioning of the structure. By the same token, a conscious experience is a single organic event; it does not involve causation of one event by another. Causality nevertheless holds, and indeed operates reciprocally, in the sense that changes in the consciously functioning experiential structure can be initiated either by the functioning structure or by the conscious quality of the function of the structure. But let us take one aspect at a time.

The experiential function of the organism is the cause of consciousness in this sense: if the experiential structure functions in the particular way that makes the experiential event present to itself, then there is consciousness, whereas there would be no consciousness if the structure did not function in such way. This is only to restate what we already knew – that the act of experience has conscious quality when it is present to itself – but stressing now that the self-presence is conferred by the act upon itself. For consciousness, being a vital process, manifests immanent causality; the experiential function that is the cause of consciousness is also the recipient of the effect. The organic function thus brings about consciousness in essentially the same way in which a muscle may be said to cause its own contraction; the will that causes the muscle's contraction is nothing other than the muscle itself,[33] but op-

33 More accurately, the will is identical with the muscle when the latter operates in

erating consciously – that is, in co-ordination with the sort of experience that is present to itself. Man's organic experiential structures cause consciousness simply by the organism functioning so as to render its experience present to itself.

To be sure, the relationship of organic experiential function to its conscious quality is more complex and less obvious than that of muscular structure to muscular function. It is more complex because the relationship is not simply that of function to structure, but that of a quality of a function to the functioning of a structure. It is less obvious because what becomes present to itself is not the structure, but only the function – that is, the active, experiential character of the event. For instance, one cannot learn how the organs of vision work by reflecting upon the experience of consciously seeing an object; one has to dissect the eye, observe its structures, and learn about nerve impulses, the role of the brain in visual consciousness, and so on. Even the bare fact that the eye is the external organ of vision is not given immediately as part of seeing. This, too, has to be learned experimentally, though it is very easily ascertained; opening and closing one's eyes is experimental evidence enough. The conscious character of seeing, however, cannot altogether escape any sighted person. Thus, since in conscious functions the act is self-revealing, though the structures are not, the conscious quality of the function can very easily appear to itself as having *functional autonomy*; this explains why consciousness is liable to misinterpret itself either by reducing itself to a function of the organism or else by mistaking itself for the function of a non-organic mind or soul somehow amalgamated with the organism.

I have accounted, however, for the causation of consciousness by organic events, but not for the reverse. For instance, I recall the time long ago when I was unfairly denied a promotion or salary increase; my conscious experience is an organic experiential event that has acquired self-presence. But as I brood about it, I become angry. The adrenalin flows; the blood boils; I rant and rave and seethe with fury. Undoubtedly, the experience has had an organic effect. Of course, the same conscious experience might not have had such effect; I might have simply recalled the events without becoming angry now. Or consider the relief from pain experienced by some – though not all – patients after dental surgery who think they have received morphine but in fact have received only a placebo. It is now known that this effect is mediated by the brain's secretion of the hormone endorphin, which has much the same effect

---

consequence of the sort of experience that is present to itself. But it is clear that muscles need not operate willfully; they can contract even when they are not used consciously.

as morphine.[34] But the secretion of endorphin could hardly be the cause of believing that one had received an injection of morphine; there can be no doubt that the experience of receiving the placebo had the secretion of endorphin for its effect. Like the causation of consciousness by organic events, however, that of organic events by consciousness can be understood in the light of the principle that consciousness is related to its organism as an irreducible quality of functioning is to the function of an organic structure. But the explanation is more complex, because now we are dealing with a more complex aspect of the on-going process – or with the equivalent, in the order of consciousness, of the organic effect (e.g., muscle growth) wrought upon the structure by the functioning (e.g., muscular exercise) caused by the structure. Let us analyse the two examples in turn.

The ability to recall and reprocess past experience is found in the higher animals; when the non-conscious recalling of past experience by an animal is fed back into current experiential processes, the animal can learn from past experience. Of itself, however, this does not amount to a present experience of the past *as such*. However, if the same recalling of past experience were conscious, part of the experience would be experiencing that it was a re-experiencing of the past; the experiencer would experience the past precisely as not-present, or *as past*. This is, of course, a very common occurrence – in humans. There is an important difference thus between animal and human memory; it is indeed almost equivocal to refer to the two by the same term. For animals avail themselves of both their past and their present experience, but their memory implies no recognition of the difference between present and past experience – whereas human memory does.

This difference, however, is not the only one. When the remembering of past experience is conscious, a further possibility arises – one that is less frequently taken advantage of than merely remembering the past as such. The experiencer can proceed, beyond the mere recalling of past experience as past, to the actual *reliving* of past experience as present – that is, to experiencing the re-experienced past *as present*. What permits an experience re-created *at* present to be re-created *as* a present experience is its conscious quality. For an experience that is present to itself is an experience that has a grip on itself, so to speak, and can manipulate itself. Or to put it less figuratively: since the conscious experiencer realizes the recollective character of his present experience, he can abstract from such character and thereby relive the experience as if it were a

34 John D. Levine et al., 'The Mechanism of Placebo Analgesia,' *Nature*, 272 (1978), pp. 826–7.

present experience of the present. Thus, if I indulge my resentful disposition, soon after I recall the events I am no longer remembering the injustice, but suffering it all over again; I am angry *now*. And if adrenalin, through some physiological mechanism the nature of which is not relevant to present purposes, could flow when I first heard the news that spelled injustice, adrenalin can flow again now for precisely the same reason and in accordance with the same mechanism.

Likewise, a conscious anticipation of euphoria or freedom from pain may be no more than a projection, on the basis of past experience, from my present experience of receiving an injection of what I think is morphine; I then experience at present that I shall later experience relief from pain. This is the kind of experience that, if it goes no further, we call hope. But since my experience of hope is self-present, it may manage to abstract from its own anticipatory character and become thus a *pre-living* of the anticipated relief from pain; it is indeed relatively easy for human beings, as we all know, to allow hope to degenerate into delusion. And a pre-living, however unrealistic, of the hoped-for experience implies all the organic functions that every actual living of euphoria requires; for it is not a faked or imagined euphoria at all, but a living of real *euphoria* now, endorphin secretion and all. Thus, the experiences of relived injustice and pre-lived euphoria are causes of organic effects but are not experiential events that cause organic events; the organic experiential function causes the conscious quality that in turn causes the organic experiential function to change. The process is essentially the same as a muscle causing the muscular contractions that cause the muscle to grow.

Other phenomena are similarly explicable. Ordinarily, when one experiences a purely imaginary object consciously, one knows of course that the object is imaginary. The self-presence of this experience, however, may be taken advantage of so as to attenuate or even extinguish its imaginative character. The object is then so realistically experienced that in some respects one responds to it as if it were real. (If one did so in all respects, which is also possible, one would be suffering from a hallucination.) Thus, I listen to Isolde's *Liebestod* upon the stage, and although I know that Birgit Nilsson's grief is feigned and that the score has been composed for the very purpose of pandering to my sentimentality, I get carried away: my chest becomes constricted and a lump forms in my throat. Indeed, I pay good money to go through this, in part, because it enables me to experience the kind of *real* – but safe – sorrow that shall, as if by magic, become unreal as the curtain falls. The self-presence of the conscious experiential event may, on the contrary, enable me to experience the real as unreal. The conscious quality of the organic experiential event may cause changes only in the functional aspect of the event, as in hysterical blindness. But it may affect the organic function even more profoundly and bring about changes in the functioning structure, in precise analogy to the muscular activity bringing about changes in the muscular structure. It is possible, for instance, for a purely psychogenic psychotic blotting-out of reality to interfere with the organic structures and functions of the brain; the immanent causality proper to the reciprocal relationship between self-presence and organic experiential function assures us that this would be as intelligible as its seeming opposite, namely, the causation of psychotic symptoms by, say, lead poisoning, post-partum hormonal imbalance, or the ingestion of LSD.

The 'body-mind' relationship is thus a circular one. Failure to understand the self-presence of experience that is its basis would create a puzzle not unlike that of trying to understand the relationship between the 'two' motions – upward and downward – of the passengers on a Ferris wheel, if one had tunnel vision and could see only one half of the wheel at a time. One's conundrum would be illusory; the solution would consist in grasping that only one motion – but a circular one – was involved. Insufficient awareness of the properties of our own consciousness prevents most of us from observing simultaneously the presence of the object to the act of experience and the presence of the act to itself. Isolated segments of a single process then appear to have contradictory characteristics, and the progression seems to run alternatively in opposite directions: bodily events cause mental events and vice versa. Likewise, what consciousness mistakes for its functional autonomy is one of its real properties, but badly so conceived. Consciousness has *phenomenal autonomy*; it is the quality of an organic function that needs no other function than itself, and no substratum other than the organism, in order to be present to itself. But this is not autonomy *from* the organism or its experiential functions; it is the self-sufficiency *of* those functions to become present to themselves. It would take, however, a more effective level of self-presence than most of us can ordinarily count upon, before we could spontaneously integrate the apparently disparate empirical facts that consciousness reveals to itself. But the seemingly contradictory indications are, in truth, complementary. To choose between them is to falsify both.

7. The assertiveness of consciousness

So far we have been concerned predominantly with consciousness in itself, or as an *act*. Thus, I have defined consciousness by its self-presence, observed that it differentiates itself from the object, and explained how it can experience the real as real and itself as itself. But consciousness can also be considered in relation to the *object* that becomes present to it. When the ability of consciousness to introduce opposition between itself and the object is thus envisaged, however, it reveals that, whenever an object of consciousness is experienced, the object is thereby *asserted* as being itself and as being whatever it is. From this coign of vantage, then, consciousness is definable as *assertive experience*. But let us consider this in more detail.

To say, as I have above, that consciousness is the sort of experience that perceives the reality of the real is true, but may be misleading; it seems to imply that reality is something contained in real things – one of several aspects of it, such as colour and size – which consciousness may take for its object. Reflexion should disclose, however, that this cannot be true. The reality of the real cannot be experienced apart from its various features; we never experience the existence of anything except as the existence of its colour and/or its size, and so on. Conversely, every self-present experience carries, as a sort of connotation, implicit or explicit reference to the reality (or non-reality) of the contents denoted by the experience. In other words, whenever our experience is of the conscious kind, we not only can, but must, experience that the object is real – or as the case may be, that it is not. What consciousness cannot do is to operate without regard to the category of reality.

By the way, this is why we can ordinarily tell the difference between the real and the imaginary; it has nothing to do with any characteristic of the object, but is a consequence of the self-presence of consciousness. A conscious sensing of the real apprehends its own non-imaginative, sensory character, whereas a conscious imagining of an object that does not exist grasps immediately its own imaginative status. The human organism, however, can also have semi-conscious experience, the sort that has enough self-presence to be conscious but not enough to appreciate whether it is imagining or sensing; to Descartes this posed a problem that was insoluble unless by relying on the veracity of God. The answer, however, should be clear from what precedes: that sometimes we cannot tell the difference does not imply that we can never be certain of it, since there is an empirically detectable difference also between semi-consciousness and ordinary consciousness.

At any rate, the reason why all conscious experience must carry reference to the category of reality is that reality means, in general, the *otherness-to* that things bear to each other, and in particular the *otherness-to* that they bear to consciousness. Thus, the reality of the real is not experienced as a result of the experiencer being informed by something called reality that resides within, yet is distinct from, the object; it is a result of the experiencer being informed by the fact that he has been informed by the object itself. Only the self-presence of consciousness, of course, can make this possible. Note, however, the implication: unlike the animal, the conscious experiencer does not simply profit from the reality of the object by accepting and using its information; he also gives credit to the object for its being real – that is, for its having informed him about itself and for its being what the information has revealed. The other side of what I described earlier as 'tagging' the object as '[experienced]' consists, therefore, in experiencing that it is real and is whatever it is. Although conscious experience does not, of course, create the reality of the real, it 'stamps' reality as real, so to speak, and 'certifies' it as such. It is for this reason that it may be properly said to be assertive.

There is, therefore, yet another difference between conscious and non-conscious experience. The relationship of a non-conscious experiencer to the object comes to an end with the reception of information; the process terminates not only *within* the organism, but also *at* the organism. Conscious experience, however, goes further. Since the process includes acknowledgment of the object's informative role, the experience, despite its taking place entirely within the experiencer, may not be said to end at the experiencer, but at the object. By this I mean that, since an essential part of the experience consists in grasping that the object is real and is whatever it is, the experience 'states' or 'declares' the object as such, even when the experiencer makes no sound or imagines no word. Consciousness must be described as assertive experience because it is not merely an experience that receives the object, but one that *affirms* it as received. The affirmation, as I have said, uses no words. It is indeed yet more silent than thought: I can look at the softly descending snow of this peaceful winter day and see the snow consciously without even thinking, let alone voicing, the sound 'snow.' The affirmation is performed by the experiential act itself, and is part of the conscious quality of the experience. It therefore refers directly to the objects themselves, without the mediation of signs; it is an *immediate assertion* of them. Although the idea noted earlier – that conscious sense experience is a wordless *repetition* of reality – is wrong as a whole, it contains, then, a kernel of truth: conscious experience is an *original assertion* of reality made by the experiencer in and through the act of conscious experience itself.

In these remarks I have had in mind primarily the simplest form of consciousness, the sensory contact we have, for instance, when we see or touch an apple. But conscious quality can accrue, of course, to the higher levels of experience, those we generically call understanding.

Now, the assertiveness of consciousness is more easily detected in the latter than in conscious sensation. For it is obvious that before understanding can become wordless by becoming habitual it requires the actual use of speech, either vocal or imagined: we can interpret anything only through reasoning and other forms of discourse that use actual worded assertions, whether sounded or thought. Nevertheless, both conscious sense experience and understanding are assertive, albeit in different ways. Conscious sensation consists in the *immediate* assertion of reality, whereas understanding asserts it *mediately*, through imagined or voiced sounds. But let us put understanding aside; in this chapter we shall continue to be interested primarily in immediate sense consciousness, simply because it is the most elementary kind.

The assertiveness of consciousness does not mean that either sensation or understanding imposes any foreign content upon its objects. The contents asserted by consciousness are the contents of reality itself, and are determined by the underlying receptivity of all experience: if I look at an apple, I do not see a pear. But the content is attributed to the object; seeing the apple affirms the apple itself as an apple, and as nothing but an apple. In other words, my attribution of reality to the real is not gratuitous, but deserved; it is based on my appreciating the object's being both other-than-me and other-than-anything-else. Without consciousness, therefore, reality is undoubtedly real, though it exists only in the dark, as it were: unrecognized as real and as being what it is. Its remaining thus unrecognized does not, of course, prevent non-conscious experiencers from interacting with it 'in the dark,' or taking advantage of the information it provides, even in the absence of conscious experience.

At the risk of appearing self-contradictory, therefore, I would even say that consciousness has not so much a cognitive as a recognitive role. I do not mean that when consciousness asserts reality experientially it restates what it had heard from the real itself, which had previously 'stated' itself for the benefit of consciousness. *Recognition* may mean a second cognition, but in this sense we should have little use here for the word. The same term also refers, however, to the acknowledgment of, say, a privilege or a right, or even to the avowal of a mere fact, but confirmatorily. Thus, a chairman recognizes a speaker, a judge recognizes a civil right of a plaintiff, and one nation extends political recognition to another – or else withholds it, asserting thereby that the other is deemed not to be real. Well, consciousness recognizes reality; it admits that the facts are facts, or else denies that the presumed facts are the facts. Of course, when it does either it may be wrong. But whether it be right or wrong is irrelevant; the point is that in either case consciousness cannot merely absorb facts; it must judge them. It must commit itself, if only doubtfully, to reality's being real and being what it is. Moreover, this *judicative* quality is part of all consciousness from the outset, not the result of a further elaboration of experience. Even the simplest, least conclusive conscious experience – the bare visual consciousness of the softly descending snow – requires assertiveness and involves a wordless 'judgment.' One does not have to wait for one's actually *saying*, either in thought or out loud, 'this is softly descending snow' before one can perceive that the object is indeed real and is whatever it is. The experience itself is the kind that 'says' it. An experience that lacked this quality would be unrecognizable as consciousness at all.

Mere experience bespeaks an organism's capacity for taking advantage, entirely within itself, of the effect that an-other has upon its senses. Its interiority is to be literally, spatially, understood; for experiencing may well result in further adjustive behaviour affecting others, but in any case the *experiencing* remains entirely within the experiencer. I have mentioned, however, that in the case of consciousness the active reaction does not stop at the boundaries of the organism; it reaches out, as it were, up to the object itself. Of course, this reaching out results in a purely experiential 'contact'; for asserting the object as such is part of the experience, not the object. But what matters is that consciousness transcends the interiority of mere experience. Contrary to what we ordinarily assume, the peculiarity of human experience is its externality; it takes the experiencer out from within himself and, as Martin Heidegger (in a different context) put it, 'casts him forth' into the world. The *transcendence* of consciousness, as some phenomenologists call it, means that although consciousness does not physically affect its objects, it nevertheless must be said, in a sense, to 'touch' them.

What I have just stated is not a deduction, but an observable fact. It is most easily verified in the least far-reaching among our senses – touch, taste, and smell – where no physical distance intervenes between experiencer and object; clearly, my touching experiences the touched at the touched itself. The same is essentially true, however, of hearing and vision, even if in these instances space separates the experiencer and the experienced. But this spatial separation affects only the physics, the chemistry, and the biology of sensation, not its psychology. Visible and audible objects are, to be sure, physically beyond the experiencing organism – but for that matter, so is the tangible object. The aural and visual objects are still farther off than the tangible, but *all* objects, be they physically contiguous to the organism or not, are other-than the sensing organism and are outside the experience. Thus, conscious experience in *every* sense modality reaches out and 'touches' the object –

though the 'contact' is not a physical relationship, but a characteristic of the conscious event. Less metaphorically described, the reaching-out of consciousness is the unique relationship between object and experiencer established when experience becomes present to itself.

The foregoing comparison between conscious and non-conscious experience may be summed up as follows. The relation of non-conscious experience and its object is mutual, though not symmetrical; experiencer and object have complementary roles in establishing the relation. On the part of the object, the relation is *prescriptive*. This need imply no purpose or will; it only means that the object's activity determines the contents of the experience; whether the experiencer is to experience apple rather than pear is prescribed only by the fruit in question. And on the part of the experiencer the relation is *receptive*. But when sense experience is conscious, the self-presence of the experience transforms the relationship: the experience becomes *ascriptive*. The organism's experiential activity in reaction to the object's prescription, unlike that of the non-conscious experiencer, returns the object to its own reality, as it were. In a perfectly valid sense, therefore, reality is profoundly affected by its being experienced consciously. It is not changed in itself, of course. But the point is indeed that, once it is experienced consciously, reality is no longer simply in itself; it has now become reality-for-us. It is thus – through its being asserted – that reality becomes, as we usually call it, the 'world.'

I have insisted that the assertion of reality in consciousness is wordless and therefore non-communicative, for the obvious reason that we can experience an object consciously without uttering so much as an imaginary word. When we speak, however, we assert what we experience in and through the uttering of words that communicate it. Asserting the object in conscious experience is, therefore, not wholly unlike speaking it in words: both are assertive acts, though one is worded and the other is not. Consciousness, then, if we examine it as closely as we have here, bears an evocative family resemblance to speech. It will be recalled, however, that we were concerned earlier with how the generation of consciousness might take place. The question thus naturally suggests itself: is this resemblance mere coincidence, or may we suspect a concealed paternity that arouses our curiosity and that we, like busybodies, feel bound to investigate? Is it possible that the ability to experience consciously is the child of the ability to speak? Or to put it plainly, do human beings, when they learn to assert their experience in speech, thereby learn to assert experientially the objects whereof they speak? If the answer should be yes, it would mean that consciousness was inherited – transmitted from one generation to the next – through the transmission of the ability to speak rather than through the transmission of genes. And if this should be true, it could well provide a hypothesis upon which might be erected a theory of how human nature originated and evolved. But this hypothesis itself, let alone its role in explaining human origins, is difficult to credit. We shall therefore consider its plausibility, in the next chapter, by studying the nature of speech.

One more question about consciousness, however, remains to be discussed. I proposed at the outset that any theory claiming to explain plausibly the emergence of man must account for the origin of both the ordered and the disordered functioning of human nature, and of a human species whose history inextricably mixes the two. We must, therefore, determine not only how consciousness operates normally, but also why it can work defectively and how its defective functioning can interfere with human life.

8. The potential of consciousness for self-misinterpretation

Since the conclusion that consciousness is definable by its self-presence requires only a little logic applied to a few universally accessible facts, it should not have been at all difficult to draw. The evidence that consciousness is self-present is provided by consciousness directly to itself. Nevertheless, our intellectual tradition has required approximately twenty-five centuries of hard thinking to discover it. Now, the self-evident is usually obvious; why should it not have been so in this case? I said earlier that cultural conditioning is part of the reason, but this only throws the question back to the origin of the discrepancy. Why was it not obvious from the outset? And why does it remain difficult for us to grasp it even now, when the facts have been highlighted and the conclusion has been demonstrated?

A first approximation to the answer is that self-understanding is possible only because conscious experiencers can, through reflexion, take their own consciousness for the object of investigation. But nothing guarantees that understanding any other object must be free from all error; why should it be different when the object of study is consciousness itself? There is, of course, some truth in this explanation – human understanding is fallible – but it cannot be the full answer. For as we have seen, consciousness perceives itself *immediately*, prior to all reflexion and all reasoning; in this unique case, therefore, where the object to be understood is identical with the consciousness that understands it, understanding should be, if not infallible, at very least easily self-correcting. The question thus becomes: precisely what is there in the nature of consciousness that accounts for its potential for self-misinterpretation despite its immediate presence to itself? Besides, why does it remain difficult for us to understand the self-presence of consciousness even after our attention has been drawn to it?

Our self-misinterpretations cannot be laid exclusively at the feet of lame reasoning; they must begin with a faulty *immediate* perception of ourselves. This means that the origin of human self-misunderstanding is a defect in the very self-presence of consciousness. In other words, since the self-provision of evidence is not enough to prevent self-mis-understanding, the self-presence of consciousness must be deemed to admit of variations in quality. Variations in the characteristics of con-sciousness in other respects – for example, in intensity of self-presence – are not difficult to observe; as everyone knows, one may be more or less conscious of the same thing at different times, and more or less conscious of different things at the same time. It now appears, however, that consciousness may also show variations that are less easily noted, namely, respecting the adequacy or effectiveness of the self-presence of the act. Perhaps the cause of these variations is that the factor that makes human experience self-present, whatever it may be – say, a certain ha-bitual way of processing information that only the human brain can develop – may be only partially effective. This defect might well result either from imperfection either in the pertinent native organic structures or else in the experiencer's culturally conditioned, acquired ability to use them. But it makes no difference which. However it may come about, insufficient self-presence would mean that when consciousness was present to itself it need not be clearly and distinctly so. Individually and in self-perpetuating societies, consciousness might come into being more or less able to discriminate between itself and its objects and, thus, more or less clear or else confused about itself.

A defectively self-present consciousness would be fully aware of ob-jects, and would even realize that it was aware of objects, but would not perceive that such realization was an integral part of its awareness of objects; it could not easily disentangle what belonged to objects and what to itself as an act. This deficiency would explain, for instance, the culturally conditioned difficulty that some readers may have experienced above, at the very beginning of section 3 of this chapter, when I set out to explain the nature of consciousness. I then called attention, it will be recalled, to the observable fact that every conscious experience is more than the experience of an object, since it also includes experiencing the act of experiencing the object. If this was not instantaneously crystal clear to every reader who understood the words, the reason must have been that, whereas the experienced object was perfectly obvious to him, the act of experiencing it was not – despite the fact that it was present to itself. And we can be sure that it was present to itself, because the reader, I dare say, entertained not the slightest doubt that he was able to experience. Being certain of it is a characteristic of all conscious experience, be it deficient in self-presence or not.

In short, within the *same* self-presence that is the ground of all human self-understanding lurks the possibility of self-misunderstanding. Consciousness contains an inherent ambivalence: the self-presence that characterizes it means that human beings, by virtue of their very nature – as contrasted with misadventure in the course of performing the operations that define their nature – may both correctly and incorrectly interpret the very characteristics that define their nature and that enable them to interpret themselves at all. Moreover, since the self-presence of consciousness constitutes, in effect, its ability to manipulate itself, self-misunderstanding may as easily be wittingly as unwittingly achieved. If wittingly, however, we should much better call it *self-deception*. But note that, in order to be effective, self-deception cannot be faked; it must be like innocent self-misunderstanding in that it must not seem to be wilfully caused. Through its self-presence, however, consciousness can easily take care of that; all it need do is to remove from the purview of its consideration the fact that it has used itself to misrepresent itself to itself.[35]

If this explanation is valid, we should be able to invoke it to account for at least some of the typical self-misinterpretations that persist in our tradition quite apart from self-deception; it should explain why the history of our understanding of human nature is not exclusively a recital of positive discoveries, but also a chronicle of our gradual overcoming of prejudices about ourselves. It should tell us in particular why we have discovered our own conscious nature only very slowly, despite the fact that we had been conscious all along. Conversely, accounting for the annals of our self-misunderstanding by reference to the inherent ambivalence of the self-presence of consciousness would tend to corroborate the validity of the explanation I have proposed. Well, then, what self-misinterpretations have prevailed in our culture that only deficient self-presence of consciousness can explain? The following, for one – a crucial one.

Everyone who is conscious can recognize in himself the typical polar duality of all conscious experience: experience is one thing, the object of experience is another. This is why even the most unsophisticated

35 Cf. Herbert Fingarette, *Self-deception* (London, 1969).

human beings have at least *some* sense of reality; it is also the reason why everyone, unless he were deranged, spontaneously enjoys the conviction that he is not the world and that the world is not he. But we have seen that this duality is, in truth, made up of (a) the *object* of experiencing, and (b) the act of experiencing the object. And the object, as I have also underlined, is the reality itself. It is at this very point, however, that most of us become confused. We cannot easily perceive that the object of experience is the object itself, attained in reality and in itself. We are likely to think instead that the object is reached *within* ourselves. By virtue of our experiencing it, it comes to exist 'in the mind' – not bodily, of course, but as an 'idea.' Thus, our culture perpetuates a disposition (*how* it manages to do it will concern us later) that inclines us to misinterpret the duality as if it were constituted by (a) an *object* in reality, and (b) the same *object*, but in experience. That is, the act of experiencing is misconstrued as the creation of a mental equivalent of the original in reality, and consciousness is mistaken for the coincidence of two different contents: (a) the contents of reality in itself, which exist in reality, and (b) the contents of the experience, which exist in the mind as a repetition of reality.

To be sure, all but the least subtle amongst us realize that ideas have no physical existence; and a little reflexion suffices philosophers to realize that the mental repetition of the object does not create a replica of the object in the mind, let alone one that resembles it. But the logic of this confusion will require even the most sophisticated of us to suppose that, since experience does after all consist in the repetition of the object, the object must be said, in some mysterious but valid sense – for instance, 'symbolically' – to be non-physically re-presented to oneself in one's mind. Once the assumption is made that the contents of reality somehow come to exist in the mind, one has condemned oneself to having to explain, by whatever name one may call it, the repetition of reality by the mind.

Not only is there no evidence at all to suppose that the contents of reality are experienced in the mind or within ourselves, but each one of us can empirically verify for himself that reality is experienced at the reality itself. It is only the act of experiencing that is within ourselves. It follows, as one of the pioneers of phenomenology once put it, that 'the first step of any [contemporary] philosophy should be to expel things from consciousness.'[36] Expelling objects, ideas, symbols, and all possible repetitions of reality from consciousness, however, entails a conse-

36 Sartre, *L'être*, p. 18.

quence that, given our predispositions, we find most unpalatable: having to admit that consciousness is self-comprising, or that its very nature is 'to be "circular".'[37]

This conclusion is difficult to accept, in part, because we know that self-containment is impossible in the case of ordinary things. But could we have expected differently? If self-presence is the specific, essential characteristic of consciousness, nothing but conscious experience could be self-contained. The more important reason, however, has to do with consciousness itself. Deficient self-presence is a sort of self-doubt that engenders self-distrust; it amounts to an inability fully to credit one's experience of one's immediately given reality. And this entails a consequence: if one does not fully accept one's experience of one's own reality, one's experience of the reality of anything else will not be convincing either – not because one has an independent reason to distrust its reality, but because one begins by distrusting one's *experience* of its reality. The self-distrust born of self-disbelief generates thus the other-disbelief from which other-distrust springs. It is also the ground of the reductionism we met at the outset of this investigation; it is, indeed, the root of all self-alienation. Since the essence of the defect is difficulty in perceiving the self-presence of consciousness except in the confused way I have described, it would not be inaccurate to refer to this disability, as I shall henceforth, as *absent-mindedness*. And since societies and traditions cannot but reflect the minds of their members, we may speak not only of the absent-minded consciousness of individuals, but also of absent-minded cultures – for instance, our own.

The self-misperception of the absent-minded consciousness is not a total mistake, but a confusion: it consists in thinking that consciousness repeats a reality which has previously asserted itself upon the experiencer – whereas the fact is that consciousness asserts reality originally and for the first time. The reduction of consciousness to the repetition of reality amounts thus to the false ascription to the object of experience of the assertiveness that in fact belongs exclusively to consciousness. This ascription is the fundamental form of the mechanism of *projection*; absent-mindedness is the basis of every other way in which human beings find it possible to attribute to objective reality what in truth is part of consciousness. It is also what permits them to foist off on others whatever part of themselves they do not acknowledge and want to disavow. A different manifestation of the same absent-mindedness is the antithesis of projection. Human beings learn to empathize as part of their learning to experience consciously; the self-presence of con-

37 Ibid., p. 20.

sciousness is, in effect, the ability of an experiencer to empathize with himself. He would necessarily, therefore, have great difficulty in fully perceiving the selfhood of others, who should lack facility in experiencing his own. And no one could treat other human beings more humanely than he knew how to treat himself, because he was insufficiently familiar with himself.

Once assertiveness has been projected onto reality, the assertiveness of consciousness has vanished. The clue has been discarded that alone can awaken the suspicion that assertive experience, consciousness, may be generated by assertive communication, speech. Through the study of consciousness, however, we have managed to rediscover this very possibility. Let us now proceed to explore it, turning our attention from the nature of consciousness to the nature of speech.

CHAPTER THREE

The nature of speech

The hypothesis that speech generates consciousness may seem strange. Most of us suppose that speech expresses in signs, and thereby repeats for the benefit of another, what has been previously sensed consciously and then cast into conceptual form. But if speech is nothing but the expression and communication of thought, as thought is the expression and conceptualization of sense experience, speech is necessarily posterior to conscious sensation and thought and, therefore, could hardly generate them. It is understandable that we should so reason: we can raise questions about the origin of consciousness, thought, and speech only after we have developed these faculties – at which time we can, indeed, first experience something consciously, then think about it inwardly, and only later communicate our thoughts and our understanding of it. But the order in which we can exercise these abilities scarcely tells us the order in which we develop them. To imagine that it did would be the same *non sequitur* as if we were to conclude, from our experience as literate adults, that the child acquires the ability to read by first grasping the meaning of written words apart from how they are pronounced, learning next to imagine silently how the words should be pronounced, and discovering finally how to read them out loud. The order is, in fact, the opposite. The same is true, I suggest, about the order in which we develop consciousness, thought, and speech.

For all its conflict with our culture's common sense, however, this hypothesis will probably not seem as preposterous today as it would certainly have in the past. Although both the scholarly and the common-sense conceptions of speech still contradict such hypothesis, our culture has managed to gain certain insights into human nature the implications of which, subliminally felt, ill accord with our traditional assumptions. These insights dispose us to think that speech does not simply communicate our experience – which it undoubtedly does, though whether by representing it is another question – but has an active role in its formation. To be sure, we do not go so far as to say that speech *generates* consciousness. Most critics of the classical interpretations are content with showing that speech – or rather 'language,' as they prefer[1] – somehow *shapes* experience as the latter is communicated, and continue to assume that conscious experience would be perfectly possible even in the absence of the ability to speak. Nevertheless, even the shaping of experience by speech implies that in some respects speech must be prior to experience. We shall, therefore, begin to inquire into the nature of speech by recalling, in the first section, our traditional interpretation of the matter – the *semantic* idea of speech, as I will refer to it – and by explaining why disillusionment with it in modern times has not resulted in a sufficiently radical critique; we have taken some steps in the right general direction but we are still not on the right track. The remainder of this chapter will then develop what I will call a *syntactic* conception of speech, which proposes instead that the distinctively human characteristic of speech is its capacity for generating the conscious quality of experience. All the other peculiarities of speech follow from this characteristic, including that aspect of the matter which modern critics have remarked upon: that speech, in ways that they do not claim fully to understand, seems to have a profound influence in the shaping of conscious experience.

The essential characteristic of speech, the source of its capacity for generating consciousness out of bare experience, does not depend on the audibility of the signals it uses (though vocal signalling is especially apt to develop such characteristic). Nor does it depend on the nature of the signal systems, or languages, that are used in speech; on the contrary, the properties of human languages depend upon those of the speech that uses them. In the second section I will show that the distinctiveness of speech pertains rather to the activity of speaking. It consists in the *assertiveness* of speech. Speech is irreducible to communication – the mere transmission of signals such as we can observe even at fairly low levels of animal life – because speakers do not simply communicate; they do so intending to communicate and being aware of the communicative efficacy of speech. And to communicate intending to achieve a communicative effect is to assert what is communicated.

1 This preference is significant. The primary acceptation of *language* refers to a system of vocal signs used to communicate, whence its second principal meaning: the use, or the ability to use, vocal communications. Equating *speech* with *language* betrays the assumption that speaking is reducible to communicating using vocal signs.

It will be remembered, however, that consciousness, too, is assertive. Conscious experience does not repeat reality, but 'states' it originally – though to be sure, unlike speech it does so immediately rather than through the mediation of signs. The third section will explain why the assertiveness of consciousness should be said to derive from the assertiveness of speech. It is clear that all communication, whether animal or human, is necessarily related to experience: reality provides the contents of experience, but it is the experience of reality that provides the contents of communication. That is, the signal made by every communicator ultimately refers to some reality, but what the communicator communicates, to put it exactly, is not reality, but his experience of reality. I will further argue, however, that when experience is communicated assertively – when the speaker *means* what he communicates – the speaker's experience can acquire self-presence. (Why assertive communication has this effect whereas mere communication does not is of course the crux of the matter; it will be studied in detail below.) Moreover, assertive experience and the assertive communication of experience become mutually involving: once experience has become conscious, the speaker can speak with consciousness of speech. A higher level of assertive speech is thus achieved, which can generate a higher level of assertive experience. As will be discussed in the fourth section, the interaction of consciousness and speech explains how *perceptual consciousness* ripens into *understanding*.

Since the syntactic conception of speech enables us to grasp the essence of the human mode of communication, it also facilitates our understanding its infrahuman counterpart more adequately than we could without this standard of comparison; it should help us appreciate the complementary side of the irreducibility of speech to animal communication, namely, the continuity between the two. The fifth section will show how all the elements of speech had been adumbrated at various stages in the evolution of animal life.

Our study of speech, resumed in the sixth section, will then suggest an alternative to the semantic supposition that consciousness mirrors the sensible and intelligible constituents of reality. I shall conclude instead that its assertiveness empowers it to develop, by means of speech, original interpretations of reality; if such interpretations obtain at two different levels – sensation and understanding – the explanation is not that a cache of intelligible meaning lies hidden behind the sensible appearances of reality, and that the mind uncovers it; the reason is that there are different levels of assertiveness in speech and consciousness. But this brings up a subject that, though marginal to this inquiry, I could not altogether ignore and that the last section will touch upon: the nature of reality. For every construction of speech and consciousness implies a corresponding conception of how reality lends itself to being consciously experienced and spoken about. If one is to maintain that reality does not have an inner meaning that speech and consciousness repeat, but that consciousness asserts such meaning originally as it interprets reality, one is bound to examine, if only very quickly, how the interpretability of reality should be conceived.

1. The traditional interpretations of speech, and their inadequacy

Since we are speakers, all we should have to do in order to understand the nature of speech is to listen to what our own speech reveals to us about itself. But the habitual absent-mindedness of our culture disposes us to lose sight of our presence to ourselves. Whenever we interpret speech – philosophically, scientifically, or commonsensically – our bent is to consider it from an outsider's viewpoint: speech is what *other* people say. What we thus learn we apply, of course, to ourselves – but taking for granted that our own speech could show nothing but what we can observe objectively in others. Having thus implicitly shunted aside our immediate experience of the act of speech, however, we could not but perceive it as the transmission and reception of communication; in this way, without quite realizing how or why, we identify speech with language, the ability to use vocal sounds as a means to communicate. Not illogically, if we should then raise the question 'What is language's main function? [the] answer is clear and generally agreed: language is the most frequently used and most highly developed form of communication we possess ... An act of communication is basically the transmission of information of some kind – a "message" – from a source to a receiver ... [Language] is human vocal noise ... used systematically for purposes of communication. Occasionally language is used for purposes other than communication – for example, to let off steam ... or to give delight ... or as a vehicle for our own thoughts when no one is present. But such uses of language are secondary.'[2] The possibility that to speak may be more than to use a vocal means of communication has been tacitly discarded.

The ontological perspective from which we usually examine speech is part of our Greek heritage. The fundamentals of the interpretation that science and philosophy have endlessly rung the changes upon were first stated explicitly by Aristotle: 'Spoken words are the signs [*symbola*]

2 David Crystal, *Linguistics* (Baltimore, MD, 1971), pp. 239, 243.

of experience [*ton en te psyche pathematon*][3] and written words are the signs [*semeia*] of spoken words. Like writing, speech is not the same for all peoples. But the experiences of which spoken words are the immediate signs [*semeia*] are the same for all, as are also those things of which experiences are the representations [*homoiomata*][4] ... A name is a spoken word that signifies something by convention.'[5]

This should be called the *semantic* interpretation of speech, because it construes speech as the outward expression, representation or signification – these three are taken as practical synonyms – of the inner experience of reality. The speaker expresses – that is, exteriorizes – his mind by embodying his thinking in certain linguistic signs; what from his viewpoint may be described as the *expression* and *signification* of his thought, from the viewpoint of the communicand may be called its *representation*, because its function is to make present to the communicand once again what had previously been present in the speaker's mind. This concept of speech is so inextricably connected with the corresponding interpretations of experience and reality, however, that we may well refer to the three together as the *semantic complex*. The relation of speech to experience is semantic, as is the relation of experience to reality and that of reality to speech. This relationship results, at each step, from the production of a 'likeness' – or more exactly, as many would insist, a sign – that communicates its antecedent. Of course, speech may be

3 Literally, 'the undergoing in the soul.'
4 Literally, 'likenesses.'
5 *On Interpretation*, 1 (16a4–9). Both *semeion* and *symbolon* mean 'sign,' 'mark,' 'token,' etc., that is, something that makes known, or points or calls attention to, something other than itself. They differ, however, in at least one connotation. *Symbolon* (literally, a 'drawing together') originally referred to a tablet on which a commercial agreement was written in duplicate; when it was broken in two, the irregularities of the break certified the authenticity of the two halves by fitting together when 'con-tracted' or 'drawn together.' (The 'indenturing' of deeds, practised in English law until the nineteenth century, made use of the same principle.) It may be significant that Aristotle calls speech and experience not only *semeia*, but also *symbola*; both allude to the mental duplication of reality by experience and speech (as does *homoiomata*), but *symbolon* connotes the mutually authenticating correspondence of two things – in this case, reality and experience. Note, however, that the correspondence of the two halves of a *symbolon* certifies their authenticity *to the parties*, hardly to each other; likewise, the correspondence of experience and reality could be authenticating only in the eyes of someone who, like the con-tracting parties, stood outside the two things that corresponded. The conception of experience and speech as the production of *symbola*, *semeia*, or *homoiomata* is possible only if the self-presence of consciousness and speech is ignored; for only this would permit one to assume that it is possible to observe from without the correspondence of the object and one's experience of it.

restricted to the silent speaker's signification of his experience to himself (i.e., thought).[6]

The foregoing is a much-abbreviated description of the process of speaking. A slightly more complete account would explain that the audible words of speech signify the inner mental words or auditory images that make up imaginary speech. Imaginary words, however, do not represent our experience directly; they represent *concepts*, which in turn represent information carried by our sense experience of reality. A distinction between imaginary word and concept – and *a fortiori*, between concept and spoken word – must be introduced because, as Aristotle noted, speakers in different languages use different vocal and imaginary sounds (*mensa, Tisch, wei*) in order to represent one and the same 'visualization' (or in Greek, the same *idea*) that all speakers share (e.g., the idea that in English we signify as *table*). Only the concept refers directly to the experience shared by various speakers in respect of one and the same tabular reality. Modern scholars have, for the most part, not departed significantly from this view, though they express it in different technical terminology. For instance, a renowned contemporary linguist, who in this respect is not atypical, tells us that there is a distinction between the conceptual 'purport' of the speaker, which is linguistically 'amorphous,' and the concrete linguistic 'form' that it has in any given linguistic code; for if we consider a variety of sentences such as 'I do not know,' 'Je ne sais pas,' and 'No sé,' we may observe that 'despite all their differences, [they] have a factor in common, namely, the purport, the thought itself.'[7] Of course, 'the same purport is formed or structured differently in different languages ... [But the form] is independent of, and stands in arbitrary relation to, the *purport*.'[8] Or to put it differently, 'the thought itself' is distinct from the sounded or imagined words in which it is expressed.

Our ordinary terminology, however, suffers from ambiguity. By *thought* we sometimes mean conceptual thought, the representation of the meaning behind the imaginary or vocal sound. This alone is the 'thought'

---

6 A further refinement has usually been added since Greek times. The experiencer's role, when he 'listens' to what reality has 'broadcast,' is not a purely passive one. Experiencing is more like 'reading' reality than 'listening' to it. 'What is read' (*logos*) is the message that reality contains within itself and 'utters' or 'speaks' to all possible readers. (*Logos*, which etymologically means 'what is picked up,' can be used to mean either 'what is heard' or 'what is read.') But if reading reality reveals its inner *logos*, then reality is structured by an inner *logos* or 'inner readable word,' much as a document is constituted by readable words that convey a message.

7 Louis Hjelmslev, *Prolegomena to a Theory of Language* (Madison, ws, 1961), p. 50.

8 Ibid., p. 52.

that is supposedly the same in all languages, the wordless repetition of reality that is itself signified by different sounded or imagined words in various languages. But we routinely apply the same term, *thought*, to imaginary speech, which invariably uses of course the words of some specific language, and which is therefore not the same for all speakers. None the less, there is agreement in the essentials. The fountainhead of speech is reality, since the process begins with reality sending information, or communicating itself, to the experiencer; when the latter experiences it, what he does is in a sense to repeat (to himself) what he has received from reality. Conceptual thought then repeats (and distils, and manipulates vicariously) the contents that reality has communicated to the experiencer through his senses. When the experiencer wishes to repeat the distilled idea to himself, he casts it in imagined sounds; if he wishes to repeat it to another, he not only thinks the word but actually vocalizes it. The listener can then repeat to himself the repetition of the repetition of the original message 'uttered' by reality. The soul of the semantic interpretation is thus the idea that speech is representative in nature: by this I mean, quite precisely, that speech communicates the speaker's experience (and therefore the reality that is the object of such experience) only because he makes such experience available to the communicand by making signs that somehow *repeat* it to the latter.

Our culture's common sense preserves the semantic view in a crude and inconsistency-riddled version. This is not true of scholars, who have unceasingly developed and modified the semantic theory in highly sophisticated ways. For example, most modern students of the subject maintain that, since the signs used in speech do not in any way resemble what they communicate, it would be incorrect to call them, as Aristotle did, 'likenesses' of the experienced reality.[9] Many would avoid also the terminology of 'representation,' as it can be all too easily taken to imply that language communicates by presenting likenesses of reality. Insisting on the progress made since linguistics became a science, they remind us, for instance, that nowadays few if any of their number suppose that speech represents the speaker's experience of reality in the sense that there is some sort of correspondence, let alone any similarity, between words and their counterparts in experience and reality.[10] The question

---

9 It is at least debatable, however, whether Aristotle was not fully aware of this.
10 But denying an oversimple version of the representative nature of speech is hardly a sufficient critique of it; the essence of the semantic concept of speech remains untouched as long as linguistic signs are deemed to be used by speakers as a means to *repeat* the speaker's experience for the benefit of the communicand. If it should help, I would gladly alter my terminology so as to refer to the 'repetitive' rather than the 'representative' conception of speech.

how signs signify that which they signify – that is, somehow communicate it or make it known – is not to be taken for granted but constitutes, indeed, the key problem of linguistic science: 'That a language is a system of signs seems *a priori* an evident and fundamental proposition, which linguistic theory will have to take into account at an early stage. Linguistic theory must be able to tell us what meaning can be attributed to this proposition, and especially to the word *sign*.'[11]

The objection might therefore be raised whether it is useful to lump together all the traditional theories of speech, ancient and modern, under the heading of 'the semantic interpretation.' So far as I can tell, however, although Aristotle may well have been improved upon in many respects, his basic assumptions about the repetitive nature of speech continue to be taken as self-evident by many linguists (and almost universally by other scientists); even philosophers, who to be sure not infrequently repudiate them, do not always do so as resolutely, consistently, and unambiguously as they usefully might. It matters little how subtle a theory may be devised to explain the way in which speech 'expresses' outwardly our inner thought and thus communicates it to another; or how ingeniously such a theory may avoid the difficulties of construing signs as 'likenesses' that 'correspond' to reality or in some other way 'refer' to it; or how forcefully it may stress the 'symbolic' instead of the 'representative' nature of speech, if it is not true that speech is reducible to the translation of experiential and cogitative processes into vocal sounds bearing meaning. The questions how speech manages to repeat reality, and what is the nature of such repetition, I suggest, are illegitimate, because the prior question is *whether* any repetition whatever is involved in any form of communication, animal or human – to which the answer, as I shall try to show in the next section, is no.

It is indeed because even in its modern variants the semantic interpretation of speech perpetuates the invalid assumptions of old, albeit cryptically, that to its adherents the hypothesis that speech generates consciousness is bound to seem *a priori* unlikely. We have seen why. The supposition that speech is but a form of communication, and that communication repeats to the communicand what had been previously present in the communicator's experience of reality, implies a strict order of priority and posteriority among experience, thought, and speech. Reality's conveyance of its contents must come first so as to determine the contents of sense experience; conceptual thought must come next as the idea is extracted from the sense information; audible speech must be last, since it repeats our thought, which is a repetition of our expe-

11 Hjelmslev, *Prolegomena*, p. 43.

rience of reality. Thus, although speech may be highly creative in other respects,[12] its essentially repetitive nature makes it utterly dependent upon its antecedents. It is patent that thought and consciousness must be in existence before speech can begin.

Not quite so obvious, however, is another implication, only recently drawn, of the semantic complex: that the ability to speak is innate. That the abilities to experience consciously and think conceptually are innate had long been assumed. If the distinction between non-conscious and conscious experience is blurred, consciousness seems to appear spontaneously in infants, through mere maturation – though precisely at what stage of growth may be moot. Likewise, if conceptual thought is prior to, and independent of, the use of imaginary words, then the ability to think conceptually must emerge through maturation, without the child's having to be taught. It has always been apparent, however, that infants do not actually speak until long after they are (as it is assumed) able to experience consciously, and that they do not develop speech unless they are taught. Precisely what learning to speak consisted in, therefore, remained unclear. What has now been pointed out, signally by Noam Chomsky, is the implication of the semantic conception of speech: though no language is innate – in the sense that children do not become able to use any language spontaneously, but must be taught how to use even their mother tongue – the *ability* to use language is.

For this ability is identical with the ability to think conceptually, which is innate. That is, prior to its having learned any language, the human organism has the genetically conditioned ability to think, or to translate experience into concepts, in accordance with 'deep' innate principles of thought that determine the functions of words and the underlying structure of sentences; this talent is, of course, universal in the species, though no language is. Actually speaking – or which is the same, using a language – consists in translating wordless categories and 'deep' syntactic rules into imaginary or audible words grammatically arranged in sentences. It follows that the only reason why children do not develop speech spontaneously is that they lack knowledge of how to use any language whatever; they do not know either the specific signs, or the specific rules about how to put them together, that each and every language requires. Conversely, they are not taught to speak; they are taught to use the language – principally the vocabulary and the syntax – without which they cannot exercise their native ability to speak: 'There

---

12 For instance, it is capable of using a 'finite means [i.e., a language, in order to realize] infinite possibilities of expression': Noam Chomsky, *Cartesian Linguistics* (New York, 1966), p. 29.

are apparently deep-seated and rather abstract principles of a very general nature that determine the form and interpretation of sentences [which may be proposed to be] ... language universals ... [There is, therefore, an] innate schematism that the child brings to bear in language learning.'[13]

The 'innatism' of Chomsky is often contrasted with the 'empiricism' of other linguists, such as Jean Piaget. For the Chomskians, to 'acquire language' is to learn, through experience, to concretize the 'innate schematism' of the human mind in a particular grammar and vocabulary; for the empiricists, it is to acquire that grammar and vocabulary through associative learning. The deeper difference between them, however, has to do with the nature of the ability to *speak*. The empiricists make no distinction between the child's ability to speak and its ability to use its mother tongue; if a child can do the latter, it is obviously able to speak. The Chomskians, to their credit, find this reasoning naïve. They keep in mind that the ability to speak cannot be identified with the ability to use any given language, because speech is universal in the species, whereas the languages in which human beings speak are contingent and variable. Therefore, they argue, behind the ability to use a concrete *language* there must be a more fundamental general linguistic ability that all human beings share; the ability to use language is innate, though the ability to use one's mother tongue has to be acquired.

What can neither be said in approval of the innatists nor used to distinguish them from the empiricists is that the foregoing reasoning hinges on the reduction of speech to communication by means of linguistic signs. The view that will be developed in this chapter is, on the contrary, that although the child does not need to learn to communicate – for this ability appears through maturation – he must nevertheless learn to *speak* and not simply *to use a language* wherewith to speak. That is, he must learn not only to use a linguistic system of signs and rules wherewith to communicate, but also to use such system – and indeed all signs – intending to communicate.

The semantic complex is deeply rooted in our culture. In the twentieth century, however, a crack has appeared in the monolith. The suspicion has gained ground that the absolute posteriority of speech to conscious experience and thought cannot be maintained; the indications that suggest the opposite are too many to be ignored. The distant background of this suspicion is to be found in certain eighteenth-century philosophic developments, particularly the epistemology of Immanuel Kant; for the vulnerability of the semantic complex was first revealed in respect of the interpretation of experience, and only much later in respect of the

13 Noam Chomsky, *Problems of Knowledge and Freedom* (London, 1972), pp. 40, 44.

nature of speech. After Kant the conviction grew that experience cannot be simply a representation of reality. Though a positive interpretation of experience as non-representative has been much less easily converged upon, most philosophers since the early nineteenth century have agreed that conscious experience is creative, in the sense that it organizes in its own way the information received from reality. It was not Kant himself, however, but his student Johann Gottfried von Herder, who took the next step; he proposed, in effect – or at least, his views on the origin and nature of speech inspired the proposal – that speech was in turn not simply the representation of experience, but the means whereby human beings creatively organized their experience. It was thus a means whereby they crafted their own humanity.

Of a piece with these trends was the nineteenth century's discovery of the possibility that truth and human values might be culturally conditioned: different human traditions, maintained through different languages, developed their humanity in somewhat different ways. Wilhelm von Humboldt, for instance, seems to have guessed that cultural differences in self- and world-perception might be related to differences in speech. But this line of thought was not assiduously pursued by many; it attracted mostly the attention of cultural anthropology, which began to flourish about this time. Only in 1940, a century and a half after Herder, did the earlier work of Franz Boas and Edward Sapir, among others, culminate in Benjamin L. Whorf's 'principle of linguistic relativity,' now more commonly known as the Sapir-Whorf hypothesis. The gist is that 'the background linguistic system (in other words, the grammar) of each language is not merely a reproducing instrument for voicing ideas but rather is itself the shaper of ideas ... [Therefore,] all observers are not led by the same physical evidence to the same picture of the universe, unless their linguistic backgrounds are similar, or can be in some way calibrated.'[14] Conversely, 'users of markedly different grammars are pointed by their grammars towards different types of observations, and hence are not equivalent as observers, but must arrive at somewhat different views of the world.'[15] In 1945, Eugen Rosenstock-Huessy independently suggested that 'languages are not means by which we represent the truth after it is perceived, but ... means to discover hitherto ignored truth.'[16]

14 Benjamin L. Whorf, *Language, Thought and Reality* (New York, 1956), pp. 212, 214. Fifty years earlier Friedrich Nietzsche had said almost exactly the same thing (*Beyond Good and Evil*, aph. 20). But, as with most of his other ideas, Nietzsche did not so much as attempt to develop this one systematically or to substantiate it.
15 Whorf, *Language*, p. 221.
16 Eugen Rosenstock-Huessy, *Speech and Reality* (Norwich, CT, 1970), p. 172.

More concrete philosophic contributions to the subject have been made since, but particular mention should be made of the critique of the semantic interpretation of speech by Ludwig Wittgenstein, Maurice Merleau-Ponty, and others who have deemed it absurd, as if the meaning of a word were an object or something contained in objects, or 'as though speaking consisted in translating thought into words.'[17] Squarely on point had also been the work of Alfred Korzybski, who had developed systematically the hypothesis that the unique sentence structure of the Indo-European languages embodies certain assumptions about the nature of reality, among them the idea that the world is constituted by substantive entities universally related by active-passive, cause-effect relationships. If so, he argued, the structure of the Indo-European sentence must be said to mould, somehow, the way in which Indo-European speakers think about the world.[18] However, since no explanation was offered by Korzybski for the peculiarities of the Indo-European languages, it has never been clear why it must be said that the Indo-European experience was shaped by the properties of the Indo-European languages rather than the other way about, as the semantic interpretation would have it. Later I shall try to show that the Indo-European languages do indeed manifest rather than cause the Indo-European form of thought, quite as common sense maintains. The Indo-European mind is, to be sure, conditioned to think in certain ways – but only because it is shaped by assumptions rooted in Indo-European speech. For *language* does not shape human experience and thought, except in secondary respects we can ignore here; *speech* does. Indeed, it does more: it generates their conscious quality.

Whorf made the same mistake: he thought that *grammar* shaped the *contents* of consciousness, when he should have said that *speech* shapes its *form* – that is, determines its properties. For they are right who insist that nothing but reality itself could determine the contents of conscious perception, understanding, and thought. But they are wrong who, mesmerized by this truth, fail to consider the possibility that speech may nevertheless determine both the conscious quality of human sense experience and the meaning that the information provided by reality holds for thought.

17 Emmanuel Lévinas, *Otherwise than Being* (The Hague, 1981), p 48. Cf. Maurice Merleau-Ponty, *The Phenomenology of Perception* (London, 1962), p. 177.
18 Nietzsche anticipated this too (*Beyond Good and Evil*, aph. 20), though he stated it in a confused and dogmatic way. For instance, he thought that Arabic was comparable in this respect to the Indo-European languages, though he provided no evidence for it. What I shall say in chapter VIII about Arabic speech will show why this is not true; it will also provide a hint about the reason why Nietzsche may have sought to assimilate Arabic to the Indo-European languages.

Appreciably closer to the mark, therefore, was the more recent work of Marshall McLuhan. For he showed that the human media are not simply what the name implies: *means* of communication. They also shape the meaning of the information that they communicate. Indeed, they do so more primordially than the source of the information itself. The medium imposes its own qualities upon the experience that it conveys – or, in McLuhan's *bon mot*, 'the medium is the message.' This formula thrives on the imprecision that should be happily tolerated in epigrams – McLuhan had a sweet tooth for hyperbole and little nose for syllogism – but the sober insight withstands the intemperate criticism to which it has been subjected. The all-important point is that a communication is not reducible to its contents. Now, McLuhan's research began with his study of the shaping of human experience by alphabetic writing, and thereafter he turned to other media; it never occurred to him, apparently, that his best-known aphorism might apply above all to the basis of alphabetic writing, namely, speech. None the less, if speech is a medium, and 'the medium is the message,' then the properties of speech have a role in shaping the properties of the experience communicated by speech. Speech, then, is not reducible to communication; it shapes the form or properties, albeit not the contents, of the experience it communicates.

For all the criticism that can be offered to Whorf and McLuhan, their words evoked the tones of truth in many different audiences; this may have been, I think, because their suggestions were in accordance with certain barely conscious expectations of our culture. What prepared us for their insights was psychoanalysis. Even those who reject the Freudian system as a whole may nevertheless agree with an observation that psychoanalytic practice first brought home to us: that speaking sometimes elevates to conscious status experiences that otherwise might never have become so. Psychotherapeutic speech makes possible a restructuring of the meaning of what is recalled. It does not simply convert the forgotten, the repressed, and the absent into the remembered, the accepted, and the present; above all, it enables the speaker to change his earlier construction of his experience. The experienced facts remain the same, but the way they are put together and the significance that may be attached to them do not. Serendipitously, psychoanalysis discovered that, although 'we often think of concepts being used to reflect or report about our experience ... concepts do not only "reflect" and report our experience ... they are *constitutive* of experience ... [Therefore] the therapist's effective introduction of a different meaning-scheme from that formerly used by the patient is a way of ... reorganizing the present experience rather than a way of revealing the truth about a hidden past.'[19] But if reflexion on our experience by means of speech helps restructure our experience, could it be that asserting our experience aboriginally is what gives it its original structure? At very least, consciousness is subject to being 'raised,' and speaking is what 'raises' it. This observable fact has become part of our culture's common sense.

The idea that speech rebounds on the speaker's experience and somehow affects it has radiated into many sectors of our culture, disseminated as it has been by our popular literature; it played a major role, for example, in George Orwell's *Nineteen eighty-four*. It is usually assumed, however, as in this novel (and as in the feminist condemnation of sexist *language*), that the operative factor is *what* is said – though George Bernard Shaw's *Pygmalion* more accurately perceived that what matters is *how* it is said.[20] Flattened by vulgarity and corrupted by self-interest, this view now enters into our everyday life as a voiceless premiss that inspires subtle techniques of interpersonal manipulation. For instance, most commercial, political, and other hucksters know that to persuade us they must first persuade themselves, so that they can speak truthfully to us and thus persuade us with their sincerity. But they also know that to persuade themselves what they have to do is to tell themselves, but *meaning* it, what they want to believe. Nowadays most of us also know that there is a more effective way to deceive than to lie (though few know why it works). To deceive skilfully, one must tell the truth, but in such a way that the hearer will assert a lie to himself: the art of the possible is nine-tenths the art of contriving to achieve this. Of course, not all the applications of our astigmatic insights into the relationship of speech and experience are malevolent or deceptive. But they can be utterly perverse, like the brainwashing techniques which depend upon such discoveries. Consider having a victim write his autobiography in minute detail, and then rewrite it over and over again the 'right' way – the way that confirms the brainwasher's interpretation of the world. One would not have thought it possible; unfortunately, it works. The victim becomes convinced of the truth of what he originally wrote believing it was false. But there are yet subtler improvements. The foregoing procedure avoids violence, but involves coercion, and brainwashers who are up to date take pride in the fact that 'for all their manipulation of ... [the victim, he] is not coerced.'[21] At the current state of the art it

19 Herbert Fingarette, *The Self in Transformation* (New York, 1965), pp. 22, 23, 25. Jacques Lacan has made the same point at length.
20 However, Shaw confused the assertive with the prosodic quality of speech, reducing thus the effects of speech on experience to largely sociological ones.
21 John le Carré, *The Little Drummer Girl* (New York, 1983), p. 142.

is possible to manipulate people into 'volunteering' to do what the manipulator wants. The peculiar effectiveness of this is that 'Volunteers find their own ways to persuade themselves'[22] that they should do as their manipulator wants.

In short, the feeling is widespread that the semantic interpretation of speech suffers from certain deficiencies; the attempt to correct it, however, has devoted most of its efforts to exploring the shaping of thought by language and the creation of attitudes by words. The results have undoubtedly had great heuristic value but a yet more radical departure from the traditional premisses is required. Moreover, the semantic interpretation of speech is only part of the semantic complex; a reinterpretation of speech would not be viable unless carried out in conjunction with a corresponding reinterpretation of the nature of experience, and indeed of the reality that is its object. The reorganization of the concepts of speech, conscious experience, and reality into an alternative to the semantic complex must begin with a phenomenological analysis of the

22 Ibid. Anticipating some of the concepts that will be developed in this work, I would describe brainwashing as a technique for destroying and reconstructing an individual's self-definition by taking advantage of the consciousness-generating properties of speech. The destructive phase is the difficult one; since human beings cannot live without self-definition, the second phase practically looks after itself. The destruction is achieved by contriving that the victim disorient himself regarding his self-identity; and this is brought about by ensuring that he assert to himself the falsity of the self-definition he has laboriously developed over many years. The victim's resistance may not be pronounced, because he is likely to assume that his beliefs about himself cannot be changed merely by lying to another about them. But he does not reckon with the fact that 'the medium is the message.' After sufficient repetition of what he originally believed to be false, the victim becomes confused about his identity; he does not know which of his assertions about himself he actually believes. The second phase begins at this point. Le Carré's novel, however, illustrates a refinement: persuading the victim voluntarily to undertake the questioning of his own self-definition. The advantage of this approach is that the reconstructed self-definition can then be all the more solidly established, because it does not result from the victim's simply allowing his new identity to be moulded by the brainwasher, but from his actively seeking to redefine himself; he will find a way to persuade himself that he is what the brainwasher wants him to be.

Observe carefully, however – for this is why I have analysed brainwashing in seemingly irrelevant detail – that the technique is successful because it takes advantage of the properties of *speech*, rather than because of *what* is said by the victim. He becomes disoriented by asserting anything about himself that he believes to be false, not specifically by asserting what the brainwasher wants him eventually to believe. It is only at the second stage, after the victim's 'brain' is 'clean,' that the brainwasher will offer statements whose contents the victim is invited to accept. If this phase is successful, the reason is that the victim, *sicut tabula rasa*, can be indoctrinated under somewhat the same favourable conditions as virgin minds ordinarily can.

experience of speaking, with the object of determining the nature of speech.

2. The assertiveness of speech

Let us conduct an imaginary experiment. Four laboratory cubicles contain, respectively, a human being, a tape-recorder, a Macintosh®-operated voice synthesizer, and a trained parrot. From each of these, in turn, the sound reaches a subject: 'The cat is on the mat.' The sound is so acoustically controlled that its physical properties are the same in all four instances. Having thus been deprived of all other information about the sources, the subject is then asked to tell which source was the origin of which transmission. Will he be able to match them correctly? The negative results are predictable. But what do the results tell us? Do they mean that there is no difference between the human and the other sources of communication? Some, apparently, are prepared to draw such a conclusion. Most of us, however, will feel that there is a difference – though few will be able to pinpoint it or to give a rational account of how they perceive it. The negative results show above all the inherent limitations of attempting to interpret speech from the viewpoint of a listener who should abstract from his own experience of speech.

Let us, however, put aside the question how we identify fellow speakers as such. There is a prior issue; for we could not very well hope to detect true speech in others unless we already knew what speech was from acquaintance with our own. If we reflect upon it, however, we may discover what would have to be missing in any speech-like sound that was not what we call speech in ourselves. The essential element is *saying* what the sounds communicate; it is making the sounds that communicate, but *intending* that they communicate it and *experiencing* their aptness for doing so. A tape-recorder produces sounds that duplicate the sounds made earlier by a human being who had said, 'The cat is on the mat,' though the recorder itself does not *say* it. The synthesizer is applied by the user of the MacinTalk™ program to produce the same sounds that a speaker makes when he says 'The cat is on the mat,' but the user does not make the computer *say* what the sounds mean to him who hears them. I need hardly debate whether parrots *say* anything. If the *saying* is absent, sound-making and its communicative effects upon a human listener who can understand speech do not amount to speech; it is *saying* that makes speech what it is.[23] Thus, when human beings

---

23 Though Martin Heidegger observed that *saying* was essential to speech, by this he seems to have meant that its assertiveness results from, and is an indication of,

speak, they do not merely convey a certain meaning; they mean the meaning they convey. To speak is to *assert* what one communicates.

To be sure, nothing can be said by a speaker except in and through his voicing, or otherwise making, communicative signs. But the assertiveness of speech demonstrates, first, the irreducibility of speech to making vocal sounds. This will be granted, I think, without much difficulty; few people think that parrots actually speak. However, it also shows, second, the irreducibility of speech to making not only vocal but any kind of communicative signs. Speech is, therefore, essentially different from infrahuman communication. For instance, a chimpanzee can be trained to make a certain sign, or a dog to bark, whenever it sees the cat stepping on the mat; these signs would communicate the same content as the human assertion 'The cat is on the mat.' But only the human communication would be speech, since only that one would be *meant* so as to communicate. (Of course, animals do not communicate only when they have been trained; human tuition merely improves upon their native ability.) If one attends to the assertiveness of speech, one cannot confuse infrahuman communication with speech or with the other forms of assertive communication that derive from it. Assertiveness raises what-is-communicated to the level of what-is-said.

What-is-said comprises two polar aspects: the content of speech, or *what*-is-said, and the saying of it, which makes the communication to be what-is-*said*. This distinction is, by another name, that between the *meaning* of what we say and our *meaning* such meaning. Now, if we pay attention to the assertiveness of speech, it should be clear that the meaning of *what* we say depends on *our* meaning it. If we are absent-minded, however, our meaning the meaning will be projected into reality. That is, the meaning of what we say will be imagined to reside within reality, and we will then interpret speech as the repetition of what reality itself *means*: as if reality spoke to us, as if its speaking to us were a prior assertion that our own speech merely repeated, and as if experience were the repetition (to ourselves) of the meaning that reality possessed in itself. But this is, of course, unadulterated fantasy: it overlooks the fact that reality cannot be properly said to mean what we say 'it means,' since the speaker alone, and not reality, speaks.

Moreover, if we take into account the assertiveness of speech, we may observe that the *saying* of what-is-said includes not only the inten-

---

its essential function, namely, to manifest reality as such; see *On the Way to Language* (New York, 1971), pp. 121ff. In the view to be developed here, on the contrary, speech reveals reality as such only because speech is assertive.

tion to communicate what-is-said, but also and more specifically the intention to make an *affirmation* – positive or negative – in relation to what one communicates. The affirmation is embodied in the speaker's intentional voicing of the audible (or in the thinker's imagining of the inaudible) sounds of speech; it is only in consequence of such affirmation that the assertion is vested in what he communicates, whether to another or to himself. Speakers, therefore, simply by speaking, implicitly hold out that their assertions are actually or potentially true. Speech may be sincere or mendacious, categorical or doubtful, and irresponsible or deliberate, but in any event includes taking a stand in respect of what-is-said. Truth is always in the background of speech. But without the assertiveness that defines human communication there is neither the truthfulness nor the lack of it that is a typical and necessary part of speech.

We may now return to the question how we recognize genuine speech by other than indirect signs. One recognizes it when one perceives reciprocity of assertiveness: if one's interlocutor asserts what he voices when he communicates with one, then he is doing what *one* does when one speaks to him. And his assertiveness is recognized when one observes that his communications are of the kind that would require assertiveness *in one*, if they were one's own communications. The most obvious manifestation of assertiveness is thus the implicit or explicit claim of the communicator to be telling the truth. Of course, anyone who insists that he is telling the truth, or who tacitly expects to be believed, may be lying. But it makes no difference whether he is. If one thinks that someone is lying, or that he is telling the truth, or if one is uncertain which is the case – but sure that he is doing one or else the other – one has recognized a speaker. To this we may contrast the coincidence of an animal's signals with reality: what the animal communicates may well be (as *we* can appreciate) true, but the animal does not thereby *tell* the truth. By the same token, although an animal's signals may as a matter of fact have a deceiving *effect*, the animal has not lied unless it has deceived *intending* to achieve such effect.[24]

24 An apparent instance of lying by a chimpanzee communicating with human beings in sign language has been reported; the circumstances could conceivably indicate that the message, which was false, had been sent for the purpose of diverting blame for misbehaviour onto another animal. But whether such intention did, in fact, dictate the chimpanzee's message is more difficult to say; controls are not easily achieved in this kind of experimental situation. However, no intrinsic impossibility should be supposed. If a chimpanzee could be trained to make signs assertively, it would have been taught to function at a certain level of consciousness. Whether

The assertiveness of speech manifests the purposiveness that characterizes all life, but in a highly developed form. It is the kind of purposiveness that has to do with achieving a goal through communication – and indeed, through communication of the communicator's experience. But it is more than this. A communication is assertive only if the communicator is guided by the facts (a) that his communicative behaviour can cause a communicand to experience what the communication signifies, and (b) that the communication of his experience to a communicand fulfils his wish to communicate. But this is possible only if his experience is present to him as experience. The ability to speak is thus the outward sign of consciousness. And since, vice versa, any communicator who is conscious must be able to do so assertively – for he must be conscious of his communications and of their being made with intent to achieve their proper effect – the necessary accompaniment of speech is consciousness. But one may be conscious and able to speak without being sufficiently aware of one's own assertiveness, or of the nature of speech, or about how one recognizes human speech, to grasp the difference between assertive and non-assertive communication. Indeed, some people who have first hand acquaintance with speech are nevertheless so confused about what they do when they speak – and therefore when they think – that they even wonder whether computers do not think.

An eminent computer scientist once thus proposed – he *was* serious, and convinced many of his colleagues – that unless one could tell the difference between teleprinter exchanges between oneself and a computer, and like exchanges between oneself and another human being, one should admit that there is no essential difference between the human's and the machine's 'thinking' processes.[25] This shows, however, the same absent-minded muddle that would be revealed by someone who wondered whether telephones did not speak and think (for, tinny voice aside, they are apt to give very thoughtful replies), or who reasoned

---

chimpanzees have the requisite organic capacity to learn this remains to be seen, though my guess is that it is exceedingly unlikely.

25 A.M. Turing, 'Computing Machinery and Intelligence,' in Edward A. Feigenbaum and Julian Feldman, eds., *Computers and Thought* (New York, 1963). However, not a few philosophical arguments to the contrary have been comparably wide of the mark, such as those based on absence of emotion, moral sensibility, and so on, in computers. Strangely, those who raise these objections rarely point out what would be more relevant: that computers are not even alive. Objections based on the supposed differences between *what* the computer and *what* human beings can do are beside the point – which is that the computer does not perform at all any of the *vital activities* that the absent-minded project onto them.

that books think (since they contain and communicate thoughts). The user is not in communication *with* the computer, any more than the reader communicates *with* the book or the caller *with* the telephone – even when he is greeted by an answering machine. Quite as the reader of the book communicates with the author and with himself, the user of a computer is in communication, first, with himself, using the machine to think more efficiently than otherwise, and, second, with the pro-grammer who wrote the application, whose thinking is embodied in the program.[26] As an abacus and a slide rule are tools wherewith the user can perform complex mathematical operations more efficiently than without, though the instruments themselves cannot so much as add one plus one, a computer is a machine *for* thinking, not a machine *that* thinks.

Evidently, those who fail to perceive the difference disregard the diistinction between the activity of thinking and the contents of thought. The latter can be objectified and embodied by the thinker – through his manipulation of, say, ink and paper, sliding beads, or electric currents and magnetic fields – in visual or other signs that *he* (and other human beings) can understand. Only such disregard would permit their ignor-ing the fact that being alive and being capable of experiencing are among the indispensable prerequisites of thinking. Nor do they seem to realize that even true communication with another would not be, of itself, proof that the communicator thinks; the latter would require evidence that the communicator communicates *to himself* what he also communicates to his communicand.

I remarked earlier that the irreducibility of consciousness to experience does not mean that consciousness can exist as a disembodied quality. Similarly, although communicative behaviour may be found both in animals and in humans without assertiveness, the assertiveness of speech is a quality of certain forms of communicative behaviour and cannot exist except as part of such behaviour; speech is not definable as asser-tiveness, but as assertive communication. It will be remembered, how-ever, that although both human and animal experience depend for their contents upon information received from the object, no experience – whether conscious or non-conscious, animal or human – is the inner

26 If Turing's hypothetical experiment allowed only limited interaction, a user may well be unable to determine whether he is in communication with other human beings through a computer or else directly. But this should be no more astonishing than the inability to determine, in like circumstances, whether one is receiving a telephone message *viva voce* or only a prerecorded one. Even with unlimited exchanges, the mediation of a computer could be detected only by a user who was more skilled at detecting the programmed nature of the responses than the programmer – not the computer – was at hiding it.

representation of outer reality. Likewise, although speech and every other form of signal-making depend for their contents on information received from objects through experience, communication does not repeat the contents of experience – not even by means of 'symbols,' whose repetitive value some scholars sedulously distinguish from that of mere signs. The supposedly important difference is that symbols have free-floating rather than fixed reference to reality, and can therefore be used metaphorically and creatively. But since such symbols remain worded counterparts of our experience, the essentials of the semantic interpretation have been retained. Is it possible, however, to dispense with this assumption? How could communication, whether animal or human, convey meaning, or signify whatever it signifies, without somehow repeating or representing what it communicates?

A terminological hazard should be noted. Besides denoting 'information transmission,' the words *communication* and *signification* have traditionally connoted 'representation'; our assumptions about the nature of speech have necessarily implied it. However, one cannot very well be open to the possibility that an organism's experience might be signified and communicated without any representation or repetition being involved, if at the same time one conceives signification and communication in a way that, prejudicially, precludes such possibility. And yet, some may be inclined to reason that every communication must somehow be representative, because the very concept of communication includes this note. Evidently, those who should so reason would be unaware that words are instruments for thinking, and would have instead allowed their words to dictate what they should think.

With this caution in mind, let us consider a typical instance of animal communication. Suppose an animal that, upon its perceiving an enemy, snarls and growls; it does not do so because it has any intention to communicate its readiness to defend itself or because it is aware of the possibility of its doing so, but only because evolution has bred into it the adaptive response of snarling and growling whenever it perceives what it now perceives. But by so responding the animal has, in fact, broadcast its experience. We can say that the animal has 'communicated' and 'signified' it, provided we do not thereby suppose that it has done anything other than to behave as it has; for in relation to the enemy that perceives it, such behaviour operates as a sign that communicates information about the snarling animal's inner dispositions. But how does the sign communicate such information? Well, the sign does not *do* anything to communicate it. What such an expression misleadingly describes is the fact that the communicand 'receives' such information. But the latter expression also is misleading. The reception of information by the communicand means simply that the second animal, upon perceiving the behaviour of the first, responds adjustively to what it has experienced. No more intent to communicate, no more awareness of its communicative powers, and no more consciousness are required for this than for the same communicand to respond adjustively to any other object of experience. Evolution breeds the ability to adjust through experience quite as effectively when the perceived object is another animal's behaviour as when it is anything else. Thus, the communicator's experience has been effectively communicated to the communicand, but without any representation or repetition having taken place and without any information having been, except figuratively, either 'transmitted' or 'received.' I need hardly add that the communicator's behavioural signs need not be visually perceptible, but may well be, for instance, sounds.

At the higher levels animals can improve their native communicative behaviour through learning. This is most obvious when they do so under human tutelage, but can happen also as the result of natural selection under ordinary environmental pressures prompting the species to adjust. But though natural selection improved the *languages* of animals, the nature of animal *communication* remained essentially unchanged until the appearance of man. The 'vocabularies' of, say, dolphins and anthropoids may be superior to those of ants and bees – not least strikingly because that of the former can be enlarged through either artificial or natural conditioning whereas that of the latter cannot – but my description of animal communication applies to all these animal species equally well.

Unlike an animal's signification of its experience, then, which is made and received instinctively, the human communicator's speech asserts his experience and is made with communicative intent; and his message is effectively communicated only because the communicand who perceives it is himself capable of asserting a like experience using the same vocal sounds, not because the signs he hears repeat or represent the communicator's experience to him. In the last chapter, however, we conceived the possibility that, when communications are assertively made, the communicative activity may render the communicated experience present to itself. The foregoing examination of the nature of speech should have strengthened this suspicion, since it has suggested that the ability to speak goes together with the ability to experience consciously. But can we go farther and conclude that this interpretation may be reasonably maintained?

3. The relationship of speech to conscious experience and thought

Granted the semantic premises, there is no possible alternative to thinking of speech as the final stage in a process of serial reproduction that begins with a consciousness constituted as such prior to all thought and speech. This way of looking at the matter may be illustrated by the following diagram:

| [Conscious] Experience | → | [Conceptual] Thought | [Worded] Thought | → | Speech |

The semantic construction is correct in part. Since there can be neither experience (whether conscious or non-conscious) nor communication (whether assertive or non-assertive) without contents, the process must begin with the reception of information from an outer or inner object. But in four other crucial respects this interpretation is incorrect. The first has been explained already: neither communication nor experience, whether assertive or non-assertive, is a repetition of reality. The other three will now be discussed.

The wordless conceptual thought supposed by the semantic interpretation must be deemed not only empirically unjustified, but also superfluous. There is no question of the existence of worded thought; it is an empirical fact. But the 'purport' or the pure 'ideas' behind words is nowhere to be found; is a a figment required by the semantic conception of speech, because otherwise it could not be claimed that speech was the subsequent representation of a prior experience, yet a representation that was contingent and variable while the experience was the same for all. But if it is true that neither experience nor speech is representative, the office that wordless concepts were invented to occupy no longer exists. The empirically justified alternative is that no 'purport' or 'idea' of anything is ever thought except in the linguistic terms of audible or imagined speech. We must, therefore, discard the supposition that wordless concepts mediate between conscious experience and speech, though we may – as I shall here – retain the term *concept* to refer to the meaning of a word, whether audible or inaudible. But let us remember: the meaning of a word is the meaning it carries because it has been asserted with such meaning; it is not a meaning that resides in objects and is thereafter represented through imaginary or vocal speech. *Thought* may thus be indifferently described either as speech in imagined *words*[27]

27 This may seem to coincide with the view expressed long ago by John B. Watson in

or as the imaginary production, ordering, and manipulation of *concepts*; it means the same as purely mental speech. Henceforth I shall use the term in this sense.

A brief aside on terminology may be helpful. The most common English usage of the word *thought* carries in part the meaning I have accepted as most proper: imaginary speech. But since thinking involves the use of imagination, our common practice, reflecting the confused self-perception from which we tend to suffer, often applies *thought* to any imagining whatever, for instance, to visual day-dreaming. *Imagining*, however, is a more comprehensive mental activity than thinking; it is the ability to reproduce (and, if we wish, manipulate and rearrange) the contents of prior sensation. We imagine, moreover, in a variety of sense modalities (though we are not equally adept at imagining in all). Thinking – that is, speaking in imagination only – is thus but one of several ways in which we can use our ability to imagine what we had previously sensed. But since human assertive communication is not restricted to the medium of audible signs, the ability to think is not necessarily restricted to the imagining of *vocal* communicative signs. Ordinarily, however, individuals acquire assertiveness through the transformation of their innate ability to communicate *vocally*, and the human species presumably did likewise.[28] The ability to think has therefore developed

---

his *Behaviorism* (New York, 1925), that thought is subvocal speech. The similarity, however, is more apparent than real. Thought is indeed subvocal speech, but not in Watson's sense that it is reducible to a 'laryngeal habit.' Both speech and thought are irreducible to organic functions. This does not imply that they are superorganic events; they are properly called mental events, in the sense that they are events pertaining to the conscious level of functioning of the human organism.

28 Though assertiveness emerged as a quality of audible communication rather than in any other sense modality, it was only natural that, once it had appeared and speakers had become conscious, they should have eventually invented purely artificial languages that made use of every other sense modality, particularly visual communication. Some of these (e.g., gestures, marks, diagrams) assert meanings that may be derived from, but which in any event become independent of, the concepts used in linguistic speech; these have a very limited role in human life. Others, notably phonetic writing, are transpositions of speech into visual signs. The visual mode of animal communication was preserved in man in its originally non-assertive form, to some extent, in the spontaneous body language of human beings (which is to be contrasted with culturally conditioned gestures and facial expressions used more or less assertively by humans). However, even body language can be used assertively, with consciousness of its communicative effects – as it is, for instance, by actors. A perfect illustration, from our own experience, of an animal's experience of communicating would be the human experience of communicating by means of body language used non-consciously. But the experience is of course a nonconscious one; for when we use body language spontaneously rather than afore-

almost exclusively in the modality of imaginary sound-making, though nothing in the nature of consciousness so demands. For instance, the ability to think visually (I do not mean simply to *imagine* visually, but to manipulate visual imaginary objects 'logically,' or with speech-like coherence) is present in human beings; but in most people it is rudimentary in comparison with the fluency of worded thought. Relatively simple spatial relations puzzles, for instance, baffle most of us. And yet, the ability to *imagine* visually is highly developed in most human beings – though in most of us it is inferior to our ability to imagine auditorily. Compare, for instance, the small number of items of visual information that most of us can reproduce accurately in visual imagination upon closing our eyes with the large number of notes of a musical composition that even a person with little musical talent can reproduce in auditory imagination – though not necessarily vocally – after the music stops. In sum, we customarily – for instance, in most day-dreaming – combine thinking with the exercise of imagination in other sense modalities. But few people are even passably clear about the various tools that make up the panoply of consciousness; to most of us, whatever goes on 'inside' our minds is 'thought.'

The third issue concerns the priority of thought over speech. In the semantic interpretation this supposition is redeemed from absurdity at the cost of ambiguity: *thought* means both wordless concepts signifying the experience of reality and the imagined words that signify wordless concepts. But in the absence of wordless concepts the supposition is hopelessly absurd: it would mean that audible speech was a translation, into audible form, of sounds that we had first learned to make in imagination only. However, we can imagine only what we have first sensed.[29] Thought – imaginary speech – can originate only in audible speech, not vice versa, and in this sense is necessarily posterior to speech. Let us consider this matter, however, a little more leisurely.

It is, of course, quite possible for human beings to speak for their sole benefit by making purely imaginary sounds; to do so they have but to suppress the audible sounds of speech. Moreover, if one is skilled at speaking both audibly and silently, one may develop the further ability to refine one's communications by 'choosing one's words.' First one thinks silently what one wishes to say, and then, after approving one's composition – or after selecting from among several – one repeats to

---

thought, we communicate without intending to communicate and without experiencing the communicative efficacy of our behaviour.

29 We can, of course, construct and reconstruct elements of sense experience to create imaginary configurations that we have never experienced with our external senses and that indeed need not exist in reality. We can creatively organize, but we cannot create, the contents of imaginative experience.

others what one had already said to oneself. But rehearsing speech is not necessary; audible assertions are ordinarily asserted and voiced simultaneously and by a single act. Does this not imply that we can speak without thinking? Yes, it does. Now in the sense that imprudent speech is possible, everyone will agree that we can. But I mean more than this; I mean that learning to speak is the pre-condition of learning to think.

The evidence is that to speak audibly is to make the same assertion, in the same words, that we could also first rehearse and then voice. The only difference between the mental event of making an assertion in speech and the mental event of making it in thought is what we have already noted: in thought the audibility of speech has been suppressed. There is, therefore, only one process – asserting by means of words – which may be given either voiced or voiceless form. But if so, we must conclude that the latter derives from the former; for if we did not know how to make vocal sounds, we would not know how to imagine them. The relationship of speech to thought is, therefore, the opposite of what the semantic interpretation supposes: thought is derived from speech. The order in which the abilities to speak and to think can be exercised after both have been acquired is not the same as the order in which they are acquired. By the same token, there is no need to postulate an ability to think conceptually – a generalized, 'deep' ability to speak – that precedes the ability to speak using a specific language. There is, indeed, quite as the Chomskians believe, an ability to communicate that is not reducible to the ability to communicate using a specific language – but it is the ability to communicate, using any signs whatever, experiencing that one is communicating, and intending to communicate.

Inaudibility is the most obvious feature of thought, but describes it only negatively. The significance of thought is positive. Because it is a means to communicate assertively not with another, but with oneself, it exhibits a higher, more distilled assertiveness than audible speech; by restricting communication to self-communication, imaginary speech enables the speaker to make assertions with greater awareness of their assertiveness than when he addresses them to another and only secondarily, if at all, to himself. For instance, we 'think things out' in order to become more certain in our own minds of what we experience and of what we mean; after communicating with ourselves in imaginary speech (we could do it audibly, but it would be cumbersome), we can assert to ourselves what we *do* think about the matter. The procedure noted earlier – rehearsing our speech – also illustrates the higher assertiveness of thought; when an assertion is made 'aforethought,' it is more definitively made, more emphatically *meant*, than otherwise. Both in nature and in origin thought is, therefore, posterior to speech. But it is significant that, at the same time, it is less communicative than speech, since it operates within the restricted ambit of self-communication. For this fact suggests that, as the ability to think grows out of the ability to speak, the progression from lesser to greater assertiveness is counterbalanced by a regression from greater to lesser communicativeness. The value of this inverse relationship should be evident; for instance, the enormously higher speed of thought and the multiplicity of simultaneous associations that it permits are the direct consequence of the thinker's bypassing the plodding pace of muscular and other physiological activities that audible speech requires. Thought, to its great advantage, trades communicativeness for assertiveness.

But if so, simple extrapolation suggests that the order of priority and posteriority among the abilities to speak, to think, and to sense consciously is the very opposite of what the semantic interpretation supposes. Conscious experience is yet less communicative than thought; indeed, it is not communicative *at all*, since it asserts the experienced reality without the intervention of any communicative signs, not even self-communicative ones. But it is supremely assertive. Thought, for its part, uses communicative signs, or words; it is less communicative, but more assertive, than speech. And speech excels in communicativeness, but is the least assertive of the three. Thus, the progression from speech, through thought, to conscious experience is the ascent from lesser to greater assertiveness, counterbalanced by a regression from greater to lesser communicativeness. I may therefore amplify my earlier statement: the order in which the abilities to speak, to think, *and to experience consciously* can be exercised after all three have been acquired is not the same as the order in which they are acquired.

Let us remember, however, that the process begins with the speaker's reception of information. More fully stated, therefore, the sequence is: from the reception of information providing the contents of experience (and of communication) to the assertion of such information, first in speech, then in thought, and finally in experience – that is, in experience that is now conscious. Since the process begins with non-conscious experience and ends with consciousness, we may conclude that speech and thought, in that order, mediate the transformation of non-conscious into conscious experience. The syntactic interpretation of the relationship of speech to consciousness could therefore be diagrammed thus:

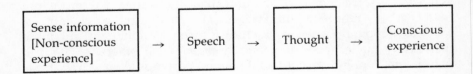

How is consciousness generated, then, in the individual human being? The concrete process will be described later, but the general principle would be as follows. Suppose an organism with a genetically conditioned ability to communicate its experience by means of (as it happens) vocal sounds. If it should develop the ability to communicate its experience by asserting it vocally, it could learn next to assert its experience to itself in purely imaginary speech. This development would ultimately enable it – rather *him* – to learn to assert the experienced reality immediately and directly, in and through the sort of experience that affirms the object in reality precisely as that which is both real and experienced. A decrease in, and eventual cessation of, the communicative function of asserting one's experience permits a correlative increase in the assertive quality of the act. Thus, although the mere communication of non-conscious experience may have no effect on the experiential abilities of the communicator, the assertive communication of it may be inherently apt to have profound effects upon them. The conscious quality of human experience would eventually result from the development of the assertive quality of the human ability to communicate. (These remarks have had reference to the individual, but the possibility flaunts itself that the same progression may have obtained in the species as well.) Of course, after he has developed a full set of human abilities, the conscious experiencer can first experience an object consciously, then make purely imaginary assertions about it to himself, which he can finally, if he chooses, communicate audibly to another. But even then the characteristics of his conscious experience would remain marked by their origin in thought and speech; all conscious experience, even in the adult individual, is profoundly affected by speech and thought, in ways we have yet to examine. In *this* sense, consciousness may be said to be not only generated, but also 'shaped' by speech and by thought. But I mean: above all by the *properties*, not the *contents*, of speech and thought.

Speech and thought have thus a role in the human process of experiencing; speech is the source of the assertiveness of conscious experience, and thought channels the former into the latter. The three remain, however, essentially different functions. The fundamental difference between speech and thought on the one hand, and conscious experience on the other, is that the assertiveness of speech and thought qualify the act of *communicating* the contents of experience, whereas the assertiveness of consciousness qualifies the act of *experiencing* such contents; all other differences follow from this. Likewise, speech, thought, and consciousness are increasingly enhanced forms of the self-presence gained by the experience of reality through its being asserted. They differ in the degree of *immediacy* of the self-presence of experience that they

respectively bring about – that is, in the directness of the assertive relationship of the act of experience to the asserted object of experience.
Thought and speech assert it mediately, through communicative signs,
but consciousness asserts it immediately. Correspondingly, whereas
consciousness is maximally self-present, speech is the least intensively
self-present of the three.[30] Speech, thought, and consciousness differ,
therefore, also in the range of sense modalities to which self-presence
can accrue. Consciousness extends to every inner and outer sense modality, whereas thought is restricted to imaginary auditory experience;
for whatever is sensed in other modalities has to be translated, through
speech, into imaginary sounds before it can be asserted in concepts.
Speech, yet more narrowly, makes experience in any sense modality
present to itself only if it is translated into actually audible sounds.

Finally, the semantic theory also misinterprets the facts in a fourth
respect: it supposes that the relationship of experience to thought and
speech is linear. But if what we have just noted is true, then the relationship is circular, in the sense that the process begins with experience
and ends with experience – albeit experience that has been raised to the
level of consciousness. The syntactic interpretation of the relationship
of speech to consciousness should therefore be diagrammed as follows,
more fully than previously, to show the interaction between the experiential and the communicative processes in man:

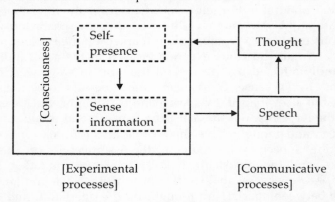

Thus, when the communication of experience becomes assertive (and

---

30 This accounts for the fact that whereas anyone who is conscious is aware that to be
   conscious is a way to experience (though he need not understand much of what
   this means), not everyone who speaks is aware that speech makes the experience
   of reality become present to itself.

why and how it so becomes, both in the individual and in the species, are the threshold questions of the study of human evolution), experience and the communication of experience enter into a symbiotic relationship – or perhaps better, into a sort of marriage, a consortium in which mutual endowment and complementary interaction produces (not always for the better, unfortunately, in the case of marriage) the unity of a dyad within the boundaries of which each member retains its individuality. The relation of speech and human experience, however, is an unusually happy mutual involvement that necessarily results in reciprocal fulfilment. Speech settles its assertiveness, like a dowry, on mere experience, enriching the latter with consciousness. But as experience acquires consciousness, the latter enhances speech in return by endowing it with its own experiential role: by means of speech the conscious experiencer can eventually *understand* what he has consciously *sensed*. Assertive communication ultimately sires the fullness of conscious life. As the quality of consciousness proliferates and an entire family of related human activities grows, the speaker becomes able to experience his own behaviour and speech consciously; he develops the power to speak, and otherwise behave, under the influence and control of the very consciousness that speech behaviour itself had originally made possible. In sum, the injection of assertiveness into human communication creates a circular, self-sustaining process: in much the same way as a fire ignites the fuel that feeds it, the consciousness generated by speech can develop itself by means of speech, while the development of speech can be brought about by the consciousness generated by speech.

The generation of consciousness by speech is thus only the beginning of the human developmental process. The interaction between speech and the experience that it communicates accounts for the fact that, as we shall now study, neither speech nor consciousness are the single-layer reality that we have so far tacitly taken them to be. Consciousness operates at two levels, which correspond to two distinct levels of assertiveness in speech.

4. The two levels of assertiveness in speech and consciousness

We ordinarily use a single term, *speech*, to refer to two quite different ways in which the ability to communicate assertively can be exercised. For reasons that will become clear, I will refer to them as *thematic* and *non-thematic* (or pre-thematic) speech. The former is both more assertive and complex than non-thematic speech, virtually containing all the achievements of the latter and more. We may surmise, therefore, that thematic developed out of non-thematic speech At the moment, however, what matters is rather how the information received from reality is asserted at each of these two levels. For if speech generates consciousness by reason of its assertiveness, then two different levels of assertiveness in speech should generate two different levels of consciousness. And it is indeed an observable fact that consciousness operates simultaneously on two planes. One parameter of human experience is conscious *sensation*, the immediate consciousness of sensible objects on which we have concentrated so far. But we also experience the sensible world meaningfully, or with *understanding*. The latter is the thematic form of consciousness, the kind that, as I propose, is generated by thematic speech. We shall see, however, that the ability to experience meaningfully is the basis of self-definition, the creation of a self that is meaningful to itself; therefore, the thematic consciousness may be best referred to as the *self-defining* mode of conscious life. But I should now explain why this should be maintained and what it implies.

We have already examined some of the common ingredients of animal communication and speech, but now we should note another. An animal's significative behaviour – say, a snarl or an alarm call – refers the communicand to an object that constitutes, in its own reality, the context of the signal. And by *context* I mean: that in relation to which the signal has its specific meaning. Thus, the snarl refers the communicand directly to the communicator's inner disposition to defend itself; the alarmed bird's chatter and flutter refer other birds to the threat constituted by the predator itself, in its own reality. The elementary form of speech adds assertiveness to this sort of communicative behaviour, of course, but does not otherwise change it – whereas speech at the higher level does. We can compare the two because, even after we rise to the fully elaborate, thematic plane, we retain the ability to speak in the more primitive way. If you raise a weapon against me, I may say, 'No! Please! Stop!' or I may call out a warning to others, 'Look out! Danger! Run!' Unlike that of animals, this communication is assertive, or thetic. I put out the signal, aware of its potential communicative effect and expecting it to have such effect. Nevertheless, it is quite like animal communication insofar as the speaker asserts his experience with *immediate*, direct reference to an outer or inner experienced object that constitutes, in its own reality, the context of the assertion. Correspondingly, when the speaker speaks in this way he can communicate only the kind of experience that can take place *immediately*, that is, within the context given to him by his situation in reality. Thus, the context of both what-he-asserts and what-he-asserts-it-about is given to, rather than created by, him. His speech is of the sort I have called *non-thematic*.

Even this basic form of speech, however, confers upon experiencers a privilege that animal communication does not provide: the freedom to determine how the information they receive shall be envisaged. What they speak about and what they shall say are determined for them by reality, in the sense that only reality can furnish the content of their speech; but precisely how they will encompass it or handle it (e.g., as 'rose' rather than as 'flower,' or as 'table' rather than as 'chattel') is determined by them. They will do so by *conceiving* the reality as they do – that is, by asserting it in accordance with one or else another among the signs at their disposal. For as we have seen, concepts signify reality only because they have been made so as to mean what they signify. And conceivers mean them *ad libitum*, since the signs at their disposal are neither furnished to them by the reality nor genetically programmed, as in animals. The signs are determined by the speakers themselves. Or to be precise, they are determined in the first instance by the community that teaches the individual to speak (for he does not invent the signs through the use of which he acquires speech), though eventually also, to some extent, by the individual speaker himself. This freedom is undoubtedly a closely delimited one; it only means that the speaker can decide, within the limits of his received or invented conceptual repertoire, the specific way in which he will attend to what reality gives to him to speak about. Nevertheless, this is more than any animal can do. The ability to mean what one communicates implies the ability to designate and delimit, in the specific way in which one means it, the reality whereof one speaks.

Once consciousness has been generated in the speaker by his non-thematic speech, however, he is by that very fact able to experience his own speech; he therefore becomes able to speak with consciousness of his speaking, and is thus able to determine the context of his assertions – that is, what he makes them in relation to. He has, therefore, become able to speak about an experienced reality not only as *given* to him, but also as *stipulated* by him. He can propose, say, 'the cat' as an *object of speech*, a topic in relation to which he intends to affirm, for instance, that it 'is on the mat,' or that it 'suffers from neurotic fits,' or that it 'had religious significance in Orphism.' Clearly, in these assertions 'the cat' does not necessarily, though it may, mean the kind of feline object that can be given in perceptual consciousness. (It does in the first of the three instances just mentioned; it may or may not in the second, depending on precisely what is meant; and it does not in the last.) This fact means that reality as immediately given is not the context of assertions made thematically. The context of 'is on the mat,' 'is neurotic,' and 'had religious significance in Orphism' is precisely the *object of speech* signified as 'the cat.'

When one becomes able to speak in this way, one's speech is not merely thetic, as all speech is, but also *thematic*; for a specified context to which assertions refer, a designated subject to which the meaning of a thesis is relative, or a selected topic in relation to which one's affirmations are to be understood, is what we ordinarily call a *theme*. Thematic speech is assertive communication in which a thesis – what is asserted – is asserted in relation to a theme, and in which the theme is asserted merely as the context in relation to which the speaker means what he says. When one says 'The cat is on the mat' one speaks thematically, because one speaks of an experienced reality only through the mediation of one's *thematization* of it. I stress that the world *about which* one speaks thematically may well be the same world *to which* one might speak non-thematically; the difference does not depend on the reality that provides the contents of speech but on how the speaker uses his ability to assert his experience of it. Confronted with the same situation in which a non-thematic speaker might say, 'No! Please! Stop!' or 'Danger! Run!' I speak thematically if I say, for instance, 'Your behaviour is reprehensible, and you should desist,' or if I yell out 'The enemy is at the gates!' The contrast is not in respect of what is communicated (though thematic speech lends itself to communicating it in a more highly nuanced way) but in level of assertiveness – and in the consequences thereof, yet to be considered, such as its enabling the speaker (and the thinker) to deal with vast amounts of information all at once. For example, since 'the cat' signifies directly an object of speech, and an experienced reality only indirectly, one and the same concept, 'the cat,' is equally apt to signify not only the concrete, individual animal lying before me on the mat, but also the intangible, generic feline nature that, for instance, held a certain religious significance for some Greeks.

Very little of what human beings say speaks about experienced reality in its immediacy; we speak mostly in 'sentences' like '*Der Mond ist aufgegangen*' rather than in expressions such as '*Himmelblitzen!*' (The latter does not ordinarily mean, of course, what it literally signifies, but communicates a state of mind.) However, non-thematic assertions need not consist in single words or convey a simple message. Nor are they restricted to signifying emotional states of mind or of inner objects; when I say, for instance, 'Someone, please, call the police!' I am not speaking about my emotions (though I may reveal them), but about the emergency. Moreover, I may or may not have strong feelings about the matter;

and if I have them, I may or may not intend to communicate them. And of course, I may convey emotional states thematically: 'I am utterly disgusted with your behaviour!' The essential differences are: whether the experienced reality is taken out of its own context as an actual reality by the very speech that asserts it, and whether one speaks of reality with, or else without, implicit reference to the fact that the reality is being experienced and spoken about. To thematize an experienced reality is thus to lift it out of its situation in real life by means of speech; it is to pick it up with the discriminating pincers called concepts or words and to hold it out as the object of assertive speech. Whereas the non-thematic speaker is simply a communicator who has learned to assert an experienced reality, the thematic speaker is one who has learned also to *abstract* it from its immediacy, so that he can affirm it as experienced and as signified.

Let us further contrast the two. Non-thematic, unlike thematic, speech contains a single though not necessarily simple element, a *thesis*, which simultaneously asserts and signifies the experienced reality. Though it has an object – namely, a reality as such (rather than as a stated object of speech) – it lacks a theme. By the same token, since the reality itself provides the context of speech, the signifying act and the sign it produces are identical, respectively, with the act of asserting and the assertive sign: 'Danger!' simultaneously *signifies* the danger and *asserts* it as a reality in itself. Non-thematic speech corresponds thus to the level of conscious experience that, like an irate victim's accusing finger, does not merely point or refer, since it also affirms, but which does so bluntly and inarticulately. Its obtuseness is what limits it to making affirmations only in relation to those experienced realities that, by their immediacy, lend themselves to being pointed to;[31] it is also what restricts the non-

---

31 But non-thematic speech is not restricted to the signification of objects presently experienced through external sensation; it may communicate the imaginative recollection of an object previously sensed but no longer present. Even the latter experience, however, must be said to take place *immediately* (i.e., with direct reference to reality); since it consists in imagining a reality precisely as having been given to the experiencer in sensation, albeit at an earlier time, even such experience would be communicated by the non-thematic speaker with immediate reference to reality. In short, the *immediacy* of non-thematic speech should not be confused with the spatial or temporal *proximity* of the speaker to the object. It is perfectly possible to speak non-thematically of absent objects, as in the example I will give in a moment, aping a primitive, exclusively non-thematic speaker telling fellow-hunters that the game was afoot. It is equally possible, however, as I have mentioned, to speak thematically of present and currently sensed objects. The difference has to do with whether the relationship of speech to the experienced objects is or is not mediated by the thematizing and thesis-making that characterize thematic speech.

thematic speaker to saying only what, by its immediacy, lends itself to being directly asserted. Accustomed as we are to paying little heed to the assertiveness of speech, we tend to think that an utterance like 'Danger! Fire!' names a reality. Some introspection is needed to verify that it does not; it signifies a reality, but simultaneously asserts it. Naming reality – signifying it assertively, yet without asserting it as a reality in itself – is possible only as part of thematic speech. For instance, 'Me, Tarzan' and 'You, Jane' are thematic assertions; their themes are, respectively, 'me' and 'you,' which set down what the assertions are about; and their theses are the proper names to be given to the generically named (i.e., thematized) objects in reality. Contrary to popular impression, therefore, these assertions do not exemplify primitive speech; a better instance of that would be, say, 'Deer! Big! Many! Watering-hole! Come! Quick! Spear! Encircling-strategy! Hurry! Food!' The Hollywood version of primitive speech is quaint, because it does not use verbs, but illustrates only the fact that verbs are not indispensable for thematic speech.

Thematic speech, on the contrary, *separates* the signification of the object of assertion from the assertion of it; this explains why it involves the twofold aspects of *thematization*, as I have called the first, and *thesis-making*, as I shall henceforth refer to the second. But by being separated, the two aspects of the assertive signification that begins with non-thematic speech become transformed. The experienced reality becomes an object of speech when the speaker, holding back his assertiveness as a sparring prize-fighter would his punch, affirms the theme with a force so discriminatingly measured that the theme will directly signify only the object of speech; the theme is designated, so to speak, as the target of the unrestrained assertion that the thesis will *then* bring down upon it. The thesis, for its part, has to be made to bear not upon reality directly, but upon the theme: an experienced reality is made into a thesis by its being asserted, specifically, in relation to the theme.

Even before we consider its second aspect, the superiority of thematic speech should be evident: it allows the speaker to delimit precisely what he will speak about. This delimitation makes possible a like precision in self-communication – and, thus, in conscious experience. And such pre-

---

Likewise, the immediacy of conscious sense experience to reality should not be identified with proximity; we can be immediately conscious of imagined as well as of sensed objects; indeed, even immediate consciousness of sensible objects does not require either spatial proximity or even temporal co-existence, as in the case of the visual consciousness of stars. But immediate conscious experience interposes no sign – neither audible nor imaginary speech – between the experience and the object, whereas the mediated form of consciousness we call understanding does.

cision is important because, although conceptualization begins with non-thematic speech, to be able to conceptualize without being able to thematize is like having an unlimited charge account in a shop that has only poor-quality merchandise and little stock. Before the speaker acquires thematic speech he can differentiate between, say, 'rose' and 'flower,' 'petal' and 'leaf,' and 'red' and 'green.' But *which* of these he will actually speak about will not depend solely on him; it will be determined above all by his immediate situation, which will call one rather than the other to his attention and create in him the need to speak about it. When a dangerous fire threatens, the fire 'prompts' one to speak and 'tells' one what to address one's speech to (though it does not determine how one must conceive what one needs to say). The thematic speaker, however, can speak even when the situation does not demand it, and when he has none but an inner motive for speaking – such as the need to understand himself, or his world, or that of others.

Thus, out of the 'rose' given to me in experience, I, a thematic speaker, can choose either 'red' or 'petal' as the object I shall speak about, and indeed can decide whether to speak at all. Of course, I also have the freedom to place the empirical information I receive from the object within the wider context of many other experiences by signifying it as 'flower.' This means that I can analytically slice the universe of my experience as nicely or as coarsely as I will, dealing mentally with an 'atom' as easily as with the entire 'universe' simply by conceiving and thematizing the theme of my speech accordingly. By the same token, I can synthetically choose to thematize the 'red' dispersed in a multiplicity of red objects and not only in red flowers, as well as the 'flower' that comprises all of them, not only roses. Thus, through thematic conceptualization I transform the whole of reality into an infinite series of possible objects of speech and thought that I can alternatively dissect or bundle as my own purposes rather than external events may require. The thematic speaker, to be sure, does not determine what the object so delimited shall contain; he nevertheless determines what his object shall be, in the sense that he selects the specific reality that he will mark off as the object he 'has in mind.'

But the creativity of thematic speech culminates in thesis-making, which requires using assertive power in a new way. Since the object of thematic speech is signified separately from what-it-is-asserted-about, the latter too must be separately signified; it no longer rides free upon the signification of the object of assertion. Quite as an experienced reality has been made into a theme, another experienced reality, or another aspect of the same one, is made into a thesis. Let us, therefore, refine our terminology. Pre-thematic speech may be said to *assert a thesis* only in the sense that it signifies an experienced reality thetically; since the pre-thematic speaker asserts theses only with direct reference to reality rather than in relation to a stated theme, he does not assert a thesis *as such*, or with consciousness of its being what-he-says. The thematic speaker, on the contrary, has to signify the experienced reality separately, or as what-he-asserts; he must *make* the experienced reality into a thesis, and therefore asserts theses *as such*.[32]

Thematic speech enables consciousness thus to function somewhat as a court of law, which distinguishes between the indictment of the accused – the specification of the charges against him – and his arraignment, that is, his being called upon to face the indictment and make answer and defence. The thematization, the preliminary part of thematic speech enabling the speaker to signify any experienced reality precisely *as spoken about*, is complemented by the conversion of any experienced reality into a separately signified thesis; this conversion enables the speaker to assert such reality precisely *as experienced*. Of course, the conceptual form of the thesis is not dictated by the immediately experienced reality, any more than is the theme's; the speaker himself determines the analytically or synthetically demarcated thesis to be asserted in relation to the similarly determined theme. The final result of the separation of assertion and signification in thematic speech is that the speaker can say whatever he selects, conceived in whichever way he selects, in relation to whatever he selects, conceived in whichever way he selects, out of whatever information he has received in any way at any time.

But we have not come to the end of the creativity of thematic speech. The speaker can make thematic assertions repeatedly, limited only by the amount of information he has empirically received and by his thematic skill. To the extent that his experiences may be organized with reference to a common theme, he can hold together in speech and thought a number of more or less systematically concatenated assertions that make up a sense-making narrative telling a more or less meaningful story. The story is meaningful to the degree that it relates a multiplicity of experiences into a pattern that unifies them all. Organizing their experiences in this way satisfies a profound need in human beings. If they cannot do it, they feel anxiety; and if the disorganization of experience is severe enough, they may be driven to extremes. We shall

32 A precisian's lexicon would therefore reserve *thesis* for what is asserted non-thematically, and refer to what is asserted thematically as an *epithesis*, that is, a thesis asserted as such, or with consciousness of its being what-the-speaker-asserts. We would then have to say, however, that thematic speech involves, besides 'thematization,' 'epithesis-making.' The benefits of scrupulous accuracy are not, I think, quite worth the higher price.

take up later the question why this should be so; but the brief answer is that human beings need to make sense out of the multiplicity of their experiences of reality, because by so doing they can situate themselves within a conceptually organized world and thus acquire self-identity; and they need self-identity in order to be satisfied with themselves. In other words, the narrative capability of thematic speech is what enables immediate consciousness to create its selfhood.

With thesis-making, consciousness becomes like a prosecuting attorney. Having been indicted and arraigned, reality is subjected to a judicial process. A case is now to be made – and if the trial is fair, supported by evidence – so that a verdict, a 'truth-saying,' can be pronounced. Prosecutors operate, however, within the framework of an established law; their point of departure is what society has previously defined as the world of admissible behaviour. The self-defining consciousness does not, through its judging of reality, construct its world-interpretation and its self-identity strictly by itself. The individual's conscious life is played out against a cultural backdrop that is already part of the stage when he first comes upon the scene; the backdrop is the lexicon and the more or less well-integrated system of propositions that add up to the society's accumulated lore, parts of which every individual acquires as he learns to speak and becomes inducted into his culture and its ways of perceiving man and world.

The system is actually a system of systems; ultimately it comprises all that society can teach to the individual; it is synonymous with the entire culture in which he lives. Of course, the individual eventually becomes able to develop novel concepts and acquire original convictions about himself and the world; having learned how to conceive and narrate, he can create new ways of organizing his empirically received information. These concepts and assertions may or may not be valuable to others; new ways to mean what one says and new ways to understand what one means may or may not survive. But if every individual had to develop his conceptual apparatus and accumulate thematic assertions about self and world starting with nothing, he would make as little headway as if he had to invent speech all by himself.

The foregoing contains a further implication: the individual's acquisition of understanding – the emergence of his ability to experience reality as carrying a certain meaning – is an essentially socio-cultural process. Culture generates the self-defining consciousness not only by transmitting the vocabulary and the stories (mythical, scientific, or in-between) that attempt to make sense out of experience, but by transmitting in the first place a syntax and a logic, and a narrative ability to speak and think in accordance with them. After he acquires the techniques of world- and self-definition, the individual can participate in his culture's definition of man and world and in his society's and his own definition of himself; he has, however, no more choice about the world- and self-definition from which he can begin to develop his independent interpretations – if any – than a child has to choose his genetic endowment.

The marvel is not, therefore, that human beings are culturally pro- grammed as strictly as they are, but that they can, at least theoretically, rewrite their programs. However, much of our self-reprogramming is less original than we would like to think. As psychiatrists point out, much human effort is invested in fulfilling in roundabout, ingeniously surreptitious ways – through ostensibly self-determined behaviour di- rected to seemingly freely chosen ends – the outlines of the life-script that was put into our hands as we were ushered onto the world-stage. Even a moderate amount of creative self-definition is relatively rare, and it can never be achieved except by dint of self-discipline, arduous labour, and the passage of time; it is a strange, almost mysterious fact – unless we are aware of the role of speech in the generation of consciousness – that human beings find it very difficult to be themselves. Traditional interpretations of the world also are proverbially difficult to change in any fundamental respect.

Note, however, that in this passage I have referred only to the cultural *transmission* of self-definition; how self-definition is *shaped* by speech is a different matter. It has not been my intention to revert to the Nietz- schean and Whorfian idea that vocabulary and syntax determine, at least in principle, our interpretations of self and world. Language merely embodies, though it also confirms, reinforces, justifies, and perpetuates – in sum, institutionalizes – principles of self- and world-interpretation that depend rather on the properties of speech.

But how does thematic speech generate not merely self-present ex- perience, but also an inwardly unified set of experiences – an experiential life – that is present to itself *as a self*? For consciousness is more than a number of discrete moments of sensory contact with reality, such as the act of consciously seeing the softly falling snow. When I experience the snow consciously, the act is not simply present to itself; it is present to *myself*; rather, I am present to myself as the experiencer of the snow. Indeed, isolated acts of consciousness are an abstraction; they are never found in real life. Once the human organism becomes a self, conscious- ness is a continuous process in which reality, ourselves, and our situation within reality are forever being adjudicated upon. In short, conscious- ness is not simply a quality of sense experience, but above all the typical quality of the human life of a human self. And thematic speech, I have said, is responsible for this characteristic of human life. But why?

The reason is that the I is nothing but the narrator of the narrative we call the meaningful world; the self is the counterpart of the world organized by means of thematic speech. Conversely, if an organism speaks thematically – and thus with consciousness of its own speech – its narrating is present to itself. Narrating a narrative *automatically* converts a conscious organism into a narrator, a 'first person' who is the subject who speaks. But narrating the narrative, moreover, makes it possible for him to become meaningful to himself (though it does not automatically ensure the realization of this possibility), because it enables him to derive his own meaning from his self-perception as part of a meaningful world – and, indeed, as the narrator of a meaningfully narrated world. Thus, the ultimate significance of the emergence of thematic speech is that, rendering consciousness discursive and interpretative, it makes possible the kind of consciousness that can experience itself as a sense-making, identifiable self. Thematic speech, unbidden and almost mechanically, creates incipient, sketchy selves who thereafter may craft themselves into adult, mature persons through the conscious use of the very thematic speech that generated their embryonic selfhood.

Admittedly, the world- and self-understanding of the self-defining consciousness are not very often original, or methodically created, or deep, or valid, and in most people they cease to develop altogether at a relatively early age – so that thereafter every new experience that fails to tally with their world- and self-concept is either denied out of existence or else distorted so as to make it fit. Human nature decrees that every individual and culture shall be appointed a judge of reality and an executive officer in charge of himself, but it cannot legislate the responsible exercise of the human self-governmental powers. Not infrequently, therefore, human beings can be observed presiding over kangaroo courts and administrative tribunals where the rules of evidence are laughed at and where the measures of truth are the smirk of the peer group and the fury of the mob. But the experience of reality as world, and of one's own conscious experience as self, need not be original, or methodical, or deep, or true, nor must it fulfil its potentiality for lifelong development, before it can discharge its most fundamental role: to enable consciousness to assert meaningfully what otherwise would be a disgregated multiplicity of meaningless transient impressions, and to bring to life the conscious self. Experience of the world without the unity of self-organization – without its being integrated as *my* experience of the world – is possible only below the human level, where the totality of experiences can be organized physiologically, reducible as they are to organic functions. If human experience is to have the unity and integrity that come to it from being a self's experience of its world – an experiential life and not a mere congeries of physiologically connected events – it must organize and unify itself.

Thematic speech is what empowers consciousness to do so; for it is only by interpreting the world that we can learn to interpret ourselves as interpreters of the world. And this requires thematic speech, because reality cannot be said to be organized – or for that matter, disorganized – in itself. Unless one were prepared to say, gratuitously, that reality exists for the sake of serving man's experiential or other needs, one should admit that reality can exhibit coherence and pattern only if it is given conceptual organization by the speaker. He does not, of course, 'give' it such organization within itself; he organizes it as *experienced* reality; he puts it in order essentially within his mind (though the possibility of arranging and rearranging reality physically – for instance to take advantage of its properties – follows therefrom). He can organize reality thus, however, only if he does not speak of it in its immediacy and in-itselfness, but rather *as spoken about* by him. Under the guise of its being thematized by him, he can assert about anything in the world whatever he may have experienced, signifying it specifically as having been *experienced by him*. But to do so is, precisely, to speak thematically. For to weld together one's experiences of reality into a world, and thereafter to fit any new experience of reality or of oneself into the totality previously put together as a meaningful world, what one must do is to lift experienced reality out of the concrete and immediate context in which it is given to sense experience. And thematic speech is what enables one to do so.

One may be able to speak thematically, however, without being necessarily very clear about what to speak thematically is; absent-mindedness makes it hard to realize that thematic speech abstracts reality from its own context, and that, unlike the non-thematic, the thematic speaker communicates the experienced reality precisely as experienced and as spoken about. Thus, everyone in our culture knows that, when we speak about reality, reality has – but *of course* – been spoken about. But most of us fail to realize that we speak about it under the very guise of its being spoken about, or as object of speech. We assume instead that, when we assert a thesis in relation to a theme, reality has been spoken about directly; we misconstrue thematic speech as a complicated form of non-thematic speech. And since in non-thematic speech reality determines what the speaker shall be conscious of and speak about, confusion between the two levels of speech yields the familiar delusion: a thematic assertion repeats what reality 'asserts' to us about itself. This mistake implies in turn the classical misinterpretation of reality as a sort of solidified thematic assertion, an objectively existing message or 'word' – a *logos*, a *ratio* – which is the original that experience and speech merely repeat. Reality itself is deemed to contain an inner meaning, a logical organization, that meaningful experience simply mirrors or duplicates.

Even non-thematic speech is not a repetition of what reality first 'tells' the speaker; for what reality 'says' to him is, to be exact, not what he must say but only what he must address himself to. All the less so thematic speech, in which reality does not communicate to the speaker even what his theme shall be. However, quite as the self-presence of consciousness may escape the notice of human beings who are un-doubtedly conscious, the self-presence of thematic speech may fade away in the ears of a speaker who, being absent-minded, should not hear his own speech loudly enough. It would then seem incredible to him that speech should be valuable, and that it should account for the typical characteristics of human life, for the very reason that it speaks directly about what speech itself proposes and only indirectly about reality itself. And yet, quite as the value of consciousness is that it can differentiate itself from the world and acquire the perspective that en-ables it to experience the real as real, the advantage of thematic speech is that, being the kind that is consciously undertaken, it can distance itself from reality and organize it narratively and as whole. To be sure, the thematic consciousness can, by the same token, alienate itself from reality. Possible failure inheres in every possible success.

If the foregoing is correct, the assertiveness that defines speech is a quality of the function, namely, communication, that provides its nec-essary base – just as mere experience is the foundation upon which consciousness can alone arise. The emergence of speech out of the non-assertive level of communication found in animals implies, therefore, no discontinuity between the two. Let us examine this, before we con-tinue to investigate the nature of speech.

5. The continuity from animal communication to speech

We use the term communication most often to mean the kind of ability to transmit and receive signals that even many animal species share with man. But the term may be legitimately taken in a much broader sense; as we have seen, it is no mere figure of speech to say that one billiard ball communicates motion to another, or that the seal communicates its shape to the wax. All communication rests on the exercise of efficient causality upon a communicand, directly or mediately, with the effect of imparting in-formation. Both the contact and the information, however, differ as we ascend from inanimate to living things, and are further transformed as life ascends. Chromosomes, for instance, are a means of communication whereby the parent imparts information to the new organism – though in this case the information takes the guise of instructions that the recipient will use to structure itself. To say that one billiard ball took instruction from another about how it should move, however, would be sheer metaphor, in the absence of any reason to think that the second billiard ball processed the information. *Receiving* the information becomes *processing* the information only when the communicand takes active part in its reception – that is, when it is alive.

The earliest form of animal communication was the sort of information-processing that biologists call irritability, out of which eventually developed the multisensory capability of the higher animals. But in all sensation, processing the information includes *organizing* it. Even the simple transmission, from the membrane to the nucleus of a cell, of the informing effect caused by contact with an object is a form of sensory processing; this primitive quasi-management of the information was the harbinger of the transmission of nervous impulses from the receptor to the effector structures of the higher organisms. With the advent of the animal order of processing, however, information underwent a corresponding change in character. The information imparted to the wax by the seal is identical with its relevant characteristics, namely, its hardness and shape; and although these belong to the seal, they are relative to the characteristics of all other things, not in particular to those of the wax. However, when the sea anemone reacts to the presence of plankton by ingesting it, the information it receives has special relevance to the communicand; for in itself plankton is merely a chunk of protoplasm; it is only in relation to the animal that plankton is 'food.' The animal's behaviour is determined not simply by the properties of plankton, but by the relationship that plankton, given its properties, has to the organism.

Communication in this sense, however, though distinct from the mere exercise of efficient causality by inanimate entities, remains a unilateral activity. Only the communicand takes part in processing sense information; as communicator, the plankton does not differ from the seal, since it provides but does not send information. The novelty of sensory communication is rather that the information, because of its relevance to the animal's needs, now has a certain *significance*. Note that the significance does not reside in the information absolutely (for instance, in the properties of plankton), but accrues to the information only when it is related (in this case biochemically) *by the communicand* to itself. Thus, processing the information involves the *self-relating* powers of animal life. Correspondingly, even at this level the forerunners of *meaning* and *interpretation* can be glimpsed. The 'meaning' is, to be sure, a strictly practical one, and the 'interpretation' is nothing more complex than the fact that the physiology of the sentient organism uses the information discriminatingly, to the organism's adaptive advantage. In return, the organism's response to stimulation involves *appropriation* of the information; in relation to the animal the facts have a relative role that they do not have in themselves. And this role is not determined by the nature of the information alone, but also by the nature of the informed: it is to the sea anemone that plankton 'means' food; to the more finicky ocean perch only shrimp 'means' food. The object or content of the communication is thus to be distinguished from its meaning; the content may remain factually constant, but its meaning may change, since it is relative to the interpretation that the communicand places upon it.

At a higher level, but still within the same realm of unilateral animal communication, sentient life becomes capable of using *signs* – that is, of taking advantage of the significance that certain objects of sensation may have. (No intent to take advantage of such significance should be inferred.) The capacity to perceive signs extends the reach and heightens the quality of sentient life and has survival value; it amounts to the capacity to obtain the benefit of sense experience vicariously. For it means that the animal can react adjustively to objects without having to experience them directly, but only through its sense experience of another object, the sign; the sign alone provides whatever sense information the organism receives directly. For instance, when a herbivore rejects a poisonous mushroom, it has become experientially related to the noxious substance, albeit indirectly; and becoming informed about a noxious substance through the mediation of a sign before one establishes direct contact with it is, of course, much healthier than having to depend on directly acquired evidence. Thus, natural selection explains why communication eventually acquired a *medium*; the processing of the information now included the processing of the sign so that a significative meaning (in relation to the reality to which it ultimately referred) might be taken from it. Or rather, so that a meaning might be *given* to it; for the meaning, as noted, does not reside in the signified object or, *a fortiori*, in the sign. Since a sign is a sign only for him who 'takes' its meaning, it is the animal's 'interpretation' that converts mere sensible appearances into signs – that is, makes them function as signs. Thus, by sensing white dots on the bright red of the mushroom cap – or however it may do it – the herbivore does not sense poison: it only senses white-on-red. But upon sensing the pattern of colours it discriminates between edible and inedible food. And this 'interpretation' – which is not, of course, experienced as such, but which is embodied in the animal's genetically determined and naturally selected rejection response – is a much higher and more properly so-described sort than the sea anemone's 'interpretation' of plankton as food. For the plankton *is* food, not the sign of food, whereas white-on-red is not poison, but a *sign* of poison.

Although signs and significance have now appeared, *signi-fication* or sign-making has not yet emerged; for signs such as the colour of mushrooms are not *made*, they happen. Only when sign-making appeared did *bilateral communication* arise – communication in the usual narrow acceptation. Below this level the signs did not make up a 'language,' even in a loose sense. The herbivore takes 'meaning' from *natural signs*; let us agree so to call them, to distinguish them from the behavioural repertoire of *communicative signs* – the language – that is a necessary part of all bilateral communication. In the unilateral communication of animals with sensible objects, even in that which is mediated by signs, there is no communicator, since nothing acts so as to communicate. But superimposed by evolution upon the sentient abilities of animal organisms, an additional level of communication appeared: now the object sensed by the communicand was another organism, a communicator, whose behaviour initiated the communicating process: it *sent* information to a communicand.

Quite as the communicator is now rightly so called, interpretation in a proper sense also arises: the processing of the information by the communicand so as to make it meaningful is relative to the communicator's sign-making. For meaning can now be taken from the sign only because it has been first put into the sign – though non-consciously and unintentionally, to be sure. We are now in the realm of such forms of communication as the dance 'language' of bees, the chirping of squirrels, and the like, where the connection between the sign and its significance is no longer natural, but in a sense artificial. The artificer, however, is not the animal; it is natural selection, of course, which determines which sign-making behaviour and which response thereto shall be preserved and which not, creating thereby both the signs that shall be sent by communicators and the meanings that shall be taken from the signs by communicands.

Bilateral communication involves, therefore, not only the novelty of sign-making, but also a new kind of medium – behaviour itself – which becomes significative as evolution converts it into signs. Whatever signs may be used by the herbivore – for all I know they may have nothing to do with colour or scent – the signs are produced by the object naturally, simply by being itself. Communicative signs, however, not only have to be sent, but also have to acquire whatever significative value they come to have; for the meaning of the sign no longer coincides with the sign itself. There is nothing in an animal's peculiar chirp or strutting that is necessarily connected with, say, sexual receptivity; nothing in the pattern of motion of a bee is naturally related to the presence of nectar in a distant field. Let us, therefore, stress the difference between the natural and the communicative sign, and the 'artificial' aspect of the latter, by reserving for communicative signs the term *signals*.

The same term is applicable, therefore, to the communicative signs used by man. In humans, however, the communicative art is their own, since the signals are not sent simply by virtue of the organism's built-in disposition to adjust, but for the conscious purpose of conveying the signal precisely as signal. A signal sent because it is a signal – and therefore with awareness of its communicative potential – carries what henceforth I shall refer to as a *message*, in the strict sense of the word. When bilateral communication evolved, then, the novelty was principally on the side of the transmission, not the reception. Taking the meaning of a sign when the sign is a signal is much the same as taking it from a natural sign; it is the ability to *put* meaning into the signal, even if only unintentionally, that distinguishes bilateral animal communication from the sense-reception of signs. Even at the animal levels, to understand the nature of communication one must perceive it primarily from the viewpoint of the communicator rather than that of the communicand.

Since the meaning carried by a signal does not depend upon the nature of the signal itself, the signals that animals can make are no more inherently limited, in respect of their contents, than human signals: a chirp or a dancing pattern can carry any meaning whatever, for the very reason that it has no necessary connection with whatever it might signify. Animals could, therefore, in principle, communicate whatever they experience. And yet, though animal 'vocabularies' are enormously richer and subtler than had been realized in the past, their signals are invariably related to a fairly narrow set of contents. Animals keep to themselves most of what they experience – whereas human beings communicate almost all of it (though not necessarily widely). Of course, only human beings can value privacy; for only he who is conscious can distinguish between self and other, and his private from his social life. But the life of consciousness is much more public than we ordinarily realize; it is lived by the individual largely outside himself, in the more or less extensive network of communicative relationships created by the need of human beings to learn what fellow-humans think and feel, and to share with others what they themselves do.

We can understand, however, why evolution has not given to animals the communicative *carte blanche* it has to man: only those signals the transmission and reception of which was apt to be rewarded with survival could have become incorporated into their genetically programmed repertoire. The individual animal does not have to learn to transmit and receive signals; it is the species that 'learns' to do so, under the 'tutorship' of evolution. The wonder is not, then, that animals communicate as frequently as they do, but that there is an abysmal disparity between their high receptive and their low transmissive capabilities – which, incidentally, accounts for the fact that animals can be trained to receive cues sent by humans that animals themselves do not transmit to each other. But the explanation is clear: there could not have been much point in evolution's producing dogs genetically programmed to sit up and beg on command or creating circus bears that were instinctively capable of seeming to perform arithmetical operations by obeying instructions contained in the trainer's barely perceptible signs.

Why should evolution have favoured not only the ability to receive signs, but also the ability to transmit them? For evolution selects for characteristics that have high survival value for the individual himself, and the capacity for *sending* signals seems, on its face, to have little. A signalling bee's own survival potential, for example, is not increased directly by its efficacious signalling behaviour, since signalling does not increase its store of information: it is the communicand that obtains the advantage of receiving information it would otherwise lack. However, a bee that survives as a result of another bee's transmitting proficiency is thereby in a position to transmit valuable signals to the bee that helped it survive. Once bilateral communication had appeared, the transformation of the species – to the limited extent to which communication had a role in it – no longer depended only on the contribution of the best adapted individuals, but also on that of the best adapted team. Bilateral communication transforms collectivities into societies and group life into consortium, life in a group that shares its fortunes (namely, the information received) for better or for worse. It would be inexact, therefore, to say that communication holds societies together, as if societies, like mere colonies, were constituted by individuals entering into collective relationships that communication helps maintain. Rather, signal-transmission generates social relationships. Bilateral communication does not arise in a social context, it creates a social context.

For all that, the evolution of communication was not the most significant aspect of the evolution of animal life. Below the level of man the development of the capacity to send signals reached only modest heights; the difference between insect and anthropoidal communication is perhaps among the least salient aspects of all that separates them. The reason may be that, until it became transformed in man, signal-making had less survival value than, for instance, intelligence, the organism's general ability to improve the adaptability of its responses. For natural signs are present everywhere in the world and impinge constantly upon the sentient organism; by sheer volume of the communications traffic, the ability to process efficiently the *signs* 'sent' by the organism's total environment would have been more important than its ability to process the relatively narrow spectrum of *signals* it could send to, and receive from, fellow communicators.

Communication becomes of the essence of life only when it is transformed into functions that surpass mere signal-transmission and -reception. In man, intelligence serves communication and the consortium that it creates – or should create, if it is to contribute to the survival of the species. In animals, however, communication remained subordinate to other modes of adaptive behaviour. This was to change only with the arrival of hominids whose intelligence had developed to the point where a momentous discovery was at hand: that signals could be transmitted with the effect and intent that they be received and interpreted by a communicand so as to take meaning from them. When this discovery was made, speech was born.

6. The two levels of interpretativeness of speech and consciousness

Let us resume the study of speech by contrasting the semantic and the syntactic interpretations in yet another respect. Having taken for granted that consciousness and speech are, respectively, the direct and the indirect representatives of reality, our intellectual tradition has had no choice but to interpret sensation and understanding as two different experiential faculties which repeat two distinct aspects of reality, namely, its sensible appearances and its purely intelligible, deducible meaning. Western philosophy has always operated, and even today in many respects continues to move, within the confines of this supposition. Science does much the same thing, in its own way; to find the explanation of observable phenomena is the same as to lay bare the mystery behind them; it is to discover the conceptually and mathematically formulable but inevident natural laws that rule the way in which reality openly and observably behaves. In the syntactic alternative, however, both these dichotomies – two distinct mental abilities and two corresponding objects in reality – are avoided.

Stated summarily, the reason is what we have already noted: that from the syntactic perspective consciousness and speech must be deemed to have, in relation to reality, an originally assertive, interpretative function rather than a repetitive one. By this I mean, first, that whereas mere experience is reducible to the reception of information from reality, conscious experience includes organizing the information in a peculiar way, to be described in a moment, in accordance with the needs of the organism. Second, what accounts for this difference is speech, which renders experience interpretative by making it assertive; for the same properties that, when considered in themselves, I have called the *assertiveness* of speech and consciousness may also be described as their *interpretativeness* in relation to reality. Therefore, third, since the assertiveness of speech obtains at two levels of elaboration, thematic and non-thematic, consciousness interprets reality at two corresponding levels. Even immediate sense consciousness is interpretative, though fully meaningful interpretation comes only with understanding. Thus, according to the syntactic interpretation, the one conscious faculty of the individual human organism renders the individual able to experience with understanding the *same* reality that he is in immediate sense contact with. There are two levels of interpretative experience, but a single reality and a single human mind.

We shall now examine how the properties of speech render both levels of consciousness interpretative, each in its own way. However, since the interpretativeness of consciousness and the dependence of interpretative experience upon speech are more readily apparent in understanding than in sense experience, I will begin with a few general remarks about the former.

It may not be patent that speech is a prerequisite of conscious sensation, but that understanding would be impossible in the absence of speech certainly is; for understanding is the kind of experience that consists in asserting, either in imaginary or voiced speech, more or less complex narratives that relate us meaningfully to the same objects that our immediate perceptual consciousness attains to. Actually asserting such narratives in thought or speech makes our immediate conscious experiences meaningful by integrating and relating them to our experience of ourselves; and being able thereafter to assert them at will in speech or thought makes our understanding of reality an habitual one. To experience reality with understanding is not, therefore, to repeat to oneself the explanation of reality that the latter hides within itself; it is to assert originally, for the first time, an explanation of it composed by means of speech out of information supplied by reality.

It follows that, undergraduate excuses for bad papers to the contrary, it is not true that anyone ever understands anything but remains unable to explain it; but if one understands only a little, and at the same time misunderstands the nature of understanding, one may mistake one's paucity of understanding for difficulty in communicating it. The exact measure of one's understanding of anything is rather the extent to which one can couch one's understanding of it *in words*; and the measure of one's understanding of someone else's explanation is one's ability to explain his explanation in one's own terms. Accordingly, one of the most efficacious ways to develop one's understanding of anything is to try to explain it to someone else; teaching does return a reward. For explaining one's experience forces one to give narrative form to it; and as the words come and the sentences flow, the information is organized and systematized: the facts 'fall into place.' The soft sound they make as they mesh and click is somehow pleasant and soothing; it yields the easy breathing, the comfort, the delight – and withal the excitement, if the matter is important – with which one experiences one's experiencing of a reality that is being understood all the better because one is facilitating others' understanding of it.

Essentially the same interpretative character is found in immediate consciousness, though much less obviously. For immediate consciousness 'speaks' the reality making no use of even imaginary, let alone voiced, words. Nevertheless, when a reality is asserted immediately in sense experience, it is asserted in a specific sense – it is experienced with a specific meaning – that depends on prior actual speech. For the experiencer first became immediately conscious of such reality in the guise that he now conceives it to be, only because he learned to use the words of speech and thought to assert it – that is, to *mean* it – in the very sense that the experience now 'states.' Consciousness is interpretative even at its simplest level, then, because one can have immediate sense-consciousness of reality only in those ways in which one has previously learned to speak and think of it. Information that has not been processed conceptually will, of course, be received just the same, but one will not realize that it has been received. One will experience – but not consciously.

Consider this illustration. Two baskets of apples lie before me on the grocery counter, selling at the same price. I cannot choose what information reality will broadcast, but depending on what I am able to say about it I can select and organize in various ways the information I do receive. For example, since I can think of 'apples' in particular, and not only of 'fruit' in general, I can treat all other baskets but those containing apples as if they did not exist; I have the power to decide which stimuli shall be allowed to remain operative and which shall be shut out; I can channel my attention at will. Moreover, because I can package the information in alternative ways – for instance, I can perceive some of the empirical facts as 'ten' in one basket and 'twelve' in the other, and think 'Delicious' in one and 'Spy' in the next – I am able to make certain discriminations that otherwise would be beyond my ken. Therefore I can use the information in ways that otherwise would not be open to me. To make apple sauce I choose 'Spy' regardless of the number; to take for lunch I buy 'Delicious,' though I get fewer for my money; to give away at Hallowe'en, skinflint that I am, I pick any 'twelve' rather than 'ten' at the same price.

My ability to organize the information in these various ways, however, is nothing but my ability to conceive it specifically as I do, by my actual or potential use of audible or imaginary words to signify it as I do. If I am unable to count, I see exactly the same ten apples as Kurt Gödel does, but I cannot see them as 'ten.' Of course, I can lack the ability to count and nevertheless be able to think of apples as 'Delicious,' 'Spy,' and so on – or, vice-versa, I may be able to count but not to discriminate among varieties of apples. But if I lacked both types of conceptual instruments, the range of my conscious experience and my behavioural repertoire would be correspondingly restricted. They would be yet more limited if I could not even conceive an apple as 'apple,' but only as, say, 'food,' or 'missile,' or 'it.' Suppose, however, that I lacked the ability to conceive them at all, or to signify objects of experience assertively in any way whatsoever (and there was a time in the life of every human being when he was in this very position, namely, before he learned to speak): what then? Well, though I would receive the same sense information as I do now (and would therefore experience it non-consciously, and be able to react to it accordingly, as animals do), I could hardly experience it consciously at all. It was only as I learned to speak of reality assertively, conceiving it in various ways, that I acquired the conceptual lexicon that I would thereafter have ready at hand to apply to reality whenever the concept might fit.

Note, then, the two ways in which concepts organize sense information. (This statement refers to all concepts; we have yet to consider the special kind of concept, the *categories*, which structure the understanding of reality, but it will apply to them also.) I acquire a concept by learning to use a vocal sign in order to mean certain sense information. The first usefulness of this, as I have already pointed out, is that it enables me to package information in a specific way; conversely, it determines one way in which I can attend to, or become perceptually conscious of, reality. But, second, by being so used the meaning of the concept becomes fixed in my mind; the meaning may change in the light of further experience and thought, but as long as I do not mean it differently it will continue to mean exactly what my assertive use has made it mean. But for the very reason that its meaning is fixed, I can also use the concept thereafter to discriminate between the information that may be so conceived and that which may not. I become able therefore to organize sense information by reference to relationships among objects themselves: this object is 'red,' whereas this other is 'not-red'; this is 'good,' whereas this is 'not-good,' or 'bad.' And although this is 'apple' whereas this is 'pear,' both are 'fruit'; in this they are both unlike 'bread,' which is 'not-fruit,' albeit 'food.' It is only because I can use concepts in this way that I can gradually build up a more or less well-integrated 'world.' This world is not yet the world we understand as such, but only its framework; the ability to understand emerges only when conceptualization becomes thematization, and the speaking experiencer learns to assert theses in relation to themes.

Organizing information conceptually does not distort or change the *contents* in any way. I have not suggested, for instance, that the 'twelve' of the apples before me is made up of twelve sense data organized by an innate concept of 'number'; and 'apple' is not made up of empirical 'red,' 'round,' and so on, organized by a non-empirical concept of 'substance.' For the 'twelve' data, the 'red' colour, and the 'round' shape are themselves so experienced only because they are so conceived; without the concepts of 'twelve,' 'red,' and 'round,' no discrimination between 'twelve' and 'ten,' between 'red' and 'green,' or between 'round' and 'square' could be *consciously* made.[33] Thus, concepts do not superimpose upon the information provided by reality an additional information provided by the mind, as Kant thought they did. To say that a concept organizes sense information is merely to say that it gives to the *experiencing* of the contents – not to the *contents* – qualities that otherwise it would lack altogether, namely, those of conscious experience. The

33 But absence of the distinct concepts 'red' and 'green' would hardly make a human being physiologically colour-blind. Assuming no distinction between experience and conscious experience, and failing to recognize that a concept which comprised several colours indistinctly would nevertheless organize sense information quite as effectively as two more discriminate ones would (though in a different way), some experiments intended to test the Sapir-Whorf hypothesis have sought to determine whether absence of discrimination among certain colours in the vocabulary of some North American Indian speakers was correlated with absence of consciousness of the visual reality in terms of such colours. But they have tried to determine it by testing the subjects' physiological ability to discriminate among the corresponding chromatic wavelengths. This makes as little sense as trying to test a chimpanzee for ability to count by handing it a basket of apples and observing whether it can handle them one at a time. Likewise, a city-dwelling hunter with normal eyesight is undoubtedly capable of seeing the same small disturbances in his path that his Indian guide can; but although he 'sees' them, he does not *see* them, let alone understand their meaning as bear tracks. But once they are 'called to his attention' – that is, once he learns to organize the information appropriately by means of concepts – he can of course do so as adequately as does his Indian guide.

conceptual form of the experience does not affect what is experienced, but only *how* it is experienced.

To say that conceptualizing reality amounts to interpreting it may seem an exaggeration: surely, it might be objected, not much interpretation is involved in packaging information as 'petal,' say, rather than as 'flower,' or as 'blue' rather than as 'blue-green,' or vice versa. And it is true, not much indeed. What justifies calling conceptualization an 'interpretation' is rather the vice versa, the fact that although no specific way of packaging information conceptually is necessitated by the reality itself, the information is conceptualized just the same. This fact reveals creativity, even if not a great deal of it; it manifests the conscious experiencer's budding ability to manage his experience, and amounts to a rudimentary ability to interpret reality – that is, to make use of it in accordance with the specifically human experiential needs. Of course, since every reality has its own characteristics, no reality can be adequately manipulated conceptually as if it had characteristics other than its own: if 'red' means a colour like that of a ripe Delicious apple, no amount of creativity could justify saying that bananas are 'red.' Nevertheless, all things whatever, even bananas, may be organized in accordance with the concept 'red,' since they all may be spoken and thought of as either 'red' or 'not-red.' The interpretative quality of even the simplest level of speech lies in the experiencer's freedom to organize the information in accordance with the way in which *he* signifies it. To be sure, if he could do no more than this – because, for instance, he could speak only non-thematically, as is the case with the very young apprentice speaker today, or as it presumably was with adults at an early stage of human evolution – his management of his experiential relations with reality would not be very deft. But even he would experience the world interpretatively, albeit in the limited sense that he could discriminate among the various ways in which he knew how to conceive reality and determine at will which among these defined the given reality, for him, at any given time.

A vastly superior kind of interpretation is afforded by thematic speech. Since the thematic consciousness can assert objects through the mediation of theses and themes, it is capable of asserting an experienced reality under the guise of its being experienced, in relation to an experienced reality under the guise of its being spoken about. When concepts are used by the thematic speaker, therefore, they are organized in relation to each other; this is what enables the experiencer to experience sensible objects not simply as facts, but as intelligible facts. Of course, the interpretative value of thematic assertions is highly variable; some types of thematic assertion contribute more than others to our understanding of the world. But such value tends to rise, and is most obvious, when discrete thematic assertions are in turn organized into logically coherent narratives such as the mechanic's 'diagnosis' of why the car will not start or the journalist's 'story' explaining why the disarmament talks have once again failed; at yet higher levels of interpretation we find ambitious, far-reaching *Weltanschauungen* like the 'system' of Copernicus, Newton's 'theory' of gravitation, Freud's 'conception' of human nature, and Christianity's 'idea' of man and his situation in the world. The simple thematic assertion is only the basic unit of human understanding. But how does the assertion of theses in relation to themes organize factual information so as to enable us to make sense out of the facts?

Observe, to begin with, that although all thematic assertions take the general form 'A is B,' there is an unlimited number of concepts that may fill in for 'A' and for 'B'; the number of possible thematic assertions relating 'B' to 'A' is therefore practically infinite. However, the number of *ways* in which 'B' can be related to 'A' is fairly small; for concepts may have very different significations in relation to reality, yet have exactly the same function in relation to other concepts. For instance, when the concepts of, say, 'toad slime' and 'the great Dalí' are considered simply as organizing sense information supplied by reality, they are utterly different; they have as little in common as, say, the concepts of 'giving you warts' and 'painting *The Outskirts of Paranoia.*' When the same concepts are used as theses and themes, however, a similarity appears. In the thematic assertion 'Toad slime gives you warts,' the relationship between the concepts that signify the thesis and the theme is the same as that which is found between the thesis and the theme in the assertion 'The great Dalí painted *The Outskirts of Paranoia.*' In the case of the two themes, two concepts that by themselves mean very different things have the common meaning of 'cause'; likewise, the two concepts used as theses have different meanings in themselves, but share the meaning of 'effect' in relation to their respective themes. Thus, whereas non-thematic speech organizes information in patterns, thematic speech organizes it into patterns of patterns. But why does this higher level of organization convert mere facts into – as we call them – 'sense-making' facts?

It was well over twenty centuries ago that our philosophic tradition became aware – though only confusedly at first – of the fact that thematic assertions are classifiable into *categories*, as the Greeks called them. (The English adaptation of the Greek word is colourless: 'ways of holding forth' would be a more idiomatic yet faithful rendering.) Since the meaning of these various ways of speaking thematically can itself be, upon reflexion, conceptually asserted, we may say that thematic assertions organize the thesis and the theme in accordance with concepts such as 'reality' and 'unreality,' 'cause' and 'effect,' 'subject' and 'process,' 'unity' and 'multiplicity,' 'quantity' and 'quality,' and so on. Even today the precise number and description of the categories are not universally agreed upon, though it is common coin that they are of the order of a dozen or so. I also mention in passing that it is ambiguous to refer to the categories simply as *concepts*, the same term by which we refer to the concepts that even non-thematic speech uses; the least we should do is draw a distinction, as I shall here, between *ordinary concepts* and *categorical concepts*. In any event, it has been only fairly recently – less than three centuries ago – that for various historical reasons the following problems arose: (a) how do we conceive the idea of relating theses and themes in the ways in which we do? (b) how is the meaning of the categorical concepts related to reality? and (c) what is therefore the validity of the categories as means of interpreting reality? The self-presence and assertiveness of consciousness, and the role of speech in rendering experience self-present and assertive, contain, I think, some implications about the sort of answer that might be given to these questions.

Like ordinary concepts, the categories are conceived empirically. The difference is that they are derived from the mind's immediate experience of itself – or more exactly, from its immediate experience of the way in which it experiences objects consciously. The categories are thus the conceptualization of contents provided not by external reality, but by the reality that is conscious experience itself. They are generated when consciousness organizes the factual information that it provides immediately to itself about the characteristics of its own activity of experiencing consciously by asserting reality using ordinary concepts. Only the self-presence of consciousness, as it learns to speak thematically, makes this possible. The contents thus conceived – 'conceived' in the sense that they constitute the essential components of the 'idea' of speaking thematically[34] – are therefore the formal properties of consciousness. Or

---

34 To learn to speak is to grasp the 'idea' of speech, in the sense that, in order to learn to communicate intending to communicate one must in effect learn what it is to communicate. I have referred to it in quotation marks, however – as I shall hereafter – because the 'idea' in question is, to begin with, merely implicit in the practical ability to speak. It is for the same reason – that we learn what it is to speak by learning what to do in order to speak, not by learning to say or think what speech is – that, as just explained above, categorical *concepts* are equivocally so called.

Our 'conception' of the categories is, to begin with, merely implicit in our practice of thematic speech; it is only after we are able to use the categories that we can,

which is the same, they are the properties exhibited by ordinary concepts precisely insofar as they function in thematic speech, in relation to each other (i.e. regardless of their actual and concrete contents), as theses and themes. Conversely, to 'conceive' the categories is the same as to acquire the essential 'idea' that defines thematic speech, or to learn to relate experienced objects in accordance with the various characteristics that consciousness perceives immediately in itself. The categories emerge at the borderline between mere immediate consciousness and the kind of consciousness that is beginning to develop the ability to define itself as it acquires thematic speech.

But after the conscious experiencer has learned to speak thematically – because he has 'conceived' the 'ways of holding forth' – the categories can be used over and over again to classify and interpret the world, discriminatingly organizing sense information that is anterior to them and that they in no way change, filter, or distort. Nor do they add any contents of their own to the contents of reality. For, as with ordinary concepts, once the meaning of a categorical concept has been established (because it has been asserted with such meaning), the concept will be found to be either applicable, or else inapplicable, to all sense information in general. In other words, the categories are like ordinary concepts in that they can be used to organize the experience of all objects whatever by measuring them against the meaning that the concept already has; the difference is that in the case of the categories the units of measurement are the characteristics of consciousness itself. The categories are, therefore, not innate, but empirically acquired. They are *a*

---

upon reflexion, make assertions about them; and it is only then that we may properly refer to the *concepts* of 'reality,' 'causality,' and so on. In other words, the assertion of the properties of consciousness that enables the speaker to 'conceive' the categories is an *immediate* assertion; it does not pertain to the order of thematic assertion. For the ability to speak thematically develops out of immediate consciousness and non-thematic speech; it cannot very well precede itself.

Moreover, since reflexion can take place in a practically infinite variety of degrees, the categories may be conceived at many different levels of reflexive thought. Long before human beings refer to concrete things as 'real' or as the 'causes' of certain effects – let alone speak of the abstractions called 'efficient causality,' 'reality,' 'existence,' and so on – the categorical concepts of *reality* and *efficient causality* have been conceived and have been effectively at work in thematic assertions that speak of things as being, for instance, 'there,' or as 'happening,' or as being 'given' (as the German *geben* reminds us even today), and as 'doing' certain things, or as 'bringing them about' (as toad slime does to warts), and the like. We may, however, ignore the differences between the more and the less abstract forms of the categories; I shall ordinarily speak of them here only in the highly abstract form that is familiar to all of us.

posteriori ways of organizing information conceptually – though in relation to the objects measured by them they are *a priori*, or preconceived.

The interpretation proposed here should therefore be distinguished from Kant's doctrine of the categories. Kant's profound insight, the fountain-head of all that is distinctively novel in contemporary philosophy, was in effect that consciousness is interpretative, in the modern acceptation of this term: consciousness does not merely 'read' reality, but 'translates' it, as it were, into the kind of language it can understand. Unfortunately, Kant was unable to shed altogether the traditional presupposition that experience must be in some sense representative as well. Thus, according to Kant the concepts used in 'judgments' as theses and themes have an empirical content, or 'matter,' which derives from reality; at the same time, however, the 'understanding ... introduces a transcendental [i.e., non-empirical, innate] *content* into its representations.'[35] That is, the empirical content of experience is organized in accordance with the 'transcendental content' – which elsewhere Kant also calls 'form' – provided by the categories. The categories are the organizational patterns of the propositions that represent the world in speech and thought, and which may be otherwise described as the various ways in which subjects and predicates can be related. These are 'pure' conceptual forms – meaning that they are not derived empirically, but are the innate dispositions of the mind to speak and think in certain patterns, and are therefore part of the necessary structure of the mind. They constitute, therefore, the antecedent conditions of the possibility of understanding what we sense. In Kant's own words, the human ability to understand is governed by certain 'rules ... [that operate] prior to objects being given to me ... [which] find expression in *a priori* concepts to which all objects of experience necessarily conform, and with which they must agree.'[36] Therefore, consciousness delivers not simply the information given by reality, but an information that has been modified, in respect of its *contents*, by the information that the human mind contributes to the final outcome of the experiential process. But, by the very fact that the categorical concepts give to the contents of experience a 'form' (i.e., a non-empirical *content*) that is foreign to them, they affect the *contents* that they represent. And this is why for Kant reality cannot be experienced consciously 'as it is in itself.'

The possibility explored here is very different: that neither sensation nor understanding is representative but that both are interpretative, and

35 Immanuel Kant, *Critique of Pure Reason*, N. Kemp Smith trans. (London, 1950), A 79,
   B 105; p. 112, italics mine.
36 Ibid., B xvii; p. 28.

that neither level of interpretativeness contributes anything to the *contents* of experience. Interpretation may be said to contribute the 'form' of experience only in the sense that it determines its conscious quality; it gives it its assertive form, both at the level of immediate consciousness and at the level of understanding. The difference between these two levels of experience depends on the kind of processing to which the information received by the senses has been subjected. But at both levels, to give assertive form to the experience of certain contents is to make it a conscious experience of the *same* contents; it is not to make it an experience of different, or modified, or hybrid contents.

The objection might be raised: if a categorical concept is formed by conceptually organizing information pertaining to consciousness itself, how can it thereafter be *validly* applied to information received from the world? And what could be the *usefulness* of so applying it? The answers should not pose much difficulty – unless we should have forgotten that the function of even ordinary concepts is not to represent reality, but to organize it. The fact that a child has derived his concept of 'red' from his experience of apples and cherries does not prevent his valid application of it to the *rambutan* that he first saw only years later, when he travelled to Indonesia as an adult; likewise, the fact that he learned of 'causality,' 'reality,' and so on, only because the self-presence of consciousness enabled him to experience various aspects of the relationship that consciousness bears to itself does not prevent his valid application of the same concepts to events like apples falling to the ground, new species emerging, and billiard balls suddenly shooting ahead on impact from another billiard ball. Although the content of every category comes from the characteristics of conscious experience itself, what is measured by the categories is not one's experience but the reality that informs one's senses in accordance with what reality itself is. But does this not imply at least that 'Man is the measure of all things, of things that are that they are, and of things that are not that they are not,'[37] as Protagoras was reported to have said? Not at all. Subjectivism is not a valid alternative to objectivism, but its equally invalid, paradoxical consequence. It does imply, however, that man himself – or more precisely his consciousness – is indeed the measure *of his own understanding* of all things. This distinction makes sense, however, only if understanding anything is not construed as the inward repetition of its meaning, but as interpretative self-relation to it by means of thematic speech.

The peculiar interpretative usefulness of the categories should be clear

37 H. Diels, *Die Fragmente der Vorsokratiker*, 5th ed., W. Kranz, ed. (Berlin, 1934), 80, Fr. 1.

also. Ordinary concepts measure reality by a standard given to us by objects themselves; by means of them we therefore take the measure of things by reference to each other. But when we conceive a category such as 'causality' and then apply it to objects, we measure the latter by a unit that we have derived from our own nature; we assimilate the world to what we have already learned to think of as 'causality' in ourselves. The result is that by implicit reference to the categories – that is, by speaking thematically – reality can be cast in *familiar* terms, in propositions and narratives that make it a world in relation to which one can experience oneself as oneself. By means of the categories the experienced world is, thus, not simply organized, and organized as a whole, but organized in relation to one's self-organization. Since we then are on intimate terms, literally, with reality – for reality is being conceived insofar as it is relative to what is innermost in ourselves – our experience of the world has the quality we call 'making sense.' Correspondingly, when reality is cast in terms whose meaning is *already* known to us, it becomes not only a world, but a world in which we can *situate* ourselves, a world that allows us to interpret ourselves in relation to it. By means of the categories, of course, we also interpret ourselves: we are able to make sense of what we perceive in ourselves.

We shall have occasion later to study how we conceive some of the principal categories; *reality, efficacy,* and *finality* will be of special interest to us. But an illustration may be useful even now. It should be simplest to take the instance of *reality,* since the matter has, in effect, been discussed already in a different context. Like every other, the concept of *reality* asserts factual information; but in this case the information concerns the fact that consciousness opposes the object of experience to the experiencing of the object, discriminating thus between self and not-self. But since consciousness is present to itself, this fact – its discrimination between the object and the act – is also *immediately* present to it. In other words, by the very fact that an experiencer is conscious, he can experience the 'otherness' of objects (in relation to his experience), and his own otherness (in relation to the otherness of objects of experience). Every experience of his will thereafter include a sense of the *otherness-to* that characterizes both objects and the conscious experiencing of objects;[38] this immediately available fact is among those that enable him

---

38 The same sense of *otherness-to* that enables consciousness to perceive real things as real also enables it to differentiate its assertiveness into, more particularly, the abilities to affirm and to deny. For every assertion is other-than every other assertion. But, if so, what one assertion asserts can be other-than what another asserts. Now, if what the first one asserts is merely other-than what the second asserts, the assertions are simply different; if, however, they are different assertions in respect

to learn to speak thematically. And when he learns, as part of his acquisition of the ability to speak, to relate theses to themes as having such otherness to each other, he has implicitly 'conceived' what by another name we call 'reality.' Moreover, upon reflexion he can explicitly conceive[39] – without quotation marks – such relationship precisely as *otherness-to*, whether in these or in equivalent terms such as *actuality, objectivity, existence*, and so on.[40] Thus, consciousness does not create the reality of the real – but neither does the idea of reality mirror or repeat what the real first 'told' us about the reality it possessed absolutely within itself. Consciousness conceives *reality* as the fundamental relationship of *otherness-to* that every thing bears to every other thing.

Moreover, the same conscious experience that reveals otherness-to also shows that such relativity is not restricted to otherness-to-experience (and much less to otherness-to-*my*-experience). For the same objects that are other-than my experience of them are shown, by experience, to be also other-to each other; likewise, not only my act of experiencing objects, but also my organism and indeed my selfhood are experienced as other-to such objects. Thus, the supposition that the reality of anything could consist in its being perceived – let alone in its being perceived by *me* – is naturally repugnant to all of us. But this is not because some instinct or irrational feeling so disposes us; it is for the very sound reason that our immediate experience contradicts it. Besides, each one of us

---

of the same contents, then the one is not simply different from the other, but contradicts it – or counterasserts it – and vice versa. Out of the ability to assert develops the ability to assert either positively or negatively.

39 But even after he has *conceived* the categories, he will not necessarily *understand* what the categories mean, or how he came to use them with the meaning that they have for him; this would require application, skill, and a high level of reflexion. For instance, most people can use meaningfully the concepts of *totality, reality, causality*, and so on, but would be hard pressed to explain what these mean; they are also likely to imagine that they learned them by experiencing the counterparts of these concepts in the world.

40 However, not all conceptualizations of reality will be equally adequate. It is only when the meaning of *reality* is asserted as *otherness-to* – which is possible only to the degree that consciousness is not absent-minded – that the reality of real things will be experienced adequately, as a relationship; it will mean indeed nothing but the fundamental relativity towards each other that is exhibited by all real things. The absent-minded, too, will perceive the otherness of objects; but since the presence of their own experiencing will not be keenly felt, such otherness will be mistaken for a characteristic that objects hold absolutely, or in themselves. But *absolute reality – that is, absolute otherness* – is a self-contradiction: nothing could be other without being other-than. Absent-mindedness will affect the conception of all the other categories analogously; the absent-minded will tend to project onto objects the absolute or ideal character that the categorical concepts can have only in human thought.

also knows, through experience, that the relation of otherness-to-one's-experience may be potential as well as actual, and indirect as well as direct. Many things I have never experienced may well be real – though if they are real it is inherently possible that, directly or indirectly, they could be experienced by me.

Now if reality is not an absolute characteristic of objects in themselves, the question may be raised again, but this time with specific reference to *reality*, how this categorical concept may be validly ascribed by consciousness to objects. Perhaps this analogy will be useful. An audience does not perform; it only watches the actors' portrayal of the characters that they alone create: their art is their own and no one else's. Though strictly by watching, however, the audience is what enables the actors to perform as such; without an audience there can be only a rehearsal or a would-be performance, not an actual exhibition of the artists' skill. Likewise, the properties of real things and the real events constituted by the real interactions among real things need no consciousness in order to take place. But the real does not enter into that particular sort of interaction we call 'being experienced as a reality' unless there should be a consciousness by which it can be experienced 'as a reality.' And this means: a consciousness for which the real can 'perform' not only *because* it is real, but also *in the role of* 'being real'; not only *because* it is itself and is what it is, but also *in the role of* 'being itself' and 'being what it is.' When the real so 'performs,' however, it is only because consciousness created the role – the category – into which the real as such could be fittingly cast. On its side, however, the real is a natural for the part. This should be hardly astonishing: the role had been written by consciousness with the real in mind.

7. The interpretability of reality

Since reality provides the objects of experience, any theory of speech and consciousness would limp unless it did at least broach the question of what kind of defensible construction of reality is required by the theory. We have seen the semantic answer, which is the keystone of the semantic complex: since experience and speech mirror reality, reality must be deemed to contain within itself the original meanings that our experience and speech, respectively, repeat and re-repeat. Thus, in addition to appleseed, Vitamin C, and the 'red' and the 'sweet' that we experience, an apple *contains* the 'causal power' or 'energy' that yields sixty calories per serving if consumed, or a fraction of a newton if dropped from the Leaning Tower of Pisa, and so on. But first and most important of all, it *contains* 'reality'; for its 'existing,' which is uniquely its own act, is the condition of the possibility of its being and doing everything else that defines what it is. The containment or owning in question can be, of course, more or less crudely understood; scientists do not think that energies and forces are contained in matter, or philosophers that existence is contained by existents, in quite the same way as apples contain Vitamin C. For instance, Thomists – who can be credited with what probably is the most sophisticated and coherent explanation of this point yet devised – say that a being contains existence in the sense that its essence *limits* an act of existing to being what the thing actually is.[41] What interests us here, however, is not precisely *how* things supposedly contain in themselves what consciousness merely mirrors, but *that*, since consciousness merely mirrors it, what consciousness mirrors must somehow or other be part of reality, absolutely and in itself. Without this supposition the semantic complex would fall apart. Well, what interpretation of reality locks in place the interconnected concepts of the syntactic complex? What is there in reality that renders it interpretable by the conscious experience that is rendered interpretative by speech?

The answer is: nothing at all. For latent in what we have ascertained so far is a conclusion that contradicts the semantic complex head on: reality is not constituted by an inner meaning that interpretative experience and speech reproduce and repeat, a cryptic but prewritten message that needs but decoding by a reader in order to be understood. This conclusion is possible, however, only because we have first reinterpreted the nature of interpretation. It is not the mind's decoding and reading of the inner meaning that reality hides within itself; it is the conscious mind's self-relation to reality by means of speech. By giving to the mere experience of reality a conceptual and categorical organization, the human mind transposes reality into its own realm, thereby making it meaningful. Therefore, reality is interpretable only in the sense that it lends itself to interpretation – in somewhat the same way in which lumber and nails lend themselves to house-building, though they do not contain, even in prefigurement, what is built out of them.

An interpretation of reality is thus created by consciousness, but whether the interpretation is valid depends on what the reality itself is. The only reason why we should imagine that something within reality makes it interpretable is the prior supposition – first stated by Parmenides,[42] but

---

41 Thomists further insist, however, that this applies only to created beings; if, by the same token, the uncreated Being, God, does not *contain* existence, the reason is that he *is* Existence itself and that his reality is therefore unlimited and uncontained.

consciously or unconsciously shared by most of us even today – that an interpretation of reality is a mental duplication of the interpretability, or inner intelligibility, that structures reality in itself. Since *we* are rational and think logically, we suppose, the reality we experience must likewise be rationally and logically structured; it must be mind-like. If, however, we make no such supposition – if we do not project our own conscious- ness into reality – reality must be deemed interpretable only by virtue of the relationship that it may come to have to a consciousness. Thus, reality can be understood, but is not intelligible in itself; it can be rea- soned about, but is not inwardly organized by logic. To say otherwise would involve a self-contradiction, namely, that reality was, *in itself*, explicable (or for that matter, not explicable) *by a mind*. For to speak of reality absolutely is, of course, to describe it as it would be if it had no relations to any other real things, and therefore without regard to any mind's actual or possible experience of it. What experience reveals is a reality that, as such, is indifferent to the presence of the human mind; there is no reason to think that it exists for the benefit of those who understand it, or else the chagrin of those who try to do so without success. It seems not to care either way.

But mark carefully: the fact that reality is not meaningful in itself does not mean that reality is absurd, positively *lacking* meaning, as Sartre thought. For reality does not need or call for meaning; the absence of intrinsic meaning leaves it totally unchanged from what it factually is. It would indeed be quite as self-contradictory to say that reality as such was absurd as to say that it was meaningful; nothing could be absurd except in relation to a conscious mind's attempt to understand it. In sum, when an experiencer acquires reality experientially, he buys only information; processing the information is not included in the purchase price. Or to put it differently: Parmenides was wrong, and Sartre realized it; but Sartre did not appreciate quite how deeply wrong, and therefore he, too, was wrong.

Let us sum up the foregoing in a formula: reality is *factual*. It is nothing but a matter of fact. But what can we say about this factuality? And since by saying it we would bring reality into relation with conscious- ness, can we say it validly? Is it possible to speak, without absurdity, of 'reality as it is in itself'? One can, indeed, so speak of it, but only if one keeps in mind that every assertion about it – even the conception of *reality-in-itself* – is necessarily relative to one's experience of reality itself. For though it would be self-contradictory to imagine that one could think or speak of reality without having, in fact, related it to oneself by

---

42 'That which can be thought is the same as that which can be,' Diels, *Die Fragmente*, 28, Fr. 3.

thinking or speaking it, one can abstract from such fact; the self-presence of consciousness enables us, even as we consider any reality, to ignore its having been given in experience. *Reality-in-itself* is, therefore, a well-grounded concept as long as it means: reality in abstraction from its relativity to experience, or as conceived under conditions that do not in fact obtain. We should not, however, mistake the abstraction for real life. The reality that is validly predicable of real things is not otherness-in-itself, but rather the fact that (at least potentially) they are related to other real things, including conscious experiencers; it is, therefore, also the fact that, under certain conditions, real things can make a difference to each other.[43] Do we human beings, then, experience reality as it is in itself? If this means, do we experience it in its factuality? the answer is that, yes, we do, but that there is neither merit nor peculiar human advantage in this. Animals do as much; their experience is a means of adjusting to reality. What is typical of human beings, and valuable for them, is rather that they are *not* restricted to experiencing reality as it is in itself. Man can experience reality as relative to him – which is to say, as real. It is therefore not important that reality is not meaningful in itself; it is meaningful in the way that matters, namely, in relation to us.

Much the same should be said about 'facts.' Since to call anything a 'fact' is to organize the information provided by reality by means of the concept of *fact*, can we be justified in speaking of facts as 'facts'? For does this not imply that we can ascribe factuality to the facts only after the facts have already been interpreted, at least to the extent of having been conceived as such 'facts'? Yes, it does, but this need not provoke the fear of scepticism in anyone who understands what it means. For it does not mean that we cannot experience the facts as such; it only means that, since conscious experience is present to itself, it is possible for us whenever we experience any facts to ignore the '[experienced]' status of the '[experienced] facts.' We can, therefore – and if we are interested in the truth we should – question, as we say, 'the factual basis' of our experience and our opinions. However, we can do so only in retrospect; one cannot be critical of one's opinions before one forms them, but at the earliest as one arrives at them. To suppose that we could question the facts from the outset, before we conceived them as

---

43 We have seen, however, that actually 'making a difference to another' by virtue of the relativity of the properties of things is the essence of efficient causality. This means that efficient causality is grounded on the reality of things; whatever is real is *apt* to enter into cause-effect relationships. It does not follow, however, that reality is coextensive with causality. Whether a reality is actually a cause, or an effect, or both, cannot be determined *a priori*, simply from the fact that it is real, but only when experience shows that it is one, or the other, or both.

'the facts,' would be like supposing that we can experience reality as it appears when it is appearing to no one. By the same token, the most intractable conflicts among human beings have to do with what shall, and what shall not, be accepted as a fact. Although the factual reality is the same for everyone, the truth is not necessarily the same for all.

Nevertheless, it is true: who can by taking thought add a cubit to his stature or make white to be black? That no one can change the facts by thinking as he may wish is obvious, and the harshest indictment of the Western epistemological tradition is that we have found it necessary to assert, and reassert, and onto this day keep reasserting, this platitude until the inner ear rebels. Indeed, the facts are immutably the same not only for all men, but for all creatures who stand upon the land; they drop down from heaven upon the wise and the foolish alike, and upon the conscious and the brute. Rain, for instance, makes all warm-blooded organisms equally wet and cold. But not everyone upon whose head it falls is conscious, when it rains, that 'it rains' – or that the statement 'it rains' asserts 'a fact.' Man is, therefore, the only denizen of earth of whom it can be said that he *knows* enough to come in out of the rain; many beasts can take cover from the weather, but even when they do they cannot *say* that they are hiding from the elements, nor can they dispute among themselves whether, 'as a matter of fact,' the rain in Spain stays mainly on the plain. Human beings, thus, are not protected from inclemency by fur or eiderdown, but by their cerebral cortex and its ability to make experience, somehow, present to itself. Thus, although they cannot do much about changing the weather by strength of fang and claw, they are able to do what is much more effective: to talk about it. Turning the weather into a theme of speech is, of course, only the first step towards setting up meteorological services, launching weather-scanning satellites, and developing a five-hundred-kilometre-long strip of summer resorts along the Mediterranean coasts of Spain. In brief, man is the only animal who experiences facts as such, and therefore the only animal who experiences the truth of facts.

It would be inappropriate to enter here upon an investigation of the nature of truth. I will mention, however, what such investigation's principal finding should be, if it were empirically grounded and critically conducted: that only the self-presence of conscious experience permits the factuality of the facts to become truth, and that consciousness has the quality of truth when it furthers its own self-presence – that is, when it facilitates, expands, and intensifies its own experience. The mark of the experience that is true is that it enables consciousness to develop, whereas the sign of falsity is that consciousness cannot expand. But I should at least provide a few indications of why I say this.

The semantic conception of truth comes in otherwise very different versions, all of which share, however, a common element: truth consists in some sort of adequation of the mind to reality. Now this conception is not altogether mistaken; it would hardly make sense to say that the relationship of the mind to its objects was irrelevant to the truth of experience, or that experience might be true regardless of whether it took into account what reality was. The objection is, rather, that this relationship is a necessary pre-condition of truth, but not the distinctive and defining element of it. For this interpretation fails to take into account the difference between mere experience and consciousness; it reduces the truth of human experience to the same objectively observable fact that *human beings* can perceive as a characteristic of certain animal experiences, but which animals themselves are unable to perceive. That is, whereas an animal's experience may be said (by human beings) to be true, only human beings *experience* the truth. For instance, when a laboratory rat chews on a food pellet but leaves a plastic imitation untouched, it gives evidence of having experienced these objects with an adequacy that *we*, the observers of the event, perceive as such and are entitled to call a true experience. But that is only because *we*, being able to experience both the pellet (directly) and the rat's experience (deductively, through indirect signs), are able also to assess the adequacy of the animal's experience to the reality. Unless the rat were conscious, however, its experience of the pellet might well be in conformity with the pellet's reality, but would not in any event include any experience of such adequation or lack thereof. By virtue of its self-presence, however, every conscious experience necessarily includes apprehending its own adequacy or conformity to reality. Therefore, the experiences we call truth and falsity arise only because *such apprehension itself* is adequate or else inadequate to what in fact is the case – namely, the degree to which the experience adequately conforms to reality. But it is the adequacy of the former, not that of the latter – the adequacy of our apprehension of our relationship to reality, not that of the merely factual relationship to reality – that we actually have in mind when we refer to the truth or falsity of our experience. If we are absent-minded, however, we may not be clear about precisely what it is that we experience when we have the experiences of falsity and truth.

✗ This conception of truth, unlike the semantic, explains the necessarily retrospective character of the experience of error. It is not without significance that we can never experience *being* mistaken, but only *having been* mistaken. Even when we are – as it later turns out – wrong, we invariably take our experience to be true. Indeed, we cannot but so take it, since the very essence of the mistake consists in so taking it – not in the lack of conformity to the reality, which is merely a factual condition prerequisite to one's *erroneously* thinking that one's experience is true. Or could it be reasonably supposed that perhaps next time one makes a mistake one will, for a change, appreciate its waywardness at the time one makes the mistake? Now, since truth and falsity are mutually relative, the retrospective nature of error points to the prospective character of truth: truth creates the possibility of yet more truth. It also follows that there can be no criterion whereby to secure the truth beforehand as one strives to reach it, any more than there can be any reasonable hope of ascertaining 'the whole truth.' (I do not mean that 'the whole truth' is an unattainable but desirable ideal, but that it is an absurdity, like 'seeing beyond the horizon.') Likewise, awareness of one's ability to experience truthfully should normally be accompanied by the humbling realization of one's fallibility. And the best safeguard against error – partially effective though it may be – is neither a proven method of rational inquiry such as science or philosophy, nor privileged communications from an all-knowing revealing source: it is a keen and respectful recognition of the inherent fallibility of all thought.

The interpretation of speech, thought, and conscious experience developed in this chapter may with some aptness be called *syntactic*, or co-ordinative, because it proposes that assertive experience and communication compose and arrange vicariously the reality that informs them, and that the orchestration of the experience of reality through the assertive communication of such experience produces meaning. Consciousness is, thus, like a musical talent that weaves harmonies by skilfully playing, with the fingers of speech, an instrument that by itself is mute: reality as it is in itself.

It is only in relation to a consciousness thus understood that the question of its origin and evolution should be raised.

The Origin
and Development of
Human Nature

The generation of
consciousness by speech:
a theory of
human evolution

The first stage of this investigation has enabled us to establish the *explicandum* of a theory of human evolution; any attempt to ascertain the process would be misdirected unless, taking consciousness and speech in the sense explained above, it tried to account for the origin and development of organisms who experience consciously and who organize their individual and collective lives by means of their ability to speak with each other and with themselves, and in accordance with the properties of such ability. But the same study of consciousness and speech has also served to raise the possibility that the ability of individual human beings to give conscious quality to their experience may be the direct effect of their prior acquisition of the ability to speak. If true, this would explain how the consciousness of individual human beings is transmitted to their offspring – which would in turn provide a hypothesis upon which a theory of human evolution might be erected.

A viable explanation of how consciousness is inherited is crucial to an adequate theory of human evolution; to appreciate why, we need only recall that natural selection is the effect of the interplay between the ability of organisms to adjust and their ability to reproduce themselves: the heart of evolution, if I may so put it, is located in the genital apparatus. Every biological theory of the origin of infrahuman species has, therefore, always rested on a prior construction of the generative process. Likewise, every theory of human *phylogeny* – the origin of man's specific nature – has invariably been conditioned by implicit or explicit assumptions about the nature of human *ontogeny*, the process whereby the individual comes into being. But the biological theories have never questioned the common-sense assumption that there is no essential difference between human and animal reproduction; they have assumed that all the essential human characteristics, including consciousness, are transmitted genetically, being reducible to functions of the organism. However, if speech should be the means whereby the humanity of human beings replicates itself, a theory of human evolution that did not assume such reducibility should be possible; for speech would be a reproductive mechanism that, being irreducible to the transmission of genes, could transmit characteristics that were irreducible to functions of the organism.

At the outset of this work I criticized the theories of human evolution developed by biology, because they force the human process into the Procrustean bed of explanations that can account only for the evolution of infrahuman life. A few additional remarks about the insufficiency of the biological theories, however, will further contrast them with my proposal and should facilitate the exposition of the latter. This will be the subject of the first section of this chapter. In the second section I shall develop the ontogenetic basis of the theory, explaining why speech should be deemed the reproductive mechanism, literally so called, of the human specificity. The general principles of human phylogenesis, the theory of the generation of consciousness in the species, will be outlined in the last section.

If the cause of biological evolution is natural selection, life does not evolve necessarily but only if certain adventitious conditions disturb its adjustment. Nor does anything predetermine which adaptive charac- teristics must appear in order for the group to survive. For characteristics survive or fail to survive only after they appear, and nothing preordains that any group, or indeed the entire realm of living things, shall endure forever. Clearly, then, no 'selection' properly so called is involved in 'natural selection.' But this is a convenient term and biologists do not hesitate to use it, as well as others that, if taken literally, would imply that evolution tends towards an appointed goal. I will likewise freely resort here to anthropomorphisms, speaking of evolution as if it had sought to create man from the outset. This practice may mislead the unwary, but is quite justified; for though the outcome of a *process* may not be fixed in advance, the outcome of a retrospective *account* of the process certainly is. Knowing as we do where evolution did in fact lead, we can explain it only under the constraint that in the end we make clear why evolution produced, specifically, man.

1. The insufficiency of the biological theories of human evolution

In *The Origin of Species* Darwin raised the possibility that the theory of natural selection might apply to man; but he positively argued that it did only twelve years later, in *The Descent of Man*. His demonstration depended on showing that 'in bodily structure and in mental faculties' the difference 'between man and the higher animals, great as it is, certainly is one of degree and not of kind.'[1] His argument hinged, thus, on the reducibility of human to animal nature.

Why did this line of reasoning seem appropriate and plausible to him? First, because he assumed that all human characteristics were 'governed and transmitted in accordance with the same general laws [of inheritance] as in the lower animals.'[2] He thought that even 'virtuous tendencies are inherited,'[3] though 'instruction' would, at least in some cases, strongly influence their development. We may surmise that behind this assumption skulked a reductionistic concept of causality in general, of which generative causality was only a particular instance. Darwin would have assumed, therefore, as some biologists do even today, that natural selection requires reductionism – though in fact it does not. But second, Darwin's understanding of man was skimpy enough to have permitted him to overlook some differences from animals. His acquaintance with the nature of consciousness was especially deficient; he assumed that experience was essentially the same in both. Thus, he was uncertain whether animals were 'self-conscious' and had 'mental individuality,' though he thought it was 'no great improbability.'[4] But given his preconceptions, he felt of course that nothing important turned on this point; only differences in degree were at stake. Likewise, he thought that 'language' was present in animals, since it is clear that animals are able to communicate; he granted, to be sure, differences of degree between animal communication and human speech.[5] With the advantage of these assumptions, Darwin was able to find a continuous gradation from man to lower animal forms – and therefore to conclude, with impeccable logic, that nothing but natural selection was needed to explain the appearance of the human species from lower forms.

By the same token, Darwin did not feel that he had to account for the appearance of human society and culture before his thesis was validated. If an individual's conscious life, having no substantiality, is reducible to functions of his organism – which is, of course, individual – all the more so man's social life. It was, therefore, no gap in his argument to admit that 'the problem ... of the first advance of savages towards

1 Charles Darwin, *The Descent of Man*, 2nd ed. (New York, 1902), pp. 21, 170.
2 Ibid., p. 196.
3 Ibid., p. 168.
4 Ibid., p. 118.
5 Ibid., p. 119.

civilization is at present much too difficult to be understood.'[6] It would be anachronistic to imagine that Darwin could have thought otherwise; even today some biologists think that social processes are reducible to individual ones.[7] The reducibility of social to individual processes long remained unquestioned in our intellectual tradition because, as everyone knows, if one looks at a group of people one cannot see a society; one can only perceive so many individuals. It was admitted that the social processes – the effects that individuals have on each other – were quite real; but they were deemed to have only the parasitic, reducible reality of 'accidents' or events accruing to the only entities that actually exist, namely, individual substantive beings. In brief, society was nothing but a generalization in one's mind. If one assumes this, one cannot but take for granted also, as Darwin did, that societies are generated by their individual members and are explicable without remainder by reference to the nature of the latter; and if so, societies can neither generate nor explain the nature of individual human beings.

During the first half of the twentieth century Darwin's theory of natural selection underwent much development at the hands of other scientists, especially after the rediscovery of Gregor Mendel's earlier work on genetics; the latter provided an explanation, not available to Darwin, of how the very reproductive process introduced variations from parent to offspring. The original theory evolved thus into that which predominates today – the 'synthetic' theory, as it is sometimes called (because it was a synthesis of population genetics and Darwin's concept of natural selection). The important novelty in this trend of evolutionary thinking, so far as concerns us, was the gradual admission by biologists – up to a point – that a reductionistic concept of causality was not required by natural selection: nowadays most biologists say – whatever they may mean by it – that evolution is an emergent process. But once differences in kind were recognized, it was necessary to explain how natural selection applied to the emergence of a human species that differed from infrahuman nature not only in degree but also in kind.

Unfortunately, not all the essential differences were taken into account; the conscious quality of human experience was again the chief omission. The principal difference remarked upon was man's socio-cultural life; the relationship between consciousness and human socio-cultural life, however, was largely ignored. Although the social sciences

6 Ibid., p. 180.
7 'A society can be described *only* as a set of particular organisms': Edward O. Wilson, *Sociobiology: The New Synthesis* (Cambridge, MA, 1975), p. 7, italics mine.

of the twentieth century continued to agree that social processes did not subsist as separate, disembodied entities – a view, I hasten to add, that I have no wish to contest – the evidence required them to admit that social phenomena were qualitatively different from individual ones; they were emergent. Under the influence of the social sciences theorists of evolution eventually recognized the irreducibility of socio-cultural processes to individual ones, and *a fortiori* to individual organic factors. Biologists concluded that human life had 'superorganic'[8] (i.e., socio-cultural) aspects, whose evolution did not depend on the natural selection of genes.

The concept of the 'superorganic' (or equivalent formulations), however, introduced an inconsistency into the synthetic theory. To admit the irreducibility of social processes to organic determinants without admitting also the irreducibility of conscious experience is illogical. For common sense is quite right: societies have no separate reality of their own; 'superorganic' processes can exist only as part of the conscious experience and behaviour of individual human organisms. The synthetic theory thus proposes, in effect, a self-contradiction: superorganic organic processes. The self-contradiction might have been more easily detected, had the introduction of a certain concept at this point not served, like the addition of new epicycles, to hide the discrepancy from sight: that two independent processes were at work in human evolution. In the theory of human evolution now prevalent, the nature of the individual's experience and behaviour is determined by the organism, but the processes so reducible to their organic causes are subject to alteration by the concurrent determination of supposedly non-organic, cultural factors. The evolution of individual processes is explained as the resultant of two different and separate orders of causality: organic evolution and 'superorganic' or socio-cultural evolution.

The synthetic theory accordingly allowed that some of the human characteristics – the 'superorganic' ones – were not transmitted genetically, but through cultural inheritance. It was 'false ... that man is *nothing but* the highest animal or the most progressive product of organic evolution. He is also a fundamentally new sort of animal and one in which, although organic evolution continues on the way, a fundamentally new sort of evolution has also appeared. The basis of this sort of evolution is a new sort of heredity, the inheritance of learning.'[9] Whereas organic variations are transmitted by means of sexual reproduction, cultural

8 Theodosius Dobzhansky, *Mankind Evolving* (New Haven, CT, 1962), p. 18.
9 George Gaylord Simpson, *The Meaning of Evolution* (New Haven, CT, 1949), p. 286.

variations are passed on through communication. Cultural evolution is 'essentially different in kind'[10] from organic evolution for the very reason that culture 'is not genetic in nature, but consists of ideas, inventions, traditions, laws, customs, and all the other learned responses by which society is regulated.'[11] But since the two concurrent evolutions exert causality by different means, they are independent processes ruled by independent mechanisms: 'Cultures ... "evolve," not according to the mechanism of organic evolution, but independently of it.'[12] (I call attention to the original's quotation marks.)

The obvious questions arise: how do cultures evolve, if not through natural selection, and how does their evolution contribute to the evolution of human nature? The answer is that, 'unfortunately, very little is known'[13] about the matter. However, since there must be a natural explanation for the origin of socio-cultural phenomena, the proponents of the synthetic theory cannot but suppose that cultural evolution must have been 'a result of organic evolution.'[14] Man's social nature announces 'a new phase of evolution, and not a new phase merely but also a new kind, which is thus also a product of organic evolution ... though its organization and activities are essentially different from those in the process that brought it into being.'[15] Now, this is a reasonable supposition; human evolution must be continuous with animal evolution. But how did cultural evolution emerge out of organic evolution? And why should natural selection have created a second evolutionary mechanism? The synthetic theory has no answers. Biologists have observed, however, the curious but so far unexplained fact that cultural evolution 'has become much the more effective and dominant'[16] of the two. Indeed, 'in a sense, human genes have surrendered their primacy in human evolution to an entirely new, nonbiological or superorganic

10 Ibid., p. 288.
11 G. Ledyard Stebbins, *Processes of Organic Evolution* (Englewood Cliffs, NJ, 1966), p. 174.
12 Bernard G. Campbell, *Human Evolution: An Introduction to Man's Adaptations* (Chicago, 1966), p. 174. It is generally recognized, however, that organic developments may incidentally have cultural consequences, and vice versa. The socio-biological theory of 'gene-culture coevolution' (see below) capitalizes on this possibility; the synthetic theory stresses that, nevertheless, the two mechanisms proceed independently, according to their respective 'laws.'
13 Paul Ehrlich and Richard W. Holm, *The Process of Evolution* (New York, 1963), p. 290.
14 Simpson, *Evolution*, p. 288.
15 Ibid., p. 292.
16 Sol Tax and Charles Callender, eds., *Evolution after Darwin* (Chicago, 1960), vol. III, p. 208.

agent, culture.'[17] Of course, it is necessary to maintain at the same time that 'the superorganic has not annulled the organic'[18] and that the evolution of human culture 'is not a thing apart.'[19] But how are cultural and organic evolution related? Indeed, *are* they related? The synthetic theory has little to say about this.

The idea that human evolution amalgamates two concurrent but separate evolutionary processes is not simply inelegant; it is fundamentally defective. It tells us that the evolution of man is partly the same though also partly different from that of other species – but it explains only the similarity, not the difference. Its failure to tell us *how* cultural evolution emerged from its organic antecedent, and precisely *what* evolutionary mechanism so emerged means that it does not account at all for the origin and the nature of the mechanism whereby the avowedly most important aspect of human evolution takes place. In other words, cultural evolution cannot explain anything as long as it itself remains unexplained. The fact that communication rather than chromosomal exchange mediates the transmission of cultural characteristics does not of itself advance our understanding of how cultural evolution operates, any more than the fact that organic characteristics are transmitted genetically rather than by the exchange of communicative signs explains, by itself, how species evolve. The questions to be faced are: what evolutionary mechanism is the equivalent, in respect of cultural evolution, of the natural selection that operates in organic evolution? And how does cultural evolution contribute to the evolution of the specifically human aspects of man?

The inability of the synthetic theory to answer the questions that it itself provokes is one of the factors that led in recent times to an expansion of the theory of natural selection by socio-biologists, principally Edward O. Wilson.[20] The basic hypothesis of socio-biology is that the genetic make-up of the organism determines not only its functional structures, but also the characteristics of its use of such structures (i.e., behaviour); natural selection explains, therefore, the evolution of behaviour as well as the evolution of organic structures and functions. This explanation is entirely plausible in respect of animal behaviour, since in the absence of consciousness even the most complex forms of

17 Theodosius Dobzhansky, 'Anthropology and the Natural Sciences: The Problem of Human Evolution,' *Current Anthropology*, 4 (1968), p. 146.
18 Dobzhansky, *Mankind*, p. 20.
19 Campbell, *Evolution*, p. 292.
20 See his *Sociobiology*, and (with Charles J. Lumsden) *On Human Nature* (Cambridge, MA, 1978).

individual and social behaviour are reducible to functions of organic structures. But whatever the merits of the theory respecting animal evolution, it was applied by socio-biologists to human evolution, at first, with no more allowance having been made for the peculiarities of human life than was provided by such concepts as that of the 'underprescription' of the details of behaviour by the genes. But 'underprescription does not mean that culture has been freed from the genes.'[21] Wilson and his collaborators professed to have no reductionist intent and to make allowance for emergent characteristics; but whatever its intent the theory, in fact, implied reductionism, since 'in the final analysis [it maintained that] all behaviour patterns evolved due to the survival of the fittest genes.'[22]

In an effort to surmount objections a refinement was then added that distinguished human from infrahuman evolution. In man, it was proposed,[23] the process is 'gene-culture coevolution.' The human mind is 'identical with physiological events in the brain';[24] but its complexity, the result of natural selection, is responsible for cultural behaviour. Once culture emerges, however, it becomes a factor in the selection of genes; for human beings make free choices in their mode of life and behaviour that have variable survival value. Thus, the culture reflects the choices of individuals; but since such choices have variable survival value – for behaviour is genetically determined, albeit 'underprescribed' – they are subject to natural genetic selection and are therefore reflected in turn in the changing genetic make-up of the individuals that integrate the culture that reflects individual choices, and so on. Like a fire, gene-culture coevolution keeps itself going once it starts.

At bottom, however, gene-culture coevolution is only a complex form of natural genetic selection; it differs from the infrahuman mechanism only in the way in which variations in the genetically determined characteristics of the human mind can be introduced into the evolutionary process. In man the natural selection of genes includes, besides environmental pressures from the physical world, the selective pressures created by culturally conditioned and perpetuated choices – the origin of which, moreover, is *somehow* to be found also in the genes. Thus, although this theory makes allowance for a specifically human evolu-

---

21 Wilson, *Sociobiology*, p. 559.
22 J.D. Baldwin and J.I. Baldwin, *Beyond Sociobiology* (New York, 1981), p. 3.
23 Edward O. Wilson and Charles J. Lumsden, *Genes, Mind, and Culture* (Cambridge, MA, 1981), and *Promethean Fire* (Cambridge, MA, 1983).
24 Wilson and Lumsden, *Fire*, p. 76.

tionary mechanism, it assumes that such mechanism is reducible to the survival of the fittest genes.

Socio-biologists are undoubtedly right when they say that the human mind and human culture have not been 'freed from the genes'; this is no more in dispute than whether culture has a role in gene selection in the case of certain characteristics. For instance, since sibling matings tend to produce genetically disadvantaged offspring, it is entirely possible that, if there should be a gene for incest aversion, the cultural institutions that tend to prevent incest would be reinforced by natural selection and vice versa. It is a different question whether the human mind is reducible to genetically conditioned organic functions, whether human culture originated in nothing but the determinism of the genes, and whether all culturally transmitted behaviour is genetically conditioned. The possibility that socio-biology discards is that the human mind and human culture have been freed from the *exclusive* determinism of the genes. Since the socio-biological theory of human evolution is in the end yet more reductionistic than the synthetic, the criticism I aim here at the latter on this score applies to the former also; moreover, this theory remains for the moment a minority view among scientists. The decision is therefore justified, I think, to criticize it separately only to the extent I have done so far.

The synthetic theory, in contrast, must for all its defects be given credit for having recognized that speech has a uniquely important role in cultural evolution: 'the inheritance of learning' depends, of course, on the transmission of messages. At least one synthetic theorist has therefore remarked that 'man has acquired what amounts to a totally new evolutionary system ... [C]onceptual thought and language constitute, in effect, a new way of transmitting information from one generation to the next. This cultural inheritance does the same thing for man that in the sub-human world is done by the genetic system, which transmits its "information" ... in the form of a DNA chain ... [B]esides his biological system, man has a completely new "genetic" system dependent on cultural transmission.'[25] Nevertheless, the difference between these concepts and the hypothesis I have advanced should be clear. In the synthetic theory the cultural transmission of information determines human nature 'genetically' only in a figurative sense of the latter term; there is a curious parallel between the chromosomal genetic system that transmits *all* the essential human characteristics from parent

25 C.H. Waddington, 'Man as an Organism,' in Tax and Callender, *Evolution*, vol. III, pp. 148–9.

to offspring, and the 'new sort of heredity,' the cultural transmission of messages. But the latter determines only the culturally dependent modifications of the experience and behaviour of human beings whose human status and nature are antecedent to such modifications. Cultural 'inheritance' therefore affects, but it does not generate, the humanity of human beings. Cultural 'evolution' is not truly a form of evolution; it is 'evolution' in quotation marks.

Accordingly, the synthetic theory does not invoke the 'new "genetic" system' to explain the origin of either the human individual or of the species. It assumes that the human ability to think and experience consciously and the capacity for cultural tradition appeared solely through the natural selection of genetically transmitted characteristics. The theory merely adds that, once man had emerged and had developed his communicative abilities to the point where he could transmit messages as complex as speech can, the human organism could continue to evolve not only in respect of its specific characteristics and abilities through natural selection, but also in respect of its behaviour and way of life through the cultural transmission of messages. There is, therefore, only one genetic system properly so called: chromosomal conjugation and exchange suffice for the generation of individual organisms in which thought and consciousness – as it is also assumed – eventually appear through maturation. Moreover, the ability to speak, which is the basis of cultural transmission, is deemed not only to have appeared through natural selection, but to have continued to be propagated genetically; it is 'a genetically determined character ... [although language,] the actual words we use, is part of culture.'[26]

The synthetic theory correctly assumes that, although the ability to communicate has extraordinary importance for human life, the *messages* that human beings transmit are radically insufficient to generate the humanity of human beings; for biologists are quite right to think that, since the information conveyed by messages does not transmit the essential characteristics of the species, such information is not genetic in any but a metaphorical sense. I have proposed, however, that the human ability to communicate is more than the ability to transmit the kind of information that is carried as the content of messages, and that a literally so-called new sort of heredity inheres in speech and is responsible for the transmission of the specifically human abilities. Speech is the reproductive basis of the evolution of consciousness. Let us consider why this can be reasonably maintained.

26 Campbell, *Evolution*, p. 313.

2. The genesis of consciousness in the human individual

In chapter II it was suggested that the ability to experience consciously is not inborn, but acquired; consciousness is a skill, an accomplishment that perfects the inborn experiential functions of the human organism. It cannot be, of course, a *consciously* developed skill; no one is in a position, before he is conscious, to make a conscious decision whether to acquire consciousness. This explains, in part, why the emergence of consciousness in the individual can be easily mistaken for the maturation of a genetically transmitted ability: it appears spontaneously, seemingly therefore in the same way as, say, the ability to walk. Now, not only organic functions, but qualities of such functions, may appear through maturation – if the qualities are reducible to the functions, as they ordinarily are. Impalas, for instance, have not merely the ability to run, but the ability to run *fast*. The quality of their running function, however, must be deemed a genetically conditioned skill, since it is reducible to the function; it does not have to be learned, but appears through maturation of the function (and, of course, the structure) of the organism. But if consciousness is not reducible to an organic function, then it cannot appear through the maturation of a genetically determined organic function. It is not like the ability to run as fast as an impala or as gracefully as a gazelle, but more like the ability to dance an Irish jig, which does not appear through maturation even in thoroughbred Irish folk. To be sure, once the young human has acquired the ability to experience consciously, he can use his organism so as to develop *consciously* his conscious skills.[27] But this is of no interest to us here; for it is the aboriginal ability to function consciously at all, even in the absence of any conscious intent to do so, that is acquired rather than inborn.

Our study of speech in chapter III, however, suggested how this may

---

27 Thus, if I see a woman's face and it reminds me of my mother, the memory comes to me automatically, yet is a conscious memory; but if I decide to tell you about my childhood, I consciously search my memory for recollections of my mother. Likewise, if you raise a weapon against me, I will consciously experience fear whether I want to or not; but in order to overcome my fear of personal inadequacy, I consciously use my brain to think about the matter. Moreover, the ability of human beings to use their brains so as to experience consciously is also the basis of their further ability to make conscious use of certain – but not all – non-experiential organic functions that can be performed non-consciously as well: they can behave consciously. The most numerous and obvious of these functions involve the striated muscles of the organism.

come about: through socio-cultural generation. The transformation of the child's native ability to communicate into the ability to do so assertively leads *automatically*, by virtue of the properties of speech, to the transformation of his ability to experience into the ability to do so consciously. The reason is, in principle, that when a communicator's communication of his experience is assertive, he enters into communication with himself. More particularly, since to speak is to communicate in the light of awareness that one is communicating, a speaker is a communicator who has managed to communicate his own communicative nature to himself; he would not have become a speaker unless he had learned to experience his signalling behaviour as the communication of his experience. The incidental result of the assertive communication of experience is, thus, that one makes present to oneself the experience that one communicates. Conversely, if, in the course of communicating one's experience to another, one experiences one's communications as such – that is, as communicating one's experience – then one's experience has thereby become present to itself. To this we may compare the animal's communication of its experience. The animal communicator is capable, no doubt, of experiencing what *in fact* is its own communicative behaviour; but it does not experience it *as such*. When it communicates, therefore, all that happens is simply that it communicates.

Since my objective at this point is merely to outline the theory, this brief account of the principle should be enough; in the next chapter the evolutionary processes whereby animal communication became speech, and speech then generated consciousness in the species, will be reconstructed in suitable detail. What we should do instead is to take note of the direct implication of the foregoing: that human generation, somewhat like that of the marsupials, is incomplete even after the organism is born. The distinctive mark of human reproduction is that the organism has the genetically determined dispositions that permit its rise to conscious life, some time after birth, by the agency of socio-cultural interaction. A human type of organism is thus the necessary but insufficient condition of human, conscious life; it must be supplemented by a process of socialization, of a specific kind, before consciousness can appear.

Our culture's assumption is, of course, very different: that for human beings to reproduce their kind it suffices that they generate a new organism. It is not remarkable that scientists have unquestioningly accepted this, given their long tradition of reductionism. It is very curious, however, that even those who believe that an essential part of a human being is a spiritual soul – irreducible to the organism, created by God, and personally infused by him into the human body upon its being conceived – do not at bottom depart from the common idea either. For their assumption means that, miraculous conceptions aside, the decisive factor determining whether a human being shall come into being or not is the biology of human reproduction: once human beings do their physiological part, God invariably obliges. In other words, even in respect of the human specificity human reproduction requires no natural processes besides the biological ones. The net result is that, for religious believers quite as for most other people, the sexual generation of a human organism coincides at all points (but, for believers, God willing) with the generation of a human being. This explains why many from both groups share the conviction that human organisms are capable of experiencing consciously and have selfhood at birth – if not indeed before – or at very least that the human organism, once conceived, has within itself all that it needs eventually to function consciously and to have selfhood. The difference between believers and non-believers who agree on this, or between the scientists and the plain folk, has to do only with the way in which the commonly supposed fact is explained. Since the interpretation of human reproduction I have proposed is uncongenial to so many, and likely to be resisted by members of very different groups, we should consider (a) some additional facts that tend to support it, (b) some reasons why the same facts are ordinarily interpreted to mean otherwise, and (c) how some of the principal objections to it might be met.

That a human organism is a necessary condition of life at the human level should not be contentious; the negative results of the classical experiments in bringing up chimpanzees in a human social environment may be recalled.[28] But what indications are there that the maturation of the human organism alone is insufficient to produce it? Since humane considerations, of course, prevent experimentation, the evidence is restricted to the observations made in the few recorded instances of 'wolf children,' 'attic children,' 'feral men,' and the like.[29] But these cases, without exception, show that when a humanoid organism matures outside a human social environment, every form of life at the specifically human level is absent. The otherwise human organism exhibits no more

---

28 W.N. Kellogg and L.A. Kellogg, *The Ape and the Child* (New York, 1933); C. Hayes, *The Ape in Our House* (New York, 1951).

29 K. Davis, 'Extreme Social Isolation of a Child,' *American Journal of Sociology*, 45 (1940), pp. 554–65; idem, 'Final Note on a Case of Extreme Social Isolation,' *American Journal of Sociology*, 52 (1947), pp. 432–7; Roger Brown, *Words and Things* (Glencoe, IL, 1958), pp. 186–92; Lucien Malson, *Wolf Children* (London, 1972); J.A.L. Singh and Robert M. Zingg, *Wolf-children and Feral Man* (New York, 1942); Victoria Fromkin et al., 'The Development of Language in Genie: A Case of Language Acquisition beyond the "Critical Period",' *Brain and Language*, 1 (1974), pp. 81–107.

signs of any ability to experience consciously, or to experience itself as a self, or other selves as selves – or, of course, to speak – than infrahumans do. I need hardly point out that much the same is true of ordinary children at birth; the difference is that the latter gradually begin to show consciousness and the ability to experience their own and others' selfhood. But we assume that there is no causal connection between their development of these abilities and their being taught to speak. Correspondingly, when feral children fail to learn to speak, and when organic maturation somehow fails to produce in them the signs of conscious life and selfhood that supposedly appear in children through maturation alone, we assume that there is no causal connection between the absence of the usual human abilities and their inability to speak. Indeed, we may not even admit that the abilities are absent; we may think they exist, but are undeveloped and do not manifest themselves.

The facts themselves are not in question; the issue is how best to interpret them. It is also clear that no amount of logic could serve to demonstrate positively that an unsocialized humanoid organism – whether an ordinary infant or a mature feral child – is not a conscious self: this is a negative proposition. But a planetary orbit can withstand so many epicycles and no more. At a certain point the obvious construction must be put upon the absence of the symptoms of human life: that they indicate the absence of human life. I do not mean, however, that the thesis that speech generates consciousness turns on the balance of probabilities. For it does not rest on the premiss that unsocialized humanoid organisms are not conscious; it depends on an analysis of the nature of consciousness as we observe it in ourselves, who are unquestionably conscious. My objective at this point is rather to show that our usual assumption – that consciousness appears in children prior to the ability to speak – is not plausible and offers no valid objection to the theory. It is at least as reasonable, if not indeed more, to suppose that an unsocialized human organism is not conscious than to suppose that it is.

A few people, including some philosophers, have proposed that all reality must be in some sense conscious. Nevertheless, absence of the signs of conscious life does not mislead many into supposing that rocks and plants are conscious; why should it do so in the case of feral children or in the ordinary human newborn? We may account for it by the conjunction of two factors. One is that confusion about the meaning of *potentiality* facilitates our misinterpreting the undoubtedly true fact that newborn children have the potential to become conscious. We shall look into this in a moment. The other is the observation, also undoubtedly correct, that they are able to experience. But it is easy to take indications of the ability to experience as if they pointed to consciousness and self-hood. In view of the importance of the question, a brief digression to explain how we recognize consciousness and selfhood in others should be justified. We do it in much the same way in which, as noted earlier, we recognize speech; the parallel is hardly coincidental.

Assertiveness enables human beings not merely to communicate, but to do so empathetically; they can experience each other not only from their own point of view but also from each other's. The ability to empathize with another is a consequence of self-presence, which may also be described as the ability of consciousness to empathize with itself – which is why no one can recognize the selfhood of others except to the very degree to which he can recognize his own. Thus, we learn to recognize that the experience of other people has conscious quality, because we can appreciate that the experience that they communicate to us requires consciousness in them, since it is the sort of experience that requires consciousness in us when it is our experience. It matters little, then, that another person's conscious experience 'is not evident to me, as it is not and never can be an experience of mine ... [Nevertheless] I experience you as experiencing. I experience myself as experienced by you. And I experience you as experiencing yourself as experienced by me.'[30] The unmistakable sign of consciousness in others is the creation of an experiential conscious life in common. This community can be established only through the specifically human mode of communication, either speech or its equivalent.

But perhaps this interpretation can be put to a modest experimental test. Based upon it I will make two predictions that time should verify or otherwise. First, I forecast that you, the reader, will one day experience with the utmost assurance, merely by reading these lines, that I, the writer of these words, was a conscious self at the time I wrote them. Why will you do so? Because you will appreciate that only consciousness would have enabled *you* to write them yourself. Second, I prophesy that any reader who shall understand, or misunderstand, or even be puzzled by, my explanation about the way in which we recognize consciousness in others, will at any rate have not the slightest doubt, while he reads it, that he is conscious. Why *you* are certain that you are conscious is plain; but why am I quite as convinced of it as you are? Because I know that only a conscious experiencer could understand, misunderstand, or be puzzled by, what my consciousness has communicated to him. Now,

30 Ronald D. Laing, *The Politics of Experience and The Bird of Paradise* (Harmondsworth, England, 1967), p. 16.

time has elapsed since I wrote these words, and my theoretical predictions can be tested against the facts. Have they, or have they not, been borne out by events? The reader may decide.

If we remain rooted in empirical ground, the fact that we cannot establish community of conscious life with the newborn and with very young children should arouse the suspicion that they have no more conscious life than animals.[31] But absence of the signs misleads us above all because, ordinarily, human organisms eventually develop the kind of experience and life that we *do* recognize as having the same nature as our own. We then become easily confused; we take this fact to mean that the specifically human abilities must have been present in the organism aboriginally, albeit only 'in potency.' Well, there *are* ample grounds for supposing that infants and physically mature children brought up in isolation have the organic potentiality for developing consciousness, selfhood, and human life – in the sense that their organisms are a fit medium from which an extrinsic causal agency can create abilities that were no part of their original endowment. But there are none for supposing that such potentiality is itself part of their genetic endowment, or that it is inchoatively human in character.

The concept of *potentiality* lends itself to confusion, because it is equivocal. There are two kinds of potentiality, which can be bracketed together only because they are both opposed to *actuality*. Consider, first, the fact that lead is 'potentially' gold. For the medieval alchemists were right after all: matter is transformable and everything is apt to become anything else. But the potentiality of lead for becoming gold is a purely *notional* one; it means only that lead may be *thought of* as non-gold – or for that matter, as non-silver, or indeed, as nothing but lead. But since there is no difference between its potentiality to become gold and its potentiality to become silver – or to become anything else – it can hardly be a potentiality that is in any true sense either golden or argentine. Aristotelians to the contrary, there is nothing actually contained in lead that is imperfectly golden, but which can become gold.

To this kind of potentiality we may contrast, for example, the potential locomotive activity of a napping cat: the resting animal's ability to move refers to a number of functional structures that are *already* part of the cat. It is not merely a notional, but a *real*, potentiality. Real potentialities,

31 The relevance of these questions to the moral problems surrounding procured abortion will have been clear from an early stage of my argument. I have abstracted from all consideration of them because they are inapposite to this inquiry: contrary to the practice of many who debate this question, I assume that moral convictions cannot be used as premises from which to deduce the nature of man.

however, come in degrees, distinguishable by their readiness to be actualized. The napping cat's locomotive potential can be activated instantly, but there was a time when the newborn kitten's organism was so undeveloped that it was unable to walk. Nevertheless, even then the kitten already had a real locomotive potentiality; indeed, the potentiality was already present in the kitten at conception, since it was identical with the properties of its genetic endowment. It was also, therefore, feline in nature; there was something in the immature organic structure of the embryonic kitten that had but to mature in order for the potentiality to become an ability that could be readily actualized. To be sure, concurrent extrinsic factors – for example, nourishment in the case of an immature organism – may be indispensable for the maturation of real potentialities. But these factors do not *generate* real potentialities out of notional ones. It is true, then, that all human organisms, however immature – even from conception – have the potentiality for consciousness and selfhood. Nothing indicates, however, that this potentiality is any but a purely notional one. We must conclude that an organism with human organic characteristics is a necessary but insufficient condition for the emergence of the specifically human level of life.

The hypothesis also runs counter to the supposition – not so much of common sense this time, but of some scholars – that children have an innate ability to speak. But this supposition is viable only in symbiosis with the assumption that the ability to experience consciously is innate. This should be enough to justify rejecting the supposition out of hand, but let us nevertheless consider independently its lack of merit. Although known cases of children brought up with little or no human contact have been very few, it is generally agreed that 'children will not learn any language when deprived of all linguistic input.'[32] It is not strange, of course, that they should not have any innate knowledge of the language of any given community. What is amazing is that neither will they create their own languages – not the simplest – even after organic maturity. This is, indeed, astonishing, since the ability to speak implies not only the ability to *use* communicative signs, but the ability to *invent* them; granted the ability to speak, any behaviour whatever can be converted into a communicative sign merely by being *meant* as a sign. Thus, a genetically carried ability to speak that even after organic maturity did not enable anyone to say *anything* boggles the mind, because the ability to speak is the ability to say *everything* one has experienced and wishes to say.

Teaching a child to speak is not like teaching a second language to

32 Fromkin, 'The Development of Language,' p. 82.

someone who already knows how to speak; it is to convey to him the 'idea' of speech, to awaken him to the possibility of using signs in order to communicate. To be sure, such an 'idea' cannot be generated in the young in isolation from their being taught to use some concrete system of signs. But what they seem to lack – altogether – is the 'idea' of speech and not only knowledge of the semantic and syntactic conventions of a language in which they can speak. Likewise, when children originally 'deprived of all linguistic input' are reintegrated into human society after organic maturity, they need to learn more than how to use a language; they must discover what it is to speak, in exactly the same way as ordinary children do. A feral child is not like a tourist abroad, who finds it difficult to make himself understood *by others*; as in the young child, it is rather the possibility of *his* saying anything that seems foreign to his mind. He cannot therefore even resort to the proverbial expedient of tourists – who unmistakably convey, by their unsuccessful no less than by their successful gesticulation, the fact that they *intend* to communicate.

What we observe in both ordinary and feral children, then, does not make it implausible to suppose that consciousness is reproduced from generation to generation through the transmission of the ability to speak; if anything, it tends to support it. The ontogeny of consciousness is undoubtedly odd, but its very peculiarities should enable us to understand the unique way in which mankind was born.

3. The genesis of consciousness in the human species

The inheritance mechanism that mediates infrahuman evolution operates under certain well-known limitations. Neither variations in purely functional characteristics (e.g., improvements in a rat's maze-running performance resulting from practice) nor modifications of structures as a result of the exercise of functions (e.g., a weight-lifter's grotesque musculature) can be transmitted genetically; for they are no part of the genetic endowment that the parent(s) settle on the offspring. In other words, reproductive cells neither learn nor reflect changes in the structures of the organism (other than, of course, changes due to maturation, which are implicit in the organism's endowment from the outset). Clearly, this reproductive mechanism would not have permitted the replication of the specifically human aspect of human nature, if it is true that the latter is acquired – indeed, learned. The first and critical step in the genesis of human nature must have been, therefore, the appearance of a reproductive mechanism suitable for the reproduction of the acquired experiential characteristic we call consciousness. I do not mean, of course, that this unprecedented mechanism had to be complete first, and then evolution began to make use of it; I mean that the development of the specifically human reproductive mechanism must have been what led the human evolutionary process. Understanding the origin of human nature begins, thus, with understanding the origin of speech.

The appearance of the human form of reproduction was comparable in novelty to the emergence of sexual out of asexual reproduction during the earliest stages of the evolution of life. However, this singularity did not emerge *ex nihilo*; as usual, evolution took advantage of what already existed. For well below the human level a means to transmit purely functional information – information on how to use the organism, or how to behave – had already appeared. I refer to signal-transmission, *communication* in the usual sense. Animal communication, however, is not suitable for communicating *genetic* functional information. (I mean: information that should not only shape the recipient's ability to behave in certain ways in accordance with the sender's instructions, but which should *create* the ability in the first place – and, indeed, that it should do so with the same inflexibility and automaticity as the information carried by the genes does.) What evolution did, however, which in turn resulted in the genesis of consciousness, was precisely that: to transform animal communication into a vehicle capable of carrying not only ordinary information, but also information about how to perform the experiential functions of the organism in the characteristically human way. The transmission of such functional information would thus have *generated* modalities and qualities of function that did not pre-exist in the recipient organism, and which would have automatically and inflexibly determined that the recipient shared in the essential characteristic of the communicator. Purely functional information would have thus been *inherited* by the offspring – information that could have been, therefore, properly called 'genetic.' I use quotation marks only to avoid confusion with the kind of genetic information that is transmitted by chromosomal exchange.

There cannot be, however, a simple equivalence between the ontogeny and the phylogeny of consciousness; in this respect the genesis of consciousness is like that of the organism, which is not a point-by-point recapitulation in the individual of the entire course of the evolution of life. The generation of consciousness in the individual presupposes a speaking community and its language; speech and its languages do not have to be invented anew by every generation and every human group. And yet, a speaking socio-cultural environment had to be invented – I mean, by evolution – if a species of conscious organisms was to appear.

Whereas now, after the species has appeared, the genesis of the individual consciousness results from the prior existence of the socio-cultural environment and speech, the genesis of consciousness in the species must have been contemporaneous, and indeed identical, with the genesis of assertive communication and of cultural society of the specifically human sort. Thus, a theory of the origin of consciousness in the species must be at the same time a theory of the origin of cultural societies and of speech.

It is beyond question that animals can experience, and that communication and social structure – differentiation and co-ordination of roles – exist even at fairly low levels of animal life. Culture has been more difficult to detect in animals, though recent observations indicate that in some species learned behaviour can be passed from elders to offspring;[33] this feat may indeed be not nearly so rare as has been deemed in the past. However, although it is much more difficult to learn from the experience of others than from one's own, of itself this achievement falls short of cultural society in the human sense; for there are no indications that learning through tradition generates in animals any new modality of experience or a specifically different mode of life that otherwise would not appear. Animal culture, therefore, where it exists, can have at best a modest role in animal evolution: as long as culture can transmit only improvements in the use of genetically determined functions, the improvements have to begin anew with each generation at the same genetically fixed starting-point as the parent generation. Note that the synthetic theory assigns no greater evolutionary role to culture than accumulating and transmitting the *contents* of experience from one generation to the next; in this theory, therefore, cultural evolution is reducible to the kind that is possible, in principle, in animal life. In the socio-biological theory, culture is assigned an even humbler function, on a par, say, with climatic changes: it is simply one more way in which events outside the individual organism segregate fit from unfit genes.

According to the theory here proposed, however, the specifically human type of cultural society does more than to enable the contents of the experience of one individual to be reproduced in another; it enables the characteristically human form of experience to be reproduced in organisms whose experience would otherwise remain infrahuman. Thus, the evolution of human nature through this mechanism need not begin

33 Among the earliest reports were K. Imanischi, 'Social Organization of Sub-human Primates in Their Natural Habitat,' *Current Anthropology*, 1 (1960), pp. 393–407; M. Kawai, 'Japanese Monkeys and the Origin of Culture,' *Animals*, 5 (1965), pp. 440–55.

anew with each generation; improvements in the *characteristics* of experience can be accumulated by the culture and preserved by none but cultural means. And as the culture generates consciousness in individuals at successively higher levels of accomplishment, the culture itself evolves. Organically, every human generation must begin at the same starting-point as its elders (except to the extent, largely negligible, to which natural selection may have continued to operate in the evolution of the human organism); in this sense human evolution has not become emancipated from the genes. But so far as concerns the quality of function of the human experiential abilities, human evolution *has* been freed from the limitations of the mode of reproduction that depends on the transmission of genes.

The theory states, then, that human society acquired its specifically human reproductive role, becoming a *matrix* or 'womb' for the generation and continued evolution of consciousness, when in the course of evolution through natural selection animal communication developed into speech. A society where communication had taken an assertive form would have thereby become a society where consciousness had come into being; thenceforth its principal and distinctive cultural functions would have been generating consciousness in its progeny and mediating its continued evolution (through mechanisms that included, but that neither were restricted to nor principally consisted of, the transmission of the contents of messages). Thus, the human social environment, the human mode of experience, and the human form of communication – culture, consciousness, and speech – acquired their distinctively human properties at one and the same time by one and the same evolutionary process: the transformation of animal communication into human speech. How natural selection could have brought about such transformation will be, therefore, the first concern of the next chapter, as we begin to reconstruct the human evolutionary process.

We have seen that the interaction between the adjustive and the reproductive functions of organisms has an inherently selective effect. When the reproductive means is the transmission of genes, the selective effect is, of course, a *genetic* selective effect. But since speech was not only a new kind of communication, but also a new mode of reproduction, its emergence was at the same time the institution of a new evolutionary mechanism. Human evolution depends upon the interaction between adjustive and reproductive functions that are qualitatively different from, and irreducible to, their counterparts in animal life. It is accomplished, therefore, through a selective means that includes, but that is not reducible to, the natural selection of genes. When it brought forth speech, evolution by natural selection had itself evolved into a higher form.

The idea that, when it created man, evolution itself had evolved is not new; the proponents of the synthetic theory remarked upon it long ago. But they seem to have treated this concept as if it were little more than a somewhat violent figure of speech. For what they literally meant was the opposite: by supposing that the 'new phase of evolution' was actually an additional process, they preserved the first intact. The suggestion advanced here is rather that evolution did evolve; organic evolution produced 'merely' a new phase of evolution, not a second process. Now, the proposition that evolution has truly evolved sounds dramatic at first; for natural selection is supposed to be a law of nature, and in the semi-conscious fantasy of most of us natural laws are even more inflexible than the Will of God, since they admit not even of miraculous or merciful exceptions. But in reality there is, of course, no such law; natural selection is merely an inherent feature of the self-reproductive capabilities of organisms. The more prosaic version of the idea that evolution has evolved is the proposition that natural selection produced an emergent form of reproduction, the complex, two-tier human mechanism. This was, moreover, not the first time that evolution had evolved; the evolution from asexual to sexual reproduction, for instance, had been a precedent, albeit on a much less stupendous scale; the emergence of consciousness was comparable rather to the emergence of biological evolution out of the lower order of evolution at work in the inanimate world. Be that as it may, the question arises: what is the nature of the human form of natural selection? How does it differ from that which operates below man?

Like infrahuman biological evolution, the human process follows the principle that adjustive characteristics tend for that very reason to perpetuate themselves; but given the human peculiarities, it does so in its own way. First, since the human form of adjustment is mediated not simply by experience, but by conscious experience, it is adjustment to, specifically, a world experienced as real. Second, since consciousness generates selfhood, conscious organisms must adjust not only to an environment integrated by objects, including other human organisms, but above all to a world constituted by human organisms who are perceived as other selves and who perceive themselves as selves and oneself as a self. Accordingly, the human equivalent of the environmental pressure that operates below man is not the external constraint to adapt or perish, but the intrapsychic pressure to adapt as a self or else suffer the consequences of maladaptation as a self. This peculiarly human quest for 'survival' *as a self* is fuelled by the need for self-identity, which can be satisfied only through self-definition rather than through the mere continuation of organic life. And the need for self-identity – the need

to create and develop our selfhood by making assertions about ourselves
to ourselves and to others, both in thought and in outward speech – is
a natural consequence of the characteristics of a consciousness that has
been generated by speech.

My use of quotation marks when I refer to the specifically human
form of 'survival' may be misunderstood; I take this expression by analogy to the preservation of infrahuman organic life, but not as a mere
figure of speech. The term is justified for two reasons. First, although
the human form of evolutionary selection bears directly only on the
consciousness of human beings, it also affects indirectly – but not less
effectively on that account – the organism as a whole and even its biological survival. For instance, since human beings are aware of their
own reality and that of others, they can seek the destruction of organic
life in themselves and in others (or for that matter, its preservation),
with premeditation and for purely psychological reasons. But second,
the essential point is that, quite apart from the ultimate effect of consciousness on man's *organic* survival, conscious selves as such are moved
above all by the need to be and remain themselves, and only subordi-
nately by the kind of self-preservation that rules in the infrahuman
world. For instance, by far the largest proportion of human behaviour
is motivated by the need of human beings to avoid threats to their self-
identity and self-esteem – posed both by themselves and by others –
than by the need to avoid danger to bodily life. The evolution of consciousness is not ruled by the purpose of surviving organically at all
costs; it depends specifically on the self-preservation of selfhood.

The emergent features of the human form of adaptation explain why
human beings can be well adjusted to their environment in every other
respect, yet mortally maladjusted to themselves and each other. Likewise, they can be profoundly maladjusted to the natural world simply
because of the way in which they perceive it; as environmentalists realize, the most deleterious forms of maladjustment to our habitat need
involve nothing more tangible, nor less likely to be transmitted through
chromosomal exchange, than our assumptions about the natural world
and our attitudes towards it. Thus, upon the appearance of even a
modest level of consciousness, generated by primitive but true speech
– and upon the appearance, thereby entailed, of the cultural matrix in
which consciousness and speech could become self-perpetuating – organic adjustment lost the stellar role it had long enjoyed in evolution.
Thenceforth the significance of genes for human evolution lay not in
what they themselves could determine, but in what could be determined
by the consciousness – and the consequent selfhood – of the organism
that they determined. The genes, therefore, did not so much 'surrender

their primacy' as they acquired a new potentiality: the ability to determine the constitution of organisms capable of having speech and consciousness generated in them by a socio-cultural matrix.

Some terminological stipulations should be made. I shall retain the plain term *genetic means* to designate those reproductive processes that involve chromosomal exchange alone, whereas I will use quotation marks to refer to the *'genetic' means* involved in the reproduction of consciousness. But I specify that this usage does not carry the implication that the latter means are not truly generative. And bowing to established usage, I will reserve *natural selection* for the selection that takes place by genetic means exclusively. One might then, with some justification, refer to the human form of natural selection as *artificial selection*. Yet more fittingly, however, I shall call it *self-selection*. My reasons are, first, that the human form of evolution involves the selective agency of the very consciousness whose characteristics are selected by the evolutionary mechanism; and second, that the process selects specifically for characteristics whose value depends not on meeting requirements laid down by the physical environment, but in satisfying the demands that consciousness imposes upon itself by virtue of its presence to itself.

It will be recalled, however, that natural selection involves no 'selection' except in a figurative sense; to be 'selected' is merely to have survived by virtue of inherited advantages. In this respect there is no difference between the human and the infrahuman mechanism. For self-selection should not be so called because, as some have supposed, 'the new evolution becomes subject to conscious control. Man, alone among all organisms, knows that he evolves and he alone is capable of directing his own evolution.'[34] This proposition describes only the way in which self-selection might take place some day in the future, if its ulterior possibilities should be realized; it may well be that mankind's survival will in the end depend on whether human beings insert a greater measure of conscious control into their evolution than hitherto, but human evolution has so far not ordinarily, if ever, come under conscious control. Evolution by self-selection proceeds for the most part in a non-conscious way, without anyone realizing that it is taking place, or how, or with what effect.

When I stress the absence of conscious control over the evolution of consciousness I do not have in mind primarily the influence of the Freudian or other repressed unconscious over human behaviour; I mean rather that speakers are not necessarily conscious of the nature or the

34 Simpson, *Evolution*, p. 290.

properties of their own speech simply because they know how to speak, and that conscious experiencers usually remain unaware of the nature and properties of consciousness notwithstanding their being conscious. Nevertheless, an investigation of the origin and development of consciousness would amount to a sort of psychoanalysis of the human race, since it would be a conscious working-out of the non-conscious factors that have affected the history of the species.

But there is a deeper reason why such a study would be aptly likened to a psychiatric diagnosis. Consciousness contains the potentiality for self-misinterpretation, and absent-mindedness actualizes it. And since absent-mindedness is a disordered form of consciousness, we can suspect that it is at the root of the self-disruptive, self-imperilling guises that human life not infrequently takes, both in individuals and in groups. Hence the requirement to which I called attention at the outset. Just as we could not claim to have plumbed the nature of conscious life unless we understood its abnormal form, we could not very well claim to have fathomed the origin of human nature unless we knew how and why absent-mindedness appeared in the species at the same time as consciousness, and with what effects. As we proceed, we shall therefore keep in mind the possibility that the origin of the individual and collective disorders of consciousness that afflict human beings may be found in evolutionary events of the distant past.

Unlike the synthetic, this is a *unified* theory. A single evolutionary process in unbroken continuity with animal evolution accounts for the origin and the subsequent development of both the individual and the socio-cultural aspects of human nature. Such a unified yet non-reductionistic theory is made possible only by a unitary but non-reductionistic conception of man: neither the consciousness of the individual nor socio-cultural relations is reducible to organic processes, but the only substantive human entities are individual organisms. For the same reason, the proposed theory, unlike the synthetic, can do justice to the socio-cultural nature of the individual; it is not only a theory of the emergence of conscious life but, more fully stated, a theory of the emergence of the kind of socio-cultural life that only consciousness can support. For socio-cultural life is not superindividual any more than it is 'superorganic'; it is the life of individual organisms, though it is reducible neither to organic functions nor to experiential events occurring in individual organisms in isolation from like events in like organisms. Since by severing the cultural evolution of society from the organic evolution of human individuals the synthetic theory renders problematic the relationship between the individual and the group, I should devote at least a few words to explaining why socio-cultural events, quite like consciousness, must be said to be organic events yet irreducible to the functions of individual organisms.

The differences among the various emergent levels of reality – non-living matter, living organisms, sentient life, and conscious life – are differences in quality and complexity of organization. If conscious life is a yet higher type than ordinary sentient life, the reason is that it is based on the *socio-cultural* organization of individual human organisms. Thus, conscious processes occur exclusively in individual organisms, but are generated and sustained only by the interaction of a multiplicity of individual human organisms. Therefore, human beings have a single life, simultaneously organic and conscious, individual and social; they do not have two lives (organic and conscious), nor *a fortiori* three (individual organic life, non-organic conscious life, and social 'superorganic' life). However, although the consciousness of the individual is a socio-culturally generated, developed, and sustained mode of life, it is generated, developed, and sustained out of nothing but the organic experiential conscious functions of individual organisms. Thus, neither consciousness nor social life is reducible to the organic life of the individual organism. Only an interpretation of human nature that respects and integrates all the facts – the organic, the conscious, and the socio-cultural – could explain cultural evolution as part of the process of the evolution of conscious organisms, which is in turn but the continuation of the evolution of organic life.

After more than a century of investigating human evolution under the auspices of a greater or lesser scientific reductionism, but reductionism at any rate, the term *human evolution* has acquired connotations that weaken its significance; from the study of evolution we have come to expect little more than the explanations of the past that it has given us in the past. This is not enough; there can be no aspect of human self-interpretation to which the study of human evolution should not be directly relevant. An adequate theory should make it possible for us to understand in particular why human cultures have come to be what they have come to be, and why human beings today behave as they behave. Indeed, since the theory interprets cultural evolution as the continuation of the evolution of human nature after its original appearance, it should enable us to gain some understanding of human history as a whole and in continuity with prehistory. The evolution of human nature through cultural means – but cultural means understood as emanating from the properties of speech – would be the concept by reference to which the facts of human history, down to the present, could be organized. The evolutionary pattern of history could then be discerned. The development of consciousness would be the standard by which to measure the meaning of historical events, and the criterion to discriminate between the fundamentally significant and the negligible cultural changes in the history of mankind. And keeping in mind the potential absent-mindedness of consciousness, perhaps we could begin to understand also the ambivalences of human history: why cultural neuroses appear and exist side by side with great achievements, and how consciousness individually and collectively creates mortal dangers for itself.

In this book, however, I shall restrict myself to the study of human evolution only up to the point at which the sort of human being had appeared whose consciousness functioned in essentially the same way as it does in us today. Far too much additional space would be needed to explore how the same theory might explain the thrust of recorded history and the rapid cultural evolution that is typical of the historical age of mankind – though a few aspects of this question will be touched upon in chapters VII and VIII. This investigation will therefore be incomplete. But perhaps it will suffice to raise our expectations of the theory of evolution, by showing the wide range of practical and intellectual human problems to which it is germane.

CHAPTER FIVE

The emergence of consciousness

We cannot, for obvious reasons, trace the process whereby animal communication became speech, and speech generated thought and consciousness; but we may be able to reconstruct it none the less. For we know with certainty what the outcome was: it was ourselves, organisms that communicate assertively, experience consciously, and behave as human beings observably behave today by virtue of their consciousness and speech. And we can safely assume that the point of departure was some sort of organism that, though lacking all the specifically human traits, was a suitable candidate for appointment to human status; it must have had highly developed abilities to communicate vocally, though non-assertively, and to experience, though not consciously. By analysing the differences between assertive and non-assertive communication, and between conscious and non-conscious experience, we can estimate the obstacles, so to speak, that evolution had to overcome before it could have created us. Following this procedure, the first section will try to show that if a communicator learns to perceive the efficient and the final causality of his communicative behaviour – and therefore his reality as a communicator – non-assertive communication can evolve into speech. This will enable us to reconstruct, in the second section, the process that created speech.

The third section will then explain how the progression outlined in chapter III – from non-conscious to conscious experience through speech and thought – would have come about once hominids had learned to speak, namely, through the mutual involution of experience and the communication of experience. When experience is communicated assertively, the opportunity arises for the communicator to identify what he experiences with what he communicates; the experience coincides with itself and acquires self-presence. At first, however, only a proto-consciousness would have emerged, an elementary form characterized by rudimentary self-presence: experience would have been present to itself only while being actually asserted in speech. The consciousness of the earliest humans may therefore be described as *linguistic consciousness*, in contrast with the *cogitative consciousness*, or thought, which would have developed out of it as speech became interiorized into purely imaginary assertion. For once a speaker learns to assert his experience while communicating it, he can experience himself asserting what he communicates. He thus awakens to his own assertiveness; from a little self-presence, fully assertive experience can eventually grow. In time, the ability to make experience immediately present to itself in *immediate consciousness* would have arisen. Conscious quality could now have accrued to experience whether it was being communicated or not; it required not even the self-communication otherwise called thought.

As we have seen, a cardinal aspect of the theory is that the emergence of speech was, by another name, the appearance of a reproductive mechanism that was not reducible to the transmission of genes. After we reconstruct the emergence of speech, thought, and immediate consciousness, we shall be concerned, in the fourth and fifth sections, with the origin and nature of the self-reproductive powers of consciousness, and of the genital apparatus – the socio-cultural matrix, as I have called it – in which such powers are vested.

I have drawn attention to the potential for self-misinterpretation inherent in consciousness. It would not be strange if consciousness were simply to remain ignorant of its nature, since the reflexive activity that produces self-interpretation is, though connatural to consciousness, not identical with it; but that consciousness should positively misunderstand itself is almost paradoxical. And yet, the phenomenon of absent-mindedness manifests this very semi-opacity of consciousness to itself despite its self-presence. Since the reconstruction of the emergence of the normal consciousness does not, without more, explain the emergence of the kind of consciousness that realizes its potential for defective self-presence, in the sixth section we shall study separately the special features of human evolution that account for it.

This will complete, however, only the first stage of the proposed investigation into human origins. For the emergence of immediate consciousness sparked the further evolution of speech and thought, since these activities could now be undertaken in the daylight of immediate conscious experience. And the evolution of speech and thought would have affected in turn the evolution of consciousness, since consciousness would then have been generated by a developed form of speech and thought. These developments – the evolutionary maturation of speech, thought, and consciousness through self-selection – will be examined in chapter vi.

1. The conditions of the possibility of the emergence of speech

Let us analyse the assertiveness of speech. Observe, first, that since a speaker is a communicator who intends to communicate, he must be the kind of communicator whose signal-making does not simply obey a communicative purpose, but a communicative purpose *experienced* as such. For an animal communicator, too, is moved to make signals by virtue of its purposive nature, in the sense that natural selection made it evolve into a communicator only because its communicative behaviour was adjustive. The animal communicator must be said thus to seek ends which, as a matter of fact, are achieved through its signal-making. But since the animal does not make signals *because* it experiences that its communicative behaviour serves its purposes, its signal-making remains disconnected, so far as its experience is concerned, from its goal-seeking. The human communicator, on the contrary, integrates the two in the experience that his signal-making is a means to achieve the end of communicating (and whatever other ends might be achieved through his conveying a meaning to the communicand).

But this implies a prior difference: unlike the animal, the human communicator perceives his signalling behaviour as having the effect of conveying his meaning. The animal behaves in a way that, as it happens, has communicative effects; but it does not experience any connection between its behaviour and those effects – whereas the speaker does. The latter synthesizes his goal-seeking and his signalling activity into a single act: the act of speech. This act integrates, therefore, communication and experience: it is a communicative act that includes (a) the experience of intending to communicate, and (b) the experience that such communicative behaviour is apt to bring about the effects that fulfil such intent.

In the *last* analysis, therefore, the emergence of speech was the appearance of a new kind of finality: the ability to intend to communicate. Note well that this ability implied not only a new way to communicate – namely, intentionally – but also a new way to intend goals, that is, through means that were themselves experienced precisely as means towards a goal. The emergence of such intentional communication, however, presupposed the communicator's perception of his signals as a means that could effectively bring about the communicative effect. Thus, the emergence of speech had introduced in the *first* place a new kind of efficient causality: the ability to cause communicative effects as such. Mark carefully also that this ability implied not only a new way to communicate – that is, with awareness of the capacity of signal-making for having communicative effects – but a new way to achieve effects as well: through activities that were themselves experienced precisely as the efficient cause of such effects. The emergence of speech was rooted, therefore, in the discovery of the *means* of communication in a twofold sense: signal-making was a means to achieve communicative *effects* and, consequently, a means to reach communicative *ends*.

The efficient and the final causality of speech are so closely related that they may seem to require each other before either of them can be realized. This is understandable. When we today reflect upon the nature of speech we already know how to speak and are indeed proficient at it; in us the two are highly integrated, and we can distinguish between them only through disciplined reflexion upon our experience of speaking. We take for granted (a) that to speak is to use means of communication that achieve a communicative *effect*, and (b) that we speak because we *want* to communicate. We tend to assume, therefore, that if one is aware that communications communicate one will necessarily realize also that a communicating will is the cause of communicative behaviour. But further reflexion may show that it is not so. The latter presupposes the former, but the first can stand alone. One can learn that one's communicative behaviour has communicative effects before one discovers that one's will to communicate underlies such behaviour, but not vice versa. The possibility therefore arises that the transition from vocal communication to speech may have had two phases. The first would have culminated in the ability to use means of communication intentionally, in the limited sense that communicators, having learned that their signalling behaviour actually had communicative effects, were able to make signals which they experienced as causes of such effects. A certain degree of assertiveness would have accrued to their signal-making even at this stage, and the animal mode of communication would have been transcended – though barely. The outcome of the second phase would have been the more intensive assertiveness of communications made not only because they had a communicative effect, but more particularly because the communicator experienced that they embodied and fulfilled his purpose of communicating; it was this purpose that caused the communicative behaviour to be directed towards accomplishing the communicative effect. We shall have occasion, as we proceed, to come back repeatedly to the distinction between these two components of assertive communication.

To sum up, the emergence of speech depended on the appearance,

in certain hominids, of a rudimentary ability to organize sense information in the light of their perception of their own *efficient* and *final*
communicative causality as such, and therefore of their *reality* as communicators. I say *as such*, because many animals are able to rule themselves by the behavioural equivalent of the ideas of reality, efficacy, and
finality; upon experiencing objects they react by exerting their causal
powers so as to fulfil adaptively their needs and wants. It is a very
different matter, however, to appreciate that reality is real, and that
behaviour achieves effects – changes in other human beings and in the
natural world – that fulfil wants and needs in oneself.

Moreover, I speak of the *perception* of their communicative efficacy,
purposiveness, and reality, not of their conception of these; for prior to
the emergence of consciousness, hominids had no ability to conceive
anything, nor hence to experience anything as a particular instance of
a general type. Thus, they could not have learned to perceive efficacy
and finality as such in the reality of their own communicative activities
by experiencing communicative behaviour as a particular instance of
efficient and final causality, or the reality of communicative behaviour
as a particular instance of reality. For the same reason, I have referred
to the early speakers' perception of their *communicative* reality, revealed
by their *communicative* efficacy and finality: before speakers had become
conscious they could not have conceived the general categories of reality,
efficacy, and finality, and therefore could not have experienced their
reality, efficacy, and finality in general.

All this suggests that human beings discovered reality and efficient
and final causality as such within themselves, and indeed that they first
learned of these from their own assertive signal-making rather than from
any other activity. We can understand why this should have been so:
only communicative behaviour was capable of providing the sort of
reality, efficacy, and finality that could have been experienced as such
even in the absence of these three concepts.[1] Indeed, it was their experiencing them as such that laid the empirical basis on which these
concepts eventually developed as categories of general application. Conversely, if these three categories remain crucially important in the conscious life of human beings, it is because their discovery was involved
from the outset in the emergence of such life.

But the role of the categories in human evolution will concern us only
in later chapters. At the moment our task is rather to apply what we

---

1 The reason why only communicative behaviour could have provided it is explained
in Appendix 1.

have just learned to a reconstruction of the emergence of speech. How could it have come about that animal communication became speech?

2. The emergence of speech

The proposed reconstruction assumes that the transition from vocal communication to speech was made possible by the exercise of the same experiential abilities that are found in the higher infrahumans. We need suppose only the peculiarity that our prehuman ancestors were unusually skilled in the animal experiential arts, able to make finer discriminations and more complex integrations than their genetically less well-endowed fellow creatures. Each step of the process was within the capabilities of other qualitatively similar forms of life. As with all evolution, the trick was to parlay the achievements, the feat was to stay the course.

All animals, indeed all living things, can take advantage of the relationships of antecedent and consequent found in nature, 'A, then B'; to do so is the same as to adapt. Beyond this is the ability not merely to take advantage of them, but to perceive the relationships. And a step yet closer to the perception of causality as such is the ability of the higher animals to learn not only that 'A, then B,' but also that 'Not A, then not B,' and to integrate the two experiences into the *invariability* that describes the two taken together: 'If, and only if, A, then B.' Of course, in animals the integration of these experiences is not conceptual; a laboratory rat that has learned to behave in function of perceived invariable sequences – for example, it invariably goes to the trough when the bell rings, having been conditioned to associate the antecedent sound and the consequent availability of food – need not be thought to have acquired the idea of invariability, even if it responds if, and only if, the antecedent is perceived. Behaviourism explains animal life very adequately. The perception of negation and absence by animals may be wondered about. Animals appear incapable of *sending* negative signals, but the higher ones at least can 'read' negative signs or the absence of a sign. A rat can be trained to expect a food pellet whenever a certain stimulus *ceases*. Many mammals engage in playful mock fights in which they nip but do not bite each other; the mock fight means, in effect, a non-fight, and the playfulness of the exchange depends on the fact that the 'playful nip denotes the bite, but *does not denote* what would be denoted by the bite.'[2]

---

2 Gregory Bateson, *Steps to an Ecology of Mind* (New York, 1972), p. 180, italics mine. I do not agree with Bateson's conclusion from this observation, however, that

There can be little doubt, therefore, that almost any hominid could have learned to perceive the concomitance of his signals and their perceptible influence on the behaviour of communicands. But this was not at all the same as learning that signals were efficient causes of such effects. The latter would have required that the communicator relate his signals to the *experience* of the communicand, so as to discover that signals had *communicative* effects. Of course, the communicator could not have perceived *that* communications communicated unless he could have perceived *the* communications in the first place. This condition, however, was hardly a stumbling-block. A barking dog can hear its own bark as well as every other dog's; a signing chimpanzee can see its own gestures as well as those of its human teacher. The problem was rather to realize that the observable effects of the signal on the communicand depended on the communicand's having the *experience* of receiving a message. Moreover, this effect had to be identified specifically as the communicand's reception of the meaning that the signal conveyed. In other words, the communicator had to learn that the communicand heard the signal *as a signal*, or that the communicand experienced the sounds as meaningful sounds. But how could the communicator have learned precisely what another person experienced? And how could he have learned that the meaning heard by the communicand was the same as that which his signal communicated, since he was not yet a speaker and therefore did not even realize that his own signals conveyed a meaning?

It is a homely, though in this context useful, truth that one hand cannot wash itself but that two can wash each other. The communicator could have learned that his signals carried a meaning when they were

---

the animals experience their signals as signals; for there is no reason to suppose that the exchange obeys a communicative purpose. It is clear that the nipped animal perceives the nipper's behaviour as a sign meaning 'not-bite,' but nothing indicates that the nipping animal *sends the signal* 'not-bite.' Bateson fails to consider communication from the communicator's standpoint, and mistakes the nipper's behaviour for signalling simply because the nipped animal takes a *meaning* from the sign.

The deeper confusion underlying Bateson's mistake may be worth unravelling. Negative assertions are an infallible indication of the ability to perceive signals as signals – and thus of the ability to speak – though the reason is that they are assertions, not that they are negative. For there is a difference between making or receiving a signal the meaning of which is negative, and *meaning* the negative meaning of such signal or receiving it as having been so *meant*. Therefore, even if animals should be observed *sending* signals that in fact were negative (as contrasted with merely making signs that had such negative content), it would be no evidence of the ability to send signals *as such*, or because they were signals. What the latter requires is assertiveness, not specifically the ability to communicate negations.

heard by the communicand, if he should have learned at the same time that his own signals carried a meaning when they were heard by himself. And both could have been learned simultaneously, if he should have managed to identify the vocal signals that he sent to the communicand, and the same signals sent by the communicand to him when the latter and he exchanged roles. That is, to appreciate the communicative efficacy of signals he had but to realize that others reacted to his signals for the same reason and in the same way that he reacted to *the same signals* when put out by them. Conversely, the key to discerning the shared meaning was learning that his signals held the same meaning *for others* that (as he now began to realize) they held for *him*, because the same signals, when made by another, had the same meaning for him that he conveyed to the other. If when I yell 'Duck!' you duck, and when you yell 'Duck!' I duck – because long ago both you and I learned to do this as ordinary non-assertive communicators – and if I can *hear myself* yell 'Duck!' when *you duck* in reaction to my yell, even as I can *hear you* yell 'Duck!' when *I duck* in reaction to your signal, I am in a position to identify what I hear with what you hear. With the benefit of nothing but enough perceptual ability, I can learn that you experience as I do, by learning at the same time that I experience as you do. I can discover, thus, that the signal you hear and the signal I hear have the same meaning, and therefore that my signal is the cause of a communicative effect on you, even as your signal has a like effect on me; I can do this because my own signal now conveys meaning to me. In sum, the early communicator would have appreciated the similarity between himself and his communicand – but only because he, too, had become his own communicand. To learn to speak is to learn the rudiments of how to empathize, whether with other selves or with oneself.

The communicator, however, need not have appreciated that the similarity was between the meaning *intentionally* conveyed by his signal and the meaning received both by the communicand and by himself; for we are still in the first phase and the communicator has not yet learned to perceive himself as a sender of signals. Indeed, hearing his own signal without any sense of his own selfhood is what permitted him both to hear his own signal as a stranger would, and to hear a stranger's signals as identifiable with his own. At this stage, therefore, he would have heard his own vocal signals without suspecting the privacy of either his experience or the communicand's. On the other hand, once he had perceived the mutual relationship of his signals and his communicand's, he had created the possibility of eventually intending to communicate.

Though at this stage the apprentice speaker had discovered that signals *told* a meaning, he had not yet learned to *say* the meaning that they carried. To do so he had further to realize that his signalling behaviour depended upon his wanting the communicand to receive a meaning. The root of the required perceptual ability can be found, however, at that earlier stage of evolution when the ability emerged in animals to experience themselves and their own behaviour from within. Proprioception is the basis of a more sophisticated and intimate mode of self-experience than the experience of oneself through external sensation only; it makes possible, for instance, reflexive sense experience and animal memory. With sufficient proprioceptive and integrative ability, the apprentice speaker could have learned to perceive his signal-making as an activity embodying his *striving* for communicative effect. We today can easily perceive the organic manifestations of our wanting to say something, for instance, when we 'ache' to rebut the public speaker's abuse of his platform but cannot for the sake of manners or practicality actually speak up. It feels like a vague discomfort; we want to 'get it off our chest'; we squirm with restlessness and sit on the edge of our chair. If this sort of perception should have been integrated by the apprentice speaker with his prior experience of signals as causally related to the communicative effect on the communicand, he would have been able to perceive that his signal-making obeyed his desire to achieve a communicative effect. And having reached this point, the communicator would have learned to speak. In the first phase he had learned that signals had a communicative effect, achieved by the communicand hearing, quite as he did, what the signal told. In the final phase he learned that signals had to be sent before they could have a communicative effect, and that they were sent so that they should bring about such effect. Signal-making had become signal-asserting, and the voicing of vocal signals now *said* what the signal told.

Undoubtedly, it is much easier for us today, when we already know how to speak, to interpret the bodily feelings created by our striving to communicate than it would have been aboriginally – but it would not have been impossible. As I interpret the results of human training of chimpanzees in the use of sign language, it appears that these animals, apparently without any inkling of their communicative causality, nevertheless manage to insert their goal-seeking into their signal-making, and therefore learn to use conventional signals invented by man and even to invent their own.[3] It should not be deemed unlikely, therefore, that

3 See, for example, R.A. Gardner and B. Gardner, 'Teaching Sign-Language to a Chimpanzee,' *Science*, 165 (1969), pp. 664–72; idem, 'Two-Way Communication with a Chimpanzee,' in A. Schrier and F. Stollnite, eds., *Behavior of Nonhuman Primates*,

the earliest human beings managed to learn as much. The difference is that such proto-humans would have been able to experience at the same time that their signals were the cause of communicative effects on their communicands. The integration of these two experiences would have transformed the mere communicator into one whose experience of communicating was present to itself.

Presumably any form of signal-making would have been apt in principle to be invested with assertiveness. Consciousness is generated in

---

vol. iv, pp. 267–77 (New York, 1971); Eugene Linden, *Apes, Men and Language* (New York, 1976). Chimpanzees learn to use signs in order to achieve a communicative end: so much is reasonably clear. The evidence for this is that the signal, *which is learned*, effectively achieves a communicative end. We must therefore conclude that the chimpanzee has acquired the ability to insert its goal-seeing into its signal-making: and this is precisely what I have described as the *second* phase in the transformation of mere communication into speech. Nevertheless, I hesitate to conclude that chimpanzees have been taught to communicate assertively, though I do not rule out the possibility. According to the theory here proposed, the communicator's discovery of his own communicative finality marks the emergence of speech only because it culminates the achievement of the first phase, in which he learns to *experience* the causal efficacy of signal-making, as contrasted with merely *taking advantage* of it, as animals do. But it is not clear that this element is present in trained chimpanzees. That is, the evidence is consistent with their having learned to strive for goals through signal-making – quite as rats can be taught to strive through simpler forms of learned behaviour – but does not go so far as to show that they have learned to strive for the effect of *conveying a meaning* to a communicand. This conclusion would be warranted if there were evidence that, for instance, the animal was capable of sending a signal with a meaning contrary to fact, not simply for the sake of procuring a desired result, but specifically for the purpose of doing so through causing the communicand to *experience* the meaning contrary to fact. The facts on which rests a well-known report of a chimpanzee's 'lying,' however, do not quite amount to this. The possibility that positive results from experimentation or casual observation may be obtained in the future, however, should not be discarded *a priori*.

But an alternative interpretation is also possible: that under human influence a true development of the animal's experiential life has been achieved, but with teratological results akin to a human-animal genetic crossing-over; their acquired ability to use sign language has some of the features of speech, but lacks others. The malformation would consist in their having learned to use sign language purposively, but without having learned *how* sign language works – whereas in man, as I have theorized, the latter is the pre-condition of the emergence of fully assertive communication. Nevertheless, the animal has learned how to make signals as such – and, if so, has acquired the potential to invent new signals – because it has learned that signal-making can bring about certain satisfactory results. Nevertheless, the animal does not *experience* that signals have a communicative effect, nor does it *experience* its own behaviour as communicative. In sum, training in sign-making has produced a superior form of infrahuman communicative activity, but one that nevertheless lacks assertiveness and is therefore not true speech.

congenitally deaf children amongst us today as they learn to communicate assertively by non-vocal means; nothing in the process we have
studied seems to depend on the signals being audible rather than, say,
visible. It is reasonably certain, however, that only these two modalities
were in evolution's short list, since only they would have permitted the
development of efficient and complex systems of hominid non-assertive
communication in the first place; the signs that human beings can make
which are receivable in other sense modalities either have much too
short a range, or are very difficult if not impossible to modulate, or both.
But why vocal rather than visual signals?

The reason may be the fortuitous circumstance that a vocal signaller
can perceive his own signals *only* in the same way as his communicand
can, namely by the signaller's *hearing* the sound of his voice through
external sensation. He cannot perceive his own vocal signal-making by
feeling proprioceptively the *making* of the sounds, as he can the making
of hand or other visible gestures. Human vocal signals are produced
mostly by the activity of the laryngeal muscles; however, proprioceptors
'are absent from ... [these] muscles, and feedback control [in vocal sound-
making] comes by way of the ear.'[4] Thus, human beings cannot learn
to control vocal sounds – and therefore cannot learn to make vocal signals
– unless they can hear the sounds that they make. This is of, course,
the reason why congenitally deaf children do not ordinarily learn to
make vocal signals.[5]

The importance of this chance condition for the emergence of speech
may be appreciated if we recall what mere vocal communicators had to
do in order to grasp the causal relationship of signal to communicative
effect – namely, to identify the meaning heard by the communicand
with the meaning that they heard in their own (and in the communicand's) vocal signals. If proprioception of vocal sound-making had been
possible, the identification would have been much more difficult. The
speaker would have controlled his sound-making proprioceptively; although he would have heard his vocal sounds, his sound-making would

4 Bernard G. Campbell, *Human Evolution: An Introduction to Man's Adaptations* (Chicago,
    1966), p. 308.
5 Most so-called deaf children are not totally deaf, and can therefore, with varying
    degrees of effort and success, learn to make vocal sounds. But even children who
    suffer from complete or almost complete congenital deafness can sometimes learn
    to speak making conventional vocal signs – though with yet greater difficulty
    and barely intelligible results – through a technique that provides a certain amount
    of artificial feedback, namely, feeling with their fingers the vibrations transmitted
    from the larynx to the skin.

have been perceived primarily as bodily effort rather than as sound. In contrast, he could have perceived another human being's signals only through hearing, not at all through proprioception. Thus the absence of proprioception in vocal signalling facilitated enormously, perhaps decisively, the speaker's identification of what he heard with what his listener heard; it made possible for him to hear the sound of his voice in the same way as his listener did, and to hear the sound of another's voice in the same way in which he did his own.[6] Now, proprioception was required at the *second* stage; moreover, it was proprioception of the striving, not of the signal-making. But proprioceptive ability in other respects, combined with its absence in signal-making, would have facilitated the emergence of assertive signal-making; and this combination obtains in vocal signalling, but not in making visible signs.

This reconstruction implies that the relation between speech and language is the very opposite of what we usually suppose. Both in the individual and in the species language precedes the ability to speak. That is, in both cases the ability can appear only because a prior system of communicative signs – a language – is already in existence and available as the raw material, as it were, that speakers can learn to process assertively. Ontogenetically, however, the language that precedes speech is a human language, the signals system of a community that already knows how to speak. In the phylogeny of speech, however, it was merely an animal system of communicative signs. Thus, there is no mystery about the origin of human *languages*, at least in principle. The various systems of human vocal communication descend from whatever systems of non-assertive vocal signs pre-humans used. The difficult question is

6 There may have been another reason why vocal communication was more suited to the emergence of assertiveness than other forms: that auditory imagination and recall are much better developed in man than the visual. For instance, photographic visual memory is rare, but its auditory equivalent is enjoyed, to some degree, by most people: almost everyone can memorize and recall fairly long dialogues with some fidelity, and some can do it verbatim; and it may take better-than-average musical ability to reproduce vocally a musical passage, but almost everyone can reproduce one in imagination in some detail. The imaginative manipulation of visual objects in space, likewise, is less well developed in most people than the ability to manipulate concepts (i.e., acoustic images, mental words) syllogistically. It is possible, however, that all this may be the consequent rather than the antecedent of the emergence of assertiveness as a quality of audible signal-making. In any event, palaeontology suggests that the areas of the brain that mediate vocal communication had developed to a high degree in hominids long before the appearance of *Homo sapiens*; it seems likely that unusually high proficiency in *vocal* communication had been reached by them before consciousness emerged.

rather the origin of *speech* – not how we came to use words, nor how words came to mean what they mean, but how they came to be used to *mean* what they mean.

Many students of speech, however, have been tempted to think that the human languages must have originated through convention about the meaning and arrangement of words. For it is certain that the signs and the grammatical rules used by speakers are arbitrary; they have no necessary relationship to what they signify. But as others have facetiously pointed out: in what language would the proceedings of the convention have been held? More accurately, the objection is that to agree on which signs and compositions should carry which meanings would be impossible in the absence of speech, because to assert what a sign or a composition shall mean, or to accept someone else's assertion to the same effect, is possible for a communicator only after he has learned that signs can be used to communicate. But no convention is needed. As early human beings acquired assertiveness they would have had at their disposal a fairly large and complex system of vocal signs that already had 'meaning' in the same sense as all other bilateral animal communications did. The signs and the way to use them had been 'invented' by natural selection and 'imposed' by it on the communicating group as its language despite the arbitrariness of the signs. A dolphin's chirp, for instance, is not a natural sign of sexual receptivity or of danger on the starboard bow, and other species use different 'words' to convey the same 'concepts.' But we can safely assume that dolphins did not hold an Aesopian convention to assign meaning to the signs that, as a species, they 'learned' to use. Now, before speech emerged, the languages of prehumans would have been limited to the range of signals that natural selection had 'taught' them; without assertiveness no language can be open-ended. As soon as speech appeared, however, languages automatically became indefinitely expandable, like the series of natural numbers – and for the same reason, namely, the self-presence of the experience involved. They were restricted only by the finite extent of assertible human experience and of the gamut of purposes to which speech might be put. By the same token, signs could *then* acquire meaning by convention and habit, and arbitrary rules could be created in the same way. For the ability to speak, being the ability to assert and compose signs, is the ability to convert anything whatever into a sign: 'One if by land, two if by sea,' and 'Tie a yellow ribbon, if you still love me.'

Why should evolution have encouraged this line of development? How did natural selection channel variations in vocal communicative ability towards assertiveness? Presumably the principle was that evolution naturally protects the organism's ability to play an increasingly determining role in its adjustive relationships to its environment. Evolution logically favours, for instance, the ability of sentient organisms to discriminate and integrate – to relate and unify, after breaking down as finely as possible – the stimulation they receive. But as we have seen, communication does not of itself give the communicator much of a role in determining its relations to its environment: the bee profits from signalling only insofar as it is a member of a team. Communication is directly advantageous to the communicator; however, when the latter acquires the ability to control its communicating behaviour; by gaining a measure of control over the information to be received by the communicand, it increases its control over its environment. Natural selection favoured the emergence of assertiveness, then, because generally it fosters the transformation of adaptive behaviour from a passive process into an active and purposive self-relation to the environment. Communication per se has relatively little value for the organism in this respect, but assertive communication has much.

Like knowledge, assertive communication is power, since it gives man's puny bodily energy an almost infinite leverage; a little human muscle power goes very far, because speech enables man to apply it with microscopic discrimination and almost magic efficacy. The emergence of speech, however, meant the metamorphosis, not merely the improvement, of communication. For instance, speech transformed the ability to utter a sound alerting a fellow hunter to danger, who might then react appropriately, into the ability to *tell* him what he might, should, or must do; the communicator's *choice* of signal, and not merely his signalling activity, influenced the outcome. Moreover, by learning that signals were signals, and that his signals were under his command, the speaker acquired command over himself as well – or at least the potential for it. For what he could assert to others he could assert for his benefit alone. More about this when we discuss the emergence of thought.

Purposive control appears in different degrees and forms at the various levels of animal evolution. But when animal life develops the human ability to communicate intentionally, the organism has acquired some sway over a new sphere, namely, the world of communicands; the range of the organism's influence now extends beyond the field of its own experience and encompasses that of others. Its power multiplies accordingly, because it can now impress into its service the power of others – usually on condition that it lend its power to others as well. Moreover, the communicator's social group – and potentially the whole species – has acquired a new significance. The society is no longer like a supra-individual organism whose members mesh together – from outside each other, like rack and pinion as it were – by virtue of their specialized functions and contributions to the whole. They are bound rather from within, by their *experienced sameness* – which depends on their capacity for empathy, their ability to experience what others experience. In short, their fundamental social bond is created by their experience of each other's reality and selfhood, by their mutual recognition as conscious, actually existing selves. He would not be human who did not recognize the humanity of other human beings; and none could recognize the humanity of others except to the exact degree that he did his own.

Finally, let us remark briefly on the evolving role of the *content* of communications as we ascend from the lower forms of communication to speech. As animal communication evolved, natural selection heightened the purposiveness of signalling behaviour, but the fact that signal-making presupposed a world remained essentially unchanged. As vocal communication became speech, however, the world was no longer merely there: it was there to be asserted and talked about. The communicator had been brought face to face with the fact that the signal had a content; he had learned that communication involved, besides the communicand and himself, the world as subject of speech. In a sense, therefore, speech transformed not only the vocal communicator, but also his natural environment. When our ancestors began to speak, only an inattentive observer of the event would have thought that the world had remained unchanged; in fact, it had been fundamentally affected – namely, in respect of its relationship to the new creature, man. For henceforth the physical environment would not be the bare world that surrounds the beast, but the cosmos that man encompasses in speech. This is but another way of saying that thereafter the principal agent of evolutionary selection would no longer be the outer environment, but the world as interiorized by the kind of experience that speech had made present to itself. And this is why, once speech had emerged, the appearance of thought and the fullness of consciousness were only a matter of time.

3. The emergence of consciousness

The advent of speech was the direct result of the operation of nothing but natural selection; but the appearance of even the most elementary level of consciousness was the outcome of the peculiar interaction into which experience and assertive communication enter once the latter has emerged. I proposed earlier that as the communicator began to experience his own communications as communications of his experience, his experience gradually became present to itself. But now I will put it more exactly: his *vocally* asserted experience became *auditorily* present to itself. The self-presence of mediate consciousness (i.e., the proto-consciousness of speakers before they developed immediate consciousness) would not have been, therefore, quite the same as the self-presence of immediate sense consciousness. It could not have been strictly so called, since it was only the *coincidence* of (a) the contents of an experience, insofar as they were signified by the speaker's act of *speech*, and (b) the contents of the same experience, but insofar as they were experienced by the speaker's act of *hearing* what he said. It was, therefore, the identity of the contents of *two* different, though simultaneous and coincident acts. (Moreover, both these acts were subsequent to the prior act of experience that provided their contents.) Thus, the act of saying, for instance, 'apple' and the act of hearing oneself say 'apple' coincide in the content 'apple,' which after being *seen* is, first, *said*, and second, *heard*. The self-presence of immediate consciousness, however, is the coincidence of (a) the contents of an act of experience, and (b) the act of experiencing the contents. This coincidence is achieved through the *single* act of experiencing the contents. The act of consciously seeing an apple reveals to the experiencer, simultaneously and by a single act, the 'apple' and the '[experienced]' status of the '[experienced] apple.' This is, therefore, self-coincidence or self-presence, properly so called.

But how was the transition made from the coincidence of the contents of experience and communication in speech to the self-presence of experience in consciousness? Our study of consciousness in chapter II suggested the answer: through the mediation of assertive self-communication, or thought. The process may be summed up as follows. Once communication has become assertive, the communicator has learned, in effect, that he is a communicator; he learns this, as we have seen, by learning that his behaviour is the cause of the same effect upon his communicand that his communicand's behaviour has upon him. But anyone who has learned this is in a good position to learn to speak to himself, or to think. And learning to think entails learning that what one communicates to oneself is one's experience; that is, it entails learning that one is an experiencer. Once this has been learned, however, the final lesson naturally follows: learning to experience while experiencing oneself as an experiencer.

But let us consider the matter at a more leisurely pace. Let us try to account for the emergence of consciousness in the unqualified sense – immediate consciousness – out of the mediate, linguistic, proto-consciousness aboriginally generated by speech, through the transformation of linguistic consciousness into thought.

A. The emergence of thought

Nowadays every human being is able from a fairly early stage to say something without telling it to anyone else but himself. We have seen that this ability cannot precede the ability to speak. But the species, too, could have developed the ability to think only out of the prior ability to assert experience vocally; the difference is that, whereas now the individual is prompted to speak inaudibly by those who already know how, the species had no elders to help it acquire the same skill. How, then, might thought have evolved out of speech?

Memory is the ability to store the contents of experience, and *imagination* is the ability to retrieve, reproduce, and reprocess the stored contents. Neither of these is peculiarly human. Animals store, retrieve, reproduce, and reprocess experience; the habitual use among the higher animals of signals with a constant meaning taught to them by humans is only one instance of this ability. But when the animal makes use of what in fact is its past experience, no intent to do so need be supposed; there are no indications that it makes use of it as past, or because it is past. All we observe is that stored past experience becomes part of the present experiential process; the animal had been 'marked' or in-formed in the past, and its having been so affected is part of its present condition as it undergoes current in-formation and then processes it experientially. And this, presumably, was all that our ancestors were able to do before they acquired the rudiments of consciousness – though we may also suppose that they were unusually skilled at remembering and imagining, albeit not consciously.

Eventually, however, they became speakers; the remembering and imagining of the sounds they had long used to communicate had now acquired a modicum of assertiveness. But their assertive reproduction of the sounds would have, at first, fallen short of thought; reproducing the sounds would have invariably taken place audibly or else not at all. That is, the imagined sounds could not have been asserted in imagination *only*, but required actual speech. Thus, in order to become able to say something in imagination only – or to think – human beings did not have to learn to remember and imagine vocal significative sounds previously learned; this skill antedated speech. Rather, they had to learn to *say* the meaning of the imagined sounds, but without making the vocal sounds; they had to learn to imagine *assertively* what they already knew how to imagine. However, if the ability to remember and reproduce past experience in imagination is supposed, then upon the transformation of vocal communication into speech it would not have been difficult for early man to discover the possibility of purely imaginary speech. The transition may have been mediated by his discovering that he could speak aloud, but only to himself – quite as children often do today. To do so is to make assertive vocal communicative signs in the absence of an apparent communicand – though there is, in fact, a communicand, namely, oneself. The transition would have been facilitated also by the uncertain control over his communication that the speaker would have had at the earliest stages: whenever he wanted to communicate, he would have blurted out what he wanted to say; to conceive the purpose of saying something to an absent communicand would have ordinarily resulted in his actually saying it. He could thus have learned to speak aloud for his own hearing alone. From this he could have passed to speaking inaudibly to himself. And this was a way of asserting communicative signs that gave wings to words.

Flights of imaginary vocal fancy are useful; thinking is both faster and freer than audible speech. Besides, once the ability to think has been acquired, the faculties of memory and recall become transformed as well. The thinker no longer simply possesses stored information that can be inserted into current processes only as the biochemistry of the brain may dictate. To the extent that he has become conscious, he has acquired a means to select and access the stored information; he can 'search his mind.' He may not know how he manages it, but he can nevertheless use the biochemistry of his brain to dictate changes in the biochemistry of his brain. In short, being able to say what he meant when he spoke, and being able to grasp the meaning of what he said to another, early speaking man must have gradually learned to grasp the meaning of what he said to himself, able to take the meaning of what he asserted even when he was not speaking audibly. The ability to *say* something in imagination only, and to 'hear' it as clearly as if it were being said aloud, had appeared. Though immediate conscious perception was still beyond him, early man could now think.

Thought, the new way to exercise the ability to speak, enhanced the rudimentary self-presence of speech by interiorizing speech: the self-involvement of consciousness begins at this point. Because I can speak to another, I can speak to myself; because I can speak to myself, I can hear myself as a speaker unto myself: the interiority of thought leads to the interiority of selfhood. The elementary self-presence of speech is heightened by thought because, once the speaker can think, he is not distracted, as it were, by the audible sound of his voice when he addresses his message to another. In an animated conversation, for instance, we can become oblivious of ourselves; indeed, unless we have more than common introspective skill we do not ordinarily hear ourselves think while we speak aloud. (This is what hampers inept public speakers; they cannot 'think on their feet.') When we merely think, on the contrary, we cannot possibly not hear our own discourse. *Making* the imaginary sounds is one and the same act as *hearing* them in imagination. Nor do we learn much about ourselves merely by making our experience known to another. But we may if, when we communicate it, we also think it; we then stop informing others about ourselves and inform ourselves about ourselves.[7] Once a thinking organism had appeared, the fullness of consciousness was not very far behind.

B. *The emergence of immediate consciousness*

Let us take note of the differences and similarities between thought and immediate consciousness, and between them and speech. Experience takes place in a variety of sense modalities. But when it is signified vocally it is translated into signs that can be experienced, by both communicator and communicand, through hearing alone: all the sense modalities are channelled into one. Since consciousness began when the vocal communicator's experience, translated into audible signs, became present to itself, the proto-consciousness of the early speaker was awakened only in the auditory mode; he continued to experience in every sense modality, but his experience could become present to itself only when given auditory form by being communicated through audible signs. Therefore, the proto-conscious quality of experience could be generated only under the twofold condition that the experience be actually communicated, and that it be communicated in audible form. The emergence of thought did not change this. The contents of experience could have been thought only by being communicated (to oneself) in imagined 'audible' signs; even today we think almost exclusively in the oral-auditory mode.[8] The changes introduced by thought were only (a) that the

7 A yet more effective way, however, is to talk to another not to make our experience known, but to facilitate our thinking our experience to ourselves by asserting it out loud, and to have the communicand reflect back, confirm, reinforce, and further facilitate our communicating our experience to ourselves. This describes, of course, the essentials of all formal or informal psychotherapeutic communication.

8 Our ordinary terminology reflects so much confusion that I should expand earlier remarks on the subject. *Imagination*, the ability to recall and reproduce past experience, is not identical with either *thought* or *fantasy*, though it is the basis of both. Thought is the imaginative signification of experience; it is an elaborate form of imagining that consists in using auditory images assertively in order to communicate with ourselves. It is not restricted in principle to the use of auditory images; indeed, most people have some ability to think – I mean, to *discourse* – in visual images. But whereas it is easy for everyone to imagine long and complex oral discourse, it is much more difficult, for instance, to work out and state to ourselves

'sounds' of thought, unlike those of speech, were not actual sounds but merely imagined ones, and (b) that the 'hearing' of the imaginary 'sounds' made in thought was correspondingly not the true hearing of external sense, but only an imaginary one.

Nevertheless, these differences were most important, for the following reason. What I have so far described in negative terms – the suppression of the audibility of speech – actually has a positive meaning: that a single assertive act, thinking, fuses together the 'voicing' and the 'hearing' of the imaginary 'sounds.' To this should be contrasted the assertiveness of mere speech, which as noted earlier depends on the coincidence of the contents of *two* distinct acts: voicing and hearing the sounds. (A prior or contemporary act of experiencing the object, which provides the content, is of course a pre-condition of both speaking and thinking; one cannot do either except in relation to something that has been experienced, in imagination if in no other way.) In thought, however, these two acts became one: the single act of imagining the vocal sound. For to make or 'voice' an imaginary sound is identical with 'hearing' it; the content of the imaginary 'sound' does not merely *coincide* with the content of what is 'heard,' because it is *one and the same* content of one and the same act. The identity of the imaginary 'voicing' and the imaginary 'hearing' means thus that imaginary 'voicing' is intrinsically assertive, in and of itself. It is not an act that, like vocal communication, can acquire assertiveness; it is an act that, like experiencing consciously, cannot be performed except assertively.

Thought, then, enjoys a more intense self-presence than speech. However, the act of experiencing the contents of thought is not an *immediately* assertive act. Since the pre-condition of thinking any contents is sensing the contents, the act of thought can be, at best, contemporaneous with the act of sensation; in any event, it is a separate act. Unlike immediate consciousness, thought asserts reality through the mediation of imagined vocal sounds. Moreover, since the self-communication of experience in thought evolved from communication-to-another in speech – which translated experience from all other sense modalities into audible signs – thought continued to signify experience primarily in the imaginary counterpart of audible signs. For this reason,

---

in visual imagination the implications of spatial relations among bodies. Fantasy is a different elaboration of imaginative experience; it is the creation of a new experience out of imaginary elements deriving from previous sense experience. Contrasted with our ability to *think* visually, which is poor, our ability to *fantasize* visually is very well developed, and frequently surpasses the ability to fantasize in acoustic images. In sum, although most of our fantasizing uses visual images, almost all our thinking is done in auditory ones.

the signification of experience in thought through imaginary signs in other sense modalities (i.e., thinking in non-auditory 'languages' such as visual imagery) is possible only under the same handicap as speaking in a second spoken language. The language of imaginary vocal sounds remains to this day every thinker's mother tongue.

Thus, the development of the ability to think out of the ability to speak did not for all its importance result in a vastly different mode of assertive experience; its true significance lay in its potential for further development into immediate consciousness. The difference between speech and thought is, in a sense, fairly small; it is only the difference between audible and inaudible, but in any event *worded*, assertiveness. Thought embodies the kind of experience that coincides with itself only through the *mediation* of words. Unlike both speech and thought, however, full conscious sense experience enjoys *immediate* self-presence. By generating thought, speech had enabled experience to be present to itself even in the absence of audible communication of the experience; but by generating immediate consciousness, thought made possible the kind of experience that could be present to itself even in the absence of *any* communication of the experience.

Like the transition from speech to thought, the passage from thought to immediate consciousness was not a result of the environmental pressure that operates in natural selection; human evolution was now ruled by the self-selection that attends the interplay between experience and communication once the latter acquires assertiveness. Natural selection, for all that, may have played a reinforcing role, since the ability to speak would have improved human communication and increased man's capacity to adjust to his physical environment; the ability to think, too, would have indirectly had organic survival value. Ultimately, however, the process must have depended on the inner dynamics of the mental life created by the transformation of vocal communication into speech; with the latter, a fountain-head of assertiveness had sprung forth that in the natural course of events was bound to spill over the entire experiential apparatus of man and suffuse it with self-presence.

I have suggested that the progression from speech to thought may have been facilitated by the practice of speaking audibly to oneself. The transformation of thought into immediate consciousness may have been fostered by another possibility implicit in thought, namely, speaking out loud what one is thinking at the same time that one is sensing it. Thinkers may at first have used both speech and thought to signify assertively to themselves the objects immediately present to their experience; eventually they would have learned to experience them assertively without having first to signify them *either* in thought or in speech. We today exploit the possibility of using both speech and thought to assert our present experience to ourselves, though the result is not that we *become* immediately conscious – for we are already so – but that we *intensify* our consciousness. We can do this with forethought; we may, indeed, with some training do it methodically and systematically. Early man could not have done it deliberately, let alone skilfully: before he had developed immediate consciousness he could not have conceived such a purpose. Nevertheless, though unaware of the inevitable results, by dint of speaking and thinking he would have achieved the same effect.

The emergence of immediate consciousness did not bring to an end the evolution of consciousness but only its period of gestation. After thought forced experience to merge into itself, consciousness had come into the world; it was scarcely mature at birth, but now it was on its own. Thereafter human nature would no longer be at the mercy of a process in which it took strictly passive part. Its conscious decisions, and in particular its conscious vision of itself and its situation in the world, would loom increasingly large in determining the course of its development. This does not mean that as soon as consciousness emerged human nature began to evolve under conscious control, but only that when evolution brought forth human nature the kind of life had appeared whose nature required it to bring itself forth; the life of conscious selfhood is the sort that must willy-nilly determine its own shape. But this should be understood in two senses. It means, first, that human nature had to be generated in every individual through his developing within himself his own ability to experience consciously – though this was possible only through the transmission to him, from without, of the ability to speak. Second, in both the individual and the group the possibility had emerged that consciousness might evolve through the exercise of consciousness itself. For, with man, the sort of experiencing organism had evolved whose typical mode of experience had the power of *self-reproduction*, on which would henceforth depend the self-perpetuation and the evolution of the human specificity. We have already seen some of the peculiarly human aspects of self-reproduction, but in the next section we shall encounter a few more.

First I comment, however, that if the reconstruction I have proposed is correct, then consciousness – but, if so, also human society, human culture, and the entirety of human life – appeared on earth fortuitously, as a by-product of natural selection. To be sure, the appearance of every species is unpredictable; evolution is an emergent causal process. But the peculiar way in which this is true of consciousness underscores, as if with heavy-handed irony, the fact that the absence of intrinsic finality in evolution is more clearly evident in man than in any other case. What justifies this remark?

Nothing in evolution suggests that natural selection brings about a predetermined end, or even that it promotes any particular line of development. The anthropomorphic term *selection* tends to obscure this absence of finality, since it lends itself to the misconception that characteristics appear *because* they are especially fit to survive. In fact the reverse is true. Characteristics survive only on condition that they should have appeared; their being 'selected' means only that, as it turns out, they have survival value. Nor does evolution 'encourage' or 'favour,' therefore, any particular 'trend.' Now, finality is at work in evolution, though in a different way from what many suppose. All life is goal-seeking, since it is inherently self-preserving: the vital functions of all organisms are the kind of efficient cause that tends to maintain itself in working order. And evolution depends on the tendency of life to survive, when such tendency interacts with the reproductive powers of life. But mark well: evolution is the effect of natural selection, not its cause; evolution does not tend towards specific advantages, not even those which at a given time may be indispensable for survival. All that natural selection can do is to 'seize' whatever survival advantages the reproductive process may churn up; natural selection is indeed nothing but the 'seizing' of such advantages.

But from the features of natural selection a logical consequence follows. Although evolution does not seek the elaboration or 'complexification' of life, as Teilhard de Chardin called it – let alone any given complexity or particular survival value or advantageous form of life – in a complex, changing environment natural selection will, in fact, produce increasingly elaborate forms of life. A mind that should subsequently inspect the 'progressive' results, the ever-more 'ingenious' ways in which evolution 'solves the problem' of adapting to supposedly 'hostile' conditions, could easily mistake what in our retrospection is a logical and intelligible outcome for an effect that the evolutionary process somehow tended to bring about. If such a mind were a little absent-minded, it would be all the more likely to do so. Even those who, like most biologists, deny that an external finality such as the will of a Creator steers the course of evolution on earth, sometimes assume that the evolutionary process contains within itself a tendency to produce conscious beings such as ourselves. They then reason, for instance, that if life has emerged elsewhere in the universe (which seems perfectly possible), it would have in all likelihood eventually developed into conscious life comparable to ours. Indeed, 'evolution is such an enormously creative force [that] there are probably also advanced [extraterrestrial] civilizations.'[9]

No 'creative force' produced consciousness; speech did. And speech was the result of natural selection, not the final cause that attracted evolution towards such result. But consciousness and human society

9 Charles J. Lumsden and Edward O. Wilson, *Promethean Fire* (Cambridge, MA, 1983), p. 53. To suppose that evolution results from natural selection and to speak of it in the same breath as a 'creative force' is at best loose thinking. As for the question of extraterrestrial human-like life, not a few scientists have been misled by the consideration that, since life tends to evolve as long as its environment changes, once life appears it will almost certainly evolve and continue evolving. This is true; what they forget is another corollary of natural selection: that the appearance of any one given life form is radically unpredictable, and that the more complex and advanced such life form, the more improbable its emergence. The emergence of every species is, thus, not unlike the outcome of a lottery held periodically, where the prize, predictably, will be won by someone every time, but not necessarily by any given ticket-holder in particular; he would reason fallaciously who thought that, having won once, he was especially likely to win again next time.

The appearance of conscious life *in our planet* was yet less likely than that of any other species; it was an exceedingly remote possibility, totally unpredictable from the fact that primitive life had emerged. If it seems otherwise to some, it is because their presuppositions about the nature of causality enable them to make an illicit transition from what *now* is an inalterable fact – namely, that human nature *did* emerge – to the gratuitous idea that it *had* to emerge. Therefore, even if we should assume that life is likely to emerge in many planets (though in the absence of any theory of why inanimate matter should develop life this would be little more than a guess), the only estimate consistent with natural selection would be that the emergence of, specifically, human-like life in any given evolutionary system was neither more nor less *improbable* than its appearance on earth. This would hold even if the human specificity consisted in intelligence, which has biological survival value and is subject to natural genetic selection (cf. George Gaylord Simpson, *This View of Life*, Cambridge, MA, 1964); all the more so if it is consciousness. But the scientists who launched the Search for Extra-Terrestrial Intelligence (SETI) project are not deterred; they believe that 'a factor of one should be assigned to the emergence of [man-like] intelligence – meaning that it would arise, eventually, on virtually any planet where there is life' (Walter Sullivan, *We Are Not Alone* [New York, 1966], p. 250). But there is, in fact, less warrant in what is known about natural selection for assigning such factor to man than there would be for assigning it to fleas, to three-toed sloths, to Monarch butterflies, or indeed, to any one given species or fauna or flora that has actually emerged on earth.

Thus, the same presuppositions that once produced the biblical persuasion that man owes his existence to predilection by a creative Force nowadays lead to an analogous scientific conviction, with but the difference that the scientific 'creative force' is deemed impersonal and uncaring and to operate in a purely natural and automatic way. The origin of these persistent presuppositions, and the reason why they are held in common by otherwise disparate religious and scientific orientations, will be discussed in chapters VII and VIII.

were not even the result of the natural selection of individual differences in the ability to experience, or in the organic structures of experience; quantitative improvements in the *communicative* abilities of the organism introduced a qualitative change in its *experiential* powers. Human nature is, therefore, doubly contingent, and the gratuitousness of human existence is yet more radical than creationists imagine: consciousness appeared as the incidental result of an unintended result. If man should experience humility and thankfulness when he ponders his evolutionary origins, he would have a much ampler, and a more deeply *religious*, reason to do so than if he deemed himself begotten by the will and design of a natural or supernatural creative force.

4. The emergence of the self-reproductive powers of consciousness

Human reproduction is most properly called *self-reproduction* because it is not only the generation of offspring that are like their generators, but offspring that, like their generators, become selves. For this means that they take a hand in the creation of their own specificity – albeit only after their generators endow them with the assertiveness that enables them to do so. I also stress that the human reproductive mechanism is properly so called, since it not only fulfils the same role as biological reproduction – perpetuating the species while making allowance for its possible evolution – but does so in fundamentally the same way. The two differ in important respects, but are more than superficially alike in the essential ones.

The evolutionary significance of the emergence of sexual reproduction was that, by ensuring almost infinite variations in the characteristics of offspring, it accelerated the pace of evolution and broadened its scope immeasurably. The key to this development was chromosomal exchange. But chromosomal *exchange* presupposes chromosomal *endowment*; the latter had been the link between sexual reproduction and the earlier, asexual mode of reproduction. In reproduction by simple cell division the original entity divides itself into two parts, each of which further divides itself, and so on. In this process it is impossible to distinguish between parent and offspring; it is not so much the reproduction as the multiplication of life, and only the species as a whole may be said to be a distinct entity. But if we should arbitrarily choose to think of the multiple individuals as the descendants of the originally single unit, we would have to say that the parent entity shares all its riches with its descendants. It is like a business corporation that decides to distribute its assets, upon dissolution, among the subsidiaries it had launched for the purpose of dividing one enterprise into several mutually independent ones – the interest in all of which, however, was to be held by the same share holders as before. In time, however, specialized modes of asexual reproduction appeared, characterized by the creation of distinct individuals – offspring properly so called – through the parent's donation of only a small portion of its capital, as it were, which could thereafter grow on its own. The offspring was, to begin with, identical with the donated assets themselves, but established by the parent as an autonomous endowment or a trust fund. The parent continued to lead its own life as an individual until it died.

The specific difference of sexual reproduction was superimposed upon this mechanism. The sexual generator is like a parent corporation that not only creates an independent subsidiary, but also passes along the parent's know-how in manufacturing the product; the parent eventually dies, but his peculiar advantages (and disadvantages) live on. In sexual reproduction the parent(s) donate no more than a cell, but inside that cell are instructions that the cell will use to develop and organize itself into a new specimen of the same nature as the parent. Moreover, the fund of genetic information is normally created by donations from two different sources, each of which provides its peculiar variations of the formula that defines its kind; the offspring, which requires a fixed quota of genetic information, takes half its quota from each parent. The offspring will, therefore, have its own unique genetic configuration, somewhat different from that of both parents yet of the same species as theirs. Endless variations are now ensured by the very mechanism that transmits them.

The transmission of genetic information, however, was not the first, nor would it be the last, communication process relevant to the evolution of life. We took note earlier that all life is based upon interactions that relate an organism to its environment through the conveyance of information. In the animal kingdom the organism's exchange with its environment rose from its crudest forms, such as those involved in metabolism and in the transmission of chromosomal material, into higher, more specialized ones. Eventually communication took the guise we now associate with the narrower use of the term: the interaction of an organism with a special segment of its environment – namely, fellow communicators – by exchanging signals instead of material products. Upon being perceived, the signals make mutually available the benefit of the experience of each. However, the principal difference between this level of information-transmission and that of sexual reproduction does not pertain so much to the nature of the *information* as it does to the manner of *transmission*. For the *information* communicated by chromosomal exchange is properly so called; it is not merely a tangible endowment, an organic structure given off by the parent; it is an organic structure that conveys a *form*, a principle of organization, from parent to offspring. Chromosomal information, however, is literally, physically transmitted, whereas in signal-making the transmission is only figuratively so called; as we have seen, nothing is given off by the informer which becomes its duplicate or 'offspring' in the informed. Thus, the appearance in man of a new reproductive system that depended upon the transmission of reproductive information *through signals* was only a refinement of the essentials of the earlier reproductive mechanism. The improvement was achieved by evolution through blending the characteristics of two forms of communication. The differences between the two modes of reproduction may be striking, but the similarities do not depend on metaphor.

The differences between the two types of communication stem from their respective origins. The kind of information-transmission involved in sexual reproduction emerged from the evolution of the inner structures of the living cell. The result was the appearance of the kind of organism that could become related to another organism – the offspring – which did not exist prior to the relation, since it came into existence through the very establishment of the relationship: in the sexual generative process the communication of information creates the communicand *ab ovo*. In signal-making, however, the communication of information evolved from the peripheral structures of the primitive cell, the structures by which it related itself to already-existing others: unlike the literal receiver of chromosomal information, the figurative 'receiver' of signals must be in place before it can be communicated with. It should not be deemed an oddity, therefore, that the appearance and development of *significative communication* in animal evolution did not affect in any fundamental way the earlier process of *genetic communication*, as I shall henceforth distinguish between them. The emergence of the former did, of course, affect the superstructures of sexual reproduction, and thus contributed indirectly to the evolution of the latter and to that of many other aspects of animal life; for instance, it made possible courtship behaviour. But the basic structure of sexual reproduction – transmission and exchange of genes – has remained the same since it first appeared on earth well over two billion years ago. From the viewpoint of the generation of the organism even the most highly developed sexuality – that of humans – works in essentially the same way as in birds and bees.

The self-reproductive mechanism of consciousness is characterized by the fusion of significative and generative information-transmission into '*genetic*' *signification*. That is, generative information is no longer imparted through the physical transmission of genes, but through signal-making. Consciousness resulted when significative communication, whose role hitherto had been solely that of carrying significative information, evolved so as to carry information that had at one and the same time a generative and a significative role. Speech is the fusion of the two. Human organisms cannot be taught to speak without consciousness being generated in them – or rather, without their being provided with the 'genetic' information that they will use automatically to give conscious quality to their experience. And human beings cannot exchange messages without thereby exchanging information that is apt to influence the development of consciousness, in both the individual and the species. But they cannot receive this kind of information except through signal-transmission. And communication through signal-transmission, as noted, presupposes an already-existing communicand.

Thus, evolution could have produced, as it did in man, the sort of communication that is both generative and significative only by superimposing its generative role upon the prior mechanism of sexual reproduction. The organism of the sexually generated human communicand is a fit recipient of consciousness-generating information, because it is an actually existing – albeit not yet human – organism that has the genetically determined organic abilities (a) to receive such information (i.e., to learn to speak), and (b) to follow its instructions in the same way as the zygote follows the instructions contained in the genes (i.e., to have its ability to experience developed into consciousness as a result of its practice of speech). I need not stress that the 'genetic' information transmitted by significative communication is apt to generate only the conscious quality of experience, and that in every other respect the self-reproduction of human nature follows the principles of sexual reproduction; but by the same token, the self-reproduction of human nature cannot be reduced to the sexual reproduction of humanoid organisms. Note also that the human mechanism is not an amalgam of two separate processes, though undoubtedly it is a complex one; its generative and its significative phases integrate a single, continuous process.

The evolution from animal communication to speech was, therefore, also the transformation of social relations and cultural tradition into an organ for the self-reproduction of human nature; it was the creation of a socio-cultural *matrix* out of an infrahuman communications network. Assertiveness transformed thus the nature of society and of tradition; it produced the kind of society whose essential cultural role was to generate the specific form of life that defines its members. The effect of this on the pace at which evolution could proceed, and on the variability of human characteristics, was of a yet higher order than that which had attended the introduction of chromosomal exchange: if the latter had given wings to evolution, self-reproduction gave it jet-propulsion and atomic power.[10]

By this I mean that the human mode of reproduction overcame the two chief limitations of sexual reproduction. The transmission of acquired characteristics through chromosomal exchange is not possible; the parent organism's genetic endowment is fixed once for all when *it* is conceived, and its reproductive cells ordinarily reflect nothing but such original endowment. Normally, therefore, what the organism passes on to its offspring is determined once for all when the offspring is conceived, and evolution can take place only at the relatively slow pace of natural genetic selection. The transmission of generative information through significative communication, however, allows the transmission of benefits acquired by the generator at any time; moreover, the advantages can be passed on even after the offspring has come into being. A second, complementary advantage is that such characteristics can be transmitted from anybody to anybody and, indeed, in principle from everybody to everybody. The kind of organism whose entire nature is generated by chromosomal exchange is shaped by its progenitors alone, but human nature is generated, *and* developed, by society as a whole; though to be sure, the socio-cultural womb generates and nurtures him only in interaction with the individual himself, who has the opportunity to participate in his own genesis and development.

The limitations of sexual reproduction have to do, thus, with *which* characteristics can be generated in offspring and which cannot, and with *whose* characteristics can be transmitted even if such characteristics are the transmissible kind. This does not curtail the amount of possible improvement in the individual's functions and structures, nor does it forbid the transmission of such improvements through learning from any member of the community to any other. But such improvements cannot be accumulated for the species, since they are not transmissible through chromosomal information. When the nature of the species is determined exclusively by genes, a limit to the amount of improvement in quality of function is quickly reached, because every generation must begin to improve its characteristics at the same starting-point as its forebears (except, of course, to the degree that natural selection may have changed the species). For instance, in a society of athletes, the average performance of its members would be much higher than in a society where everyone's favourite hobby was writing books on philosophy;

10 This alludes to the *possibilities* opened up by consciousness. It does not imply that consciousness will necessarily evolve indefinitely, or that human evolution is necessarily accelerated, or that consciousness necessarily develops in adaptive or healthy ways.

but an upper limit in athletic prowess and in musculature would eventually be reached, because all children would be born with a normal and untrained organism whose finite lifetime imposed a limit on how much it could improve. However, if the nature of the species is determined by characteristics transmitted through signal-making, then the evolutionary possibilities rise to a new order of magnitude in respect of both the range of variations and the speed of change.

Evolution through socio-cultural reproduction should not be confused, therefore, with the 'cultural evolution' of the synthetic theory, the simple possibility of cultural transmission of learned behaviour; the latter is observable, though on a small scale, even at the higher levels of infrahuman life. When the socio-cultural matrix generates consciousness by transmitting the ability to speak, it does not merely improve upon the native abilities of the organism; it imparts 'genetic' information about how the organism can acquire an ability that otherwise it would not enjoy at all. And as the quality of function of the individual is subsequently changed through the interaction between him and his socio-cultural environment, the matrix becomes constituted by individuals whose quality of conscious functioning may have developed: the womb of humanity has itself evolved. Therefore, when it now generates consciousness, it does not merely change the quality of the conscious functions of individuals; it generates individuals whose native endowment may include a somewhat different quality of conscious functioning than that of their elders. In short, the socio-cultural matrix not only develops the consciousness of individuals, but may also change the nature of consciousness. Human cultural society operates so as to render possible the evolution of the essential nature of man.

Reproductive powers such as these could not have come into being, any more than sexuality could, unless vested in appropriate organic structures. And, of course, the individual human organism could not have served as an adequate organic base for them. But the implication of what we have studied is that there is, nevertheless, a reproductive organ, properly so called, within which the human specificity is literally conceived. The socio-cultural matrix is not, to be sure, an individual organism, but an organization of individual organisms that is created, maintained, changed, and made to operate by the speaking activities of such organisms. Its nature and origin will now be briefly discussed.

5. The emergence of the socio-cultural matrix of consciousness

The phenomenological analysis of the experience of reality we conducted earlier implies what might well be called a principle of universal relativity.[11] Nothing real is truly absolute, altogether independent of other things. It follows that the universe is not simply the totality of all things but also the environment of each; all things are present to each other, albeit more or less so. Understandably, therefore, the relativity of reality is reflected in the process that generates anything – that is, the process whereby it becomes real. Now, this is true at every level of reality; we have seen, for example, that the physical changes that take place in the world of inanimate entities are explicable by the concept of relativistic causality. But it is especially evident in the case of living things. Every individual organism comes into being within an environment that plays a more or less passive but indispensable role in its generation; a regional portion of the ocean, say, or of a lake provides the medium – the space – within which certain forms of life are generated. As the scale of life is ascended, evolution develops yet more restricted – and therefore yet more controllable – receptacles of the reproductive process. Specialized structures appear that create a boundary zone that, by separating hostile from favourable environmental conditions, protects the embryo and enhances its viability. At the yet higher levels, however, the negative, protective function of the boundary layer is complemented by a nourishing one. A highly specialized generative system evolves, centred on the 'mothering' or matrix function, which positively facilitates the self-organization and maturation of the embryo in accordance with its genetic instructions.

In mammals the generation of offspring is, of course, hardly complete at conception. Their reproduction has two quite distinct phases; the male parent participates only in the provision of genetic information, but the mother has an additional generative function that she alone performs. Strangely enough, many take this function as the ground for extolling man's motherhood above the responsibility of all human beings for each other, and for assigning to the female sex of man peculiar parental duties from which they absolve not only the individual male, but even society. For human generation requires more than motherhood added to paternity: the potentially human organism can become actually human only if, passing at birth from the organic matrix into the matrix of consciousness, the human reproductive process enters its final, socio-cultural stage; if a human organism should have been obstetrically speaking born, but not into the matrix of humanity, it would have humanly speaking aborted. Ordinarily, of course, the biological mother and father are,

---

11 I do not call it a *principle* in any of the traditional senses of the term; it is neither a self-evident metaphysical truth nor an *a priori* judgment. It is a generalization that can be derived from the experience of reality through critical reflexion.

at least at first, the leading – though rarely the sole – personators of the socio-cultural matrix. But no mother, no parental couple, no extended family group, can perform the entire generative task. The womb of consciousness is a complex apparatus, of which many individuals – potentially all members of the species – are integrating parts; this includes earlier generations, to the extent that their experience has been virtually preserved in the form of culturally transmitted assertions that enable the human individual to become himself.

The relationship between the human individual and his society would be paradoxical, were it not rendered intelligible by the circularity that defines the human specificity; the individual consciousness is created by society, but once created it becomes part of the matrix that generates conscious individuals. In other words, society generates consciousness and consciousness generates society: these are two complementary phases of a single cyclical process. There is, however, an important, if obvious, difference between the individual consciousness and the socio-cultural matrix: consciousness has physical existence in the functions of individual organisms, whereas the social matrix has no *individual* organism of its own in which it can exist separately. Nevertheless, the social matrix could not lack an organic base; if it did, it would have no other reality than as a concept or an abstraction, and could hardly perform the function of generating real human beings. The organic base and physical existence of society, however, are those of the individual organisms whose consciousness integrates the socio-cultural matrix. Society does not have an independent individual organism; this is true. Society has an organism integrated by individual organisms.

X If we agree, then, that speech generates consciousness and that human nature is reproduced socio-culturally, we must also say that the stuff of all human society and culture is speech. For society and culture are nothing but the sum total of the conscious states of an organized group of individual organisms – which states include, however, the individuals' experience of each other's experience, and indeed, their experience of each other's experience of each other's experience, and so on. All human relations are based on the exchange of assertive communications by individuals, and on the institutionalized assertions of a speaking community. Society and culture are, at bottom, simply what people say, to themselves and to each other, about the world, themselves, and each other.

To be sure, human beings perform many actions other than speaking, thinking, and listening to the spoken thought of others; and they have many relations other than those of communicator and communicand. But human beings do *nothing* that does not depend for its specifically human modality on its being asserted by them, at least to themselves and usually to each other as well; all human activities and all human relations directly or indirectly involve speech as their essential element. Speaking is, therefore, not one among many other possible forms of human behaviour, but the one that underlies all others. No behaviour can be called human but for its actual or potential conceptualization in thought and speech, and no cultural artefact can be deemed human but because it has been given its specifically human meaning, disposition, order, or shape, by an organism whose experience and behaviour were conscious. The most important of these artefacts are indeed the most obviously constituted by speech: the interpretative traditions that, like common sense, religions, sciences, and philosophies, perpetuate the culture's world-views. ⟩

It is clear, then, that once speech had appeared, the nature of society had been profoundly affected – indeed, in two ways. First, whereas the infrahuman community consists of a multiplicity of individuals related by differentiated but co-ordinated roles, the human community is constituted by individuals who are, to be sure, so related, but for whom their *experiencing* that they are so related becomes the essential element of their relationships. The son behaves as a son because he perceives his father as his father and himself as his father's son; these perceptions are not given by the biological facts, but worked out in the interpersonal transactions – in the assertive communications – between father and son. Likewise, a criminal is a criminal because of the way in which he defines himself in relation to others and others in relation to him, and in which others define him in relation to themselves and themselves in relation to him. The rulers and the ruled are equally ruled by what they assert to be the rules of ruling and being ruled. Many of these rules are, of course, tacitly asserted; these are the most inflexible of all. In the human species, social, economic, political, legal, and all other roles, organization, and transactions are determined by the kind of information that is not transmitted genetically, but assertively.

Second, whereas in infrahuman life 'culture' (to the extent that any may exist) is in the service of, and depends upon, social organization, in man the relationship between society and culture is reversed: society is determined by the turning-over and the handing-down of experience. It is significant that social organization appeared very early in the evolution of animal life, for it needs only the most elementary levels of communication, whereas culture is apparent only among the higher species and is rudimentary except in man. In man, however, social organization and tradition are fused into a single reality – but with culture in the lead, since it is speech, which is generated culturally, that unifies the two. Thus, in the human species social organization is not imposed from outside, or from above, the tradition of the society itself. The human social order is created by human beings *saying* what the social order is. It may even be created by people *saying* that they do not create the social order, but that it has been predetermined for them, for instance, by God, or else by nature, or by man's animal ancestry, and so on, according to their particular faith. Under the right conditions, therefore, the principle of the divine right of kings can as effectively organize a stable, efficient, and satisfying society as those of representative democracy or totalitarianism. (Catholic religious communities, at least until recently, would have exemplified the last very well.) The condition is that it be commonly asserted as the proper social order. The assertion, however, has to be *meant*. I stipulate this, because human individuals, who deceive themselves at least as often as they do others, are collectively self-deceptive as well. It has been frequently said that people always get the political – and indeed, the economic, and the entire social order – that they deserve, not necessarily the one they think they should get. The reason is that the order they get is the one they actually create, because it is the one they truly assert – which is not always the same as that which, self-deceptively, they merely vocalize.

6. The origin of the defective self-presence of consciousness

If consciousness is generated by the assertive properties of speech, then the defective self-presence that characterizes absent-mindedness in the individual must result from defective assertiveness in his speech. Correspondingly, absent-mindedness in the species must hark back to the aboriginal generation of consciousness by defective assertiveness in speech. But since the assertiveness of speech results, as the theory supposes, from the non-assertive communicators' perception of their communicative efficacy and finality as such – and thus of their reality as communicators – then defective assertiveness must have originated in insufficiently sharp perception of these. Its roots reach down to the earliest stage of human evolution, when mere communication was being transformed into speech.

The emergence of a defective form of consciousness can be explained, therefore, by supposing that those hominids who were destined soon to acquire speech, but with a flaw, were somewhat lacking in perceptual acuity. (Whether this affected the whole species or only some groups is another question, but in any case our own culture's ancestors were included.) Although they would have had enough ability to discriminate

among and integrate the pertinent facts about their communicative behaviour, they would not have done so very clearly or accurately. The
consequences would have been that their experience of their own efficient and final causality as communicators would have been a little
snarled, and that therefore they would have had a somewhat insecure
grasp of their own assertiveness. As for the reason why they should
have mustered less-than-ideal perceptual acuity, genetic factors can be
assigned as the not implausible cause. This is, therefore, only a special
form of the same hypothesis as that on which the reconstruction of the
emergence of consciousness in general has been based: absent-mindedness originated in the *confused* perception, by non-assertive communicators, of what they had to perceive in order to develop speech. But
what could have been the nature of such confusion? And in what might
have consisted the tares it bequeathed?

Their shortcoming was that they could not perceive the efficacy of
their communicative behaviour well enough to discover precisely how
communication worked; they did not fully realize that signals communicated only because they were made by the communicator. But it will
be recalled that, in order to grasp his causality as a communicator, the
prehuman signaller had to perceive not only the relation between the
signal and the communicand's reception of the message, but also the
fact that it was *his behaviour* – his making the signal, not the signal itself
– that was the cause of the effect worked on the communicand. To
appreciate this, however, he had to hear his own message as if he had
been his own communicand. But if his perceptual abilities should have
been deficient in this very respect, he would have grasped only confusedly the relation between the cause (his signal-making) and its effects
(a meaning being conveyed). When he voiced a signal he would have
readily identified *what* the communicand heard and *what* he heard, but
he could not have perceived distinctly the connection between what he
heard and his act of *voicing* it. Since such hominids perceived, however
dimly, that they communicated, and since they were not altogether
unaware of the purposiveness underlying their signal-making, they would
have acquired speech – but only the kind whose assertiveness was wanting. They developed a speech impediment, as it were, because they
suffered from a sort of hearing defect.

Our elders' confusion, then, may be summed up in the formula that
when they spoke they were not quite clear about precisely who was
truly speaking or to what end. By this I mean that they were uncertain
about the *real* assertiveness, the *real* efficient and final causes of speech;
for they could have had little doubt about the fact that it was they
themselves who uttered the sounds that repeated reality and who vo-

calized the messages received by their communicands.[12] Nevertheless, since they could not perceive that they were the original and sole source of the *saying* of what they said, they would have experienced their own speech as the repetition of the *déjà dit*, their reiteration of a reality that in some mysterious way had been 'said' before. In sum, it was reality itself that *meant* the meaning that their speech merely reproduced. The confusion I have described is, therefore, the primordial source of the semantic interpretation of speech; it potentially contained the entire semantic complex. Conversely, if anyone should find it difficult to believe that our forebears could have grasped the fact that their signals had communicative effects, yet not fully realize that the reason was that the signals had been sent by them – for surely, it might be objected, this is obvious – and if he required monumental evidence before he so believed, the reply to his objection is an epitaph commemorating the ancestral absent-mindedness: *circumspice*.

Although the defect in speech that is responsible for absent-mindedness must have originally resulted from organic, genetic factors, once human beings had learned to speak it would have been perpetuated socio-culturally by being passed on to the young as part of the culture's common 'idea' of speech; more about this later. This is why we in our culture do not, even at this late date, advert readily to the assertive properties of speech, though infinitesimally few individuals amongst us, if any – and certainly no groups – are genetically pure descendants from our prehistoric Indo-European linguistic fathers.

Absent-mindedness, come to think of it, is a remarkable phenomenon; if we do not find it so the reason can only be that we are enured to it. It is a sort of mental stammer that afflicts a consciousness that *does* experience assertively, but whose self-presence is slightly out of phase, always a little behind itself. But since the stammer is congenital, we cannot easily diagnose it: we never have much opportunity either to hear ourselves speak normally or to hear normally our abnormal speech. We take for granted, therefore, that we should be obscure to ourselves despite our being conscious, and that we should positively mistake our-

---

12 However, it is possible that they may have had difficulty in attributing their own thinking activity to their own ability to speak soundlessly and to their ability to do so at will – that is, to their efficient and final causality as thinkers. If so, thinking would have been for them the hearing of voices which they could not have identified as their own imaginary speech; they would have suffered endemically from auditory hallucinations. The possibility that at least some early humans were chronically hallucinated is one aspect of Jaynes's theory of the origin of consciousness that, if totally removed from its original context, could be incorporated into the theory proposed here.

selves for what we are not. But this is thoroughly anomalous, a living self-contradiction in the kind of experiential faculty that provides to itself the evidence of its own nature. However, it is not, at least in our culture, an abnormality in the statistical sense.

Whether absent-mindedness is universal in the species will be discussed later. Note, however, that there is no reason to suppose, as we commonly do, that the conscious quality of human experience remains identically the same throughout the range of human cultural strains; indeed, it would be unusual if it did. Ordinarily the characteristics that make up the specific nature of every life form vary in degree among individuals and groups; group differences are often wide enough to warrant dividing species into varieties and races. Should consciousness be an exception? It is not inherently improbable, let alone impossible, that evolution might have split mankind into races, in the only sense in which this term could be properly applied to man; I mean, in respect of consciousness, as contrasted with the characteristics usually but wrongly called racial in man, which are not even distantly related to the human specificity. But I have argued only that this is possible. We should of course require positive evidence before asserting it as a fact.

Absent-mindedness could not but have had the most profound effects on human self-interpretation and thus on the everyday conduct of human life. But this is not yet the proper time to examine the practical consequences of this hindrance. Their vastness may be surmised *a priori*, however, by recalling the magnitude of the role of self-presence in the generation of culture. A little learning is, poets to the contrary, actually quite safe, but an absent-minded consciousness is a most dangerous thing.

CHAPTER SIX

The emergence of the
self-defining consciousness

In all cultures of whose speech we have notice, whether living or dead, recent or ancient, primitive or civilized – even in those that most probably reflect what late Palaeolithic human life was like – human beings have been able to speak both thematically and non-thematically. It will be recalled from chapter III that the latter form of speech asserts reality immediately, and that it generates immediate consciousness, the experiential assertion of sensed objects directly and in themselves. Thematic speech, however, does not bear on reality directly, but only through the mediation of objects of speech, or themes; its higher level of assertiveness enables it to generate a consciousness that virtually contains, but is more than, immediate consciousness, and whose distinctive mark is self-definition. Self-definition is achieved through the speaker's understanding of the world and of himself in relation to his world, and understanding is the kind of interpretative experience that only thematic speech and thought can mediate.

The fact that historical man speaks both thematically and non-thematically, however, scarcely implies that the human ability to communicate assertively included from the outset the ability to speak thematically. Since thematic is more elaborate and assertive than non-thematic speech, it must have evolved out of the latter at some prehistoric time. If so, the evolution of human nature has passed through two quite distinct stages. The first began when certain hominids developed non-thematic speech, and was complete when their speech had succeeded in generating thought – I mean, non-thematic thought – and immediate perceptual consciousness. The second phase began when thematic speech and thought – logically flowing, narrative thought, as ours now is – appeared. When these in turn elevated consciousness to its self-defining form, a new plateau of humanity had been reached. Since human beings have not transcended thematic speech – it is indeed an open question whether they will ever do so or whether their future evolution, if any, will not take an altogether different direction – it is clear that we still exist within the ambit of this second stage.

Having omitted consideration of the difference between non-thematic and thematic speech, the reconstruction proposed so far has been only a first approximation. The same general principle – that experience becomes self-present to the degree that the speaker's communication of his experience facilitates his experiencing his own reality as the efficient and final cause of his assertiveness – explains the generation of consciousness by speech at the level of both immediate consciousness and self-definition. But the last chapter was concerned only with the simplest and most primitive way in which the principle applies, which explains specifically only the first human evolutionary age. We still face the task of reconstructing the inception and course of the second. That is the objective of this and the next two chapters. I remind us that we shall accomplish it, however, only in part, since we shall stop short when we arrive at that point in human evolution where consciousness, having become fully self-defining, had acquired all the essential characteristics it has displayed since at least the beginning of the historical period and most probably long before. Of course, consciousness continued to evolve thereafter, even if it has not changed so profoundly during historical, or even late prehistoric, times that it must be deemed to have entered a new age. For practical reasons previously mentioned, however, the application of the theory to recent human ages will be excluded from this work.

The great achievement of the first stage had been that, at its end, human evolution was no longer regulated by natural selection nor dependent on natural environmental factors – except of course in the sense, which may be taken for granted, that without the survival of its organism consciousness can neither survive nor evolve. Evolution was governed rather by *self-selection*, and depended on the *self-adjustment* of conscious life. Even in respect of the physical world what counted was adjustment to it as an object of consciousness; the environment in which the individual existed was no longer merely the world of nature, but mostly an utterly intangible, purely mental one of his own making. For all of a human being's life, even his interactions with his material surroundings, is lived within the experiential field created by (a) the presence of his experience to himself, (b) the presence of other selves' experience to him, (c) the presence of other selves' experience to themselves, and (d) the presence of his experience to other selves. This *inner environment* of consciousness is, by another name, human society, which unlike animal society depends for its existence upon its being interiorized in the mutual experience of its individual members.

Animals experience each other, but do not experience the fact that they experience each other; animal societies, therefore, are integrated by individuals whose experience is reducible to what they themselves perceive. In human societies, on the contrary, the individual's experience comprises also the experience that belongs to others, to the degree that the latter is empathetically shared in by him. Animal societies, therefore, *make use* of their members' ability to experience each other, but are not *constituted* by their experience of each other – whereas human societies are. Accordingly, animal societies are determined in all essential respects by the genetically determined nature of their members, whereas human societies are ruled by their members' interpretative experience of what their own nature is; human beings are self-defining not only individually, but above all as groups. Note, however, that the complexity of the social field of consciousness is much greater than I have just described; for I have abstracted from the fact that, when an individual experiences the experience of another individual, the latter's experience includes the experience of the former's and vice versa. For instance, a most important aspect of every person's experience of himself is his experience of the way in which others experience him. Nor is this the end of the complexity; for I can experience you as experiencing me as experiencing you, and so on, indefinitely.[1]

If we can say, then, that with the emergence of consciousness the evolutionary mechanism had itself evolved, it is because self-selection operates in the inner environment of consciousness. And since the adjustment that counts towards the evolution of consciousness is to this environment, the variations that human evolution selects for pertain to those characteristics that facilitate or else hinder the adjustment of consciousness to itself. This is true not only of individuals; since the sociocultural matrix is integrated by individual conscious organisms, every society must reckon with the consciousness of its individual members. The group must adjust to itself. Indeed, the adjustment of the species as a whole to the inner environment created by the interaction of its member groups is the adjustment on which the evolution of human nature ultimately depends.[2]

1 Cf. Ronald D. Laing, *Self and Others* (Harmondsworth, England, 1971), pp. 174ff.
2 To judge by what we can observe in contemporary primitive societies, the idea that early man was locked in a titanic struggle with a hostile natural world, with physical survival at stake, is a myth. Primitive human life may be harsh, but is not particularly dangerous, since even the most elementary level of consciousness has overkill capacity in the requisite respects. This reflects the fact that consciousness

In the first section of this chapter I shall invoke self-selection – the mutual involution of assertive communication and assertive experience – to reconstruct the origin of thematic speech. In general terms, my suggestion will be that thematic speech emerged as an evolutionary response to the fact that, once non-thematic speech had generated immediate consciousness, the inner environment of the speaker had been altered. Since the speaker was now conscious, he could speak with consciousness of speech; and to do so is, in effect, to speak thematically. The immediate consciousness generated by non-thematic speech caused thus the transformation of non-thematic into thematic speech. In the second section we shall study the next step in the ascent of man. To the degree that thematic speech had appeared, the inner environment of consciousness had been altered again: the generation of consciousness was now effected by the assertiveness that characterizes thematic speech. The self-defining consciousness thus emerged.

We shall then be ready to examine, in the third section, the specifically human need – the need for self-definition – that appeared in evolution once consciousness was being generated by thematic speech. Satisfaction of this need is the typically human motive; it alone explains such seeming paradoxes of human conduct as the fact that human beings can find pleasure painful and be pleased by pain; indeed, human life can seek deliberately to terminate as well as to prolong itself. Any theory that claimed to account for the emergence of the human peculiarities would have to explain how organic life, whose inherent purpose is biological self-preservation, could have evolved into the kind that finds it possible to deny as well as to affirm itself. Conscious life is able to do so, I shall propose, because its being generated by thematic speech endowed it with emergent purposes that were not reducible to the self-preservation of biological life; even the latter can be subordinated to the need of human beings for experiencing their identity as a meaningful one. I stress that this is not merely a want, but a need, and that it is indeed a need that inheres in human nature since it is a consequence of consciousness. Thus, in the evolution of the human specificity this need is

---

emerged as a by-product of natural selection, not as its direct result; when exercised consciously, general intelligence and ability to learn become multiplied. It cannot be overstressed, however, that man's self-adjustment ultimately involves organic survival. Individuals, groups, and even the species as a whole are subject to extinction for reasons that have nothing to do with adequate response to challenge from the physical environment, but with the adjustment of individuals and groups to themselves and to each other, and of the species as a whole to the conditions of conscious life that it creates for itself. The direst threats to consciousness are created by consciousness itself.

the equivalent of the built-in purpose of surviving that moves the evolution of organisms as such. It is, therefore, also the criterion whereby the human self-selective process discriminates *inherently*, not necessarily consciously, between what is 'fit' to be preserved and what is not.

The emergence of the self-defining consciousness implied corresponding developments in the socio-cultural matrix and in the nature of the human evolutionary process; these will be our next concern. With non-thematic speech the function of culture had already been transformed from that of merely transmitting learned behaviour to that of handing down the specific kind – assertive communication – that generated new experiential powers. However, once conscious life was being generated by thematic speech, the culture not only generated but also developed the consciousness of individuals; it did so by creating both the individual's ability to define himself and the collective self-definition of the society, which is embodied in the traditions of the group. Culture became thus the more or less coherent system of self-perpetuating assertions made by its individual members – about themselves, the world, and each other – by means of which they gained self-identity both as individuals and as a group; it became the institutionalized self-definition of a society. We shall see, however, that a culture institutionalizes self-definition above all in the 'idea' of thematic speech that it perpetuates, and only derivatively in the contents of specific thematic assertions. The reason will be discussed in the fourth section, but briefly stated is as follows.

To acquire not merely the language wherewith to speak, but the very ability to speak, the child must acquire an 'idea' of what he should do in order to speak. (I have explained that I use quotation marks because I am not referring to a concept, but to a purely practical skill; if children could conceive ideas before they knew how to speak, it would not be absurd to try to teach them to speak by explaining to them what speech was.) But the child acquires his 'idea' of speech when he learns to experience his communicative behaviour as (a) his *intentional* and (b) *effective* communication (c) of his *experience* (d) of *reality*. Learning to speak amounts, thus, to developing an 'insight' – a purely practical and unconceptualized one, to be sure – into one's nature as an experiencer and speaker, and into the nature of reality, the objects of experience and speech. Therefore, as the socio-cultural matrix endows the young with the ability to speak, it automatically transmits to them deep-seated, non-conscious assumptions about man and world. And when it endows them, specifically, with the ability to speak thematically, it teaches them in particular certain conceptions of reality and of efficient and final causality. For, as will be remembered, to be able to speak thematically is the same as to be able to relate theses to themes in accordance with the meaning of categorical concepts – the principal of which are these three – which are learned through experiencing the assertiveness of one's own immediate consciousness and non-thematic speech.

The assumptions about the nature of reality and of efficient and final causality are transmitted, received, and held by their recipients non-consciously, because they are not handed down as messages but as implications contained in the speaking of messages: they operate as part of the elders' and of the child's unquestioned 'idea' of what to say *anything* is. That merely learning to speak creates assumptions or 'pre-understandings' – *Vorverständnisse* – in the mind of the speaker is of little moment at the non-thematic stage; but when the socio-cultural matrix generates thematic speech it means that the child has been en-dowed not only with the ability to make interpretative, categorical as-sertions about self and world, but also with presuppositions about them that will inexorably determine in all fundamental respects the limits within which such interpretations must be contained. We may thus distinguish the *primary* institution of self-definition, which is thematic speech itself, insofar as its properties embody the premises of all self-definition, from *derivative* secondary and tertiary institutions, which carry, transmit, and perpetuate the self-definition of human beings only by virtue of the *contents* of thematic speech. Culture is a message whose meaning depends fundamentally on the form of the primordial cultural medium, speech, and only secondarily on the contents of the message itself.

The bearing of these findings on human evolution during its second stage can be easily guessed at. Whereas everyone, when he makes a thematic assertion, is conscious of *what* he says, hardly anyone is conscious of what is implicit in his *saying* it. Operating all the more relentlessly because they work by way of tacit implication, the 'pre-understandings' underlying all human understanding determine the basic features of the overt self-definitions communicated and perpetuated by the secondary and tertiary socio-cultural institutions. This explains why the evolution of the self-defining consciousness has never been con-sciously self-directed; to date it has proceeded, and in the foreseeable future will in all likelihood continue to unfold, entirely with non-con-scious determinism, having been 'genetically' constrained by the prop-erties of speech. Cultural variation in self-definition has been possible, so far, only within the limits of logical consistency with the presuppo-sitions created in the speaker by the process of acquiring thematic speech.

And yet, evolution feeds on differences; if offspring were exactly the same as their parents, all the 'options' available to the selective process, whether human or infrahuman, would by definition be exactly the same and the species could not change. The theory must therefore explain how culture functions so as to perpetuate human self-definition, and withal to permit variations in it. The explanation, as we shall see, is that when evolution created thematic speech it also made provision for the introduction of variations in its form. But variations in the properties of thematic speech imply variations in the presuppositions about self and world acquired by the individual as he learns to speak thematically; and variations in these presuppositions create different cultural orientations in different human groups. The evolution of the self-defining consciousness is possible, then, for the same reason as organic evolution: that the universality of the nature of the species does not forbid variations in its form. But this is to run ahead of the argument. The study of these questions, moreover, will require that we take into account a second observation that was intentionally disregarded in the last chapter, since it was not relevant to the first stage of human evolution: that there is, as a matter of fact, more than one form of thematic speech – more than one way in which the experience of reality can be communicated by asserting theses in relation to themes. Indeed, the fact that thematic speech is not uniform throughout the species is of so great importance for the study of the evolution of consciousness that we shall devote to it a chapter of its own. Meanwhile I shall conclude this chapter by explaining, in the fifth section, the significance of the emergence of self-definition as part of the evolution of life.

1. The emergence of thematic speech

We have seen that speech processes reality by giving a certain organization to the information received by the speaker. This organization must be supplied by the latter, because reality provides no information on how the information that it does provide is to be organized. It is true that reality may do more than merely obtrude upon the experiencer; it can also become insistent, 'suggesting' to the speaker *that* he speak and *about* what; a loud report, for instance, 'calls attention' to itself and 'prompts' the speaker to address himself to it. Even then, however, reality does not so much as hint at *what* he should say.

If the speaker does nothing but simply assert the information received, he will speak non-thematically; this is but another way to say that non-thematic speech does not organize information beyond packaging it conceptually. The organization effected by thematic speech, on the contrary, is quite intricate. The process begins when some information received from reality is conceived as a theme, while other information is constituted as a thesis; but it is achieved only when the thesis is asserted in relation to the theme in accordance with one or else another preconceived category. We have seen also that the contents of the thesis and the theme are not changed by the categorical relationship that the thematic speaker gives to them. A thematic assertion is an interpretation of reality that consists in taking its measure in relation to consciousness itself, but the validity of such interpretation depends on whether reality can support the construction put upon it. Accordingly, the manner in which the thematic speaker uses his utter freedom to organize the information has the gravest practical consequences. Some thematic assertions are totally useless for living in a real world whose reality and identity are not created by consciousness but given to it; others are useful, though not always in the same way or to the same degree. Yet others are positively noxious. To say that 'Arsenic is a harmless condiment' is a perfectly possible and sense-making way in which one might organize information; all that is wrong with it is that *meaning* it renders one a danger to others and to oneself.

So far as concerns the relationship of thematic speech to reality, the speaker may organize the information in three basic ways. First, he may give it a purely formal thematic organization, for instance, 'The broom drank two flowers off the fried shoe.' Though the information is derived from experience, it has been organized in a way that is not referable back to reality. A different type of formal organization would be shown, for instance, by 'Slithy toves gimble wabily agyre.'[3] This organizes information – provided by the experience of speaking English – about the form of English adjectives, nouns, verbs, and adverbs. Another variant of purely formal thematic organization is a lie; its unreferability back to reality is, of course, the essential means to the speaker's end: hampering the communicand's adjustment to reality. The possibility of giving purely formal thematic organization to every kind of information shows that although thematic speech is bound to inner or outer objects as its only source, it is free to organize the information as it may decide (within the limits of its assumptions about the nature of thematic speech and about the ways in which theses can be asserted in relation to themes). But purely formal thematic organization cannot obey the purpose of facilitating the life of consciousness in the world of reality, though its very meaninglessness – except as to form – can be used for an ulterior purpose, such as to lie or to amuse.

3 I have altered the text of Lewis Carroll's 'Jabberwocky,' removing its last traces of semantic adequacy in order to contrast sharply its formal sense and its semantic nonsense.

Since the essential function of thematic speech is to facilitate human adjustment, organization is given to information more fundamentally for the substantive purposes it can serve than for the sake of its purely formal value. But the range of purposes is wide, and the possible kinds of substantive thematic organization make up a spectrum. Here, however, I shall arbitrarily divide them into *factual* and non-factual – or *fictional* – thematic assertions. The former are more basic; but strangely enough, fictional assertions are yet more valuable for human life than factual ones. In neither type is the purpose simply, as it is in non-thematic speech, to communicate information received; the intention is rather to communicate it with consciousness of its relationship to the reality whence it derives. However, the two types refer back to reality in very different ways.

In factual thematic speech the assertion refers to reality in the latter's actuality and concreteness, or in itself; for instance, 'This situation is dangerous,' or 'At the end of the *Liederabend* Marilyn Horne chose spirituals for her encore.' As in all thematic speech, the speaker's *assertion* of the thesis does not refer directly to the reality itself, but to the theme. However, the *information* refers directly to the reality that supplied it. In the scale of assertiveness, thus, factual thematic speech is only one step above non-thematic speech, because it is removed from reality by only one step. Fictional thematic speech, however – some instances will be analysed in a moment – organizes the information so that it can be referred back to reality only indirectly, through prior translation into factual thematic assertions (or even into non-thematic ones). Thus, fictional thematic speech is doubly removed from immediate reality – though its usefulness and truth are not necessarily impaired on that account. On the contrary, this kind of speech is useful for the very reason that it is not concerned with relating the speaker to factual, immediate reality; its truth is all the more enlightening because it is the sort of speech that, unlike non-thematic, enables the speaker to relate himself to reality as world.

The essence of fictional speech is its hypothetical quality; the speaker's relationship to the world is mediated by a special sort of thematization, namely, his supposition of imaginary surrogates and alternative versions of reality. Different forms of non-factual assertion do their work differently, but without the ability to make up fictions human life would not be what it is. We manage our existence as much, if not more, by resorting to fanciful realities and by using them to compose minor scenarios as by asserting facts as facts: 'If we don't leave now, we'll miss the last bus,' 'Either you stop or I'll scream,' 'It should be interesting to have them at the cottage, but I hope they'll not bring their kids.' And as we all have had occasion to muse, 'My decision may have been a mistake.' The ability to ask questions, also, is rooted in the thematic speaker's power to detach an assertion from factual reality, so that the assertion be made only under the guise of its not being necessarily true: 'Did I or did I not turn the headlights off before I parked?' By speaking and thinking in this way we can organize factual information, for instance, to plan the future and learn from the past, and to evaluate the worlds that might have been and those which may yet be. Our lives are spent indeed, for the most part, within such imaginatively made-up worlds rather than in the one that does in fact exist. Of course, living in imaginary worlds is dangerous; it becomes maladjustive when it ceases to be a means to managing our relationship to reality and becomes a pretext for not dealing with it.

But fictional speech is useful in the first place for constructing, out of mere facts, a totally unreal, abstract world altogether removed from concreteness, individuality, and time. Every generalization falls in this category – whether made by common sense, old wives, or myth-makers, at one end of the spectrum, or by disciplined and rational thought such as science and philosophy at the other. Facts are singular, transitory, and bound to the moment; factual assertions take account of this. Nothing in reality corresponds, however, to the timeless, universal ministory told by the assertion 'Sodium combines with chlorine to make table salt.' This is a work of fiction; it is useful and true, but its truth is that of an interpretation which may be applied and verified in factual reality; for instance, it could be translated into factually true assertions about the contents of this salt-cellar. Likewise, nothing in factual reality corresponds to the compact fables told by the second law of thermodynamics or the principle of natural selection. An untested hypothesis is also a work of fiction; its peculiarity is that one does not yet know whether it is referable back to reality, though one thinks it may be.

Other fictions discharge their function in other ways. A novel, a totally imaginary construction though it is, may convey a most important truth about the nature of man. But the distinctiveness of the type of fiction to which we usually, but without good reason, restrict this term – stories, tales, and the like – is not that it consists in an imaginative construction, but that it casts its asserted meaning (namely, the artist's perception of a certain aspect of the world or of human life) in pseudo-facts. That is, it translates the meaning of reality into thematizations referring to facts that are, though imaginary, proportional to real ones. The fiction writer's creative skill lies in this prorating of the imaginary to the real. But a scientific principle is an equally imaginative construction; it is quite as removed as a novel from the concrete facts that provided the information. The difference is that the scientific interpretation *remains* removed from factual reality; it is not – or at least, ideally should not be – translated into pseudo-facts, and therefore is not metaphorically but univocally true.

Thus, the thematic speaker, unlike the non-thematic one, distances his experience of reality from reality for the sake of experiencing reality in patterns and as a whole. Standing off from reality in order to surmount and judge it is what enables him to *manage* his relationship to it. Of course, the opportunity to manage necessarily opens the window to mismanagement and abuse; the same self-distancing from reality that, in one way, provides depth of perspective may in another bring alienation from reality, a peculiarly human disability. At any rate, once man had developed thematic ability, he had become a story-teller and a creator of myths. I need hardly explain that stories and myths – for that matter, scientific and philosophical interpretations – may be more or less critically composed and more or less adequate, useful, and true. And true narratives can be superseded by truer ones. None of this denies the fact that a valid explanation of reality is a story – I mean, a true story – that we tell ourselves about it.

Since thematic speech is more complex than non-thematic, we cannot but suppose that the former developed out of the latter. This is suggested also by the fact that in individual children today the 'first stage of [speech development] is one in which the maximum sentence length is one word; it is followed by a stage in which the maximum sentence length is two words.'[4] Thus, the earliest speakers must have been able to speak exclusively non-thematically. We can scarcely imagine what their experience of speaking must have been like, even if as adults we retain our infancy's ability to speak non-thematically; the inarticulateness of exclusively non-thematic speech is eclipsed for us by our ability to use non-thematically all the conceptualizations available to us after we have developed complex world- and self-interpretations using thematic speech.

---

4 B.A. Moskowitz, 'The Acquisition of Language,' *Scientific American*, 239 (1978), p. 95. Thematic speech does not consist in arranging two or more words together, but in making assertions integrated by two functional elements, thesis and theme; but since the thesis and the theme must be signified separately, a thematic assertion must be at least two words long. Of course, a string of two or more words, each asserted non-thematically, is also perfectly possible. A child's two-word assertion – say, 'doll, pretty' – could be either a simple thematic assertion or a complex non-thematic assertion; knowledge of the contents alone would not enable us to determine which it was. It is possible, if not indeed probable, that children normally pass through an intermediate stage of two-word non-thematic assertion before they begin to make simple two-word thematic assertions. But in any event, the first stage in their speech is non-thematic, since it uses single words.

An early, exclusively non-thematic speaker could hardly have made such non-thematic assertions as 'Death to the enemies of the people!' and 'Go to the ant, thou sluggard, and consider her ways!' Conceiving each of the elements and asserting them one at a time would have been well within his capabilities; but organizing them artificially, as in these examples, would have approached the thematizations of the higher form of speech. Conversely, the signification of a great deal of our non-thematic speech today is pseudo-articulate. 'God damn you to Hell,' for instance, is non-thematic speech upon which the trappings of thematic conceptualization and organization have been superimposed; what it truly means is: 'Anger! Hate!' For the same reason, our non-thematic speech today is often deceptively specific, semantically misleading, and conceptually inappropriate: 'Fuck you!' asserts and conveys the same meaning as 'Damn you!' And neither means what it supposedly signifies.

How did thematic speech develop out of merely non-thematic speech? The theory explains that it was the result of the mutual involution of experience and communication, the same principle at work in the passage from non-assertive communication to non-thematic speech. The latter transformation had taken place when the freshman speaker had as it were successfully completed a program of two courses, Introduction to Communicative Efficacy and Survey of Communicative Finality. Having now been promoted to the sophomore grade of humanity, he was prescribed the same two subjects again, but at a more advanced level: he had to appreciate his efficient and his final causality not merely as a communicator, but specifically *as a speaker*, so as to experience *consciously* his assertive reality. In other words, knowing already how to speak, he now had to learn to speak with consciousness of speech. The process whereby he did so should be deducible from a comparison of the two levels of speech. As we have seen, the differences between them concern, in general, how the speaker relates himself assertively to reality. But, more particularly, they have to do with how he (a) *communicates* the experienced *reality*, (b) *asserts* the experienced *reality*, (c) *communicates* his *experience* of reality, and (d) *asserts* his *experience* of reality. Let us compare thematic and non-thematic speech in these four respects.

Non-thematic speech communicates an experienced reality and asserts the speaker's experience of it in a single act that simultaneously asserts the reality and communicates the experience of it. That is, a single act, embodied in making a single (though not necessarily simple) sign, achieves the following, all at the same time: first, it communicates *indistinctly* the experienced reality both as experienced and as reality; second, it asserts *indistinctly* the experienced reality both as experienced and as real; and third, it *indistinctly* both asserts and communicates the experienced reality. For instance, I am confronted by a dangerous situation and am moved to speak. My act of non-thematic speech consists in my uttering a vocal sign, 'Danger!', which indistinctly communicates the reality (i.e., the danger itself) and my experience of it (i.e., my alarm). Inevitably, therefore, it must also assert indistinctly the reality of the dangerous situation itself, and my experience of alarm. Thus, when I call 'Danger!' I indistinctly mean both 'I experience danger' and 'This situation is dangerous' (as we would discriminatingly say in thematic speech). Non-thematic speech fuses together the [experienced] reality and the experience [of reality]. Likewise, it fuses together the communication [of the asserted experience of reality] and the assertion [of the communicated experience of reality]. For as long as I speak non-thematically I cannot simply propose 'Danger!' as an object of possible assertion; if I propose it, I necessarily affirm it also, since proposing it and asserting it are one and the same act.

If non-thematic speech is not only confused, but also inconsiderate and crude, the reason is that its tongue is tied to immediate reality. Lacking distance, it lacks perspective; and lacking perspective, it lacks judgment and delicacy. This is what makes it singularly apt for the expression of feelings with feeling, or for assertively signifying emotions emotionally; I mean, immediately, rather than as thematized objects of speech. Conversely, thematizing one's feelings tends to make them 'dispassionate.' But note that non-thematic speech can as adequately signify outer as inner experience, external realities as well as our feelings about them, and experiences holding much emotional charge as well as those that have practically none.[5] But though anything that can be said non-thematically can also be said thematically, it is not always practical or desirable to speak with purpose aforethought or to experience with finesse; non-thematic speech continued to have an indispensable role in human life even after thematic speech had appeared, for the very reason that it can pour forth incontinently. Thematic speech, for its part, is imperative if one wishes to disguise, deny, distort, suppress, repress, or otherwise distance oneself from one's feelings. These properties are the obverse of the inarticulateness and rudimentary self-presence of non-thematic speech.

5 But no conscious experience is ever entirely lacking in affect. Being self-present, the experiencer's valuing of his experience is necessarily included in the experience of any object. This is true even when the object is an inner one. Thus, we have feelings not only about outer objects, but also about our own experiencing, our selfhood, and even about our feelings; for instance, one can be angry at oneself because one is afraid; one may worry that one is not worried, if one feels that one should be.

An analysis of thematic speech in the same four respects, on the contrary, shows how it discriminates with razor's-edge precision among the various aspects and functions that non-thematic speech fuses together. The discriminations are not necessarily consciously made, since few speakers reflect upon their 'idea' of speech; they are nevertheless made, in the sense that they are implicit in what the thematic speaker actually does. By the same token, they constitute the curriculum that the non-thematic speaker must master in order to speak thematically. They may be enumerated as follows. When I speak thematically, I implicitly discriminate, first, between the *reality* assertively experienced and communicated by me, and my *experience* of such reality; second, between the experienced and assertively communicated reality as object of *experience*, and the same but as object of *speech*; and therefore, third, between my speech as *assertive* in relation to the experienced and communicated reality, and my speech insofar as it is *communicative* of the experienced reality that I assert. But now I will explain, one by one, how these discriminations are embodied in each of the two functions – thematization and thesis-making – that make up thematic speech.

The first discrimination – between the experiencing [of reality] and the [experienced] reality – is implicit in the fact that the thematic speaker does not assert his experience with direct reference to the reality itself, but specifically in relation to the theme. Communicating in this way is possible only because the theme is asserted in a peculiar manner: its affirmative force is reined in or held back. For to thematize is to assert an object of speech – for example, 'this situation' – but positing it precisely as something to be spoken about, withholding reference both to its being experienced and to its being real. The thematization merely creates the context in which the communication is to be understood. But to create the context of one's assertions is to take the experienced reality out of its own context, in itself. And in order to do so it is necessary to discriminate between reality in itself and reality as given to the speaker in experience. Therefore, discriminating between experience and reality is the first condition of the possibility of thematizing reality.

Second, the thematization of experienced reality also implies the ability to differentiate between speaking and experiencing. For as just noted, the theme refers the communicand immediately to an object of speech, and is specifically asserted as object of speech. But if a speaker can signify and assert objects of speech, he must be able to differentiate – at least functionally, not necessarily in the sense that he could conceptualize the difference – between his speaking [about a reality which is an object of experience] and his experiencing [such reality]. Thus, the thematization of an experienced reality such as 'this situation' reveals the speaker's ability to discriminate between experience and speech. Thematization also implies a higher level of self-presence in the speaker's experience than non-thematic speech does; for one can speak thematically only if one has learned to experience, be it more or less clearly, the assertiveness of one's speech. The graduated, controlled assertiveness typical of the theme would not otherwise be possible. In order to propose an object of speech as such, the speaker must restrict the assertiveness of his speech so as to communicate the theme only as a theme. This, then, is the third discrimination implicit in the ability to conceive reality as a theme: awareness of the assertive as distinct from the communicative aspect of speech.

The conditions to be satisfied before an experienced reality can be made into a thesis are the mirror image of the foregoing. To be able to assert 'is dangerous' in relation to 'this situation' I must be sensitive to the difference between my experience [of reality] and the [experienced] reality. For the thesis is asserted with direct reference to an object of speech and only mediately in relation to the [experienced] reality; and in order to take reality out of the context of its own reality it is necessary to attend specifically to its being an object of experience. The same discrimination that permits my thematizing an experienced reality also makes possible my making a thesis out of it and my asserting it, precisely as experienced, in relation to the theme. This discrimination between experience and reality implies in turn a discrimination between experiencing [reality] and communicating [the experience of reality]. The discrimination is made by communicating the experience, precisely as experience, in relation to a proposed object of speech that is asserted merely as such object; only differentiating between asserting and communication permits this. However, the ability to make theses out of experienced reality implies particular awareness of the assertive, as distinct from the communicative, aspect of speech. This is the counterpart of the discrimination between assertion and communication implicit in thematization, where the focus of the speaker's intention is to communicate rather than to assert. For the distinctive function of the theme is *to communicate an object of speech* (in relation to which a thesis is to be asserted), whereas that of the thesis is *to assert an object of experience* (in relation to the proposed theme).

These discriminations imply each other; a speaker could not speak thematically unless he made all of them at the same time. Thematic speech appeared when speaking communities, like the detective who puts all the clues together for the guests assembled in the library, synthesized all the suspicions that their experience as non-thematic speakers had gradually aroused. Nevertheless, the discriminations exhibit a logical order, and it should be possible to deduce the sequence of the various stages of the process. The progression seems to be: from the experience of reality to awareness of the difference between experience and reality; from the latter to awareness of the difference between experience and speech; and thence to awareness of the difference between assertion and communication. As non-thematic speech rendered the speaker's experience increasingly self-present, and as he experienced the difference between reality and experience, the speaker learned to experience consciously his own speech, becoming especially aware, at first, of its communicative function; the condition of the possibility of learning to thematize his experience of reality was thus satisfied. The process culminated with heightened awareness of the assertive function, and hence with the ability to convert an experienced reality into a thesis. The process was, in short, the rise of speech to a higher level of assertiveness, as the self-presence of experience became intensified. Once natural selection had created non-thematic speech, the interaction between the speaker's experiential-adjustive functions and his communicative-reproductive functions would have gradually satisfied the conditions of the emergence of thematic out of non-thematic speech. Natural selection had nothing to do with it.

This could have happened in evolution only very slowly. The chronology of human evolution is not essential, of course, to an understanding of the principles at work in the process; nevertheless there are some indications, albeit scant and indirect, of the order of magnitude of the temporal scale by which the origin of speech and consciousness is measurable. Judging by the development of the inferior-posterior parietal area of the cortex, which is the principal speech-integrating area of the brain (as such development can be deduced from endocasts of fossil skulls), biologists deem it 'highly probable [that speech] was selected and evolved in the Middle Pleistocene,'[6] roughly 500,000 years before the present. Whether 'speech' in this context means truly assertive vocal communication, however, is unfortunately not a question that this sort of evidence can resolve. But it is clear that an unusually high level of vocal communicative ability had appeared in hominids as long ago as this. The earliest positive indication of consciousness, however, can be found only much later; I refer to the burial customs of the Neanderthals, which began much less than 100,000 years ago. These practices cannot but imply that the Neanderthals experienced the death of fellow humans as a significant event; and it is difficult to explain how anyone could so

---

6 Bernard G. Campbell, *Human Evolution: An Introduction to Man's Adaptations* (Chicago, 1966), p. 313.

experience it unless he had at least a minimal awareness of his sharing the mortal nature of the deceased, and of his own reality, which death could take away. (Some scholars think that these rituals also point to belief in the self's survival after death, but their reasoning seems to me to take an excessively long leap.) Self-identity, however, was a later development than awareness of reality as real and of one's own reality; the selfhood of him who had but recently acquired a sense of reality would have been weak and uncertain as long as it remained unthematized in the pronoun 'I,' or some equivalent, by means of which the speaker could attribute anything to himself as part of himself. We need suppose, therefore, only that the early Neanderthals had developed non-thematic speech and some degree of immediate consciousness.

The earliest positive indications of thematic speech go back only to the Upper Palaeolithic – say, about 25,000 years ago. This estimate is based on the flowering of art during this period. When an artist takes some reality – stone, ivory, pigment – and organizes it so as to put it to a communicative use that it does not have in itself (e.g., makes it into a figurine, a toy, or a painting), he demonstrates thematic ability; his work is the practical equivalent of a deliberate, albeit somewhat inarticulate and elemental, thematization of reality. Like the thematic speaker, the artist asserts his experience as such; and he asserts it not with direct reference to the reality itself, but through the instrumentality of an artistic medium (corresponding to the theme), which he impresses with the peculiar disposition that signifies the very experience he wishes to assert (corresponding to the thesis). Thus, the ivory carving no longer signifies ivory, but a human being or an animal; and it no longer asserts the reality of the human being or the animal in itself, but refers specifically to the artist's perception of it. At the same time, however, art is inarticulate, and to that extent reminiscent of non-thematic speech; it joins thesis and theme, and the medium and the message, in the single reality of the work of art. The emergence of art, then, probably marks the time when the transition was being made from exclusively non-thematic to thematic speech.

At any rate, whereas the road to thematicity is traversed by children today in a matter of months, the evolutionary path had to be negotiated by the species one laborious step at a time. Perhaps we can best comprehend the experience of those who trod it by analogy with the intensification of consciousness in an individual nowadays when, after much travail, he makes a major discovery about himself. Most of us have had this experience, if we have lived so long and have been open to learning about ourselves. Our hard-earned wisdom then feels like the realization of something long suspected yet not known at all, and we liken our

newly found freedom to an awakening. The gradual awakening of speakers to the *assertive* character of their *communication* of their *experience* of
reality was, by another name, the transformation of non-thematic into
thematic speech.

Of course, semi-wakefulness was possible as well. The torpor of consciousness I call absent-mindedness first became a liability only when
speakers developed thematic speech; it was the less-than-full awakening
of certain speakers to the assertive nature of their speech. But let us put
this aside until later and examine instead the natural consequence of
the evolution of non-thematic into thematic speech. I refer to the evolution of consciousness from its aboriginal to its thematic, interpretative,
and self-defining form.

2. The emergence of self-definition

After thematic speech appeared, the next step was the emergence of the
self-defining form of consciousness; immediate, perceptual consciousness acquired the ability to define itself by interpreting itself in relation
to its interpreted world. Let us recall that non-thematic speech is interpretative only in the sense that conceptualization organizes empirical
information in bundles whose composition is determined by the speaker
alone; full interpretativeness is conferred upon consciousness only by
thematic speech. When the latter appears, the conceptual patterns of
information are themselves organized into patterns of patterns in accordance with principles of organization derived from the speaker's prior
idea of how his own conscious experience is organized by (non-thematic)
speech. For instance, in the assertion 'Toad slime gives you warts,'
information is organized not only by means of the concepts 'toad,' 'slime,'
and so on, but also, at a higher level, by the categorical concept of
causality; the latter determines that, in this particular assertion, 'giving
you warts' means an effect in relation to its cause. Note that 'giving you
warts' does not of itself carry this meaning; for instance, if 'you' refers
to a pathologist, the assertion that 'The surgeon gives you warts' conveys
no causal meaning at all. Consciousness adopts thus its own constitution, and the ways in which it operates and describes itself to itself, as
standards for measuring all things interpretatively – even itself. The
speaker's interpretations are meaningful because they relate whatever
they interpret to what is immediately and directly familiar to the interpreter: his actual and immediate reality as conscious experiencer and
thinker.

The process whereby the self-defining consciousness arose is therefore not difficult to reconstruct. In the last section we saw that immediate

consciousness enabled the speaker to have conscious experience not only of other objects, but also of his own assertiveness and of the characteristics of his own experiencing and speaking mind. This enabled him to discover the possibility of relating theses and themes in certain categorical patterns. And the emergence of the categories is the same as the emergence of the interpretative means whereby sense information could be meaningfully organized and consciousness could define itself. Thus, at the first stage of evolution the mere experiencer had become a conscious experiencer; he had learned to relate himself assertively to the [experienced] world. Now, by developing thematic ability, he had become the conscious experiencer who related himself interpretatively to whatever he was conscious of. Quite as the interplay of non-thematic speech and immediate consciousness had naturally tended to create thematic speech, the elevation of immediate consciousness to self-defining status was the natural consequence of the interplay of immediate consciousness and thematic speech.

Though the general character of the process is clear, one aspect of it should be examined in more detail. Since the categories are the principles of all world- and self-interpretation, we should at least consider how the most important among them – reality, efficient causality, and final causality – are conceived.[7] These are the most important, because they assert the fundamental characteristics on which conscious life is established; I shall, therefore, call them the *constitutive* categories. We hardly need deal with reality, however, since the topic has been discussed already in other contexts. I will simply remind us that we conceive *reality* when, by virtue of the self-presence of consciousness, we become informed about the relationship of mutual otherness between objects [of experience] and the experience [of objects]. Reality is the *otherness-to* that binds together all real things.

The empirical ground of the concept of *efficacy* is the fact that consciousness *does* its own experiencing. Being conscious consists in doing something; for unless one's experiencing be done, one will not experience at all. More particularly, conceiving is an act, because a concept is

---

7 The emergence of the categories may be described as their being 'conceived' in the sense that they originate when the non-thematic speaker, having made the necessary discriminations and integrations, discovers the 'idea' of thematic speech. Conversely, anyone who knows how to speak thematically has thereby a practical 'idea' of the various ways in which he can relate theses and themes. Thus, the categories are, to begin with, implicit in the practice of thematic speech; it is only when he reflects upon his practice of speech that the speaker may be properly said to *conceive* the categories, that is, to signify them assertively to himself by means of words such as *reality*, *causality*, and so on.

conceived by the mind's assertion of it. However, even before *conceiving* and *being conceived* are themselves conceived by consciousness as *doing* and *being done* (or as *activity* and *passivity*), they are conceived as *causing* or *effecting*. The reason is the strict proportion between the doing of the experiencing and the experiencing that is done. For there is, of course, no difference between an *act* of consciousness and the corresponding conscious *state*; one and the same consciousness that appears to itself as the former also appears to itself in the latter guise, since these are but two ways in which consciousness can be present to itself. Thus, act and state correspond perfectly, and cannot but so correspond. The categorical concepts of *activity* and *passivity* assert each of the two aspects separately, in abstraction from each other, whereas the concept of *efficient causality* asserts them in the first place as mutually related, or as found in real conscious life; it signifies the mirror-image proportion between doing and being done, or between cause and effect.

Of itself, then, the category of efficient causality includes no reference to necessity. The latter, too, is a category, though not a constitutive one. Like *sameness* and *unity*, which will be considered in a moment, *necessity* is conceived when the identity of the act of consciousness and the corresponding conscious state is experienced. Since the cause and the effect of experience are one, it is impossible both to experience and not to experience at the same time, or to experience anything but what in fact one experiences. This is the way in which, as a matter of fact, consciousness operates, given its self-presence: the experiencer must *necessarily* experience whenever he experiences, and he must *necessarily* experience whatever he in fact experiences. This impossibility – or its diametric opposite, necessity – is absolute. There cannot be any exception to it, for the very good reason that the standard by which possibility and impossibility are measured by consciousness is the self-identity that conceptual thought *in fact* exhibits.[8] Necessity is, therefore, not a prop-

8 This does not imply that the possibility or impossibility of real events depends on whether they are actually conceived; it means that we think of an event as possible or impossible depending on whether we find it conceivable or not. Nor does the absolute character of the category of necessity imply that the reality of consciousness is absolute; this is why I have stressed that the self-identity of thought, which is the ground of the concept of necessity, is itself nothing but an observable *fact*; that is, thinking must abide by necessity in the sense that one of its characteristics is, *as a matter of fact*, to be self-identical. Indeed, all the categories have a perfection or absoluteness that empirical reality seems only to approximate; the reason is of course that in the categorical measuring of reality by consciousness, the nature of consciousness is adopted as the unit of measurement. For instance, the self-coincidence of every concept is perfect because the self-coincidence of *acts of conceiving* is what provides the contents of the definitions of 'self-coincidence,' 'self-identity,' and

erty of the reality interpreted by thought, but only of the thought that interprets reality. This is true even when the reality interpreted by thought is thought itself (or more generally, the processes of consciousness).[9] In short, necessity has a purely 'logical' reality – that is, as a property of the organization that the thematic consciousness gives to its own processes – and efficient causality does not imply the necessitation or compulsion of the effect by the cause. It would be easy for an absent-minded consciousness, however, to imagine that it did, projecting thus onto all causal processes a characteristic that only conscious processes showed.

The active constitution of consciousness has another side, which is the basis of the concepts of finality and purposiveness. When we do our experiencing, we do it *wanting* or *intending* to experience what in fact we do, or else despite our *not wanting* to do it. What no one can do as long as he experiences consciously is to take no interest whatever in his experience. At the bottom of this phenomenon is the fact that all life has needs. The higher animals, however, experience their needs; they have *wants*. Being able to experience both their wants and the objects that satisfy them, they learn to behave so as to attain such objects. The self-presence of consciousness means, however, that human beings not only experience wanting and not-wanting; they also experience *that* they want and *that* they do not. They therefore not only seek objects that satisfy their wants and reject those that frustrate them, but experience some objects as desirable and others as undesirable. In other words, a human being, unlike an animal, not only takes advantage of the relationship between satisfaction and the means to attain it, but also experiences this relationship as such. The deliberate postponement of gratification is only one of the many possibilities opened up by this experience. At any rate, once the conscious experiencer has learned to relate means and ends, he has discovered his finality and can thereafter organize sense information in terms of *desirability, value, purpose, intention*, and so on.

Together with *otherness-to* – or however we may conceive reality – the constitutive categories of *efficacy* and *finality* assert the *ante-logical* properties of consciousness. For even before immediate consciousness develops thematicity, it is present to itself as other-than its objects, causing its own states, and undertaking to achieve goals. The *logical* properties

---

'sameness.' Likewise, the characteristics of consciousness that are conceived as its 'unity,' its 'finality,' and so on, are no more absolute than those of other entities. Only the categorical *concepts* are absolute.

9 For instance, although consciousness can cause effects in reality, its causality is no more absolute than that of other causal agents.

of consciousness, however, arise only with thematic speech and thought. There is, thus, a second type of category, which asserts the *sameness* and *difference*, the *unity* and *multiplicity*, and the *totality* and *partiality* that consciousness can perceive in its own functions when the experience of thinking and speaking include the meaningfulness that is typical of understanding. Since these concepts determine the rules of logic, they may be called the *regulative* categories.[10] Of course, the 'rules' of logic merely describe how consciousness in fact works when it speaks and thinks thematically,[11] not how it must willy-nilly work – as if the rules existed first and consciousness had then been designed in accordance with the rules. But the absent-minded consciousness is likely to imagine otherwise – just as it is likely to mistake mathematical, and sometimes even grammatical, 'rules' for objective constraints that determine from without how human beings may and may not think.

We have already seen how *necessity*, the negation of *factuality* or *contingency*, is conceived. *Sameness* or *equality*, and its opposite, *difference*, arise empirically when consciousness asserts to itself the fact that every concept coincides with itself – that is, is the *same* as itself. For instance, if I think 'rose,' and then think 'rose' again, I experience that the concept 'rose' is the *same* as itself; whereas if I think 'rose,' and then 'red,' the two do not coincide. They are *not-same*, but *different*. It is thus an empirical fact that, in respect of its contents, no concept can be more or less than itself; every concept is precisely *equal* to itself. And yet, in the reality of the world, as Plato rightly observed (drawing therefrom, however, the wrong conclusion),[12] nothing is ever exactly the same as anything else; indeed, nothing is quite the same as even itself, since it is

---

10 The relation between the constitutive and the regulative categories may require some elucidation. The most fundamental properties of consciousness – reality, efficacy, and finality – are enjoyed by consciousness, of course, even before it develops thematicity, though it is only when it learns to speak thematically that it conceives the corresponding constitutive categories. It is, however, only when it acquires narrative ability – and for that very reason – that consciousness develops logical properties, becomes able to experience logically, and conceives the categories that regulate its narrative, logical processes. Thus, both the constitutive and the regulative *categories* appear at the same stage of evolution; but the former assert the ante-logical, whereas the latter the logical, *properties* of consciousness.

11 Although all thematic speakers are 'ruled' by the logical properties of thematic speech and thought, they do not all take the same advantage of their capacity for learning to reason consistently with the logic of their thought. Likewise, not all cultures develop logic – or mathematics, or grammar – to the same degree, or at all, by reflecting upon the properties of their speech and thought.

12 Namely, that the concept of *same* represents the self-sameness of a reality beyond both consciousness and the empirical world; see *Phaedo*, 75A ff.

always changing. But it does not matter that in the real world identities and differences are always relative; by means of the categories of *sameness* and *difference* we are able to relate ourselves to reality precisely insofar as reality is relative to us.

Other facts of the inner life of consciousness provide the original meaning of the categories of *unity* and *totality*. A concept may be the same as, or different from, another in content, but the second is in any event not the first – for example, 'rose' now is one concept, whereas 'rose' again is another. Each of the two is one. Moreover, a concept that is both *one* and *self-same* is a *totality*; for, being *same* (as itself), it is neither more nor less than (i.e., is *not-different* from) itself. At the same time, being *one*, it holds its self-same contents in itself, rather than both in itself and another. In other words, it is in itself *all* that it is or can be: whatever coincides with itself, or is self-identical, is also a *whole*. Thus, given the regulative categories, a thematic thinker would experience his attempt to assert a self-contradiction such as 'A rose is not a rose' as meaningless. The reason is not that things in themselves are self-identical, but that *concepts* are. Likewise, a syllogism makes no sense if neither premiss is universal; for this means that the middle term would be undistributed (i.e., *not-a-totality*) twice, and equivocity would result; a seemingly constant term would have *different meanings* in each of two propositions. By the same token, *one* plus *one* is *equal* to a *total* called two; this assertion does not correspond to any property of the real world, though it is nevertheless applicable to it. Thus, reality is neither logical nor mathematical in itself, but can be interpreted by means of logical and mathematical thought. Its contents are not distorted simply by being so interpreted. But they would be, if the logical and mathematical properties of thought were projected onto objects and ascribed to them as their own.

Categories of a third type conceptualize the *post-logical* characteristics of thematic speech. Their list is not closed; for as consciousness evolves, new categories of this sort may be conceived. They measure the experience of thinking and speaking, as conceived in accordance with the constitutive categories, by the units provided by the regulative categories. Since they unfold before one's own eyes the ways in which one has elaborated one's thematic abilities, they may be called the *descriptive* categories. The most likely to be developed in the majority of cultures, because they are the most elementary, are *quantity* and *quality*, *structure* and *function* (or *subject* and *accident*), *space* and *time*, and *absoluteness* and *relativity*. Since the meaning of these categories depends not only upon the nature of consciousness, but also upon the categorical thinker's prior perception of his reality and his efficient and final causality, the misinterpretation of the latter categories by the absent-minded will compound their misunderstanding of the former. Since their handicap prevents their appreciating the relativity of reality, they will inevitably assume that only one of the terms of each pair – that is, *quantity, subject, space,* and *absoluteness* – is truly and unqualifiedly applicable to reality. The prejudice that *quality, event, time,* and *relation* are somewhat less real than the foregoing is among the most deep-seated that the human mind can acquire as it develops thematic speech.

3. The need for self-definition

Following common practice I have repeatedly used the terms *identity* and *self-identity* as if they referred to a human peculiarity; I have said, for instance, that the acquisition of thematic speech is the cause of the emergence of the level of consciousness that develops self-identity. But this is a little inaccurate; it would have been better to speak of 'the identity proper to persons or selves.' For all things whatever, even if they are not conscious – indeed, even if they are not living – have to some degree and in some sense the continuity, coherence, and integration that define self-sameness; they all exhibit a constellation of 'traits,' a pattern of consistently observable features that gives them a distinctive 'personality' or 'character.' But of course, the self-sameness of a non-living being is not the identity of a self, since it is not even experienced – let alone present to itself – as such self-sameness. Moreover, the identity of a thing in itself does not make it meaningful in itself; as we have seen, the meaning of a thing is not the meaning in the thing, but the meaning-for-consciousness of the thing. In sum, all things, even inanimate beings, have some sort of identity, although their meaning depends upon our relating ourselves meaningfully to them. What is distinctive of consciousness, then, is not that it can have identity, but that its identity is *self-given* and that it is the sort that can become *meaningful* to itself.

Since the means whereby consciousness can give itself its own identity and meaning is thematic speech, the reconstruction of the emergence of thematic speech has enabled us to explain how the self-defining consciousness originated. But in the light of what we have just noted – that all things have identity, but no inherent meaning or explanation, and that they can be meaningful only in relation to human understanding – the fuller significance of the emergence of self-definition in human evolution may be appreciated. I have in mind the fact that, with thematicity, an organism had appeared that was stirred into motion by a new kind of mainspring.

The essence of mere organic life is organic self-preservation; however, with the emergence of the kind of life that was not reducible to organic functions, self-preservation itself was transformed. Human beings are not ruled by an unimpeachable built-in orientation towards preserving their existence; it is a fact that they are capable of deliberately disposing of it. Indeed, only one thing reveals more starkly the irreducibility of consciousness to biochemical processes than does the fact that human beings are capable of managing their biochemical processes so as to terminate their ability to manage their biochemical processes. And that one thing is the fact that they can do so for the most inane and reprehensible reasons as well as for noble and selfless ones. Human beings are ruled instead by the need to create, preserve, and enhance their selfhood.

The construction of their own meaningful identity is for human beings not only a possibility, but a vital necessity; the satisfaction of this need is the specifically human motive and that which qualifies all the other wants and needs that may animate conscious behaviour. The reason is almost paradoxical, as so much in human nature is: that when consciousness first appears it comes into being not only without having any intrinsic meaning (as all other things do), but also (unlike all other things) without having its own identity. The human organism has, of course, the material identity and the organic individuality that can be found in all material and organic entities. As noted in chapter II, however, not only is the human organism originally not a self, but even consciousness has no selfhood when it first comes into being. For the *ego* cannot antecede consciousness. Since selfhood in the human sense requires the ability to experience oneself as an experiencer, consciousness is a *precondition* of selfhood. Consciousness is therefore born, I then said, as nothing but what-the-other-is-other-than; it comes into being as a mere negation, as *not-being* the object that it experiences.[13] Consciousness is thus hungrier than mere organic life when it comes into the world; it is radically needy, dispossessed to the ultimate degree.

In contrast, inanimate things come into being already owning whatever identity they can have; they need acquire nothing in order to be what they are. Infrahuman living beings do need others in order to keep themselves alive, to be sure, but their identity does not begin at nothing. For organic reproduction works through the parent's passing on to the offspring a part of itself that is already living. That is, since offspring come into being already alive, there never is a time in the life of any infrahuman organism, not even at the very moment of its origin, when

13 See Jean-Paul Sartre, *L'être et le néant* (Paris, 1943), pp. 57–84.

it does not have at least one thing that it could call its own, as it were – namely, its identity as a living organism. The consciousness of human beings, however, is not generated through the parents' endowing the offspring with a small amount of consciousness or with an immature seed of it; the human being's *only* native endowment is his organic one. And the socio-cultural matrix transmits to the young no 'genetic' endowment other than speech, the wherewithal for *it* to grow its own consciousness. Therefore, when the experience of the human organism first becomes self-present, the organism contains within itself not even a nucleus of inherited *human* identity that, like a gamete, could thereafter grow, mature, and in time become self-supporting. Unlike all other things, then, living and non-living, consciousness comes into being having no name at all; all it has is a capacity for eventually attributing to itself the names by which it becomes conscious of itself. The self-defining consciousness is fittingly so called for reasons already seen, but not least of all because it creates its own identity as a self.

The explanation of the human need for explanation, and the meaning of the human hunger for meaning, are therefore the obverse of the fact that, in man, the drive for self-preservation has been transcended; survival in the usual biological sense is not the most powerful human 'instinct.' Human beings need above all to make sense of themselves, to integrate their experiences of themselves, and thereby to acquire the identity of a self. Conversely, in the absence of self-definition human beings experience the discomfort of meaninglessness; in order to be truly satisfied with anything else that otherwise might be of value, even organic life itself, they must experience themselves as having significance. And since they can integrate their experiences of themselves only by situating themselves in the world as experiencers of it, their first need is to integrate their experiences of the world.

The need for self-identity replaces none of the other motives built into the human organism, but transforms them all by elevating them to the status of self-present want. So far as a human being wants consciously, he does not want objects for their own sake, as the animal does; what he actually wants is to have certain conscious experiences (and not to have others). Objects will be wanted (or otherwise) only insofar as they may be instrumental in procuring those experiences he wants (and in sparing him the others). Underlying a human being's wanting anything is, therefore, his wanting to be the experiencer of his experiences – or, which is the same, to be himself. But many of us do not quite realize this; we may then attempt to satisfy our need for self-identity by striving to possess, consume, and accumulate human and non-human objects. No amount of success of this kind can bring satisfaction, however, if one remains unable to determine precisely whom one wants to be and what one really wants, and if one has not learned to want only what one wants to want. Our self-misinterpretation would be all the more stultifying if we mistook our deepest aspirations for the wish to transcend our mortality and thus ascend to a different order of reality than that which we and our world have, and one in which satisfaction might be obtained through the endless accumulation of 'higher' values. What we actually want, and what we can realistically hope to attain, is rather the *self-possession* that places one's self-respect even above one's own life and death. If one achieves it, then one values nothing – not even the enjoyment of everlasting existence in a world that should provide an infinite supply of spiritual consumer goods – more highly than one's consciously self-given identity as a self.

Creating and appropriating one's identity is an arduous task. But it offers proportionate rewards. By integrating themselves living organisms merely stay alive, whereas by integrating itself consciousness enjoys being alive. This implies, of course, that man is also the being who can find life a burden. Whereas the absence of intrinsic meaning is no hardship for mere organic life, for human beings meaninglessness is unbearable. If they cannot perceive meaningfully the real world, therefore, they will invent out of whole cloth one to which they can relate themselves. And they will conjure up a pseudo-identity if they do not have one of their own, or if they cannot tolerate the one that otherwise they would have to acknowledge. Man can seek relief from meaninglessness in any of the myriad ways in which reality and existence can be symbolically or literally denied – even in madness. Unique opportunities are open to man, but he might not take advantage of them. The possibility of failure is implicit in the possibility of success.

4. The institutions and the limits of self-definition

The kind of consciousness generated by non-thematic speech could have been removed from animal life by only one step; the individual would have had no self-identity other than as a member of his group. Individuality of the sort we now take for granted – that of selves who experience themselves as being uniquely themselves – requires thematic speech. This hardly means, however, that as soon as human beings developed thematicity they began to create their selfhood exclusively, or even principally, by themselves. Indeed, we have not reached this condition – not remotely – even today. If anyone should think that simply because human beings have freedom of choice they actually determine for and by themselves what they are, what they do, and what they become, he would demonstrate both insufficient understanding of the nature of freedom and excessive capacity for ignoring palpable facts. The self-creativity of human beings is severely restricted. There are two reasons for this.

The first is that the same thematic ability that enables human beings to make thematic assertions to themselves about themselves also enables them to make assertions about each other to each other; and to the same degree to which assertions made by others are assertively repeated by oneself, they become one's own. It is only after a human being's selfhood has matured considerably – if ever it does – that he can define himself autonomously. But to begin with he can define himself only by asser-tively repeating (to himself) what others explicitly – and, most important of all, implicitly – assert to him about himself. Every member of a the-matic community participates, therefore, more or less directly and de-cisively in everyone else's interpretation of himself and the world. Thematic speech transformed society in no way more dramatically than by con-verting it into a system of cultural institutions that define and regulate, sometimes in minute detail, almost every moment of human life between birth and death; there are, indeed, right and wrong ways of coming into the world and of retiring to one's final resting place.

Thematic speech *did* create the opportunity for the individual to define himself – but only in interaction with others. And the degree to which individuals take advantage of the possibility of participating actively in this process is as varied as the degree to which they help create the kind of society that does not merely permit, but also facilitates, the individ-ual's autonomous self-creation. The primary identity of many – perhaps most – people continues to depend on their experience of themselves as members of groups rather than on their independent idea of them-selves. The advertising flackery, the public-relations circuses, and the propaganda machines that governmental, commercial, financial, and other interests turn to their profit did not invent the penchant of most people for letting others do their thinking for them; they merely take advantage of weaknesses in the design of human nature. Nothing in this implies, however, that the essentially social character of self-defi-nition is doomed to conflict with the individuality of the self. Everyone's self-definition must begin, but need not end, with his induction into his culture's ways. Groupthink is not attributable to the social nature of the individual, but to his failure to develop his selfhood beyond its juvenile stages. Of course, the *possibility* of conflict between the individual and society does inhere in the structure of the thematic consciousness. The integration of the two has had to be worked out in history as human beings have continued to evolve. And human beings, individually and collectively, have been more or less successful at this endeavour in different places and at different times.

Not everything that people teach their young and each other is equally relevant to their world- and self-understanding, though even pedestrian truths – 'The nearest bus stop is two blocks away' – and transient facts – 'The bus is late again today' – are more or less distantly related to everyone's idea of what world and self are like. The more comprehensive a thematization or narrative, the greater its bearing upon self-definition. And the compass of even the highly relevant assertions is very wide. It embraces, for instance, simple propositions such as 'Motherhood is a good thing,' as well as the encyclopaedic explanations of why it is (or is not) so. The culture perpetuates humble verities about the body ('To cure hiccups, hold your breath') and about the soul ('A soft answer turns away wrath') as well as noble ones ('Religion is the opiate of the people,' in some societies, or according to others, 'Man was made to serve God.') It transmits theoretical interpretations ('The world was born of the copulation of Tiamat and Apsu,' and 'The CERN experiments confirm that gluons W and Z exist') as well as practical advice ('Crime does not pay,' 'The family that prays together stays together,' and 'It's only human nature to look out for number one'). But somehow they all coalesce into a *Weltanschauung* and a self-interpretation – or at least, depending on the individual and the culture, into a number of more or less well-integrated, partial definitions of world and self.

Without a doubt, societies differ greatly both in the degree to which uniformity of self-definition is enforced and in the degree to which it prevails. But, in any event, with thematic speech the socio-cultural matrix became the repository of assertions and narratives that more or less authoritatively, coercively, and uniformly propose to people how they ought, should, or might perceive themselves and make sense out of the world. Even the transmission of information guiding the members of the culture in their organic adjustment to the physical environment is subsumable under the same heading. The young tribesman learning to make utensils out of clay is doing more than adjusting to his physical environment, since he will use his ware only in part to draw water or to store grain; he will put it to work also to construct his identity as a member of a group that uses pottery jugs to draw water or store grain. Every artefact functions in human culture as 'genetic' information determining self-definition, by virtue of its direct or indirect dependence upon thematic speech. Culture is the institutionalized self-definition of a group.

The wide spectrum of thematic assertions directly relevant to human self-definition, however, can be divided into two main categories. Some aspects of culture institutionalize assertions that collect, proclaim, systematize, develop, and perpetuate the narratives and the interpretations that govern day-to-day human life; they make up the economic, political, legal, social, familial, and other institutions of every society, which do more intensively and systematically what the community's common sense does in an informal and general way. Important though these are, however, they are only the superstructure of tradition; they particularize and draw the quotidian, practical consequences of yet more basic thematic assertions: 'Language ... constructs immense edifices of symbolic representations that appear to tower over the reality of everyday life like gigantic presences from another world. Religion, philosophy, art and science are the historically most important systems of this kind ... [But] despite the maximal detachment from everyday experience that the construction of these systems requires ... symbolism and symbolic language become essential constituents of the reality and the common sense apprehension of reality.'[14] These or equivalent systems of assertions are concerned with the fundamental principles of self- and world-interpretation, the all-encompassing basic ideas that define the orientation of individuals and groups and that determine, at least in outline, all else that they will think and not think. Expounding more or less methodically derived and firmly held convictions about human nature and values, they are more or less consistently presupposed by legal, economic, political, and social conventions, and the like.

But we have not yet reached bottom. These two levels of self-definition embody and transmit self- and world-understanding to new generations by virtue of the *contents* of thematic speech. Their effectiveness should not be underestimated; it is not by chance that the wisdom of dialectical materialism is best appreciated in the Soviet Union and that of Adam Smith in the United States, that God gives to most Spaniards the grace to become Catholics yet the gift of Lutheran faith, if any, to Swedes, and that scientific humanism fares best in countries with a low illiteracy rate. But their influence is not absolute; conversions to, and apostasies from, the basic systems of religious and secular self-definition, in one or another of which all of us receive infant baptism, are not rare. Strictly determinative of one's self-definition, however – in respect at least of its general orientation – is the *primary* institution of self-definition, speech, by virtue of its inherent consciousness-generating properties. In the final analysis, all the thematic assertions whose contents

14 Peter Berger and Thomas Luckmann, *The Social Construction of Reality* (Garden City, NY, 1967), pp. 40–1.

make up the *secondary* and *tertiary* levels of institutionalized self-definition – as the earlier-mentioned may be called – are subject to the constraints imposed on them by the *form* of thematic speech. This brings us to the second way in which the exercise of human self-creativity is restricted.

The second factor that makes it difficult for human beings to give themselves an independently constructed identity operates yet deeper below the surface of consciousness than the first. When the individual is taught to speak thematically, his identity is thereby automatically prescribed for him by his socio-cultural matrix – I do not mean in detail, but in certain fundamental respects of which he ordinarily remains unaware (and which for that very reason are almost impossible to change). This prescription is a side-effect, of special importance only at the level of thematic speech, that accompanies the socio-cultural generation of the ability to speak. Let us recall that thematic speech emerges only when the speaker becomes able to make the discriminations that are its pre-condition – namely, among *reality*, the *experience* of reality, the *communication* of the experience of reality, and the *assertion* of the communication of the experience of reality. But, if so, the thematic speaker's purely practical 'idea' of how to speak thematically embodies equally practical 'concepts' of reality, of conscious experience, of communication, and of the assertiveness of speech. The same process that habilitates him as an interpreter provides him with the fundamental premises on which his interpretations will depend.

Thematic speech operates as a means to self-definition, therefore, in two ways at the same time. Insofar as assertions have certain contents, self-definition is transmitted through the speaker's and the listener's *conscious* understanding of what is said. Non-conscious factors may well affect it, but it remains conscious none the less. Speakers and listeners, therefore, remain free – theoretically fully free, in practice only more or less so – to make the assertions or not, and to accept or reject what is proposed;[15] for instance, not everyone in our culture agrees that 'Holding your breath cures hiccups' or that 'Man was made to serve God.' But

---

15 Rather, they are theoretically free to reject it, upon critical reflexion and in the light of experience, only after having originally accepted it; for the traditional self-definitions perpetuated by the culture come to them, and are accepted, before they have defined themselves autonomously for the first time. This, too, is inevitable; no individual and no generation could evolve if they had to work out their self-definition – or their thematic ability, or their vocabulary and grammar, or their ability to speak – all by themselves. Significant change in self-definition can be made only with great difficulty, even within the limits of the constant presuppositions created by the form of thematic speech.

at any rate, since speakers learn thematic speech with no conscious awareness of how they do it, they cannot realize that by learning to speak they have acquired presuppositions that are implicit in their ability to speak. Their *Vorverständnisse* will operate as inalterable, unquestionable, seemingly self-evident principles, within the confines of which the human mind must needs interpret self and world.

The nature of these presuppositions can be ascertained. Since they are contained in the speaker's 'idea' of thematic speech, they are part of his 'idea' of how to assert theses in relation to themes: the *Vorverständnisse* are identical with the meaning of the categorical concepts assumed by the speaker; the most important of these are the constitutive categories of reality and efficient and final causality. On the one hand, therefore, these presuppositions have an empirical basis; they are not necessarily invalid simply because they are non-consciously held – though like all other products of experience they may be more or less adequate, depending at least in part upon the experiencer's skill. On the other hand, as long as they remain non-consciously held, they cannot be subjected to critical review. Any inadequacies (or for that matter adequacies) in the speaker's most basic assumptions will then be endlessly repeated, unwittingly handed down from one generation of speakers to the next. They will be as inflexibly transmitted by the self-reproductive mechanism that perpetuates the human specificity as are the genes that determine susceptibility to sickle-cell anaemia and colour of skin.

I have said that the presuppositions are non-consciously held, but this should be more precisely put. A speaker who learns to say such things as 'The cat frightened the mouse' makes use of the category of efficient causality, though he may never have become conscious of 'efficient causality.' But if he reflected upon it, he *could* become conscious that cats 'cause' fear in mice. Indeed, if he were philosophically inclined he might even inquire into the nature of 'causality'; our intellectual tradition began to do so many centuries ago. What will escape his conscious notice altogether, even if he should be a philosopher – unless he should have become aware of the consciousness-generating properties of speech – is *why* he means what he means when he says 'on account of' or 'because,' or when he relates theses and themes as causes and effects. That is, he will not be conscious that the fundamental meaning of his concept of causality is *presupposed* by him, let alone that it is implicit in his 'idea' of thematic speech. He might even imagine that he learned it by experiencing through his senses, or discovering with his reason, a 'causal force' that resides within things themselves. Likewise, he might suppose that he conceives the reality, the being, or the existence of things by reproducing within himself, in experience, something within things themselves called their 'reality,' 'being,' or 'existence' – despite the fact that it is invisible, intangible, and altogether undetectable by any sense.[16]

I have also said that the categories are 'premisses' implicit in the speaker's 'idea' of speech; but since the categories are not propositions used by speakers when they reason, this, too, should not be taken literally. The point is rather that, as long as the speaker takes for granted his 'idea' of speech, he cannot but automatically and uncritically accept the presuppositions that it embodies. Moreover, as long as speakers and listeners fail to become sufficiently conscious of the properties of their speech, the presuppositions will continue to be conveyed and received below the threshold of consciousness; for their meaning will not be transmitted as part of any message, but will be implicit in the properties of the medium. Development and variation in the contents of self- and world-interpretation may thus take place – but within the boundaries of a fairly constant fundamental meaning, the latter having been inexorably predetermined by the underlying, unchanging assumptions implicitly carried by the form of speech.

This is why the rigorous operation of these assumptions does not forbid variations in the concrete thematic assertions and narratives that add up to the self-definition of individuals and groups. For instance, ultimate realities that are uniformly absolute and transcendent, but otherwise very different, can be commonly found in such independently developed systems of self-definition as Hinduism and the religions of the primitive Western Indo-Europeans. The reason is that the cultures that produced them shared the presupposition that the reality of the empirical world was less than real *tout court*. (I will show later how this assumption was implicit in their 'idea' of thematic speech) Therefore, they could not but have reached essentially the same conclusion – that

16 One of the most sophisticated explanations of how we experience the existence that supposedly belongs to real things as their absolute property is that of neo-Thomists, who try to avoid the objections that can be levelled at the simpler theories by stressing that existence is not the object of simple apprehension but of judgment. Existence (*esse*) – the act whereby a thing is and is what-it-is (*essentia*) – is not represented by a concept, but by the act of judgment itself, which 'intellectually *reiterates* an actual act of existing': Étienne Gilson, *Being and Some Philosophers* (Toronto, 1949), p. 303, italics mine; cf. Jacques Maritain, *Existence and the Existent* (New York, 1948), pp. 15–35. In other words, it is the very *act* of judging that reproduces, imitates, or acts out, as it were, the thing's *act* of being (*esse*). This explanation reaffirms, however, that in the case of existence no less than in any other the human mind simply re-presents or repeats – it 'reiterates' – what reality itself first contains in itself; it only adds that the mind's reiteration of existence differs from its reiteration of every other aspect of reality.

there was a higher, *really* real, order of reality other than this world –
though they diverged in the details. By the same token, even if a speaker
should appraise and critically judge the whole or any part of the world-
and self-interpretation of his culture, he would not ordinarily be able to
question its basic assumptions. He might well use his initiative and
imagination to devise alternatives more in keeping with his experience,
but any such alternative would be only a variation on the same fundamental traditional theme. One might thus reject the idea that man
was made to serve God, and conclude that he was made to serve the
omnipotent will of history – or vice versa. My suggestion is not that
differences of this type do not matter, but that they matter less than
whether their common underlying assumptions are correct.

To question the adequacy of the *Vorverständnisse* that his speech creates in him, the speaker would first have to realize that he is prepossessed of such assumptions, and then criticize them. But since he must
conduct all his reflexions, and in particular his critical thinking, using
his own form of speech, is it not impossible for him to become aware
of them? And is it not doubly impossible that he should be able to criticize
them? No, not quite, for reasons that will be considered later. But it
would be almost as difficult for human beings to define themselves
without following the instructions contained in the 'genetic' information
that generates their ability to define themselves as it would be for any
organism to integrate itself biologically ignoring or changing the chromosomal information it received at conception. This explains why un-
derneath wide and obvious variations in detail the self-definitions
perpetuated by human cultures are monotonously repetitive. Human
nature *has* evolved since the inception of its second evolutionary age –
but it has changed remarkably little. Even the conventional wisdom
comments upon it: *plus ça change, plus c'est la même chose*. That, indeed,
may be the problem of the human species today: that it has changed a
great deal in ways that do not much count towards self-adjustment, but
perhaps not enough in those that do.

These matters will be dealt with in the next chapter. Meanwhile let
us pause for a moment and reflect upon the meaning of the emergence
of self-definition by situating it within the larger context of the evolution
of all life.

5. The emergence of the self-defining consciousness as part of the evolution of life

According to the conception of causality developed in chapter II, the
characteristics of every reality are relative to those of every other reality;

therefore, whatever is real is, in point of fact, capable of exercising efficient causality. But there is an important difference between the causality of inanimate agents and that of living things: the former cause effects, but do not act *so as to* cause them. When life somehow emerged out of non-life, however, what came into being was an irreducibly novel kind of efficient agent, one that exercised *purposive* efficient causality; for life, as I have repeatedly reminded us, is the sort of efficient causal process whose proper effect is to keep itself operating as a causal process. At the lowest levels of life this inherent purposiveness is, of course, not mediated by experience; and even in the highest animals it does not amount to any sort of conscious intention to achieve a goal. But regardless of modality, all life tends to achieve a goal; and in the final analysis its goal is to realize itself. Misleadingly, we call this phenomenon 'self-preservation' – misleadingly, I say, because it falsely suggests that the activity of preserving itself is superadded to life. The truth is rather that life is the process of self-preservation itself.

Unlike inanimate reality, then, life naturally tends to coincide with itself; its essence is *self-orientation*. This is indeed a defining characteristic of all forms of life, from the simplest and most primitive to the most recent and complex. But if so, I suggest, consciousness is the logical – though neither the predetermined nor the sought for – outcome of evolution, in the sense that its self-presence is explicable as an emergent form of self-orientation. And this is most especially true insofar as consciousness is capable of self-definition. Let us consider why.

As life evolves, it tends to become increasingly self-directed. This is a consequence of the inherent tendency of life to protect itself, because natural selection protects whichever activities contribute to their own self-preservation. In other words, the adaptability of life results in the evolution of life, because the inherent purposiveness of the activities that define life naturally protects characteristics that enhance the adaptability of the organism. No force compels life to become increasingly adaptive, but unless it did so it would not evolve. Conversely, the nature of life is such that, though it need not evolve, if it evolves at all it must do so in the direction of increasing its survivability (not absolutely, but in relation to whatever environmental conditions prevail). Thus, although evolution achieves no particular purpose – that is, it tends to bring about no given form of survivability – it nevertheless evolves in accordance with its purposive nature. This means that evolution tends to make the efficient causality of organisms to converge upon itself. Purposiveness or goal-seeking is indeed nothing but the convergence of efficient causality upon itself.

Every stage of evolution can be envisaged, therefore, as an episode in the development of the self-preserving purposive efficacy that defines life. For example, the emergence of sentience in animals meant that the self-sustaining character of life had become a function of the organism's ability to process the information it received. Correspondingly, *want* no longer denoted mere *lack* or *need*, but implied goal-seeking behaviour, actively working towards the satisfaction of tendencies that ultimately redounded to the benefit of the organism. In the last analysis, experience is simply a way in which the self-orientation of life can be served; sentient organisms use their ability to experience in order to direct their efficient causality towards the attainment of goals that fulfil their wants, foster their welfare, and enable their life to sustain itself. If we can say, then, that with sense experience the purposiveness that had originally come into being as primitive life had evolved considerably, it is because the convergence of efficient causality upon itself had come, to a very large extent, under the control of the organism itself. Though all life is in some sense or other self-governing, the lower kind of life governs itself automatically, without having any opportunity to intervene purposively in its own adjustive processes. The emergence of sense experience of animals, however, amounted to such opportunity. The organism's self-government being now mediated by experience, the organism participated in the shaping of the events that, in turn, had a bearing on whether it would live or die.

Without self-presence, however, animals could experience what in fact was their wanting, as well as objects that in fact might satisfy their wants, but could experience neither their wants as such nor objects of want as such; this is merely to say once more that, even at the highest point reached by infrahuman evolution, want was not any more conscious than had been the inherent purposiveness of primitive life. When experience became conscious, however, the organism not only *was* alive and able to experience, but also *experienced* that it was alive and able to experience; it therefore experienced its needs as needs, its wants as wants, and the objects that responded to such needs and wants as objects that so responded – that is, as desirable objects. Conscious life may thus be defined as the *integration* of efficacy and finality. When the efficient, purposive causality of organic life became present to itself, the mere *convergence* of efficient causality upon itself became the *congruence* of efficient causality with its purposiveness.

This explains why proto-consciousness appeared when communicators learned to hold together, in their experience of communicating, their ability to *cause* communicative effects and their ability to *intend* to cause such effects. Likewise, the process I described earlier as the subsequent emergence of thought and immediate consciousness could be

restated in terms of the further intensification of the primitive assertiveness of speech – assertiveness being, in effect, a synonym for the
ability to integrate efficient and final causality. Self-direction towards
goals had reached thus a higher, emergent form: it was *deliberate* self-
direction, or self-direction that experienced itself as such. Conversely,
the purposiveness of life was now conscious; it had evolved into what
we usually call *will*. Thematic speech and the power of self-definition
crowned the appearance of will and endowed it with *freedom*; for by
means of these, human beings could now govern their ability to govern
themselves.

The human will is thus but the inherent tendency of all life to operate
as a self-sustaining functional unity – but with the transforming difference that such tendency is present to itself. Hence, to experience consciously is not merely to cognize an object which, as it happens, is of
value or disvalue to the organism; it necessarily includes experiencing
it as such value or disvalue. Only absent-mindedness enables us to think
of conscious experience as if it were reducible to the factual representation of inner and outer objects, followed by an affective reaction to
them. Purely cognitive human experience is an abstraction; it is *never*
found in actual human life. Cognition and appetition can remain separate in animals only because their experience lacks the self-integration
of consciousness.[17] In man, however, the self-presence of consciousness
brings the organism's needs and wants face to face with themselves,
and enables the inherent purposiveness of life to experience itself as
such. In actual human existence, then, conscious experience and conscious purposiveness are *identically* the same thing. We have but one
conscious life. Consciousness is the kind of experience that wills.

The emergence of conscious self-direction, or *freedom*, as a new dimension of life did not mean that the determining causality of every
other factor impinging upon the organism from within and without had
vanished. It meant that the self-determination that at the higher levels
of animal life enables the organism to govern itself had been transposed
into a new key; it now was a function of the organism's awareness of
its purposiveness and of the objects of which it might avail itself to fulfil
it. But with the new possibility came a correlative requirement: a new

17 We saw the reason earlier in another context: since animals are not conscious, they
   are unable to experience that their experience is related to their purposiveness;
   they cannot experience that their experience has the quality of being good or bad.
   Their purposiveness remains thus extrinsically related to their experience. They
   can guide themselves by their experience so as to achieve goals; but since they are
   unaware that they can do so, they cannot experience anything as a means to achieve
   goals.

level of initiative had to be taken by the human agent before he could exercise his power to seek goals deliberately. For conscious purposiveness merely *enables* human beings to manage their self-direction; it does not provide automatic deliberate self-direction, the sort of contradiction in terms that the classical conception of free will supposes. That is, consciousness enjoys freedom in the sense that it is not predetermined to want whatever it wants; it has the capability of deciding what it shall actually want. It would be absurd to suppose, however, that it is predetermined to exercise such capability.

Thus, the human will is not born free, any more than it is born a self; it is born with a capacity for self-identity and for self-liberation. Moreover, the integration of efficacy and finality – or which is the same, genuinely free and deliberate behaviour – is, like self-presence, a matter of degree. Whether the possibility of becoming a free self is realized, and to what degree, is not given by the nature of consciousness, but by what consciousness individually and collectively does with itself. Self-definition is not to be understood as mere self-knowledge or as reducible to erudition about the ways of man. Self-definition is above all the means through which human selves create their own identity and become free selves.

CHAPTER SEVEN

The emergence of the
self-defining consciousness
in variant forms

In the preamble to the last chapter I said that to reconstruct the emergence not only of conscious perception, but of the full conscious life that human beings exhibit today, it would be necessary to take into account two facts I had thereto ignored. I have just concluded making use of the first – that human beings speak thematically as well as non-thematically – so as to explain how the self-defining consciousness of the species came into being. To complete such explanation, however, and thus to pursue the reconstruction of human evolution up to the portals of history, we shall have to make use of the second: that thematic speech is not uniform in the species. But the complexity of this matter is exceeded only by its importance for understanding the evolution of consciousness. In this chapter we shall be concerned only with analysing and interpreting the observable fact that there is more than one way to speak thematically; its implications for human evolution will be investigated in the next.

Scholars have long been aware that the known human languages[1] – both the historically recorded and the currently spoken – can be classified into two kinds in accordance with certain grammatical dissimilarities between them. There are several such differences, but they all cluster around the fact that a verb or verbs 'to be,' or analogous copulas, are

---

1 Appendix 2 shows some of the principal linguistic divisions of the human species; Appendix 3 illustrates those of the IE linguistic family in particular. The classification of human languages is, of course, a complex and difficult problem, and experts do not agree in every respect. These tables are offered only as a rough linguistic map of the world and should not be taken as expressing an opinion on any of the contentious issues involved. Readers who require reliable information on the topic should consult competent sources. A useful introduction to the subject is Kenneth Katzner, *The Languages of the World* (London, 1986).

found only in some languages; contrary to what most of us who use them are likely to assume, they are absent in others. Indeed, 'to be' and like copulative verbs are exceedingly rare; only the languages of the Indo-European (henceforth IE) family, and outside these only Sumerian[2] – the language of the first human civilization, which emerged in Mesopotamia about 5,500 years ago – can be confidently attributed this feature.[3]

2 At one time it was widely held that Sumerian was among the IE languages; cf. C. Autran, *Sumérien et Indo-Européen: l'aspect morphologique de la question* (Paris, 1925). Currently the almost unanimous opinion of linguists holds that this is most unlikely, and that Sumerian should remain unclassified as to family until further evidence should appear. I shall assume here that this view is correct; I know of no theoretical reason to the contrary, and in any event the truth of the matter has no bearing on present purposes. However, the possibility of common ancestry, going back to the pre-thematic stage of human evolution, cannot be discarded simply because Sumerian is not an IE language.

3 Three closely related questions should be distinguished. The crucial one is whether verbal predication – asserting theses in relation to themes by means of verbs – is the only way in which thematic assertions can be made. Many linguists think not; others, principally Chomskians (who comprise a very large school of thought), hold the contrary view. Another is whether all languages use a verb 'to be.' (So far as concerns my argument the importance of this issue is that whether a language uses verbal predication at all can be resolved only by determining whether it uses a verb 'to be.') The position that many languages do not, and that indeed verbs 'to be' are relatively rare, is not uncommon – though again, Chomskians tend to think that, since verbal predication is essential part of all thematic speech, 'to be' must be at least implicit in the 'deep' structure of every language. This chapter's discussion will be directly concerned with these two matters.

A third and collateral problem will be considered here only to the extent of this note: granted that non-verbal assertion of theses is possible, and that 'to be' need not be part of every human language, precisely which languages include 'to be' and which not? It is beyond debate that all the IE languages and Sumerian do. Of the remainder, specific instances have sometimes been disputed by linguists, because they exhibit constructions that at least on the surface can be assimilated to the use of 'to be.' But the answer to whether they actually have a verb 'to be' in the same sense as the IE languages do hinges, of course, on the definition of the IE 'to be.' And this is a question whose philosophic dimensions should be apparent to anyone who has a nodding acquaintance with the history of metaphysics. For reasons to be given later, a thesis could not be considered the equivalent of an IE predicate using 'to be' unless it were intended to function, like every other IE verb, so as to reflect objective reality by means of speech. 'To be' achieves this both when it functions as a copula (i.e., when it is intended to reflect in speech the relationship that supposedly exists in objective reality between the referents signified by the thesis and the theme), and when it functions existentially (i.e., when it is intended to reflect the objective reality of the theme). Linguists who have inquired into the matter taking these philosophic considerations into account tend to share the conclusion that a 'verb "to be"' which serves both as a copula ("X is Y") and as

Linguists are not agreed on the significance of this difference, but this need not detain us: we are not interested in language for its own sake or from the viewpoint of linguistics, but philosophically and for what it may tell us about the nature and evolution of speech. In the first section of this chapter we shall discover that the grammatical differences between the two kinds of language reveal, upon philosophical analysis, two variant types of speech. By this I mean that human beings use at least two different thematic speech techniques embodying different kinds of assertive intention; mankind seems to have developed at least two somewhat different 'ideas' of what it is to assert theses in relation to themes. Note, however, that variations in the 'idea' of speech are not variations in what people merely *think* speech is. Since their 'idea' of

---

an indicator of [objective] existence ("*X* is", "There is *X*") is almost confined to Indo-European languages': A.C. Graham, ' "Being" in Linguistics and Philosophy: a Preliminary Inquiry,' *Foundations of Language*, 1 (1965), 223–31, p. 223; see also Ernst Locker, 'Etre et Avoir: leurs expressions dans les langues,' *Anthropos*, 49 (1954), 481–510. Some linguists, however, adopt philosophically lax criteria of what distinguishes verbs 'to be.' It is not difficult then to run into claims like 'the Mandarin verb "to be" is "shi", as in *ta shi xiansheng*, "he is a teacher".' A.C. Graham has shown why this is incorrect, to wit, because the predominant idea conveyed by *shi* is not that the subject is *in objective reality* what the predicate states, but that *the speaker's* attribution of such predicate to the subject is justified – in other words, that *his perception* of the matter is true; see his ' "Being" in Classical Chinese,' in John W.M. Verhaar, *The Verb 'Be' and Its Synonyms*, part 1 (Dordrecht, The Netherlands, 1967), pp. 1–9. I add a further indication to the same effect: that the first acceptation of *shi* is as a pronoun meaning 'the aforementioned,' or 'the one in question.' The use of *shi* as a so-called verb 'to be' depends on its reduplicative value; *ta shi xiansheng* can be idiomatically translated as 'he is a teacher' only because unidiomatically but literally stated the meaning it actually carries is 'he, indeed a teacher.'

I know of no instance of a non-IE language other than Sumerian where the proper criteria have been applied and equivalents of 'to be' have been found. But I stress the difference between the proposition I have actually put forth – that the presence of 'to be' is unquestionable only in the IE languages and Sumerian – and the unqualified contention that 'to be' does not exist anywhere in the world outside these languages, a proposition that would be practically impossible to establish, that for all I know may be false, and that in any event I have not subscribed to. My point is rather that, as long as the presence of 'to be' in other languages has not been positively established, we cannot very well attribute to any but IE and Sumerian speakers the form of speech – verbal predication – and the way of thinking that 'to be' symptomatizes. Moreover, if a genuine equivalent of the IE and Sumerian 'to be' were found outside these languages, the bare fact would militate neither for nor against the thesis I shall develop here concerning the cultural differences between societies that use verbal predication and those that do not; whether it supported one side or the other would depend on what sort of cultural pattern accompanied the linguistic fact.

speech is identical with their assumptions about what they must do in order to speak, different 'ideas' of speech means: differences in how people in reality speak, differences in what they actually do when they assert theses in relation to themes. For reasons that will appear I propose to refer to these two ways of speaking as the *apodictic* and the *depositional* variants of thematic speech.[4]

The fact that thematicity emerged, and to this day exists, in two guises is explicable by the proposed theory. It is the outcome of prehistoric developments that can be deduced from the differences between apodictic and depositional speech. Apodictic speech results from the sort of 'idea' of thematic speech that could have been conceived only by an absent-minded consciousness, whereas depositional speech indicates the sufficiency of self-presence that the human mind can be ordinarily expected to exhibit. We shall see the evidence of this: to judge by the characteristics of his speech, the apodictic speaker speaks as if his assertions – both his experience and his speech – were but the repetition of what reality itself first asserts to him, whereas the depositional speaker is mindful of his own assertive nature as a speaker and experiencer and does not project his own assertiveness onto the world.

The explanation of the appearance of thematic speech in variant forms is, therefore, that differences in the intensity of the self-presence of immediate consciousness in different human groups, as the thematic level of speech was being attained, produced different – more or less insightful – 'ideas' of thematic speech. We have seen that thematic ability grows out of the non-thematic speaker's conscious experience of his own speech; but since consciousness obtains in degrees, inherent in the properties of consciousness is the possibility that non-thematic speakers might be more or less vividly aware of the assertiveness of their speech. Thus, if in any given community, while it was in the throes of acquiring thematic ability, the statistically normal level of self-presence should have registered below a certain critical point – the point at which the speaker experienced a need to express that his assertion was a repetition of reality's own assertion, for otherwise he would not have felt that he was making an assertion at all – the community would have devised the linguistic means that so communicated. If, on the contrary, the

---

4 It is possible that with increased understanding of the nature of speech finer discriminations could be made within each of the two. This is especially likely in the case of depositional speech, which probably has only the unity of a genus, and which can be described as if it were a single form of speech only by opposition to the apodictic.

community's normal assertiveness should have been high enough to require no such expression, its syntax and vocabulary would have so reflected. Grammatically different apodictic and depositional forms of speech would have emerged as a result of differences in the 'idea' of thematic speech that prevailed in different groups.[5]

The reconstruction of the emergence of thematic speech and of the self-defining consciousness developed in the last chapter abstracted from these considerations. In the second section I shall therefore amplify such reconstruction to include specifically an explanation of their emergence in variant forms; we shall be especially interested in how absent-minded speakers proceeded to devise verbal predication in general and verbs 'to be' in particular, while others developed syntaxes that lack copulative verbs and that do not require verbal predication. We shall then be ready to pursue, in the next chapter, the cultural consequences of this development.

To anticipate their thrust, however, we need but recall a conclusion previously drawn. Once human beings had developed thematic speech, they had become able to create and develop their identity by interpreting their situation in the world – but only in the light of assumptions about themselves and the world implicit in their 'idea' of thematic speech. If thematic ability emerged in at least two variant forms, however, then the self-defining consciousness must have appeared in precisely as many variant forms, distinguishable by differences in the presuppositions created by the form of speech that generated each. This means that, as early thematic speakers established their institutions of self-definition – and in particular their religions and their more or less sophisticated equivalents of philosophy and science – they did so on the basis of alternative preconceptions about reality and efficient and final causality which effectively determined the general orientations that their cultures would take. In short, two forms of thematic speech imply two types of human mentality and two types of culture. I will refer to the form of consciousness and culture mediated by apodictic speech as the *ontic* variant of the self-defining consciousness, and to that generated by depositional speech as the *phenomenal* one. The aptness of these terms, too,

---

5 Differences in the statistically normal level of assertiveness in speech and in the self-presence of consciousness would have also existed, of course, in non-thematic communities before the emergence of thematic speech, but nevertheless did not result in variant forms of non-thematic speech. The reason is that the rudimentary nature of the assertiveness of non-thematic speech does not allow variations in its form: there is only one way to assert a thesis in immediate relation to reality, namely, by means of a single act that lacks all the discriminations that define thematic speech.

should become apparent as we ascertain the inclinations of each form of consciousness to interpret reality and efficient and final causality in its own distinctive way.

A caveat should be registered before we proceed. That only absent-minded speakers could have developed apodictic speech does not at all imply that only apodictic speakers can be absent-minded; this would be a *non sequitur*. I need not repeat, I take it, that consciousness is not a disembodied entity, but simply the quality of certain brain processes; genetically conditioned differences should be enough to explain the aboriginal appearance of deficient as well as normally sufficient self-presence in the species, and their more or less sporadic recurrence thereafter in all human groups. Thematic speech, however, through mechanisms we shall examine, made possible the *cultural* transmission of both present- and absent-mindedness independently of genetic inheritance; it afforded the means for the *institutionalization* of variations in the level of self-presence prevailing in different human groups as they entered the second stage of evolution.[6] This means, incidentally, that thematic speech amounted to a mechanism whereby group differences in respect of the characteristics of consciousness could become self-perpetuating quite apart from individual variations; the bearing of this on the continued evolution of consciousness is part of what we shall investigate later.

I stress, therefore, that it is not at all impossible that individual apodictic speakers should become aware of the assertiveness of their speech and advert to their own reality as conscious experiencers, in the sense that nothing in the nature of their consciousness bars it. But they are hampered by their culturally created assumptions, which function as 'genetic' predispositions to the contrary. For example, since empathetic sensitivity to the humanity of other human beings is but the other side of sensitivity to one's own, one of the practical concomitants of present-mindedness is high capacity for making common purposes with others – whereas absent-mindedness fosters rugged individualism. Therefore,

6 It would be in accordance with the explanation of the 'body-mind' relationship suggested in chapter II, however, if such cultural transmission of the quality of consciousness were to have in turn an effect on the organization of brain functions in individuals. Interestingly enough, Tadanobu Tsunoda, a Japanese neurophysiologist, has reportedly concluded that 'Japanese brains function differently from other people's not because of inheritance or conditioning but because of the peculiarities of the Japanese language ... What Tsunoda has found, he claims, is that the language one learns as a child influences the way in which the brain's right and left hemispheres develop their special talents': Atuhiro Sibatani, 'The Japanese Brain,' *Science 80*, 3 (1980), p. 24. A review by Sibatani of Tsunoda's untranslated book, *The Japanese Brain: Brain Function and East-West Culture*, may be found in *Journal of Social and Biological Structures*, 3 (1980), 3.

although nothing forbids apodictic individuals' being highly co-operative and socially minded, their being so runs against their culture's grain. Our own culture exemplifies this very well: kind, gentle, and empathetic individuals abound amongst us, though our society as a whole is highly competitive and believes implicitly in the effectiveness of force.[7] We are not unaware that an inner contradiction lurks somewhere, but we do not often locate it at the heart of a culture that forces us to conclude simultaneously that, for some strange reason, although altruism is good, selfishness is normal. We thus require explanation for the fact that 'the good I would do, I do not, but the evil I would not do, that I do.'[8] Some take this for a consequence of 'original sin,' whereas others, including many scientists, attribute it to atavistic instincts or to other residues – genetically transmitted, of course – of animal ferocity in man. The proposed theory, however, offers an alternative to all of these.

Depositional speakers, for their part, have a different cultural bias; but this hardly means that either as individuals or in groups they infallibly escape perils that are, after all, built into the very structure of consciousness. They are not noble savages. Since they are conscious agents, nothing human is alien to them; even whole traditions can develop dysfunctional forms of consciousness. The phenomenal cultures are none the less of an observably different type. Nothing I shall say hereafter by way of contrast between the cultures created by the different types of speakers should be taken to detract from the foregoing stipulations, and he would mistake my meaning who thought otherwise.

1. The apodictic and the depositional variants of thematic speech

It is easy to suppose that every culture's 'idea' of thematic speech is the same as one's own; ethnocentricity affects most of us, and it is understandable if we tend to take for granted that our form of speech is

---

7 We do not, as a group, believe that might is necessarily right, but only when might is guided by right reason; nevertheless, we take it as self-evident that power is effective to bring about results. Hence, whenever we deem our ends to be right – say, the restoration or preservation of social order – we are inclined to think of the application of force as the obvious means to achieve it, and the use of violence as a justifiable last resort. The institutionalization of power, and if need be violence, includes its measuring, tempering, and regulating – for instance, by means of the law – but is in any event the practically inevitable result of the presuppositions of the ontic form of consciousness. A very different approach to the maintenance and restoration of social order is possible, but only on the basis of different presuppositions.

8 Romans 7:19.

universal in the species. At least on the surface, however, the way in which we IE speakers relate theses to themes is decidedly uncommon: we invariably do it by means of a verb, and seem unable to speak in any other way; the verb may, of course, be suitably complemented, but the complements are not essential whereas the verb is. Thus, if I say in English 'The flower, red' or 'The dog, the barking,' I have not affirmed anything in relation to anything else; in each of these two examples I have merely named two things. To assert them in relation to each other I must say 'The flower *is* red,' or 'The dog *does* the barking' (or, more idiomatically, 'The dog *barks*,' or some other finite verb), unless perhaps convention or context should permit the omission of the verb because the verbal relationship of 'predicate' and 'subject' – as we call them – was tacitly understood.[9] The omission of an explicit verb, however, does emphatically not mean its absence. The tacitly understood verb is present and operative in the speaker's assertive intent and in the listener's understanding of it; without at least such tacit intent there would be no assertion at all. Apodictic speech may thus be described as verbally predicative speech – whereas depositional speech, as we shall see, does not permit making assertions in verbal form.

Verbal predication, moreover, is mandatory; an apodictic speaker who wishes to make a thematic assertion has no option but to do it by asserting verbal predicates in relation to subjects of verbs. He is not compelled to do so, however – as he is likely to assume – by the universal and necessary nature of thematic speech, but by his particular and questionable assumptions about the nature of thematic speech. That is, the verbally predicative character of his speech is *not* the effect (as Whorf would have deemed it) of the grammatical properties of the verb. In the light of what has been established so far we must maintain, on the contrary, that the latter are a consequence of the apodictic speaker's 'idea' of what it is to speak thematically. This is why we are not interested in the grammar of verbal predication, but in its phenomenology. What is the *experience* of speaking when one speaks apodictically? What does one do when one *means* a verbal predicate in relation to a subject?

Reflexion shows that the essential aspect of the speaker's intent is to attribute the predicate to the subject as *belonging* to the subject – or better still, as *proceeding* or *issuing forth* from it. Apodictic speakers assume that the subject is the ground, the active cause, or performer of what the

9 Convention permits in some circumstances the regular omission of 'to be,' but not ordinary verbs, in some IE languages, for instance, Greek, Russian, Sanskrit. However, convention does not permit the regular omission of any verb in English, though context exceptionally may.

verb signifies, whereas the verb is that which is attributed to the subject as its own, having proceeded from, or been caused or performed by, the subject. I do not mean that these speakers attribute the vocal utterance they call the predicate to the vocal utterance they call the subject; rather, the *reality* signified by the predicate term is attributed to the *reality* signified by the subject term by means of a verb that signifies the *real* relationship between such realities. Thus, if I am an apodictic speaker and say, for instance, 'The dog barks' or 'The flower is red,' what I am doing is to assert a predicate term intending it to signify what a certain reality, which is represented by the subject term, does or is in itself – namely, to *do* the barking or to *be* red. Correspondingly, I signify the subject under the supposition that my vocal utterance stands for the reality that, in fact and in itself, does or is what the predicate ascribes to it in speech, namely, *really* barking or *really* being red. Therefore, in 'The dog barks' the subject and the predicate put together duplicate the reality, a barking dog; and to say 'The flower is red' is to repeat, by means of words, the reality of a flower's own being red. The assertion of the predicate in relation to the subject carries thus the 'idea' that the relationship in speech between what-I-say and what-I-say-it-about is the repetition of the real relationship between the two realities signified by the subject and the predicate terms. And this relationship is definable by the fact that the reality represented by the predicate has its source in the reality that the subject represents: the former belongs to the latter, or issues from or is caused by it.

This 'idea' of thematic speech contains a twofold negative implication. Since the predicate is asserted as repeating what the corresponding reality is or does in itself, it is *not* asserted primarily under the guise of its being what the speaker experiences. Likewise, the subject is *not* proposed specifically as what the speaker is going to make an assertion in relation to, since it is proposed instead as that which in itself is or does what the predicate will represent it as being or doing. In other words, although I, an apodictic speaker, would not necessarily deny – if the matter were brought to my attention – that my assertions in fact asserted what I experienced, and that they were made in relation to a proposed object of speech, I do not make them mindful of their having these characteristics, let alone *because* they do. My assertions appear to me instead as articulate repetitions of what reality itself articulates by *doing* or *being* whatever it really does or is; or more precisely, they appear to me as my repetition of an experience that had in turn been a repetition of what the reality had communicated to me about itself. Accordingly, reality is that which 'tells' me about itself by causing me to experience it. The implicit construction that apodictic speakers put on their speech is, therefore, the same as that which philosophers, linguists, and others have traditionally made explicit by reflecting upon their practice of speech: the semantic interpretation of speech. Philosophers have not been wrong when they have judged that such interpretation accurately described how their fellow speakers – how they themselves – experienced their own speech. If they have been mistaken, it was rather in assuming that speakers in all cultures spoke as they themselves did, and that apodictic speakers perceived correctly the nature of thematic speech. Their interpretations of experience and of reality have been conditioned, of course, by their interpretation of speech, and have coalesced with the latter into the semantic complex.

Verbs ordinarily signify actions. The apodictic speaker, however, does not absolutely have to use an ordinary or action-signifying verb; 'to be' is always at his disposal. But I have put this tendentiously: many philosophers have said that even 'to be' is an action-signifying verb – and indeed the epitome of all other action-signifying verbs – since it represents the dynamic activity whereby a real thing is real and actually is whatever it is. Metaphysics, the study of reality as 'being,' depends on this interpretation of 'to be.' In any event, this verb is especially useful to apodictic speakers because it has no other semantic function than to signify the verbal relationship; it means nothing but the essence of what verbally predicative speech represents, namely, the *being* of real things. 'To be' is therefore uniquely suited to the verbal predication of qualities, states, and passive conditions, and to assertions in which there is no question of true action but the metaphorical ascription of action is either not readily available or is undesirable. For instance, the normal, almost mandatory way to predicate the quality signified by 'red' in relation to the reality signified by 'the flower' is, of course, 'The flower is red.' This is why 'to be' is not definable merely by its copulative or connecting function – some linguists seem content with so defining it – but by a copulative function that supposedly mimics the objective reality of things: with a complement it repeats what the subject itself *is*, and without a complement it re-enacts the existential fact that it *is*.

Hence the grammatical peculiarity of the apodictic languages: they include one or more special verbs, the principal of which is 'to be,' that maintain the relationship of verbal predicate to subject even when the predicate neither is an action nor is otherwise likened to an action performed by subject. 'To become' is also usually available for the same purpose, and may (as in English) be derived from 'to be,' or altogether distinct from 'to be' (as in Sanskrit, Spanish, and French). Factive verbs such as 'to do' and 'to make' (in the sense of 'to cause to become') and others, such as, in English, 'to grow' (in the figurative sense of 'to become') may also be used as copulas, but they depend on assimilating the predicate to an action, or to the effect of an action, performed by the subject. It is therefore the presence of a verb or verbs[10] 'to be,' not that of verbs in general, that can be taken as a reliable shibboleth to test whether a language requires verbal predication and is spoken apodictically. For all human beings, including depositional speakers, have occasion to assert theses signifying actions literally or figuratively performed by the agent signified by the theme; the semantic content of such theses, when asserted depositionally, would be indistinguishable from that of the corresponding verbs in the apodictic languages. For instance, if the thesis signifies the action of 'barking' or 'eating,' semantic content alone would not serve to indicate the difference between the verbs 'to bark' and 'to eat' used by apodictic speakers, and non-verbal theses signifying the actions of 'barking' or 'eating' used by a depositional speaker. But only the apodictic languages need – or can make provision for – a verb that, like 'to be', can be used for predicating verbally even when the predicate does not signify an action. In these languages, therefore, 'to be' is the essential verb. It alone can be used to assert any verbal predicate, since even assertions using an ordinary verb can always be expressed by means of 'to be' (e.g., 'The dog is barking' instead of 'The dog barks'). But verbs 'to be,' as it appears, are found invariably in the IE languages; outside these, they have been positively identified only in Sumerian. Only these can be reasonably included, therefore, among the languages of apodictic speech.

Since depositional speech underlies the immense majority of human languages, the construction of thematic assertions in the depositional cultures is not grammatically uniform – at least, not in details. Nevertheless, a common negative feature can be observed: nothing is ever used, even when the thesis is not an action, to signify the attribution of the thesis to the theme as proceeding from, or as being caused or performed by, it. These languages lack, therefore, the verb 'to be' or any equivalent verbal copula; the juxtaposition of thesis and theme usually suffices to convey the assertion of the former in relation to the latter.[11] A preferred if not mandatory word order is usually followed, so as to make clear which is the thesis and which the theme; for this is, of course, as essential in depositional as in apodictic speech. In the

---

10 Like French, English has only one verb 'to be,' but a language may have several. Spanish, for instance, has two.

11 Sometimes the *speaker's* assertiveness is explicitly signified for the sake of emphasis or clarity; but nothing is used to signify what apodictic speakers imagine as the relationship of the reality represented by the thesis to the reality represented by the theme.

apodictic languages this objective is often accomplished by the inflexion of the verb, though word order has acquired considerable importance in those which, like English, have lost almost all verbal inflexion for person. In resorting to a standard word order for this purpose, the Malayo-Polynesian family is typical. In Indonesian, for instance, a dialect of Malay, the theme is usually proposed first and the thesis follows: *Bunga itu, merah* ('Flower this, red') is the Indonesian equivalent of 'The flower is red.'[12]

Word order, however, is often supplemented by other devices, including prosodic means, to avoid the ambiguities that abound in complex assertions. In Indonesian a brief pause after the theme (which here I will normally reduce to writing by a comma) together with a change in intonation are used. The same may be achieved, however, by very different means. Arabic, a representative of the Hamito-Semitic family, uses simple juxtaposition of thesis and theme – as in the paradigm 'A [nominative], B [nominative],' translatable as 'A is B' – but in certain circumstances it also uses emphatic devices to mark the difference between the non-verbally related thesis and theme. One of these is to interpose a third-person pronoun (masculine *huwa*, feminine *hiya*), as in 'A, *huwa* B' (that is, 'A, which [or he] B'), meaning 'A is B.' This reduplication of the theme by a pronoun, so as to mark it as such, is found in many depositional languages.[13] Chinese, for instance, like Arabic, resorts both to the juxtaposition of thesis and theme and, as noted earlier in another context, to the reduplication of the theme by a pronoun. Under other conditions it achieves much the same effect by means of a particle, *yeh*, which has approximately the force of 'indeed,' and which therefore makes explicit the speaker's assertiveness. 'A, B *yeh*' can be translated as 'A is B,' because it means: '[In relation to] A, [I affirm] B indeed.' Among the African languages, Sechuana uses a complex version of the same general idea. Simple juxtaposition is used if the theme is a personal pronoun: *Ke kopa madi* is literally 'I, wanting money.' With a nominal theme, a particle that repeats the prefix that accompanies the class of noun to which the theme belongs is inserted between thesis and theme; normally the same particle is also attached to the thesis. Thus, *Se-tlhare se se-tona* (approximately, 'The-tree, it large-one') means 'The tree is large,' and *Lo-kwalo lo lo-tona* ('The-book, it large-one') means 'The

12 I use throughout the pre-1972 spelling of Indonesian words, based on Dutch phonetic values.
13 Is this not the same assertive technique frequently used in French, as in *L'état, c'est moi*? Not at all. This French construction uses reduplication, but the assertion does not depend upon it; it depends on the verb 'to be,' whereas in Arabic and Chinese the assertion is made by means of the reduplication, and there is no 'to be.'

book is large,' while *Mo-sadi o kopa madi* ('The-woman, she wanting money,' for *mo* becomes *o*) means 'The woman wants money.'

A common 'idea' of what it is to make thematic assertions can thus be detected among depositional speakers throughout the world. The generalization may be proposed – it will be explained and supported in a moment – that in these languages the thesis is not offered to the communicand under the guise of its conveying at second hand what the reality named by the theme is in and of itself; it is offered precisely as the speaker's assertion, in relation to the theme, of what he experiences. In other words, although their grammars may otherwise differ, the depositional languages uniformly imply that the thesis B, when asserted in relation to the theme A, is not intended to mean simply or primarily 'what A itself is or does'; it is meant to convey 'what I, the speaker, assert about A.' Correspondingly, the theme does not mean 'that which is or does B'; it means 'that in relation to which I, the speaker, assert B.' In the IE languages and Sumerian, on the contrary, the speaker asserts the thesis B meaning specifically 'what A is or does,' and he asserts the theme A intending to convey precisely 'that which is or does B.' Unless the IE or Sumerian speaker does this, he feels that he has not asserted anything at all.

The depositional 'idea' of speech is what accounts for the absence of 'to be' in the depositional languages even when the thesis does not signify an action. Nothing is used, because nothing is needed, to signify that the assertiveness of the act of speech parallels the relationship in reality between what the thesis and the theme represent. For the speaker does not suppose that his act of experience repeats the assertiveness of reality and that his act of speech re-repeats it; he assumes instead that his act of experience asserts the reality originally and for the first time, quite as his act of speech asserts his experience originally and for the first time. If he did signify his assertiveness – for instance, to avoid ambiguity or for emphasis – his signification would refer to nothing but the assertiveness of *his* act of speech. But ordinarily even this would be superfluous, since the actuality of his speaking necessarily conveys it: no listener can hear speech without thereby perceiving, in addition to what is said, the fact that the speaker is speaking. The apodictic speaker, on the contrary, needs to signify his assertion for the very reason that he intends to convey that what he says is not truly *what he asserts*, but *what is*; he merely *repeats* what is.

Before I further explain the difference between the two forms of speech I call attention to a beckoning pitfall: it is always tempting to foreclose the problem of how to explain a mischievous difference by doing away with the difference. Only a little ethnocentricity is needed to assume, for instance, that when an Indonesian speaker says *Bunga itu, merah* his assertive intent and his experience of speech must be the same as that of the English speaker who says 'The flower is red.' Many of us would gladly suppose that he really *means* 'The flower is red,' but that he omits the 'is,' much as a Russian speaker does when he says *Krasnyi čviet* as a complete sentence instead of *Čviet iest' krasnyi*. But let us think again. Like every other ie, the Russian speaker has 'to be' at his disposal; and like many (though not all) ies he can under certain conditions choose either to use it or omit it. It is true, therefore, that when the ie 'to be' is omitted, it is nevertheless tacitly understood. However, the Malayo-Polynesian, the African, and the North and South American Indian speakers, like the Chinese, the Japanese, and indeed most others, lack 'to be' altogether. They cannot very well omit what does not exist, or tacitly understand what they cannot understand at all. Thus, they cannot mean what we mean when *we* make tacit use of 'is.'

Nevertheless, some linguists – signally transformational grammarians – have insisted that in reality there are no 'nominal sentences' (i.e., without a verb) in any language, and that such assertions are in truth verbally predicative though cryptically so. The contrary appearance, they have often said, 'arises from confusing deep structure and surface structure ... [But] there is no "nominal structure" in the deep structure'[14] of thematic assertions. This conclusion is understandable. The analytic procedure devised by Chomsky and known as the grammatical transformation of sentences rests on the postulate that the composition of a sentence by a 'verb phrase' predicated of a 'noun phrase' is a 'linguistic universal,' a characteristic of all speech; and this postulate seems reasonable to Chomskians because they assume that all human beings make thematic assertions in the same way. But their postulate is at bottom nothing but a generalization from the properties of their own – the ie – form of speech. Against the circularity of their reasoning stands the empirical fact that innumerable languages lack verbs 'to be.' The depositional languages demonstrate that, strange as it may seem to us, thematic assertions need not have a verb.

But what does the Indonesian speaker *mean* when he says *Bunga itu, merah*? Well, the process begins with his experience of a flower which – as *we* would say – 'is' in reality red. He experiences it, of course, in the same way as any other conscious human being would – I mean, receiving the same information. The respective experiences of the depositional and the apodictic speakers would thus have the same content.

14 Ferenc Kiefer, 'The Verb *van* "to be" in Hungarian,' in John W.M. Verhaar, ed., *The Verb 'Be' and Its Synonyms*, Part 3 (Dordrecht, The Netherlands, 1968), p. 54.

The only difference we need suppose does not have to do with the object, but with the speaker; the Indonesian would be more vividly aware of the self-presence of his experience and of the assertiveness of his speech than apodictic speakers would normally be. Having experienced the red flower, the Indonesian speaker may have occasion to assert, quite as his apodictic opposite number might, 'the [experienced] red' in relation to 'the [experienced] flower.' There is no more question in his mind than in the apodictic speaker's that his experiences of 'flower' and 'red' depend on information received from reality. But since he speaks with reasonably normal and adequate consciousness of the nature of experience and speech,[15] he is implicitly aware that his thesis signifies immediately his experience of reality – though mediately it signifies, of course, the reality itself. He likewise supposes that his assertion is directly relative to a theme – though it is also mediately relative to the reality signified by the theme. If so, to assert what he wishes to assert he simply states the object of speech that he is going to make an assertion about (*bunga itu*), and then states what he wishes to assert about it (*merah*). And having so said, he has said *exactly* what he wanted to say. The simple juxtaposition of thesis and theme embodies and communicates his intention perfectly, since his intention was (a) to communicate what he experienced precisely as what he experienced, and (b) to assert it precisely as what he asserted.

I have so far considered only the type of depositional thematic assertions that linguists generally call 'nominal sentences,' which are translatable into the IE languages only if a copulative or other verb is supplied. But of course, depositional speakers often have reason to assert theses that signify true actions, and they are able to use analogy and metaphor to speak of active processes 'performed' by inanimate agents, and to describe as an action what is no action or process at all.[16] Thus, depo-

15 Only in the sense that his 'idea' of speech will be fundamentally correct; unless he should have reflected on the subject he would lack conscious *understanding* of the nature of speech. However, just as philosophers who are apodictic speakers ordinarily develop semantic interpretations of speech, depositional speakers develop a syntactic one, if they do any at all. But they do not often do so; depositional speakers are not inclined to philosophize. Nevertheless, I may point to the Chinese philosopher Hsün Tzu, who in the third century BC had already arrived at a conclusion that Western thought has only recently begun to entertain: that speech serves to organize sense information so as to yield an understanding of the world; see H.G. Creel, *Chinese Thought* (New York, 1953), pp. 99–100.

16 For instance, Indonesians commonly say *Mesin, berdjalan* ('Machine, walking') to mean 'The machine is running.' To say that the path *berdjalan* along the pond, however, would probably occur to an Indonesian poet more readily than to an ordinary speaker – though to an English speaker 'The path runs along the pond' feels

sitional speakers often make thematic assertions of the type than can be translated into an IE language by means of an ordinary verb; for instance, in Indonesian, *Kuda, makan rumput* ('Horse, eat grass'), or *Annakku, tidur* ('Child-I, sleep'), and *Andjing, menjalak* ('Dog, bark'). Some linguists therefore say that a distinction should be made between these sentences, which alone are truly 'verbal sentences,' and 'nominal sentences' like *Bunga itu, merah.*

Theirs is a milder ethnocentricity than that of transformational grammarians; it admits that speakers in certain languages do not always predicate verbally, though it assumes that at other times they do. This position is perhaps the most common one taken in recent times by linguists other than Chomskians; it is now widely admitted that in many languages, for instance, in Indonesian, 'there is no reason why the "slot" of a Predicate ... will have to be filled by a grammatical word class such as the verb as a "filler." In fact, in the absolute use of certain words which are verbs morphologically, one may doubt whether we have a verb at all, rather than, say, an adjective.'[17] But in the same breath they usually add: verbal predication is possible in all languages, if not indeed 'prototypical' and 'normal.' And it is true, of course, that from the viewpoint of content nothing differentiates an apodictic from a depositional 'verb.' To appreciate what these linguists overlook – that there are no empirical grounds for differentiating between the 'nominal' and the 'verbal' sentences in languages that lack 'to be' – it would be necessary to attend instead to the assertive relationship between the thesis and the theme. If they did, however, they might observe that, although an Indonesian speaker saying *Kuda, makan rumput* is well aware that the horse *does* its own grass-eating, he does not take his assertion as a repetition of *what the animal has told him* of its own figurative mouth; he takes it as an original affirmation of *what he has experienced* – the horse eating grass – which he wishes to communicate precisely as such. His assumption is that his assertiveness has no source besides his own ability and willingness to speak.

Apodictic speech is not merely a distorted conceit, but also a defective way to practise thematic speech. This explains certain oddities it occa-

---

more like a literal statement than a metaphor. However, one would never say in Indonesian that 'This newspaper reports [*mengabarkan*] that ... ,' or 'This book says [*berkata*] that ...' It would sound ridiculous, as if the speaker thought that newspapers and books could speak. One would say, for instance, *Menurut suratkabar ini, ialah bahwa* ('according-with newspaper this, it [is] indeed [the case] that'), and *Didalam buku ini, tertulis bahwa* ('within book this, [it has been] written that').

17 John W.M. Verhaar, *Teori Linguistik dan Bahasa Indonesia* (Yogyakarta, Indonesia, 1980), p. 21.

sionally exhibits. Consider the following. When apodictic speakers reflect upon their thematic speech they are unlikely to analyse it using the concepts of 'thesis' and 'theme' (or equivalents such as the categories of 'topic' and 'comment' used by a few linguists). This is, of course, for the very good reason that ordinarily they do not experience their own speech as the assertion of theses in relation to themes. Instead they use terms that, as 'subject' and 'predicate' do, refer to the supposed relationship in reality between 'a doer' and 'what a doer does,' or between 'a being' and 'what a being is.' What is strange, however, is not this, but the fact that the verbal subject and the predicate not infrequently fail to constitute, respectively, the actual thesis and the actual theme of the assertion; in other words, the grammatical properties of the language are out of phase with the speaker's assertive intent. For instance, imagine that a certain shameful behaviour, 'doing x,' has been incorrectly attributed to me, and that I wish to deny it. But several possibilities arise. I might wish to convey that, although I did not do x, the action may well have been done – which implies that, if done, it was done by someone else. In the alternative, I might want to admit that I did do something blameworthy, though not x. Or I might want to state merely that doing x was incorrectly attributed to me, without indicating whether it may have been done by someone else or whether I myself did do something other than the act in question. These are of course three different meanings. And yet, I would almost certainly use the same construction, 'I didn't do it,' to convey all three. To differentiate between them I would therefore be reduced to using appropriate emphasis. In the first instance I would say 'I didn't do it'; in the second, 'I didn't do it'; and in the third, 'I didn't do it.' Now, why would I speak this way?

I would use the same construction in all three cases, because in all three my assertion had to do with the performance or non-performance of an action by me. Since I am a verbal predicator, I will automatically make 'I' the subject in every instance – which leaves me no choice but to make the predicate 'didn't do it' regardless of which nuance I may wish to convey. In other words, instead of paying attention to what I am speaking about – the theme – and to what I want to say about it – the thesis – which are not the same in the three cases, I will be inclined to construct my assertion in terms of the doer of the action and the action performed by the doer, which remain the same. The result is that, out of the three assertions, the predicate and the subject coincide respectively with the thesis and the theme only in the first, 'I didn't do it.' For only in this case am I actually speaking about myself, asserting in relation to myself the non-performance of the act; this is what leaves open the implication that, if done, it was done by someone else. When I say 'I didn't do *it*,' wishing to imply that I may have done something else, the theme is 'it,' and the thesis is 'not what was done by me.' And in the simple denial, 'I *didn't* do it,' the theme is actually 'doing it,' whereas the thesis is 'not I.' Yet none of us would say – as an Indonesian would – 'the doing of it was not by me,' instead of 'I *didn't* do it,' though it is exactly what we should say if the subject and the predicate were to signify, respectively, what we were speaking about and what we were actually saying about it. Appropriate emphasis is thus critical, because our grammatical construction is at odds with our speaking intent. Moreover, as apodictic speakers we would be a little hard put to explain why the three assertions had different meanings, despite the fact that in all three cases the subject and the predicate were exactly the same.[18]

The profusion of metaphorically used verbs, which is typically apodictic, and the preference for the active voice indicate likewise a certain constraint upon the speaker to fit his themes into the mould of a subject, and his theses into that of a verbal predicate, regardless of what the intended theme and thesis actually are. But this, if we come to think of it, is not a little absurd: it is to execute an intention without having regard to whether the execution actually fulfills it. That an apodictic assertion might turn out to affirm something even slightly different from what the speaker wants to affirm betrays his uncertain control over his own speech; it cannot be described except as a confused way to speak. But we must take care that we ourselves do not become confused about the nature of the confusion.

The confusion lies – metaphorically, of course – in our speaking the words, not in the words we speak; it is not *caused* by the grammatical properties of the languages used to predicate verbally. On the contrary, these properties result from the prior confusion that contaminates our 'idea' of speech. Thus, every apodictic speaker is apt to say, for instance, 'The winding path runs around the pond,' but we can be reasonably certain that few have been misled by this grammatical form into thinking that the path actually moved along the ground, weaving right and left, as it pumped its legs at a fast rate. This is not to say that confusion in our speech does not manage to consolidate itself because, having twisted our theses and themes so as to fit into the mould of actions and agents, we take ourselves much too literally; but this is only a backlash effect, a reinforcement of a confusion already at work at a much deeper, non-conscious level of our thought. The confusion cannot be dispelled quite

---

18 We might put it down to a disparity between grammar and rhetoric reflecting the opposition of logic and emotion. The disparity, however, is between what we do and what we think we do when we speak.

as easily, therefore, as Korzybski and others have deemed, namely, by becoming critically conscious of *what* we say. What we should instead pay attention to is *how* we say what we say.[19] But if one is absent-minded, this is sooner prescribed than understood, and far more easily agreed to than done.

The essence of apodictic speech is well described as *verbal predication*; for as the etymology of the these words makes clear, the 'predicate' is that which is conveyed by a *praedicator* – someone who heralds, albeit in his own words and with his own voice, a message that he does not originate – while the *verbum* is the word that 'words' (i.e., ex-presses or issues forth) what reality contains within itself. The reason why the apodictic speaker may be aptly so called should also be plain: that he speaks *demonstratively*. This is to be understood with all the connotations of the Greek *apodeiksis*, which its Latin equivalent, *demonstratio*, brings to the English term. Even when he speaks thematically he speaks as if

19 It is for the same reason that the perpetuation of sexism through speech cannot be as effectively countered as those feminists think who – Whorfians by osmosis, if not always by deliberation – mistake the semantic symptoms for the assertive disease. If I, for one, do not accede to their usual requests, it is not for lack of sympathy with their cause but because I think that their major premiss is wrong. Moreover, their strategy is deluded; their 'non-sexist' terminology will become sexist as soon as its novelty wears off, because sexism is not carried by the semantic content of particular words, but by how any words are meant. They should remember how 'fool' became 'moron,' how 'moron' recovered its antecedent's contemptuous connotations and had to be replaced by 'feeble-minded,' which then gave way to 'mentally retarded,' which is no longer quite acceptable and now seeks to be replaced by a *truly* non-prejudicial word. ('Developmentally delayed' seems to be the leading contender.) Moreover, the feminists' mistake is compounded by faulty semantics; they object to the inclusive use of 'man' to mean 'human being,' but gladly accept the exclusive use of it meaning 'a male human being,' a sense that derives from the prejudice that 'male human' and 'human' are convertible. Yet more strangely, they do *not* object to 'woman,' although this word's very origin – it comes from 'wife-man,' that is, a female human – presupposes that, since only males are properly called 'men,' a female human being's sex must be specified or else the necessary connotations of 'man' will result in a wrong attribution. It seems to me, on the contrary, that women should object to being called, in effect, 'female humans' and never plain 'humans,' even when the context makes their sex irrelevant; and they should protest when males continue to be called simply 'men' instead of 'males' even when their male sex is part of the intended denotation.

If changes in usage should nevertheless be deemed desirable – and if for no better reason, then for their reassurance value – they should be theoretically well-grounded. For my part, I use 'man' to mean any human being regardless of sex, I never call a female a 'woman' but a 'female,' if sex is relevant, and never use 'man' but 'male,' if reference to maleness is required. Other usages might also be profitably modified – but only if a suitable effort of thought and some linguistic sensitivity are allowed to play a role in any proposals.

he were simply showing up reality, using speech as a pointer to bring it to the communicand's attention but letting the reality speak for itself. He uses thematic speech, then, as if it were but a complex form of non-thematic speech, distinguishable from the latter only by its articulateness; its breaking down and recomposing reality in speech is, supposedly, simply the repetition of what reality articulates within itself by doing what it does or being what it is. He tends to speak, therefore, with all the self-assurance – and sometimes even the dogmatism – of him who, after all, is only the channel through which the truth manifests itself. In short, apodictic speech is objective speech.

The depositional speaker, on the contrary, is present-minded; he has no need to ponder the matter before he can decide that he is, in fact, speaking. His speech may be called depositional because he is somewhat like a deponent who swears an affidavit. Unlike a trial witness, who is admonished by the court to keep his opinions to himself and to confine himself to the facts (as if he had no need of opinion in order to decide what is and what is not a fact), a deponent is permitted to subscribe his assertions under the rubric of speaking 'to the best of his knowledge and belief'; moreover, he is allowed to speak for his own stated purpose rather than, as the witness, in order serve the purposes of a court that enjoins him to let the objective facts speak through him. The absence of 'to be' is therefore only the grammatical index of the *adjectival deposition* that defines this speaker's 'idea' of what to speak thematically is. The substance of the matter is that he who speaks like a deponent does not assume that he is a spokesman for the truth. Since his thesis betokens the pledge of his word – his commitment to his assertion – he implicitly accepts responsibility for being the original source of what he says and not only for repeating it accurately.

An anthropologist – one of not a few who has contrasted the North American Indian 'attitude of humility and respect toward reality' with our own – has accordingly related this cultural difference to the respective 'ideas' of speech: 'We are aggressive toward reality. We say *This is bread*; we do not say like the Wintu, *I call this bread* ... If [a Wintu] speaks of reality which is not within his own restricting experience, he does not affirm it, he only implies it. If he speaks of his experience, he does not express as categorically true. Our attitude toward nature is colored by a desire to control and exploit. The Wintu relationship with nature is one of intimacy and mutual courtesy.'[20] This statement of the matter, however, is a little inexact. In the North American Indian languages, as

20 Dorothy Lee, *Freedom and Culture* (Homewood, MD, 1959), quoted by Jamake Highwater, *The Primal Mind* (New York, 1981), p. 74.

in other depositional languages generally, it is entirely possible to signify the depositional equivalent of 'This is bread,' and not simply 'I call this bread,' which is a different assertion. It would be more accurate to say that when a depositional speaker affirms 'This is bread' he does so under the guise of his assertion being what he asserts rather than under the guise of his merely repeating what is. Moreover, there is indeed a nexus between his speech and his attitudes towards the world; but the way he speaks is not the cause of his attitudes; rather, his self-perception as a speaker and experiencer is the cause of both his attitudes and the way he speaks.

Finally, the apodictic languages share another peculiarity that can be explained by the same hypothesis – absent-mindedness – that has enabled us to understand their verbally predicative character. By way of background, however, I should first amplify earlier remarks on the origin of the category of *time*. Its basis in all human beings is of course the self-presence of consciousness: since an act of conscious experience is one that is present to itself, an invariable accompaniment of every conscious experience is that it is felt to be taking place *now*, or at what we call the *present time*. Note that the present is therefore the only real time when consciousness can exist – in the sense that it is the only time when anything can ever be actually experienced consciously[21] – though presentness is not the only temporal relation that objects can have to each other and to our organisms. However, the same self-presence of consciousness that requires us to perceive the act of experience as having presentness entails a further consequence: that we are able to tell the difference between the sort of experience we call sensing and the kind we call imagining. That is, simply by being present to itself, an act of conscious experience includes reference to the imaginative or else sensory character of the activity involved.

This consequence is the origin of the differentiation of the *past* and the *future*, which do not exist, out of the present that does exist.[22] For

21 I have expressed this accommodating our usual terminology. A better statement would be: the experience of 'present time' being identical with the experience of the self-presence of consciousness, it follows that nothing could be experienced consciously except in and through an experience that has the quality of taking place 'at present.'

22 It is probably obvious that when I say that only the present exists, or that the present is the only real time in which consciousness can exist, I do not mean that time has objective reality in the classical sense that it is a standard of duration antecedent to experience by reference to which we can order and measure changes in reality. I should leave no doubt, however, that neither do I mean the diametric opposite, the Kantian doctrine that time is an *a priori* subjective disposition of the human mind that cannot be validly extended to reality in itself. In my view, the

discriminating between present sensing and present imagining amounts to differentiating between (a) an experience that is taking place now because its object is informing the organism *now*, and (b) an experience that is taking place now despite the fact that, as the very character of the experience reveals, the object is *not now* informing the organism. Moreover, a further discrimination can be made between two kinds of imaginative experience. Imagining, as I previously explained, is an experience that necessarily refers to another experience (namely, a sense experience that supplies its contents). Well, in the first kind, (a) the imaginative experience taking place now connotes reference to a prior sense experience that, when it occurred, included reference to the organism's being informed *now*; whereas in the second, (b) the imaginative experience taking place now connotes reference to another experience that at present is itself purely imaginative, but which might well become the sort that includes reference to the organism's being informed *now*, (namely, a sense experience). Thus, the *act* of conscious experience always occurs at present, but does not always refer to present *objects*. The objects will be experienced *as present* if they are sensed; but if the experience is an imaginative one, they will be experienced either as what *has been* sensed, or as what *may yet be* sensed. Or in more familiar (though misleading) terms, imaginative experience may refer either to *what is past* or to *what is to come*.[23] The ability to experience in terms of past and future temporality develops out of the ability to experience in the present, as the conscious experiencer's immediate grasp of the properties of his own consciousness becomes increasingly firm.

----

concept of *time* – or more precisely, *present time* – originates empirically in the immediate perception by consciousness of its presence to itself; further differentiations, which I am in the course of explaining, result in the concepts of *past* and *future*. By means of these concepts, however, we can measure and interpretatively order a reality that is in no way the creature of consciousness, namely, the presence of objects to each other that is the basis of, for instance, their real causal interactions. Hence, though *time* has no more objective reality than, say, *causality* or *existence*, our interpretations of reality in temporal terms are valid when they are warranted by the relations of presence (or absence) that real things bear to each other, and invalid otherwise; this parallels the way in which assertions about causal processes, and about what is real and what is not, depend for their truth or falsity upon reality and not upon what the human mind may fancy or wish.

23 This terminology is misleading because it implies that reality in itself is either past, present, or future. It is thus a symptom of the projection of the temporality of consciousness onto objective reality as its absolute possession. (By the temporality of consciousness I mean: its presence to itself insofar as it is the basis of its experience of the relationship of presence and absence that things bear to each other and to consciousness.) Why and how this projection takes place will be explained in a moment.

These universal characteristics of consciousness, however, result in somewhat different concepts of time in the absent- and the present-minded; and the differences are manifested in certain grammatical divergences between the languages of apodictic and depositional speech. In the apodictic languages every thesis – rather, every verbal predicate – includes a temporal index; the verb must contain, as part of its meaning, reference to *when* the 'doing' or 'being' occurs. This is true even when the assertion 'represents' (as the apodictic speaker would put it) an event that he is not currently experiencing, but only one that he remembers or one that he fantasizes about. To be sure, other words – adverbs and adverbial phrases such as, in English, *now, later, some time ago, yesterday, one day*, and so on – are available to convey the present, past, or future tense of the predicated activity; but the verb itself will, in any case, signify the tense. The inclusion of temporality is indeed so typical and indispensable a part of the verb's meaning that for Aristotle it was the specific difference that defined this part of speech.[24] In the depositional languages, however, the general rule is that if the speaker wishes to convey the time to which the assertion refers – which is far from the usual case – he must signify it by supererogation, for instance, by using the appropriate 'adverb' or 'adverbial phrase' (as *we* would describe it, though in fact it would be an adjective). Most commonly, perhaps, only the past and the future are specified; otherwise the assertion is understood either as present or without reference to time (though it is usually possible to emphasize its present character, provided it be signified separately). And this holds when the thesis signifies an action as well as when it does not. In other words, in these languages the thesis does not, of itself, ever carry an indication of time; the differentiation between the present, the past, and the future, if any, must be conveyed separately, because it does not refer to the temporality that supposedly inheres in objects absolutely, but to the temporal relationship that they have towards each other and towards our experience of them.

We can understand why. Since for all human beings the present is the only time when experience occurs, both the absent- and the present-minded speaker will, in what pertains to temporality, signify in basically the same way what they are currently sensing: both will assert a thesis in relation to a theme without either of them experiencing the need to specify that the event is taking place at present. What they thus do, however, will appear differently to each. Assuming that his speech is but the specular counterpart of reality, the apodictic speaker will not

24 *On Interpretation*, 3 (16b6).

simply use his own temporality to measure reality, but will imagine that his experience has the quality of *now* only because reality itself 'is' or 'does' *now* what he is experiencing *now*; he has projected the temporality of consciousness into objects. (This, incidentally, is the basis of the concept of a universally simultaneous world, or which is the same, the idea of *absolute space*.) In truth it is the other way about: he can experience that reality 'is' or 'does' anything at present, only because he has already conceived the presentness of his own consciousness. (Therefore, as Einstein – following a very different route – was compelled to conclude, events that one experiences as simultaneous will not necessarily be experienced simultaneously by every other conscious experiencer.) It follows that when his experience is either an imaginative recollection of previous experience or an anticipation of future experience, the absent-minded speaker will take for granted that his assertions reflect, likewise, what reality itself 'was' or 'did' in the past, or 'will be' or 'will do' in the future. Even when the experience refers to the past or the future, therefore, the verbal predicate itself will be *meant* as including temporal reference; that is, in every case the predicate will be supposed to represent the temporal character possessed by reality absolutely, objectively, and in itself.

Observe, however, what has happened: as if by legerdemain, the temporality of consciousness – the actuality of self-present experience and of assertive speech – has been palmed upon the object while attention was being focused on the contents of experience. In other words, the fact that *one's acts* of experiencing and asserting are taking place now has vanished from one's own sight, and all that remains is the fact that these acts refer to *real events* that are taking place either at the *present* moment of time, or else have taken place in the *past* or will take place in the *future*. This unintended but fully effective self-deception, this prestidigitation in which the *act* is replaced by its *contents*, is of course the essence of absent-mindedness.

Since depositional speakers, on the contrary, have a normal level of self-presence, they keep in mind the fact that all consciousness – all human experience and speech – takes place at present. They assume that *no* assertion requires, of itself, that any temporality be specified; for it always signifies an experience that is taking place at present. If the present experience refers, however, to contents that are not being experienced as present (because it is a present experience of what is imaginatively recollected or else imaginatively projected), communicating the experience's temporal quality requires that one so specify. In Japanese, for instance, one would say 'Pinkerton, a departure' to speak of a certain naval person's present caddish behaviour either as present or without reference to time; but to refer to past or future events as such one would have to say the equivalent of, for instance, 'An abandonment of me by him, some time ago,' or 'A ship in the horizon, one fine day a seeing by us.' Specifying that the first event occurred 'some time ago' and that the other may perhaps happen 'one fine day' is mandatory, because the speaker does not intend to represent the temporal characteristics that inhere objectively and absolutely in earlier human acts or in hoped-for ships' looming into view; she intends rather to communicate which of the two different types of imaginary experience is involved in her present remembrance of betrayal and in her currently anticipated reunion with her fickle lover. And unless she signified it 'adverbially' (or more exactly, in some supererogatory way), the imaginary nature of her experience, and the type, would remain unexpressed.

This way of speaking is much more faithful to reality than the apodictic. For it implies that, although reality can be validly spoken of in temporal terms, temporality is not an absolute characteristic possessed by real things; it is a relationship that they bear to each other and to consciousness. Apodictic speakers, on the contrary, cannot very well avoid supposing that time has some sort of gossamer but objective reality that flows from the future through the present into the past – or vice versa, sometimes we find it hard to tell which – and consequently that there is an empty but real space within which all things exist simultaneously. These suppositions are part of their 'idea' of what it is to speak. If we understand how absent- and present-mindedness result in different 'ideas' of thematic speech – because they determine the degree to which speakers are conscious of their speech – we should understand also how the grammatical differences between the two types of languages emerged, as non-thematic evolved into thematic speech.

2. The emergence of the apodictic and the depositional variants of thematic speech

In what pertains to the genesis of the depositional variant of speech, very little need be added to what was said in chapter vi about the way in which all thematic speech emerges; depositional speech is the sort that would have developed in human beings in the normal course of evolution. But quite as evolution through natural genetic selection sometimes fails to proceed normally – in the sense that disadvantageous characteristics, genetic defects, can appear – human evolution is apt to produce its own version of 'genetic' abnormality. Special explanation is needed thus to account for the kind of thematic speech that emerged when the process did not unfold as smoothly as it might have. To incorporate the peculiarities of apodictic speech into the proposed theory, however, all we need suppose is that as thematic speech was emerging out of non-thematic there were differences among human groups in the self-presence of the immediate consciousness generated in them by their non-thematic speech. In most groups thematic ability would have been manifested in the sort of syntax devised to express the standard level of consciousness of speech created by a standard level of self-presence; other groups, a few, would have been handicapped by a lower level of self-presence in their immediate consciousness. This deficiency would have been institutionalized and rendered self-perpetuating by the kind of grammar that defines the apodictic form of speech.

Granted, however, that absent- and present-mindedness are at the bottom of the difference between the two forms of speech, can we account also for the origin of the *linguistic* differences that manifest the differences in speech? Again, there is no great difficulty in reconstructing how the grammatical structure of thematic assertions in the depositional languages must have developed. Since the depositional speaker does not project his assertiveness, once he conceives the possibility of asserting theses in relation to themes he has automatically created the device of adjectival deposition: juxtaposition of thesis and theme. In other words, there was no intricate grammatical artifice to create; to satisfy the requirements of his 'idea' of thematic speech it would have been enough that he speak assertively. Accordingly, all the depositional linguistic families use fundamentally the same linguistic technique, though they are dispersed throughout the world and presumably developed thematic ability independently of each other. It is, however, far from obvious how the linguistic features of verbal predication followed from the properties of apodictic speech. Through what process would the IE languages and Sumerian have developed the unusual grammar that requires that all thematic assertions be made by means of verbs, and that 'to be' must be used, at least tacitly, when the predicate is neither literally nor figuratively an action performed by the subject?

Let us recall that words signifying actions are not peculiar to the apodictic languages. Indeed, they are not exclusive to thematic speech or to human communication: chimpanzees learn to make hand signs for such actions as 'come,' 'go,' 'open,' 'hurry,' 'drink,' 'eat,' and so on.[25] The vocabularies of the human groups that eventually became apodictic speakers would have included, besides vocal signs used non-thematically to signify qualities, states, agents, events, and relationships,

25 John E. Pfeiffer, *The Emergence of Man* (New York, 1969) pp. 397ff.

signs that signified actions. However, action-words used by pre-thematic speakers could not have been verbs; *ex hypothesi,* they could have been used only non-thematically. What we need to explain is indeed how words used by non-thematic speakers to signify actions came to perform the function of verbal predication, and why only such words and 'to be' came to carry the assertive function in apodictic speech. The explanation is suggested by the fact that 'to be' is apt to substitute for any ordinary, action-signifying verb; for this hints at the possibility that 'to be' (and any other words that became copulas) may have been the original and sole linguistic expression of verbal predication in the apodictic languages. That is, 'to be' would have been used at first in all thematic assertions, including those where the thesis signified an action; but eventually, for reasons I will make clear in a moment, 'to be' would have been perceived as a redundancy whenever the thesis signified an action, and would have been customarily omitted in these cases. Conversely, 'to be' would have been used regularly thereafter only when the thesis did not signify an action literally or figuratively ascribed to the theme as to a subject – though it would have remained open to the speaker to ascribe actions to subjects by means of 'to be,' for example, 'The dog is barking,' instead of 'The dog barks.' But why would 'to be' have been used in this way originally? And why would it have become obsolete when the thesis signified an action?

A word is not a verb because it signifies an action, but because it is used as a verb – that is, to relate the thesis to the theme as what the latter is or does. Until apodictic speakers began to use 'to be' as a verb, there could have been no *verb* 'to be.' Nevertheless, before 'to be' there could well have been 'be,' a word that was not a verb but that was available for transformation into the original predicative verb of apodictic speech because its original signification in non-thematic speech rendered it apt for signifying the supposed relationship between the realities to which the thesis and the theme referred. The plausibility of this hypothesis tends to be obscured by the semantic indigence of 'to be' today, now that it has come to be used as a copula. At present it signifies only that the remainder of the semantic load of the predicate (i.e., the complement), if any, is ascribed to the reality signified by the subject as what the subject in itself and in reality is; and without a complement it means the same as 'to be real' or 'to exist.' But some memory of the inherent signification of 'be' has been preserved in a few languages which, like Sanskrit, are closer to the original language of the proto-IES than its more modern descendants. And enough has been reconstructed by scholars of the language of the Sumerians to support the hypothesis that verbal predication emerged among them through a process strikingly similar to that of the IES. Let us consider separately the possible origin of the Sanskrit and the Sumerian 'to be.'

Most of the inflected forms of 'to be' in the later and the modern IE languages go back to two IE roots, the Sanskrit forms of which are *as-* and *bhu-*. The former is the foundation of *asmi*, the principal Sanskrit copulative verb; from the other comes *bhavāmi*, 'to come to be.' As a copula *asmi* carries no more meaning of its own than does the English 'to be,' of which it is the close equivalent (though under certain conditions it may function as the equivalent of 'to become'); and like 'to be,' it can be used to mean 'to exist' 'to happen,' 'to be real,' and 'to live.' Quite unlike 'to be' in the younger IE languages, however, *as-* can also be used with its own meanings. Some of these are: 'to belong to,' 'to turn out,' 'to result,' 'to tend towards,' and 'to fall to the share of.' We shall consider additional evidence presently, but this should be enough to justify the conclusion that the semantic content of the ancestor of *as-* made it a most suitable means for IE speakers to develop verbal predication. Why?

Let us recall that IE speakers operated under the handicap of certain misconceptions. To speak thematically, they assumed, was to paint word-pictures of objective reality; and the difference between non-thematic and thematic speech was that the former consisted in using words merely to reproduce objects or aspects of objects, whereas the latter consisted in relating words so that their relationships in speech should reproduce relationships among objects or aspects of objects in reality. These speakers therefore *had* to signify that the reality itself was responsible for creating the relationship that their speech merely imitated; otherwise they would have felt that they had not asserted anything at all. On this point we need not speculate, because this 'idea' of speech survives to this day. Exceptional conventions or context aside, if we read a sentence from which the verb has been omitted, we a feeling that something missing – I mean, we *have* a feeling that something *is* missing – whereas an Indonesian who heard the assertion 'we, a feeling that something missing' would not feel that anything was missing. And if it should seem implausible that a speaker should want to say something, yet not say it precisely as what *he* says but as what he merely repeats, let us call to mind those amongst our fellow speakers who sometimes seek to reassure us about the truth of *their* assertions by telling us, without adverting to the paradox, 'That's not *my* opinion, that's a fact!' and 'That's not what *I* say, it's what God says!' – or for that matter, 'That's not what *I* think, but a scientifically ascertainable truth!'

But if reality itself, and not the speaker, bore the responsibility for the relationship that obtained among objects or aspects of objects – a relationship that speech merely repeated – then *as-* was ideally fit to represent such relationship. The reason is that it denoted *attributability*, the sort of relationship that connects the owned to its owner, the result to its factor, or the effect to its cause. To the mind of the apodictic speaker, the predicate *belongs* to the subject – as we ourselves not infrequently put it – in the sense that the reality signified by the predicate *springs forth*, or *results*, from the reality signified by the subject. The IES developed thematic speech, therefore, by learning to say things like 'The flower, red, a belonging [of the one to the other],' and 'The dog, a barking, a springing forth [of the latter from the former].'[26] Simply by being used in this way – namely, as a means to make assertions apodictically – *as-*, a word that was not originally a verb, began to function as a verb.

According to this explanation all IE thematic assertions would have originally required 'to be,' even when the predicate signified an action actually or figuratively performed by the subject; only the word (or words) signifying 'to be' had become verbs. But once verbal predication had emerged, the possibility of verbalizing all words signifying actions automatically arose. There is no need to say, for instance, 'The dog, a barking, a resulting [of the former in the latter],' because 'a barking,' being an action, necessarily includes its being the result or effect achieved by the performer. Action words had thus acquired a verbal function in their own right, and 'to be' was indispensable only when the thesis was not an action. To acquire the full grammatical form that it eventually took, the verb had but to become inflected to agree with the subject and to signify time – that is, to include reference to whether the 'resulting' or 'springing forth' of the predicate from the subject was or was not taking place at present (or to put it precisely, whether the speaker was *experiencing* the 'springing forth' at present or not). More about this below.

There may be other indications of the aptness of *as-* for being used as the original verbal predicator. I mention, for what it may be worth, that in a second acceptation (conjugated somewhat differently), *as-* means 'to throw,' 'to cast,' and 'to shoot at.' And in a third (more commonly spelled *aṣ-*) it means 'to go,' 'to move,' 'to shine,' 'to take,' and 'to receive.'[27] A constant central idea, conveyed in somewhat different modes,

---

26 The verb is normally placed last in Sanskrit and in some other IE languages, and presumably also in proto-IE. The medial position, which is now standard in many modern IE languages, is a much later development.

27 *As-* can also mean 'to breathe.' This is a very rare usage; many Sanskrit dictionaries

is therefore signified by this root; it envisages either the sort of event or process that consists in projecting, issuing forth, bringing about, or being the cause of, some result; or else the action of originating that which is projected or cast forth. A more distant, but possibly related meaning, is carried by *aś-*, which can be translated as 'to reach,' 'to come to,' 'to arrive at,' and therefore also 'to get' and 'to obtain.'

The other usual Sanskrit copula, formed with the root *bhu-*, is *bhavāmi*. In some contexts it can be translated by 'to be,' but its distinctive note is more particularly 'to come to be,' or 'to have come into being;' therefore, it can be translated as 'to happen,' 'to arise,' 'to occur,' and 'to take place.'[28] Much like the English 'to become,' then, it presupposes 'to be,' in the sense that it expresses an idea that depends upon the prior assumption that things themselves 'are' whatever they are truthfully said to be. Now, if this were the only meaning of *bhavāmi*, *asmi* would have been the only Sanskrit verb 'to be,' and its ancestor would have been the only proto-IE 'to be.' An indication to the contrary, however, is the fact that in many IE languages 'to be' is etymologically a mixture of both roots.[29] This suggests that originally the two may have been more or less interchangeable, but that for some reason *asmi* became the standard Sanskrit copula 'to be' and *bhavāmi* became what it now is.

---

do not mention it at all. Julian Jaynes nevertheless suggests (*The Origin of Consciousness*, p. 51) that *asmi* depends for its meaning of 'to be' upon an animistic metaphor. It seems to me, however, that animism is not a premise of apodictic speech. On the contrary, animism may well be a result of it, since it depends on a confusion of efficient and final causality that absent-mindedness facilitates; for absent-mindedness, as we shall see, predisposes human beings to perceive efficient causality as a force – that is, as a striving to produce certain effects – from which follows that even inanimate agents act for an end. The so-called animism observed in contemporary primitive societies, which are depositional in speech, does not suppose that inanimate nature exerts a will-like, compelling causality; it expresses rather the consubstantiality, as it were, of all entities in the world – the continuity of man, animal, and inanimate nature – and the qualitative nature of all processes. It is not properly described as the idea that all things are in any sense alive, but that all things share in a common quality that binds them together in kinship and that accounts for their relationships.

28 Anticipating certain issues that will be discussed later, I underline that this refers specifically to the objective reality of events. The 'happening' or 'occurring' in question does not carry the connotation that the event of 'coming into being' is what 'happens to' or 'befalls' either the speaker or those who observe the event; the subject of the thematic assertion alone is what either *does* the 'coming into being' or else is *caused* to 'come into being.'

29 For instance, English 'am,' German *sind*, Spanish *soy*, and French *suis* descend from the same IE root as *asmi*. English 'been,' German *bin*, Spanish *fui*, and French *fut* come from the same root as *bhavāmi*.

The conclusion that indeed they probably were interchangeable is reached as soon as one considers some of the other meanings of *bhavāmi*. They tell their own story: 'to fall to the share of,' 'to become the property of,' 'to belong to,' 'to cause to be or become,' 'to call into existence or life,' 'to originate, produce, cause, or create,' and indeed 'to manifest, exhibit, show, or betray' and 'to present to the mind.' The two roots were thus about equally apt to serve the purpose of IE speakers, because they envisaged basically the same situation: reality *issues forth* into manifestations; these manifestations are at one and the same time the *effects* or *results* of the reality that causes them and to which they *belong*, and the causes of our experience of them.[30] By means of either the speaker could therefore attribute predicates to subjects objectively, or as their own.

There is, however, a slight difference between the two roots that may explain why, if not in the IE languages generally at least in Sanskrit, the forerunner of *as-* became the standard copula while the principal meaning of *bhu-* was narrowed down to 'to become.' An analysis of the nuances of the various meanings noted above suggests that, although the two roots contemplated the same sort of process of 'issuing forth,' they envisaged it from opposite perspectives. Whereas *bhu-* connoted 'issuing forth' particularly as the flowing of the predicate out of the subject as an effect does from its cause (or as what-is-said flows from a speaker), *as-* took the viewpoint of the causal activity in the subject that was responsible for the predicate's flowing from its source as an effect. Thus, *as-* connoted the *efficacy* of efficient causality more pronouncedly than did *bhu-*, which paid attention instead to the *outcome* of the causal process. Or which is the same, unlike *bhu-*, which focused on the supposed fact that the predicate was 'uttered' by the subject, *as-* stressed that the subject *did* the 'uttering.' Therefore, *bhu-* would have been somewhat

---

30 I have repeatedly noted how this implies the projection of the speaker's assertiveness into reality, since it means that we speak about reality only because reality first 'speaks' to us by uttering or issuing forth manifestations that we in turn receive. It is interesting that there is a Sanskrit verbal root, *bhā-*, a variant of which is *bhās-*, whose most common acceptations are 'to shine,' 'to be bright,' 'to appear,' 'to show,' 'to show oneself,' 'to seem,' 'to look like,' 'to exhibit,' 'to manifest,' 'to cause to appear,' and 'to come to mind,' which therefore is most likely a cognate of *bhu-*. The Oxford Sanskrit-English dictionary, however, compares this with another verbal root, *bhāṣ-*, which means 'to speak,' 'to say,' 'to tell,' 'to announce,' 'to declare,' and, indeed, 'to cause to speak.' We can recognize the same parallel in the Greek *phainein*, 'to show,' and *phanai*, 'to speak,' and in the Latin *parere* and *fari*, the Western IE cousins of *bhās-* and *bhāṣ-*. It is possible, therefore, that *bhu-* and *bhāṣ-* are cognates, and that the proto-IES *consciously* likened the 'issuing forth' of manifestations by reality to the 'uttering' of words by speech.

more apt than *as-* to signify the thesis as 'coming into being' or as 'happening' simply as a matter of fact, whereas *as-* more pointedly alluded to the subject's actively 'being' what the thesis proclaimed.

I will deal only summarily with the sequel to the verbalization of the IE thesis, namely, the temporalization of the IE verb. (It will be convenient to mention at this time a few cultural phenomena directly attributable to this development, even if I have reserved to the next chapter a more systematic account of the cultural implications of the form of speech.) Linguists tell us that, generally, the IE verbs were not originally inflected for the future tense, but only for the past and the present – or rather, for two tenses which, in my opinion, should be more exactly described as follows. One tense expressed the idea that reality's utterance of itself was in the course of being currently experienced and spoken about by the speaker; this was the *present*. We have already seen why this should have been so, and if my theory is correct this would have been the original IE verbal tense. I underline that the present tense, therefore, took account, if only absent-mindedly, of the fact that reality was being experienced and spoken about by the speaker as he spoke – as the etymology of *present*, 'being in front of,' indicates. The other tense expressed, purely negatively, that reality was *not* being spoken about under the guise of its being currently experienced by the speaker; it was, in effect, the *not-present* or, as we might also call it, the *absent*, tense. No distinction was originally made, however, between the past and the future – that is, between the two kinds of absence we are apt to experience – because the speaker had not yet learned to discriminate imaginative experience of past sensation from imaginative experience of possible future sensation. But since he was absent-minded, to speak in total abstraction from the fact that reality was being experienced and spoken about seemed to him to describe reality absolutely and in itself – or as it appeared when it was 'not before' the speaker. Only a defective consciousness, of course, permitted the speaker to imagine that his speech was most faithful to reality when it represented the latter as absent – that is, as it appeared when he was not-present to it, or indeed as it appeared when it was not-appearing to anyone.

Since to speak in the not-present tense was to take the viewpoint of a reality whose utterance was anterior to man, it was, in a sense, to speak in what we now call the past tense. But since reality in itself had no reference to human experience, to speak in this tense was, more precisely, to speak without reference to the temporality of human experience, in which events are successive; it was to portray reality in a sort of timeless, all-at-once present, or in an infinite objective 'now' otherwise called *eternity*. The 'time' designated by the original not-present tense of the IE verb may therefore be described, in the categories we now use, as simultaneously encompassing the past and the future within the perpetual present of eternity, which is not-present to us (or from which we are absent). Speaking of reality apodictically tended thus, by its own inner logic, to generate the concept of eternity as the duration proper to an absolute reality above time and altogether outside succession and change. The further, direct implication was clear, and escaped not a single IE culture: man is absent from his true home, namely, that other plane of existence that is definable by its eternal duration and absolute reality; here below, in the world whose duration is always a fleeting present, we are in exile.

In due course, moreover, yet another implication would be drawn: that eternity included not only past events (i.e., whatever has already happened and is therefore anterior to current human experience and speech), but also those events which, though having already happened from the absolutely objective viewpoint of reality itself, have not yet been experienced – and a fortiori, have not yet been spoken about – by man. The importance of these mental processes for human self-definition is obvious: those who thus suppose that there is a transcendent order of duration – eternity – are necessarily bound to think also that what for them is in the future has already been predetermined and is no more avoidable than what has already happened. The concept of *fate* is inseparable from the concepts of eternity and absolute reality, and like these two logically follows from the properties of apodictic speech. (The scientific version of the same idea is not called *fate*, but *determinism*.)

At any rate, the linguistic consequence of drawing this implication was that the IE past and future verbal tenses became differentiated out of the not-present tense. The original not-present tense furnished the grammatical forms of the past tense; the grammatical forms of the future tense were created *ad hoc* by the device of appending auxiliaries (most often 'to have,' in the imperative sense of 'to be obliged')[31] to the stem or to the infinitive of the verb.[32] The relatively late origin of the future tense is obscured in many IE languages by the fusion of the future auxiliary and the stem to produce the illusion that the stem has been inflected (e.g., Latin *am-abo*, Spanish *amar-é*, French *aimer-ai*). This is not

31 The implicit reasoning may have been that the future already contains within itself the necessity that it eventually happen; that is, even now it *has* all that it needs in order to happen.
32 On its face it might well have happened differently; the original not-present might have provided the grammatical forms of the future, and the past forms would have had to be created *ad hoc*. But there may have been a reason why it happened as it did.

true, however, of all the IE languages. For instance, English regularly uses two future auxiliaries – whose imperative meaning is plain – and upon occasion 'to have' (as in 'I have to do it'), but none of the three has become fused with the stem.

But I return to my principal subject. The ancestors of the Sumerians seem to have followed a roughly parallel route to much the same destination reached by the IEs. In Sumerian, theses are verbal predicates. Every sentence must contain either an ordinary verb or a copula;[33] without a verb, 'which almost invariably ends the sentence,'[34] no thematic assertion is possible. Indeed, the Sumerian verb plays in a sense a yet more assertive role than the IE. The latter is essential, but only rarely does it attempt (as it would in *veni, vidi, vici*) to convey the meaning of the entire sentence. For, apart from its own semantic content, the IE verb contains within itself, at most, reference to the subject and to time. (In English, reference to the subject has largely disappeared.) For instance, in the English sentence 'He praises the goddess in the presence of the priests with a beautiful hymn,' the signification of the verb 'praises' extends beyond its own radical semantic content (i.e., 'to express a favourable opinion of') only to the present time and to a third-person–singular subject. In Sumerian, however, the same sentence would be structured in a way illustrated roughly by the following schematic form: 'He; of him, goddess; priests; of them, presence; hymn beautiful; by him, her, in theirs, with it, a praising.'[35] The last element or 'complex,' the *single word* signifying 'by him, her, in theirs, with it, a praising,' is the verb – or as some Sumeriologists understandably call it, the 'verbal complex.' In other words, the Sumerian verb 'strives to epitomize within itself every part of the sentence,'[36] and amounts to 'a sort of synthetic résumé of the proposition in which it is found.'[37]

In Sumerian the verb is thus not only essential, but almost absorbs the whole of thematic speech. We can appreciate, then, why at least one Sumeriologist has concluded that 'the objective positing of ideas – that is, the way in which they are considered above all in themselves,

33 Adam Falkenstein, *Grammatik der Sprache Gudeas von Lagaš*, 2 vols. (Rome, 1950), vol. II, p. 5.

34 Stephen Langdon, *A Sumerian Grammar and Chrestomathy* (Paris, 1911), p. 131.

35 I have separated by commas what in Sumerian would be single syllables, and by semicolons the elements or 'complexes' of the sentence (as Sumeriologists often call the Sumerian equivalent of words). A Sumerian sentence is ordinarily no longer than its English equivalent, and indeed frequently contains fewer syllables than the latter.

36 C.J. Gadd, *A Sumerian Reading Book* (Oxford, 1924), p. 40.

37 Raymond Justin, *Abrégé de grammaire Sumeriénne* (Paris, 1951), p. 29.

with a minimum of elements manifesting the presence ... of the speaker ...
– constitutes one of the basic characteristics of the spirit of this language.'[38] This points to a yet lower level of self-presence than that of
our own IE ancestors; the Sumerians' projection of their assertiveness
onto reality seems to have been almost totally unqualified. The Sumerian
interpretation of self and world, as it can be ascertained from their
religious and philosophical beliefs, confirms that such was indeed the
case. Reality – what we IES call 'being' or 'that which is' – was for the
Sumerians *literally* 'that which asserts.' I mean: the Sumerian verb that
we translate as 'to be' meant 'to assert.' Perhaps more precisely, it meant
'to assert imperatively,' or 'to command.'[39] In Sumerian, to say 'A is B'
is the same as to say 'A commands B.'

The root of the Sumerian 'to be' is *me*. In particular contexts words
having this root would be translated as 'law,' 'decree,' 'order,' 'effective
power,' 'causality,' 'necessity,' 'force,' 'compulsion,' 'might,' 'will,' and
the like. It also connoted – hardly a mere coincidence – 'the sacred' and
'the other-worldly.' As a copula, however, *me* was used in exactly the
same circumstances as are the IE verbs 'to be,' namely, when the predicate was neither an action nor assimilable to an action. An emphatic
form of it, *na-nam*, means 'to be most surely,' or 'to be necessarily,'[40]
whence the noun *nam*, usually translated as 'fate,' since it literally means
'that which has been spoken or commanded';[41] the principal difference
is that it denotes much more explicitly than the latter that fate is 'spoken'
or 'asserted' in commanding terms whose effectiveness is absolute. Accordingly, to the Sumerians (and to the Akkadians and Assyro-Babylonians who perpetuated the Sumerian world-view), it was self-evident
that 'each man is allotted ... at birth ... an individual and definite share
of fortune and misfortune. This share determines the entire direction
and temper of his life ... It is in the nature of ... the individual "share,"
that its realization is a necessity, not a [mere] possibility.'[42] The individual's destiny, however, was only part of the scope of fate: it was the
entire 'course of the world [that] was governed by the ... *me*-powers ...
a universal and cosmic order which was then to be realized in the activities of men.'[43] Conversely, the corner-stone of Sumerian self-defi-

---

38 Ibid., p. 30.
39 Gadd, *Sumerian*, p. 187.
40 Ibid., p. 37.
41 Ibid., p. 188. The English *fate* comes, of course, from the Latin *fatum*, the neuter
   past participle of *fari*, 'to be spoken'; therefore, it literally means 'that which has been
   spoken.'
42 A. Leo Oppenheim, *Ancient Mesopotamia* (Chicago, 1964), p. 202.
43 Helmer Ringgren, *Religions of the Ancient Near East* (Philadelphia, 1973), p. 43.

nition was the idea that 'man is the slave of the great cosmic forces; he serves them and obeys them; and his only means of influencing them is by prayer and sacrifice, that is, by persuasion and gifts.'[44]

Now, in *all* the known religions of the primitive IEs – and indeed, in those developed by the IE civilizations also, though nuancedly in the latter – a basic religious concept has always been that 'that which has been spoken' comes to pass inexorably; simply by having been spoken, it happens necessarily. Or in the terms of the three biblical religions, fate betokens 'omnipotence,' since fate is nothing but the effect of the irresistible Will of God. But whereas in the IE languages the absolute necessity that fate be accomplished is only a connotation, in Sumerian it is part of the denotation: as we have seen, *me* means simultaneously 'that which has been spoken' and 'that which necessarily is.' Correspondingly, when one speaks of reality in Sumerian, one speaks simultaneously of its objectivity and of its causal-effective structure: reality is at the same time 'being' and 'causal power,' because 'to be' is synonymous with 'to command.' More particularly, since the immediately given reality of the empirical world depends for its reality upon an ultimate order of reality beyond all possible experience, to speak of objects of experience in Sumerian is to allude simultaneously to 'that which commands [us human beings to experience what we experience and to say what we say]' and to 'that which has been commanded [so to command].' The world of reality is thus a chain of being – that is, a chain of command, or of deterministic cause-effect relationships in which human beings are willy-nilly and inextricably enmeshed.

The aptness of *me* for signifying the subject-predicate relationship scarcely needs underlining. What I should stress instead is the implication that the Sumerians seem to have been perceptibly more absent-minded than the IEs, yet less aware of the assertive causality of their speech. For they ascribed their own assertiveness to objects of speech without so much as the vacillation with which the IEs did; they assumed, in effect, that objects *alone* – and, to be sure, the ultimate reality behind them – had any assertive power. They may have been in no more doubt than the IEs that the *voicing* of their speech was theirs, but the speaker was literally – not metaphorically, as with us – the mouthpiece of reality. By the same token, objective reality, the world, was yet more anthropomorphically conceived by this subvariety of apodictic speaker than by the IE. Since in Sumerian 'to be' means the same as 'to assert' or 'to command,' it follows that, merely by 'being,' reality automatically 'com-

44 H. Frankfort, H.A. Frankfort, John Wilson, and Thorkild Jacobsen, *Before Philosophy: The Intellectual Adventure of Ancient Man* (Baltimore, 1949), p. 216.

mands.' Reality is thus not merely that which *causes* man to experience as he does, but also that which *wants* him so to experience. The Sumerians, as scholars have observed, felt 'that there was a will and a personality in each phenomenon – in it and yet somehow behind it.'[45] The explanation lies in the properties of their speech.

To divine a few of the further cultural consequences of this way of thinking we need but consider that in such a universe 'obedience must necessarily stand out as a prime virtue ... [A]n orderly world is unthinkable without a superior authority to impose his will.'[46] The reason is that the social, moral, legal, and political orders descend to human affairs from above; and they enjoy the status of indubitable truth because they flow from a transcendent and eternal will, *me*, rather than from a merely human and transient one. We should have little difficulty understanding what the Sumerians felt; for in the history of the IE peoples – and more particularly, in our own Western culture – analogous ideas, cast in otherwise very different moulds, have recurrently appeared and have been rationalized by means of the IE equivalents of *me*. They continue indeed to be asserted by many even today, though they are no longer unquestionably or unanimously held. Other features of Sumerian tend to confirm that this was how the Sumerians perceived their speech, their experience, and the reality they experienced and whereof they spoke.[47]

There are indications that *me* was not the only word that was suitable, by reason of its original semantic content, for the purpose of embodying grammatically the verbally predicative function, but that a process much like that we have reconstructed for the IES resulted in the redundancy of the others and the eventual supremacy of *me*. It seems that three other roots were used at one time as signifiers of assertiveness: *dug*, which means 'speaking';[48] *ag*, which refers to 'making' or 'doing'; and *du*, which denotes 'going along' or 'continuing [along a path],' and

45 Ibid., p. 143.
46 Ibid., pp. 217–18.
47 For instance, according to Thorkild Jacobsen, the Sumerian verb can be conjugated in twelve moods, one of which is indicative, the other eleven being variations of the imperative; see 'About the Sumerian Verb,' in his *Toward the Image of Tammuz* (Cambridge, MA, 1970), pp. 245–70. It could be argued, however, that even the Sumerian 'indicative' is actually a form of the imperative. This mood, to be sure, manifests the mere assertion of fact, in the sense that it takes no account of either the speaker's or any other concrete agent's will; nevertheless, it asserts necessary facts, namely, the events willed by fate. In Sumerian, *nothing* can be said except with reference to someone's will – the abstract and impersonal will which is 'being itself' (as *we* would say), if no other as well.
48 That is, 'voicing,' as contrasted with 'saying,' 'telling,' or 'commanding.' The cuneiform that represents it derives from a pictogram of an open mouth.

therefore also 'fulfilling,' 'coming to completion,' and 'coming to pass' – that is, 'to happen.' It should not be difficult to understand why these were nearly as apt as *me* to signify verbal predication. Indeed, two of them, *dug* and *du*, overlap appreciably with Sanskrit *as-* and *bhu-*, respectively; and the usefulness of 'to do' (*ag*) in order to signify the activity of the subject that 'utters' the predicate could not be more obvious. But we can estimate why *me* should have eventually prevailed, namely, for the same reason that *as-* did in Sanskrit: that it corresponded *exactly* to the speaker's 'idea' of thematic speech. To the IES the assertiveness that they projected onto reality was above all what 'did' or 'caused' their repetitive experience and speech to be such as it was, whereas to the Sumerians it was what 'commanded' them to experience and speak as they did. Conversely, for the IE speaker reality played principally the role of efficient cause of experience and speech, which is why experience and speech were explained as the *representation* of reality. As we have seen, however, for the Sumerians reality discharged predominantly the office of a finalistic cause determining experience and speech, and therefore experience and speech denoted, above all, *obedience* to reality.

This explanation is supported by certain features of Sumerian that 'should go back to the early period of the language.'[49] Although in historical times *me* alone was the normal copula, and although ordinary verbs were usually formed without *me* or any expression of the relationship of subject and predicate other than their own semantic content, it was optional to add *dug* or *ag* to the ordinary verbal root 'without the meaning of the latter undergoing any modification whatever.'[50] It was somewhat like saying in English 'It does work,' instead of 'It works,' which adds emphasis but which does not change the meaning. This may be interpreted, therefore, as a vestigial use of *dug* and *ag* from a time when they were copulative verbs and when copulative verbs were not redundant even when used with predicates signifying actions. *Du*, however, possibly by virtue of its signification, performed a somewhat different role in historical times; it survived as a copula which, when combined with adjectives and participles, and with some substantives, carried the special connotation of realizing or fulfilling 'the nature or essential and distinctive quality'[51] of something. For instance, *zid* means 'fair,' and *erim* means 'foul' or 'evil.' With these roots the verbs *zid-du* and *erim-du* could be formed, meaning, respectively – as a weak translation would have to put it – 'to be fair' and 'to be evil.' But the idea is

49 Justin, *Abrégé*, p. 69.
50 Ibid., p. 68.
51 Ibid., p. 69.

that of *necessarily* realizing the essence of good and evil, as if by compulsion or fate. Thus, like all the other copulas, *du* became superfluous as Sumerian speakers realized that action-words in general included the idea of imperative causality, but continued to be used in order to emphasize the compelled and compelling nature of reality in respect of qualities and states.

The parallel between the IE languages and Sumerian is remarkable also in respect of the temporalization of the verb; the differences in their respective confusions, however, are very interesting. The Sumerians made only a 'rudimentary'[52] distinction between past, present, and future. So far as the verb indicates time, Sumerian distinguished instead between the 'actualized' and the 'non-actualized' tenses.[53] The actualized tense comprised indistinctly what in the modern IE languages is differentiated into present, past, and future. The reason is that, to the Sumerian mind, in every present event 'it is an agent external [to the events], as it were, that manifests itself, always with power, and often suddenly.'[54] And this means that the present is so charged with the power manifested by 'being' that the future is, so to speak, as much a foregone conclusion as the past. In other words, whatever shall be, already is and always has been; the 'actualized' tense describes what has been commanded from all eternity to have occurred in the past, to be occurring at present, and to occur in the future. In contrast, the 'non-actualized' tense – marked, perhaps significantly, by the absence of any affix of tense – indicated events envisaged in their pure essence and outside time, or as they eternally were. It abstracted from the reality of the world given in experience in order to reach to the ultimate reality behind it, which 'utters' the reality we do experience. This tense was mandatory 'if one wanted to stress the objective nature of an action considered in itself, maintaining its immutable meaning independently of its historical situation in time.'[55]

The superficial differences but profound similarities between the Sumerian and the IE tenses can be explained as the result of the independent development of thematic speech in two different human cultural strains, but in the light of common assumptions created by the same cause. Both peoples began, as all cultures do, by differentiating between the present and the absent; this is in accordance with the universal properties of consciousness. But because of their absent-mindedness

52 Ibid., p. 30.
53 Ibid., p. 73. The same tenses can be described of course in other categories.
54 Ibid., p. 71.
55 Ibid., p. 72.

they both assumed that reality as such is correctly represented by being spoken of objectively (i.e., as it is in itself or, which is the same, as it appears when it is not-appearing to us). From this common basis, however, the IES and the Sumerians proceeded in opposite directions by emphasizing one or else the other aspect of objective reality, namely, either its being present to itself or its being most properly described when it was spoken of as not-present to human experience. The IES were especially impressed by the thought that a reality that is absent to us is none the less present to itself. Therefore, the present tense was used to refer both to the ever-changing succession of human nows, and to the totally simultaneous, perpetual, unchanging now of eternity; this left them free to differentiate eventually between the past and the future out of the original not-present tense. The Sumerians, however – and this is another indication that their absent-mindedness was deeper than ours – were swayed by the consideration that reality as such and in itself is not-present to human experience. They therefore used one tense to speak of 'non-actualized' or altogether absent reality, namely, eternity.[56] Their other tense correspondingly covered the present, successive, 'actualized' temporality of the world of human experience in all its forms; it comprised indistinctly the experiences that IES break down into present, future, and past.

These parallels between the IE and the Sumerian subvariants of apodictic speech are all the more striking if it is true that Sumerian is not a member of the IE family. It is also noteworthy that the aboriginal apodictic groups were in any event very few in number; if there were others besides the IES and the Sumerians, they either did not survive to historical times or for some other reason have failed to come to our notice. Their paucity would have been in keeping with their subnormality. Their subnormality, however, need not have stayed their success – at least, not if we measure the latter simply by the effective use of causal power, regardless of the kind of purpose to which the wielding of causality may be put. With absent-mindedness comes difficulty in channelling power towards ultimately satisfying ends, but no difficulty whatever in amassing it. On the contrary, if it is true, as I remarked earlier, that absent-mindedness can be most dangerous, part of the reason is that, like a little madness, it can be a most useful and convenient thing.

This statement is not intended cynically, as if it meant only that

---

56 Eternity, as we IES think of it, is of course 'actualized'; it is indeed the perfect and infinite actualization of reality in itself, as it endures perpetually present to itself. But in relation to human experience eternity is, on the contrary, 'not-actualized'; it is absolute *absence*. The latter consideration rather than the former was evidently the one that weighted heavily on the Sumerian mind.

absent-mindedness has promoted the false self- and world-perceptions that have traditionally inspired and justified the conquest and enslavement of the phenomenal peoples by the ontic – though it *has* meant this. I mean rather that evolutionary advantages and disadvantages can be ambivalent. Absent-mindedness is truly a human disvalue, but nevertheless it can have results that, from a long and comprehensive evolutionary perspective, should be deemed positively valuable for mankind as a whole. The full reasons for this will be explored later, but the question is important enough to justify adducing a telling instance of it even now. It is significant, I suggest, that whereas ideographic writing was invented independently by both the Sumerians and, later, by the Chinese, only the Sumerians succeeded in making the transition from ideographic to the vastly more efficient phonetic writing. The Sumerian invention – perhaps the most valuable single technological innovation of all time – has, of course, benefited all mankind. The explanation, strange though it may seem, is that absent-mindedness paved the way to the Sumerian development. This should be clear from an analysis of the difference between the two media.

An ideogram conveys no particular vocal sound; it conveys directly a meaning which, upon being grasped, serves to recall the vocal sound that the reader has previously learned to use to assert such meaning. This is why ideograms can be used to communicate not only by those who share a common tongue, but every whit as adequately by those who do not; for example, Chinese characters are used to communicate by Chinese speakers of mutually unintelligible dialects. Likewise, a certain Arabic numeral conveys the same idea to people who variously think of it as 'five,' 'cinco,' and 'lima.' But I have expressed this in our traditional terminology, which is misleading. We may tolerate the traditional metaphor of 'conveying an idea,' but we should understand clearly what it means: since the same arithmetic experience can be assertively meant quite as adequately by the vocal sign 'five' as by 'cinco' or 'lima,' various speakers can use the same visible sign, an Arabic numeral, to communicate equivalent experiences which each one of them asserts by means of his own vocal sign. By asserting the meaning in his own audible or imaginary sounds the reader shares thus the meaning asserted earlier by the writer when the latter wrote the visible sign. Ideographic writing presupposes, therefore – whether its users be able to say so or not – that *both* the writer and the reader are capable of asserting the same meaning. The function of the ideogram is to enable the writer to specify which meaning the reader should assert if the latter wants to grasp the former's meaning, and to enable the reader to assert it using his own words even if his words are different from the writer's.

Phonetic writing, however, does not of itself convey a meaning; it conveys instructions to the reader to make certain vocal sounds – whether audibly or in imagination only – which in turn enables him to recall the meaning that he has learned to assert by means of such sounds. Thus, whereas to read an ideogram one need only assert its meaning in one's own speech, to read phonetic writing one must first of all obey the sign's phonetic instructions – that is, to voice (audibly or in imagination only) the sounds originally made (or imagined) by the writer to assert what he meant. In this system it is essential, therefore, if communication is to take place, that the communicand use the same language as the communicator.[57] It is only upon hearing himself *repeat* the sound, audibly or inaudibly, that the reader can assert (to himself) the meaning of the sound. To the reader, then, his own assertion of the meaning appears as a compliant *repetition* of the meaning inserted by the writer into the sign. As McLuhan put it, phonetic writing gave man 'an eye for an ear.'[58] The phonetic sign is a vicarious 'voice' through which the absent writer speaks from beyond the here and now. And to read phonetic writing is to allow one's obedient, repetitive voice to be shaped by the instructions uttered by the written signs and heard by the mind's ear in accordance with the writer's original assertive intent.

It is difficult to suppose that mere coincidence accounts for the fact that the idea of using visible signs in this way occurred to a culture for which to speak was to repeat the message that reality enjoined upon the speaker through experience – a message that reality conveyed only because it itself had been previously commanded to do so – and that this idea did not occur to a culture for which to speak was to assert a meaning originally and for the first time. As depositional speakers the Chinese would have been much too mindful of the fact that written communication depended upon the reader's assertiveness and not only upon the writer's, whereas the Sumerians were not. The transition from ideogrammatic to phonetic signs was enormously facilitated by a certain degree of *unawareness* of the assertiveness of speech.

57 Conversely, a reader who did not understand the language, but who knew the phonetic conventions, could vocalize a message out loud without understanding what it meant, yet conveying the meaning to those of his listeners who understood the language. He would be following the phonetic instructions, but his vocal sounds would not mean anything to him, because he could not assert their meaning; the latter cannot be done except in one's own words.

58 *The Gutenberg Galaxy* (Toronto, 1962), p. 27. It would have been much more exact to say, however, that certain human beings invented phonetic writing because they suffered from a hearing defect that, by making it difficult for them to hear their own speech, bred into them the delusion that visible objects spoke to them. It would also have been much less memorable.

CHAPTER EIGHT

The consequences of the emergence of the self-defining consciousness in variant forms

As thematic speech appeared in two variant forms, the ontic and the phenomenal forms of consciousness came into being. The human species had become culturally differentiated into moieties, distinguishable by the divergent cultural orientations generated in them by the presuppositions with which their respective forms of speech endowed them. The courses were thus set that the two types of human culture would thereafter naturally tend to follow. If we wish to understand, therefore, how later human developments down to the present have been conditioned by man's evolutionary past, we must ascertain how these two different cultural orientations began. But to do so what we must determine is how the meaning of the three principal categories – reality, efficacy, and finality – was affected by the absent- or else present-mindedness of non-thematic speakers as they began to develop thematic speech. The tasks allotted to the three sections of this chapter are thus defined. In earlier chapters we had already studied how these three categories are conceived, but without taking into account how defective self-presence affects the process; now, however, we shall focus on it.

We can surmise the thrust of what we shall discover if we recall what was established in the last section of chapter VI: the self-defining consciousness is the sort of experiential life that, unlike animal life, integrates the experience of fact and the experience of value; it synthesizes the ability to experience what reality is like, and how it behaves, with the ability to experience such states of affairs as desirable or undesirable. The unification of the two not only enables human beings prepensely to steer efficient causality towards the realization of their conscious wants, but also, and more fundamentally, it creates in them the inherent requirement that they direct their efficient causality to the satisfaction of their specifically human needs, under pain of starvation and disintegration of their selfhood. Thus, it was to facilitate the welfare and de-velopment of their conscious life that, as they reached the second stage of human evolution, human beings spontaneously and automatically – by virtue of 'genetic predispositions' otherwise describable as the prop-erties of thematic speech – developed religious and intellectual traditions and the secondary and tertiary socio-cultural folkways and mores that derive from these. Their creators could hardly have realized it, but these institutions came into being because they foster the kind of everyday human experience that, in principle, serves to enhance selfhood; for they cultivate, improve upon, and perpetuate a people's understanding of the meaning of man and world, and human beings require such interpretations to satisfy the specifically human needs, the inherent re-quirements of conscious life.

When human beings learned to speak thematically, therefore, but did so in different ways, what was at stake was not merely the greater or lesser theoretical validity of the various world-views they would even-tually develop in the light of different presuppositions. It was rather a supremely practical matter: differences in the human ability to wield efficient causality so as to fulfil effectively the inherent purposes of conscious life. In other words, the two 'races' of mankind differed in the extent to which their institutions of self-definition – their cultures as a whole – could have functioned satisfactorily. One division of the human species, the largest in numbers by far, could count on the un-impeded exercise of the abilities that normally accrue to consciousness. To the same degree that certain other human groups institutionalized their absent-mindedness, however, they became burdened by a hered-itary infirmity that has not handicapped the other human branches either to the same degree or in the same inevitable, 'genetically' transmitted way.

This infirmity is properly called *cultural neurosis*, since it exhibits es-sentially the same vicious circle of self-defeating behaviour that typifies the neuroses of individuals. There are countless ways in which societies and civilizations experience pain as a result of their own conduct and would therefore change it, yet are in a sense impotent to do so. This is not because they actually lack the ability to behave differently; it is because they lack the inner organization, the *integration* of the faculties and resources they do possess, effectively to do what they think they would, but which unfortunately will not, do. They have, thus, all the power that their conscious nature confers on them, but not enough consciousness of their conscious nature to manage their power effec-tively. An especially noteworthy symbol of contemporary cultural neu-rosis, because it involves a literally mortal danger to all of mankind, is the Cold War. No one wants nuclear destruction or enjoys living in the fear of it; therefore we are all determined to abolish this and indeed every other form of armed conflict, and the economic and social evils that provoke it. But somehow, for all our good intentions and all our strenuous efforts over several generations, we 'cannot.' To say that the inhuman economics and the paranoid, dreadful symmetry of international politics in the twentieth century amount to a form of collective mental illness is neither exaggeration nor metaphor.

Now, in any culture, be it ontic or phenomenal, it may well come about that the ability of human beings to exert power over external reality, and over themselves and each other, exceeds their ability to manage such power in accordance with their own and other people's best individual and collective interests. The theory accounts, however, not only for the origin of 'the streak of insanity which runs through the history of our species,'[1] but to some extent also for its uneven distribution in space and time. For it explains why ontic speakers are especially susceptible to this ailment, why as a matter of historical fact the ontic cultures have distinguished themselves in this unenviable respect, and why cultural neuroses have appeared in Western culture and in our own age in acute form and on an unprecedentedly large, global scale. I hasten to forestall, however, if I can, several mistaken impressions that these remarks may produce.

Too facile a translation could be made from what I shall suggest here about the ontic and the phenomenal cultures in their original form to what their descendant cultures have come to be today. After all, the evolution of consciousness did not come to a halt with the appearance of thematic speech in variant forms. The fundamental ideas that now shape, for instance, modern Western civilization could not very well reflect exactly the same assumptions that ruled over our prehistoric proto-IE ancestors' attempt at self-definition; the assumptions themselves have evolved. Indeed, an evolutionary interpretation of the history of human culture would be, in effect, an account of the evolution of such assumptions. But though the ways of thinking of a contemporary culture such as ours are not totally reducible to those of its ancestors, they are intelligible only by reference to the characteristics of the form of consciousness from which they stem. The latter is the aspect of the subject I shall emphasize here at the expense of the former – an emphasis that is justified because, as will be remembered, the study of human evolution during historical times is outside the scope of this investigation.

We should likewise beware of supposing that the theory would not

1 Arthur Koestler, *The Ghost in the Machine* (London, 1967), p. xi.

be valid unless perfect correlation could be found nowadays between the form of speech and the form of consciousness. Apodictic speech – which is now coextensive with that of the IE linguistic family, since Sumerian disappeared several thousand years ago – continues to be a most reliable, indeed unerring, index of an ontic, or at least predominantly ontic, heritage. But history attests that at certain times some peoples whose linguistic filiation was originally depositional, and whose languages remained grammatically depositional in form, came under the cultural influence of either the Sumerians, or the IEs, or both, from whom they adopted ontic, or mainly ontic, convictions about self and world. The most important instances of this are the Hebrews[2] and the pre-Islamic Arabs. Their acculturation – which led directly to the systems of self-definition of Mosaic monotheism and Judaism, on the one hand, and to Islam, on the other – is sufficiently well known for us to determine that it accounts for what otherwise would be an anomalous disparity between the form of their thematic speech and that of their self-definition. The same is true, by extension, of those non-IE cultures converted to Islam, such as the Turks and the Hamitic peoples of North Africa, and of the very few non-IE cultures that accepted the Christian version of Judaism, such as the Basques and the Magyars. (I need hardly remind us that Christianity, a typically ontic religion, has flourished almost exclusively among IE speakers.) All these depositional-language groups are now to be included, therefore, among the contemporary predominantly ontic cultures – though their ontic character was acquired, rather than congenital, through processes we shall consider below.

The phenomenal cultures – originally all but the Sumerian and the proto-IEs – are today represented mostly by primitive or at least relatively undeveloped peoples. Though a number of phenomenal cultures reached highly civilized status in the past (e.g., the Egyptian, the pre-Hellenic

2 The Bible itself is one of the principal sources of the conclusion that the Sumerian tradition held sway over the Hebrews during a period which can be counted in centuries and which goes back to earliest known times; nothing contradicts the Old Testament memory of patriarchal ancestors 'who lived for generations in Ur or other Sumerian cities ... [and] there is no reason to doubt that these proto-Hebrews had absorbed and assimilated much of the Sumerian way of life': Samuel N. Kramer, *The Sumerians: Their History, Culture, and Character* (Chicago, 1963), p. 299. Contact between the Israelites and the Assyro-Babylonians continued, of course, throughout historical times. If it is true, however, that 'in the course of the third millennium B.C. the Sumerians developed religious ideas and spiritual concepts which have left an indelible impress on the modern world, especially by way of Judaism, Christianity and Mohammedanism' (Kramer, *Sumerians*, p. 112), part of the reason is that the IE recipients of those ideas were ideally well disposed to receive them by virtue of their native presuppositions.

Minoan, the Etruscan, the Incan, the Meso-American),[3] almost all the phenomenal civilizations disappeared long ago, having invariably perished at the hand of ontic conquerors. (It is, of course, common historical coin that the IES have been extraordinarily violent peoples, and the most successful, blood-thirsty, world-empire builders recorded in history, rivalled only by Islam.) China and Japan are the noteworthy exceptions, culturally beleaguered though even they now are. Geographical isolation from the Eurasian, IE-dominated world contributed for a time to the cultural survival of the phenomenal peoples of Africa, Oceania, and the New World. In more recent centuries, however, they, too, have been threatened with either cultural assimilation into, or extermination by, the ontic peoples – though in the last few decades not always through the crudely oppressive means that formerly were the rule. Nevertheless, it would be difficult to find many phenomenal cultures today, however geographically inaccessible – not even in the upper Amazon, one of the last redoubts – that have not been subjected to IE or other ontic influence of one or another kind.

At present ontic influence means mostly Westernization, since after a long internecine struggle among the IE peoples for world domination, or at least ecumenical supremacy – the Persians, the Indians, the Greeks, and the Romans each had their day – the coveted, bloody sceptre passed to us. Not unrelated to the general course of world history, which is definable by the steady expansion and ever-growing ascendancy of the IES over all other peoples, is the fact that most of the 'gigantic presences' – the imposing, majestic, highly sophisticated, theoretically intricate, and usually proselytizing systems of self-definition that have been most influential in human cultural evolution in historical times – have been creatures of the ontic mind. Hinduism, Buddhism, Zoroastrianism, Greek philosophy, Judaism, Christianity, Islam, and modern Western scientific secularism and humanism are the principal among these. (Contemporary subvarieties of the last-named include dialectical materialism, national socialism, and democratic capitalism.) But it is clear, I trust, that the ontic systems of religious (or for that matter, secular) self-definition are no more the *cause* of cultural neuroses than delusions are the cause of paranoia; rather, their dysfunctionality is itself the result of a prior affliction of consciousness that interferes with the health of the religious and secular life of man. But because religions manifest such affliction in its purest and most concentrated form, the study of religions – if I may

---

3 Since the language of the pre-Hellenic Minoans has not been deciphered at all, and that of the Etruscans too imperfectly for us to understand its structure, it is only a conjecture that they were depositional, and that the cultures were phenomenal.

paraphrase Freud – is the royal road to understanding the unconscious processes that have caused consciousness to evolve since late prehistoric times. Nor does anything prevent – in principle – the self-reformation of the ontic religions even in respect of their most fundamental assumptions, so that they might fulfil their aspiration to facilitate the enlightenment, welfare, and ennobling of mankind. But I say 'in principle'; nothing within the horizon indicates that this is at all a likelihood.

It would require, of course, a systematic review of the cultural history of mankind, with particular reference to the religions, sciences, and philosophies that manifest the properties of the self-defining consciousness, to verify what I propose as a corollary to the theory: (a) that the historically recorded world- and self-interpretations of all human cultures have been either wholly or at least predominantly of either the ontic or else the phenomenal type, (b) that apart from a few exceptions the type into which they fall invariably correlates with the apodictic or else depositional form of their speech, (c) that all of the few exceptions can be accounted for as a result of the acculturation of certain phenomenal traditions to the ways of thinking of the ontic mind, and (d) that, therefore, the course of human history and the contemporary cultural configuration of the species as a whole can be explained by the same theory that has helped us reconstruct the prehistoric evolutionary process. But my point is, indeed, that what shall be established here about the ontic and the phenomenal forms of consciousness does not of itself bring the study of human evolution up to date, nor is it intended to do so. This will be attempted, or so I hope, only elsewhere.

The question will nevertheless continue to nag us how deficiencies in self-presence may be reconciled with the uniquely influential role that the Sumerians and the IES have played in the history of the human species. The exploits of the IES in general and of contemporary Western civilization in particular do not end with the Herculean labour it took to have disrupted almost every other human culture on earth, or with the magnificent *tour de force* of our having exported social, political, economic, and ecological chaos on a world scale. Our positive achievements are undoubtedly real and justly to be proud of, and must be recognized as potentially permanent contributions to the species. But even the bare fact that the IES have long and increasingly held sway over depositional mankind, and that in recent centuries an IE civilization has come to dominate the entire planet in almost every conceivable respect – a fact whose evolutionary significance may not be self-evident, but whose evolutionary importance should be recognizable *a priori* – would seem incongruous with the suggestion that the ontic form of consciousness operates under deluded assumptions about the nature of reality and under confusions about the nature of man that phenomenal thinkers are more likely to escape.

Part of the answer is that the self-mystification that spells absent-mindedness, and the attitudes towards self and world that it generates, are apt so highly to motivate human beings to reflect upon themselves, to inquire into the nature of the world, and to engage in a compulsive quest for mastery and progress, as to enable them to reach spectacular levels of achievement – the same derangement that also accounts for the unbalanced, self-maladjusted forms that their grandeur frequently takes. The fuller explanation, however, is that the human equivalent of survival value – namely, the contribution that human characteristics can make to the self-adjustment of consciousness – is like biological survival value in this respect: that it is not absolute, but relative to given environmental conditions (which in the case of the properties of consciousness means, of course, inner environmental ones). It would, therefore, be inaccurate to say, with Arthur Koestler, that 'something has gone wrong' in human evolution; absent-mindedness is doubtless a disvalue, but everyday experience should suffice to alert us to the ambivalence of all values and disvalues. I have already given an illustration of the fact that under the right conditions and in the short run even absent-mindedness can be an asset[4] (though in the scale of human evolution centuries

4 Other examples closer to home and from more recent times could be adduced, such as the invention of the computer, and in particular of computers having what is misleadingly called 'artificial intelligence.' This event may be deemed a close parallel of the invention of phonetic writing not least of all because it may prove to be the cause of cultural changes comparable in magnitude only to the Sumerian innovation. It is already possible – though with limitations that are certain to be overcome before long – to build computers that (to put it loosely) understand spoken instructions and reply in kind, that can translate from one human language to another, that exercise judgment on the basis of previous experience (for instance, they offer medical diagnoses and prescribe medical procedures), and that seem to think and reason in ways that are distinguishable from the human processes only in being more reliable and exceedingly faster. Of course, a computer that takes verbal instructions and responds with intelligible vocal sounds – either in the same or in another language – discoursing on, say, medical subjects, no more *understands* speech or medicine than a typewriter *thinks* and then *communicates* its medical wisdom by typing out a medical textbook. It is the human beings who use it, and who interact by means of it, that alone *perform* these activities; the computer could be attributed 'artificial intelligence' only in the same metaphorical sense in which levers might be ascribed 'artificial muscle power.' Thus, using a computer that has been appropriately programmed to lend him the skills of human medical experts, a person can produce results that surpass what he could do on his own – the very thing that a medical textbook can help him do, though on a much smaller scale.

But many people are unclear about the difference between the activity and the contents of thought; they therefore assume that 'artificial intelligence' is possible, and

and, indeed, millennia need not amount to a very long run). In brief, we should beware of premature and unqualified assessments of what is good and bad for mankind, and of precipitate judgments about what superiority and inferiority mean when measured in evolutionary terms. In the concluding chapter we shall consider this question again at greater length.

1. The ontic and the phenomenal
concepts of reality

We have ascertained the empirical basis of the concept of reality: being present to itself, every conscious experience reveals to itself the opposition between its content and the act. Since this mutual relativity is constituent part of all consciousness, not even the absent-minded can fail altogether to appreciate the experiential character of conscious experience – nor, therefore, the otherness of the object in relation to experience and of the experiencing in relation to the object. The experience of *otherness-to-another* of both object and self – otherwise called *reality* – is thus the necessary concomitant of conscious life. The categorical concept of reality asserts what consciousness exhibits to itself about its relativity to others, and about the relativity of others to it and to each other.

The process whereby absent-mindedness interferes with the conceptualization of reality is rooted in the impaired ability of certain speakers to differentiate between the act and the object of consciousness.[5] They

---

are inspired to create it. My point is that their not knowing better facilitates their success. For instance, they analyse human speech and thought in order to recreate these processes electronically in computers. Now, if they took into account the assertiveness of speech and thought, they would realize that the threshold requirement for producing these is some sort of self-oriented causal process – in other words, the purposiveness that is found only in living entities – and would therefore deem impossible the creation of a machine with artificial intelligence. Their unawareness of this impossibility, however, holds a paradoxical advantage: speech and thought as they mistakenly conceive them are the kind that *can* be electronically reproduced. In the end they do not, to be sure, create a true counterpart of the human processes; but what they actually achieve is a marvel none the less, and multiplies immeasurably the power of human beings to bring about change. Now, *why* should 'artificial intelligence' be created? And for what *ends* should it be used once it is created? These questions are not likely to be adequately answered either by scientists who are so confused about themselves that they conceive the idea of creating it, nor by the equally perplexed, eager consumers of scientific technology who defer to them.

5 To put it more exactly, they have difficulty in differentiating *accurately* between the two: they can without undue effort perceive that an act is somehow involved,

are able to focus either on *experiencing* or on the *object* of experience, but not both at the same time; likewise with *speaking* and *what is said*. The result is that the speaker learns to speak thematically in the light of a faulty self-experience, embodied in faulty categorical concepts. In respect of the category that now interests us, difficulty in simultaneously keeping in focus both object and act means that the apodictic speaker will be by definition one who, though able to experience the object as other and himself as a self, will not find it easy to experience himself specifically as that in relation to which the object is other. He will, therefore, not readily perceive that otherness is a *relationship*, nor that the reality of the real is the *relationship* of 'otherness-to' that simultaneously binds the real to, yet delimits it from, both the experiencer and every other real thing. In other words, 'otherness-to' will be cut down to mere 'otherness.' Reality is thus converted into an absolute, objectified into something that things have or do 'in themselves.' The fact that the reality of the real does not reside *within*, but as it were *between*, things has been lost sight of.

The first consequence of this is that substantiality becomes the paradigm of reality. Substantiality may or may not be identified with materiality; for immaterial, but nevertheless substantial, realities may be admitted, such as the human 'mind' and other mind-like 'spiritual' substances. But in any case transient events merely 'accrue' or 'happen' to the figuratively or literally more solid and enduring reality of those things that, whether material or spiritual, exist 'in themselves.' It also follows that the reality of real things is that which separates them from each other; whatever is real is, as such, isolated, atomic, monadic, and independent. By the same token, things are deemed to be lacking in reality to the very degree that they lack self-sufficiency; if anything is finite, contingent, or changeable, it must be lacking in reality. What we actually witness in the world is, of course, precisely the opposite: all real things are, as such, interdependent, related, blending into each other – fuzzy at the edges, as it were – and participants in each other's properties to a greater or lesser extent. For the same reason, the higher and more elaborate the reality, the greater its vulnerability. But the absent-minded are not moved; they either pay little attention to these observable facts or else explain them away; for they are prepossessed of an idea of reality

---

but the *assertiveness* of the act eludes their grasp. Experience is reduced to its contents when the assertiveness of experiencing is discounted and objects are deemed to have intelligibility in themselves; speech is reduced to language when the assertiveness of saying is discounted and what is said remains behind as having meaning in itself.

that necessarily converts whatever is finite or contingent – let alone what is mortal – into something less than really real and really itself.

The second consequence is that the ontic mind will interpret itself as having only a second-rate, qualified reality. Even our everyday terminology gives us away: we do not ordinarily contrast 'the reality of experience' with 'the reality of the object of experience'; we oppose 'reality' to 'experience' as if objects alone were truly real. It could hardly be otherwise, if when we think of 'experience' we automatically discount the act itself and reduce 'experience' to its contents. Since we cannot, however, altogether ignore the opposition between our experience and its object, we think of the contents of experience as a diaphanous, flimsy representation of reality. If we are philosophically sophisticated we may realize that the re-presentative value of experience cannot depend on any *similarity* between an original reality and a corresponding copy in experience. We then explain in some other way, or if need be leave unexplained, what we presuppose in any case: that the experiencing mind *repeats* the objective reality. Conversely, since no one can deny altogether the reality of his experience, experience is ascribed the secondary, dependent reality of an 'accident' that happens to a subject; the latter may be variously construed as the organism, the soul, the mind, or at very least the substantive *ego* – but in any event as a subsistent subject whose prior existence 'in itself' supports its experiential acts. In short, the self-alienation of the ontic consciousness, its deficient sense of its own reality, means that by *reality* it must necessarily mean: that which is more real than it itself is. This paradoxical self-derealization of consciousness – the bizarre delusion that the self that one experiences oneself to be is not one's true self, but that one's 'really real' self is an objective, self-subsistent reality beyond one's own experiential reach – is the logical outcome of converting reality into an absolute under the promptings of absent-mindedness.

But ironically implied by these misinterpretations is a third: that the reality of anything given in experience – the entire empirical world – cannot be fully real either. For if someone does not accord full recognition to the reality of his conscious experience, he cannot very well accord full recognition to the reality of anything he experiences; he is by logic bound to discount *his experience* of their reality. Thus, although to the ontic thinker stable objects may well seem more real than his transient consciousness of them, *nothing* around him can be unqualifiedly real; the world as a whole will be felt to be lacking in the firmness and solidity it ought to have. And since he will find such impermanence and contingency essentially unsatisfactory – because by definition they betoken a radical imperfection, a deficiency in the very reality of the empirical world – he will easily beget within himself what he at times calls a 'yearning for the absolute.' The ontic mind is, therefore, sorely tempted to reason that, since no reality could be really real unless it lay altogether beyond experience, an *ultimate reality* must be posited. Besides this world there is another, an order of reality beyond the immediately evident, but conditionally real, 'appearances' that pullulate 'here below.' Conversely, being absolutely real, the reality beyond all possible experience is absolutely other. One well-known version of this idea puts it in those very terms: the ultimate reality is *totaliter aliter*. A more familiar vocabulary speaks of it as the 'transcendent' Being whose reality is utterly beyond all we could possibly think of as real in the world and in ourselves. This is, of course, a self-contradiction. Otherness is a relationship; nothing can be *other* unless it be *other-than*.

The logic of the mental process is not less inexorable merely because it need not be consciously pursued; the implications of the tacit premises make themselves felt even in the absence of reflexion. Thus, the absent-minded experiencer projects his faulty self-perception onto the objects of his experience; but since he projects onto objects a reality that he deems less than fully real – namely, that of his experience – he must needs tar the world with the brush of his defective experience of himself. The plight of the ontic consciousness is thus not unlike that of the comic stage character who resolved to join no club that would have him: he would not respect, he explained, those who had no self-respect. Absent-mindedness functions, then, somewhat like an inferiority complex. Let us remember, however, that the latter disorder does not lead, as some imagine, to diffidence and self-effacement, but to aggressiveness and hostility. These are a defence against the anxiety that one's deficient self-perception has managed to procure for oneself. Absent-mindedness poses a threat – disconfirmation of one's own unqualifiedly true reality – that is none the less real because it is self-posed.[6]

6 Considering that the mechanism of projection does play a large role in my interpretation of the origin of the fundamental ontic cultural institutions, an inattentive reader might well reduce the view developed here to the proposition for which Ludwig Feuerbach is well known: that man's projection of his ideal nature, in abstraction from its imperfection and finitude, is the origin of the concept of God. A better understanding of my argument may be facilitated by my contrasting my views with Feuerbach's in a few respects. What I have suggested, for better or for worse, is very different: that man's projection of his assertiveness leads to the ontic, or objective, conception of the reality of *the world*. This does not necessarily lead to the concept of an ultimate, transcendent reality (though admittedly, it is practically certain to do so), let alone to the idea of the concrete and personal transcendent reality usually called God, which is far from universal among the ontic cultures. If it does, however, it is not through a projection of human nature, but through

We have already noted a few instances of the mythological and religious interpretations of man and world that the Sumerian and the primitive IES eventually devised in the light of their *Vorverständnisse*. The more sophisticated ontic systems, such as Greek philosophy and Hinduism – and the latter's descendant, Buddhism – managed further to identify the nature of the ultimate reality: it is Speech or Utterance (*Logos, Brahman*). We can reconstruct their implicit reasoning. Although empirically given objects assert to us the meaning that our experience and speech merely repeat, they do not, of course, make actual vocal sounds. It is not so much, then, that they voice a message, but that they *are* a message; they are like signals or 'words' that mutely broadcast their meaning only because they themselves have been 'spoken' prior to all human experience and speech. The ultimate reality is, therefore, the Speech that 'speaks' them, or issues them forth into reality. That the Greeks and the Indians reached – independently, so far as is known – this conclusion is a good index of their perspicacity. For in a sense they were, of course, quite correct. Having originally projected their assertiveness onto reality, reflexion upon their experience of reality enabled them to discover that reality was constituted by assertiveness. The ultimate reality is, therefore, definable as the primordial Speech.

Identifying Speech as the substance of the ultimate reality, however, does not necessarily imply belief in a concrete Speaker of the Speech, an actual and active agent who can be ascribed its performance. Personal and anthropomorphic ultimate realities are indeed rare; to find them we must go principally to the biblical tradition. We shall consider in a moment the origin of the *monotheism* that Moses gave to his people, the

---

ordinary reasoning and hypothesizing on the basis of a conception of worldly, empirically given reality into which the assertiveness of consciousness has been previously projected. Unlike Feuerbach, moreover, I do not ascribe this projection to the nature of consciousness as such, but to its deficient self-presence; and I provide an explanation of the origin of the capacity of consciousness for projection as part of the process of human evolution. I argue, therefore, that upon the premiss provided by the ontic idea of reality can be erected many different systems of self-definition (though to be sure, all such systems will exhibit fundamental characteristics in common). The absent-minded projection of assertiveness explains not only the emergence of biblical religion, but also that of the other 'great religions' of the IE civilizations. The same explanation, moreover, renders intelligible also the eventual appearance of such 'post-Christian' Western world-views as scientific secular humanism and antitheistic systems such as dialectical materialism and atheistic existentialism. (As an atheist, Feuerbach would have especially disagreed with this view.) All these are different – and evolving – manifestations of the same form of consciousness, and instances of the principle that the properties of consciousness depend upon the properties of the speech that generates it.

idea that there was a divinity who was the one and only God because his 'name' was Yahweh – that is, because his nature was that of the absolute Reality. The reason why the Hebrew word *yahweh* conveyed this idea with exquisite elegance will also be explained presently, but we can appreciate even now that it was a feat of extraordinary ingenuity on the part of Moses to manage to convey the idea of absolute reality in this language. The problem was not simply that Hebrew lacked the vocabulary – this is easily remedied, since the ability to speak necessarily entails the ability to invent words – but that as a depositional language Hebrew created in the speaker the predisposition to think of reality as a relationship, and hence to find the idea of an absolute reality self-contradictory.

The Old Testament conception of reality – the world given in experience has been sired by an ultimate personal and father-like being beyond all possible experience, an uncreated Creator God whom 'no man shall see and live'[7] – became of course an integral part of Christianity. So did the Greek identification of such ultimate reality as Speech (*Logos, Verbum*). But eventually, as Christianity stocked a distinctive conceptual shelf of its own, on which the Bible rubbed shoulders with the *Metaphysics*, the Christian God became *ipsum Esse subsistens* and creation consisted in his making created 'beings' (*entia*) to 'be' or 'exist.' Christianity, however, unlike the Old Testament, expressed these ideas in languages that were – but how could they not have been? – so naturally suited to the task that divine favour has been suspected by some. Now, since the ontic religious traditions do not cause, but manifest – though to be sure, they also reinforce – the ontic way of thinking about reality, it should not astonish us to learn that the medieval Christian concept of reality, albeit scotched, has survived the secularization of the Western mind. Even some *phenomenological* philosophers continue to inquire into the meaning of 'Being,' wishing to know why there is something rather than nothing and marvelling that languages such as German and Greek are, in what concerns intellectual suitability, 'the most powerful and most spiritual'[8] of all. Indeed, having learned that 'being' is nothing but 'the collection of appearances that manifest it,' they conclude that, nevertheless, the 'legitimate problem of the *being of such appearing*'[9] remains to be solved.

Since the phenomenal consciousness does not project its assertiveness onto reality, it does not condemn itself to having to conceive reality as

7 Exodus 33:20.
8 Martin Heidegger, *An Introduction to Metaphysics* (Garden City, NY, 1951), p. 47.
9 Jean-Paul Sartre, *L'être et le néant* (Paris, 1943), pp. 13, 14.

'being,' or as 'what is' or 'what exists'; it automatically escapes the snares of metaphysical thought by failing to set them for itself. And since it does not assume that objects have any priority over conscious experience in what concerns their otherness-to, it will not suppose that there are degrees of reality. It is, therefore, typical of the phenomenal religions to take for granted that there cannot be 'another world'; the empirically given world is the only real one. Within the world there are, to be sure, realities of different kinds; for instance, some are living and others are non-living; some are higher and some are lower than man. But the various ranks of reality are uniformly real, and reality is ascribed univocally to all real things. Among the inhabitants of this world are to be included, therefore, the finite entities whom *we* IES, when we study cultures of this type, usually call 'gods,' and whom *we* often describe as 'supernatural' entities. But we mislead ourselves by so doing, because the 'gods' of the phenomenal cultures are not imperfect versions of the Supreme Being whom we are accustomed to think of as God. Indeed, not even the 'gods' of the polytheistic *ontic* cultures should be so understood; their equivalent of God is rather the absolute reality, in whichever form it may be conceived. Both the phenomenal and the ontic 'gods,' notwithstanding their exalted status and wonderful characteristics (e.g., extraordinary powers, elusiveness, and, not infrequently, immortality), are man's fellow inhabitants of this world and neither more nor less real than all other worldly entities; *invisibilia* rather than 'gods' would be a much better name for them.

Nowadays not everyone in our culture is committed to the belief that a Supreme Being actually exists; our typical position is rather some form of agnosticism – which assumes the possibility that God might exist. Now, why should this be so? It is partly because, as our everyday terminology reveals, we retain the idea that a thing's reality is something it holds in itself. To us it is self-evident that a real thing 'has' something called 'reality,' or that it 'does' something called 'to exist'; if it did not perform the activity of existing, we reason, it would not be real. At the same time, however, we perceive that things do not exist necessarily; they come into being and they cease to exist; and to us this means that they *acquire* existence and *lose* it. Inevitably the questions arise: how did things first *acquire* existence? And why should even human beings, who appreciate that they exist and do not want to die, nevertheless *lose* their existence? Our culture is sufficiently empirically minded to find it difficult to affirm with certainty that an ultimate, transempirical reality exists – but its idea of the nature of empirically given reality inclines it to concede that perhaps it does. To the phenomenal mind, however, it would not make sense to say that things 'existed,' or that they contained 'reality' within themselves – as if things were not identical with their reality or as if it were possible for anything to be real yet unrelated to everything else. The reality of a thing is rather its relativity to other things; this includes, but is not restricted to, its relativity to human experience.[10] (We are especially concerned with the latter, however, since only our experience reveals reality to us as real.) In these cultures, therefore, the concept of an ultimate reality is not thinkable; it is a contradiction in terms. The differences between the two forms of consciousness concerning a supposed other world are but manifestations of more basic differences in respect of their views of *this* world.

The phenomenal perception of the reality of the real as a relationship is reflected in the etymology of the terms used in the depositional languages to refer to it; they usually convey such meanings as 'presence to,' or 'availability,' or 'that which one may come across.' Not infrequently reality is also spoken of as 'that which comes to pass' or 'that which happens, or eventuates.' But when used by phenomenal thinkers, expressions such as 'happening,' 'event,' or the like, are not understood, as we are likely to imagine, merely in the sense that 'what happens' or 'what eventuates' is the outcome of a process; they are taken in the sense that reality is 'what happens to' those who witness it or are otherwise affected by it. Reality is that which 'befalls' us. (It also 'befalls,' of course, every one and everything else in the world and not only human beings.) In Arabic, for instance, the quality that describes the real as such is *wujud*, from the 'verb' *wajada*, which means 'to find' and, conversely, 'to lie in one's path' (i.e., 'to be apt to be found').[11] *Wujud* means, in effect, 'findability' or 'availability.' Nothing can be found, however, except by a finder, and nothing can be called available except in relation to someone or something that could avail itself of it. Though *wajada* can be translated into the IE languages by 'to be,' it could not be said to mean the same as 'to be,' as it lacks the objectivity of 'to be.'

Almost exactly the same idea is found in the Hebrew 'verb' *hayah*, which is most often translated as 'to happen,' 'to eventuate,' or 'to come

10 I have already explained, in chapters II and III, why the relativity of reality does not imply the Berkeleyan view that *esse est percipi*; though reality is essentially relative, it is not relative to perceivers exclusively. However, the relativity of reality does imply that whatever is real is subject to being experienced, whether directly or indirectly, by those who are capable of experiencing it. If Berkeley had said *esse est referri*, he would have been much closer to the target.

11 In Arabic, as in Hebrew, some 'verbal' roots can envisage the same kind of activity alternatively from the viewpoint of the speaker or from that of the object of speech, somewhat as do in English the related pairs of verbs signifying 'to lie' and 'to lay,' 'to drip' and 'to drop,' 'to fall' and 'to fell,' and so on.

to pass,' so that reality – the world – would be 'that which comes to pass.' I stress, however, that *hayah* is among the 'verbs' that grammarians of Hebrew call 'stative,' which do not signify actions but qualities, conditions, and states. Much less than ordinary 'verbs,' therefore, are these true verbs. At any rate, it is undisputed that the 'happening' or 'coming to pass' of reality envisaged by *hayah* describes nothing that reality does, but the quality or condition of being real. But in what does this condition consist? The usual translations tend to hide the relativity of 'that which happens' to those *to whom* (or *to which*) it happens – though such relativity, quite as in Arabic, is part of the connotation of the original. According to Hebraists *hayah* derives from a root meaning 'to fall' and, conversely, 'to be a stumbling block' or 'to cause to fall'; it can be translated as 'to happen' only because it actually means 'to befall.'[12] And albeit tacitly, the latter alludes to something or someone to whom the events befall when they eventuate or come to pass. Notwithstanding this as well as the fact that it cannot be used existentially,[13] *hayah* is very frequently said to be the Hebrew equivalent of 'to be.'

In keeping with this perception or reality, the ancient Hebrews did not conceive what we call 'the world' – the whole of reality – as most of us naturally do, namely, as a spatial totality constituted by whatever independently existing substantive entities there may actually be at any given time. They thought of it rather as the indefinite succession of 'happenings,' the endless eventuation of events. The logic is clear: since the condition of 'being real' is the same as the state of 'befalling,' the universe as a whole is the unceasing flow of all the events that 'befall' us and each other. Had the Hebrews and the Israelites wanted to refer to what we call 'the world,' therefore, they would have said in effect something like: 'the continuous happening' or 'the continuous coming to pass [of events].' I stress that since it was no part of this interpretation to suppose that 'happening' or 'coming to pass' is an act, the 'continuous coming to pass' does *not* refer to a subject that performs such 'coming to pass.' The Hebrews' original idea of the world was, thus, not unlike that which is typical of phenomenal cultures such as the Chinese, who speak of it as *t'ien-hsia*, '[the things] under the sky,' and who affirm that a thing is real by saying that *t'ien-hsia* 'has' it (i.e., it is in the world, standing in relation to others and available for interaction with them).[14]

12 'The original sense of the verb [*hayah*] was probably "to fall," from which comes the meaning "to befall," "to become," and hence "to be" ': Raymond Abba, 'The Divine Name Yahweh,' *Journal of Biblical Literature*, 80 (1961), 320–8, p. 324.

13 *Hayah* 'never means "pure existence:" rather it has the sense of "happening," "becoming," "being in a certain state or place," "being present" ': ibid., p. 325.

14 A.C. Graham, '"Being" in Classical Chinese,' in John W.M. Verhaar, *The Verb 'Be' and Its Synonyms*, Part 1 (Dordrecht, The Netherlands, 1967), p. 7.

Unless speakers of Hebrew should have learned from apodictic speakers how to do it, they would not be able to think of reality as 'that which is.' We shall have need to remember all this in a moment.

The Indonesian vocabulary of reality is also instructive. Apart from *wudjud*, an Arabic borrowing used in much the same sense as the original, Indonesian uses principally two terms to speak of it, *keadaan* and *kenjataan*. The first is the abstract form of the base word *ada* – which is, I underline, an adjective – meaning 'present' or 'available'; it refers to the quality of that which is, or could be, before one. Understandably, it is often translated by the verb 'to be': *Ada bir dingin? Ia, ada*, 'Is there [any] cold beer? Yes, there is.' But the literal meaning of the answer is: 'It, available.' Thus, if anyone should ask for me at the gate, and the porter informs him that *tidak ada*, he does not mean that I do not exist, but that I am not available: the reason could as well be that I have died as that I have gone out for a cold beer. *Kenjataan* comes from the adjective *njata*, often translated as 'real.' But the connotations of *njata*, which are twofold, explain what it truly means. *Njata* refers to clarity or evidence, which obviously supposes relativity to an experiencer; for instance, *menjatakan* means 'to clarify' or 'to explain.' But it also refers to factuality, as shown by the reduplicative form *njata-njata*, which means 'indeed,' 'assuredly,' or 'as a matter of fact.' Most significant, perhaps, is the fact that *njata* derives in turn from *ia*, the genderless third-person pronoun, 'he, she, or it.' Thus, *njata* means literally 'it-ish,' and *kenjataan* is therefore 'it-ness,' the quality proper to 'it.' The aspect of 'clarity' accrues to it because to explain something is to point to the facts, or to exhibit the 'it-ness' of it.

In the above remarks I have had in mind only the original idea of reality of Arabic and Hebrew speakers as it can be deduced from the etymologies of *wajada* and *hayah*, an idea that is very different from that which has predominated in these cultures since later – though still relatively early – historical times. The explanation of the difference, as I have indicated, is that the acculturation of both these peoples led to modes of self-definition, and in particular to religious convictions, that mixed characteristics of both forms of consciousness – though the ontic have tended to dominate and the phenomenal to remain latent. This accounts in particular for Mosaic monotheism, which originated when anthropomorphic characteristics such as ordinary gods were deemed to have (e.g., intelligence, purposiveness, moral sentiments, feelings towards human beings) were ascribed to the transcendent ultimate reality that embodied the omnipotent, but blind and uncaring, higher Law of Mesopotamian religion. In other words, monotheism was born of a conflation of the impersonal and abstract Sumerian *me* with the idea of a god, a superior though concrete and finite personal divine entity. The *tertium quid* was 'God,' a supreme personal divinity whose reality was ultimate and whose will was identical with 'the Law,' in the same transcendent sense in which the Sumerians (and their Akkadian, Assyrian, and Babylonian cultural descendants) had understood 'the Law.' Though there can be many gods, there can be, of course, only one such God, because there can be only one ultimate reality.

Note, however, the almost paradoxical fact that the oneness of God was actually tangential to Moses's monotheism; for the defining characteristic of God is the ultimacy or transcendence of his reality, not the uniqueness that necessarily follows from such transcendence. The very choice of 'monotheism,' the singleness of God, as the fundamental symbol of the Mosaic faith was thus symptomatic of the cultural miscegenation that produced it; the idea that a correct enumeration of all the true gods would have to stop after the first one had been counted was the aspect of the matter that the Israelites could readily comprehend, debate, and accept, doubt, or reject. Mostly they rejected it. Before Judaism, the spontaneous convictions of most Israelites continued to echo the uncomplicated ancestral ways of thinking; the transcendent nature of God was at this time, and for several centuries after Moses remained, a strange, foreign conception, far removed from their everyday religious life.[15]

It is not essential to my argument, but nevertheless it may be useful, if I append further comments on the birth of what is, after all, the single most important idea to have conditioned the origin and evolution of the Western world. I mention, then, that the first-person singular imperfect of *hayah* is *ehyeh*, which is used at Exodus 3:14 in the phrase *ehyeh asher ehyeh*. Scripture puts this formula in the mouth of God, speaking in the first person, for the purpose of his 'naming' himself – that is, revealing his nature. The archaic third person of the same 'verb,' as scholars believe, was *yahweh*; this is, of course, the word that would have been used by the Israelites when, speaking in their own person, they wanted to express the name that God had given to himself speaking in the first person.[16] Many authors are of the opinion that the formula *ehyeh asher*

---

15 The Old Testament itself documents the fact that 'the mass of [Israel's] population were never conscious of the dependent status of creation, and that it was only a few historians and prophets who fought against the seductions of idolatry or the cults of foreign gods ... [H]ardly a generation fully understood the world's created status. In this matter Israel was in a constant state of flux, and one can distinguish a whole series of advances, thrusts forward to a specifically new understanding of the world': Gerhard von Rad, *Old Testament Theology*, 2 vols. (New York, 1965), vol. II, p. 341.

16 For the same reason, this form is also put in the mouth of God at Exodus 3:15 when he, speaking in the person of Moses, refers to himself in the third person.

ehyeh was intended to convey, somehow, the absolutely essential characteristic of God – that is, his transcendence. Nevertheless, biblical scholars have long disputed the exact meaning that the Israelites took from it, and the precise reason why it should have served to signify either God's transcendence or at least an especially important truth about him.[17] However, if we read it keeping in mind the fact – which both Christian and Jewish biblical scholars have largely ignored – that Hebrew was spoken depositionally, the following interpretation would not be an altogether implausible one.

In Hebrew grammar the so-called imperfect state is used to indicate the continuing condition of whatever the 'verb' signifies; *ehyeh*, as I have said, is in the imperfect state. Let us remember also that *hayah* is a 'stative verb,' the kind that signifies no action but only the state or the quality of that to which it refers. Of course, if one assumes that Hebrew 'verbs' are true verbs, *ehyeh* must be taken for a predicate even if it signifies no action; and if so, the theme to which *ehyeh* refers automatically becomes the subject of the verb. To the ontic mind it would seem, therefore, as if the literal translation of *ehyeh* should be 'I [i.e., God] continue in the state of eventuating' (or of happening, or of being real). And since *asher* is a relative, it would follow that the literal translation of the entire sentence should be: 'I continue in the state of happening [or being real], who continue in the state of happening [or being real].' By assuming that *ehyeh* has a verbally predicative relationship to the implicit subject 'I,' however, and that the antecedent of *asher* is the same subject, this translation ignores the difference between apodictic and depositional speech. The result is that the meaning of the original is distorted in three ways.

In the original, *ehyeh* is related to the implicit 'I' as a quality or state that *accrues* to 'me'; it is not an action literally or figuratively *performed* by 'me.' Therefore, first, *ehyeh* cannot mean 'I continue ... ' etc. or 'I am in the continuing state ... ' etc. It can only mean: '*my* continuing state ...' etc. And this is important, because it implies, second, that the theme of the assertion cannot be 'I'; it can only be the first *ehyeh*, '*my* continuing state of happening, or being real.' That is, the speaker does not assert the thesis in relation to 'me,' but in relation to '*my* continuing state of happening.' But if so, third, *asher* does not relate the second *ehyeh*, which is the thesis, to the 'I' implicit in the first *ehyeh*; rather, it relates the

---

17 The literature on the subject is voluminous. A brief summary of the principal positions taken, and introductory bibliographical information, are given in Brevard S. Child, *Exodus: A Commentary* (London, 1974), pp. 60–70. A short bibliography is also available in Georg Fohrer, *History of Israelite Religion* (London, 1973), pp. 75ff. An earlier but fuller one may be found in T.C. Vriezen, *Theologie des Alten Testaments in Gründzugen* (Wagenigen, Germany, 1956).

thesis (the second *ehyeh*) to the theme (the first *ehyeh*). In other words, if the depositional character of the assertion is taken into account, then it is clear that the function of *asher* is to make explicit that the second *ehyeh* is the thesis, and that the first *ehyeh* is the theme; its role is, in effect, to signify, as a depositional speaker would, that 'in relation to *ehyeh*, [I affirm] *ehyeh*.' Therefore, the proper translation of the formula is: 'In relation to my continuing state of happening, or being real, my continuing state of happening, or being real [is affirmed, or is to be affirmed].' This is not a paraphrase, but as close to a literal translation as the differences between the two languages and the two forms of speech permit. But what would this formula have conveyed to the Israelites?

When read by an apodictic speaker, even the literal translation I have suggested is bound to be misunderstood; his predispositions will inevitably lead him to accepting 'my continuing state ... ' etc. as if it had the same meaning in both the thesis and the theme. He would not necessarily deem it a meaningless tautology; he could interpret it as describing, for instance, the self-identity of God. But his point of departure would be the assumption that the formula asserted a tautology, and that the problem was what sense to make of it. But no tautology is involved. *Ehyeh* could have been understood by the Israelites in either of two equally legitimate senses – though both would probably have been neologisms at this date, before intensive speculation on religious questions had begun. *Ehyeh* could have properly been taken to mean, first 'my reality,' that is, God's 'continuing to happen.' To understand the second sense, however, let us recall that (a) what we call 'the world' was conceived by the Israelites as 'what happens,' the ensemble of successive events that 'befall' us, and that (b) in *ehyeh* the relationship between the 'continuing state of being real' and the implicit 'I,' as I have just explained, is not verbal, but adjectival. Thus, *ehyeh* could quite as legitimately been taken to mean, second, 'my continuing state of being real,' no longer in the sense of 'the reality by virtue of which I am real,' but in the sense of 'the reality by which *the world*, which is mine, is real.' In brief, the formula played on the equivocity of *ehyeh*. Its meaning would be faithfully conveyed by a slight paraphrase of the literal translation suggested above: 'To my continuing reality is to be attributed the continuing reality which is my world.' A somewhat freer, yet fully justified, alternative would be: 'My continuing reality is that by which all things in my world are, and continue to be, real.' The same explanation accounts for the abbreviation of the full formula into the tetragrammaton, and the use of the latter as the proper name of God. For granted that 'the reality of all worldly events is [to be affirmed in relation to] my reality,' it follows that the proper name by which God can be referred to in the third person is: *Yahweh*, 'He by reference to whom all worldly events eventuate.'

The idea conveyed by Exodus 3:14 is thus not exactly that God is the efficient cause of the world – though this is not excluded and is a possible deduction from it. The meaning is in part – but only in part – that God is the ultimate and absolute reality; moreover, it is conveyed only by implication. The essential and explicit element of the formula – the very element that became obscured by the Greek of the Septuagint, *egō eimi ho ōn*,[18] and rendered utterly impenetrable by the Latin of the Vulgate, *ego sum qui sum* – makes a statement about *the world*: that nothing can be said to 'come to pass' except by reference to his reality. The reason is that things have only a deficient reality. To be sure, they *are* real; but their reality is actually *'his'* – not in the sense that they share a common reality with him, but in the sense that their reality is his property. In short, God's creatures do not own themselves; their reality belongs to him.

Although this meaning would have been reasonably clear to the contemporary listeners of Moses and his preachers, it would also have seemed absurd. For it proposed what to native depositional speakers would have appeared as a radical contradiction in terms: that the immediately given reality of the world was less than fully real. This explains the deep and protracted resistance of the Israelites to Mosaic religion, and their eventually forgetting the meaning originally conveyed by the tetragrammaton. Nor was it the singleness of Yahweh as such that they found difficult to accept, but the self- and world-perception that the doctrine of Moses proclaimed. How could man and world be less than pure and simply real, the Israelites must have recurrently objected, when 'reality' means, in effect, 'the worldly events that befall us'? But by the same token, the genius of Moses – or of his group of Jahwists, or of whoever invented the tetragrammaton – can be best appreciated by considering that the formula went straight to the heart of the matter: it attempted to convey to depositional speakers, in a depositional language, a direct denial of what depositional speech led them to assume. Moses had, in effect, divined – though he could hardly have been con-

---

18 It was obscure, but not altogether opaque. On the one hand, it was bound to be understood as if *ho ōn* meant 'he who is'; it was, on the other, not entirely unjustified, if *ho ōn* connoted: 'the being by virtue of whose reality all things in the world are real.'

scious of it – that their conception of reality depended on the properties of their speech, and that to teach them his new interpretation of reality he had to take advantage of such properties in order to rebut head on their perception of self and world.

Much less is known about the religion of the Semites of the Arabic desert before Islam than about the religion of the Hebrews and Israelites. Nevertheless, the 'extant evidence in no way suggests that in ancient Arabia there was any marked preoccupation with the idea of ... Destiny ... [Theirs] was a view naïve in its concern for material prosperity [rather than for elevation to a higher level of reality] and also in its appreciation of the universe of its experience [as contrasted with belief in an ultimate reality beyond experience].'[19] This is, of course, the very thing one would expect in a religion developed by depositional speakers. Unfortunately, there is a long hiatus in our knowledge of Arabic religion between the period to which the above statement refers – about the first millennium BC – and the centuries immediately preceding Muhammad's reform. We do know, however, that the Prophet's biblically inspired monotheism clashed with a widely held contemporary belief in fate. Since the Arabs lived continuously under the cultural shadow of Parthian and Sassanid Persia after the end of the Seleucid Kingdom in the second century AD, remaining under Persian suzerainty until the sixth, Iranian – and thus quintessentially Indo-European – origin is the obvious hypothesis to account for the widespread pre-Islamic conviction that fate ruled over worldly and human affairs. The Qur'an itself makes clear, moreover, that such fate was a capricious allotment of fortunes and misfortunes by an impersonal, abstract disposition of nature, without the slightest regard to fairness or justice; it was the standard IE version of fate. Muhammad's patent motivation was moral indignation against this view of life. Therefore, although his positive doctrine – total 'surrender' (islam) to the will of God – included of course belief in fate, its instant success is not difficult to understand. For his was the biblical version of predestination. The Qur'an's principal recurrent theme is the mercy and justice of a God whose decreeing of fate harms only the wicked; those who love him and prove it by believing in him and following his commandments are predestined to eternal happiness. To the Israelites, given their native assumptions – and even in early Judaism, for a time – the biblical doctrine of fate must of necessity have seemed not only strange, but (as Job highlights) harsh and of at least problematic fairness; to the Arabs, however, in view of their previously imported

19 S.G.F. Brandon, *Man and His Destiny in the Great Religions* (Manchester, 1962), pp. 239–40.

convictions, the same idea could not but have appeared as welcome relief from the injustice of a blind and uncaring fate. This may explain why Muhammad's doctrine gained immediate acceptance among his people, whereas the religion of Moses took centuries to achieve comparable success.

In the absence of a concept of transcendent reality the religions of the phenomenal cultures are predicated upon the premiss that this world is the only real one. Though these religions may otherwise differ widely, especially regarding the degree of sophistication with which they develop their systems, they uniformly propose at least two characteristic teachings that derive from such a premiss; in this as in other respects, religions may vary greatly in superficial lineaments, yet remain recognizably constant in gist. One is the idea that, for all the differentiations that may be found within it, the universe is a single, orderly unit; the 'Navaho view [of] the universe as an orderly unitary system or continuum of interrelated events'[20] is typical of the species. Totemism is but one manifestation of this conviction. For instance, among the Australian aborigines, from the 'basic fact or premise ... that man and nature share a common life and belong to one moral order ... [follows that] specific segments of nature, that is[,] species and objects belonging to the tribal environment [,] are linked with specific human segments ... [The totem is] the symbol of that common inheritance of flesh and blood that they have received through their mothers.'[21] The concept of *mana* illustrates another guise of the same doctrine, since it presupposes also that all things are related, of the same kith and kin. In respect of their reality, though not necessarily otherwise, 'all beings and objects [are] homogeneous, ... participating either in the same essential nature, or in the same ensemble of qualities ... Thus beneath their seemingly strong diversity [all things] present an essential homogeneity.'[22]

The second doctrine complements the first: man is an integral component of such a world. And the certainty that man *belongs* in this world necessarily implies that this earth is man's true and only home. This attitude is most clearly revealed by the absence of all preoccupation in the phenomenal cultures with the attainment of 'salvation' – that is, deliverance from the finality of death through ascent to a higher, transcendent level of reality.

20 Leland C. Wyman, 'The Religion of the Navaho Indians,' in Vergilius Ferm, ed., *Ancient Religions* (New York, 1965), 343–61, p. 344.
21 A.P. Elkin, 'The Religion of the Australian Aborigines,' in Ferm, *Religions*, 273–84, pp. 276–7.
22 Lucien Lévy-Bruhl, *The 'Soul' of the Primitive* (London, 1965), pp. 19–20.

To understand the difference between the two types of religion in this respect, however, we should first note that it has always been typical of all cultures, whether ontic or phenomenal, to interpret death as the separation of two elements, the visible body and the invisible (or barely visible) 'breath,' 'spirit,' 'soul,' or other principle of life. It is not difficult to see why: the observable differences between a living human being and a corpse lend themselves to being perceived by all peoples as if something intangible yet active in nature – the body's 'life' – had literally exited at death from the thereto living body, leaving behind a lifeless human being, a corpse. But the usual assumption, even in many ontic cultures, is that only the living body, the composite created by the union of animating soul and animated body, is identifiable with the *ego*; the 'spiritual' or breath-like remains do not amount to the person, any more than the corporeal remains do. When body and soul are separated, therefore, it is precisely the *I* who dies. The fact that the soul continues in existence after death, at least for a while – the body does, too, though briefly – does not invariably have the religious significance that we are apt to project upon it: it is no indication of the immortality of the *self*. The separated soul is, like the separated body, simply part of the detritus left over by death. By the same token, belief in reincarnation, which is not at all rare among both ontic and phenomenal peoples, does not necessarily have the meaning that Westerners are apt to invest it with; it merely expresses a sort of principle of the conservation of life that parallels the conservation of matter as it were – 'all flesh is grass'[23] – that even primitive peoples are able to observe.

In isolated ontic religions, however – for instance, in Orphism – the soul has been identified with the self; and in a few others, as in Christianity, it has been deemed to be, though not quite the same as the whole person,[24] at least the carrier of a human being's potential selfhood.[25] This, not the mere temporary or even indefinite endurance of the soul after death, is what opens up the possibility of salvation; for it means that the world of transcendent reality can be attained when the true self, or at least the potential self, is carried by the soul across the gates of death into the other world. Needless to say, hardly any other ontic idea more directly depends on absent-mindedness than the supposition that one is not really whom one experiences oneself to be, but that one's true self is hidden from oneself. For this requires one to think,

23 Isaiah 40:6
24 Cf. St Thomas Aquinas, *Summa Theologiae*, 1, 29, 2 (ad 5um).
25 Cf. Aquinas, *Summa*, 1, 89, 1 (ad 3um).

in effect, that one is not truly oneself; one is 'really,' for instance, one's soul, or yet more preposterously, as in Hinduism, the Absolute. Not even all the ontic peoples have gone so far. If, on the contrary, none of the phenomenal religions seems to have confused the persistence of the soul with the immortality of the self, the reason is not difficult to suppose.

Unless an ontic religion devises a doctrine of salvation, it can only promote pessimism and despair; for it can only suppose that human existence is an unavoidable problem to which there is no possible solution. Sumero-Akkadian and Assyro-Babylonian religion are notorious instances of this; but the gloom of the early IE religions was not much less profound. The so-called world religions have been unusually successful among the ontic cultures in part because they have offered to the ontic mind the very hope that its deficient self-perception made it crave. The Buddhist form of salvation is especially interesting, because it illustrates the certifiable extremes of self-alienation to which the ontic mind can go. In the other ontic religions, salvation is usually the overcoming of the evil of this world by denying the finality of death, and thus by affirming the continued existence of the self in another world. For Buddhism, however, the deepest evil is rather man's inability to escape this world of suffering (*duhkah*) even at death, since he is condemned to keep coming back to life in an endless flow (*saṃsāra*) of reincarnation. Man's problem is thus not death, but the fact that death is not really final; it is that, seemingly, we are condemned to unending life, or which is the same, to everlasting evil. Salvation cannot lie, therefore, in the survival of the self that we experience ourselves to be (*jīva*), but which is not our truly real and substantive reality (*ātman*); on the contrary, it can be attained only through the genuine and total 'extinction' (*nirvāṇa*) of the self. Only this allows our true reality, which is identical with the ultimate reality or Speech (*Brahman*), to realize itself. Our fulfilment depends, then, on the final and irrevocable dissolution of ourselves in the bliss of a true death beyond the apparent death of the grave. The necessary premiss of this logic is, of course, the conviction, inherited from Hinduism, that one is not *at all* who one thinks one is, but actually is something altogether different and beyond all experience, namely, the ultimate reality itself.

Although the phenomenal religions provide no salvation, this is not exactly a disadvantage; lacking a solution for a problem they do not have can hardly interfere with their positive value for enabling human beings to adjust to their own reality and that of others, even in respect of their inherent mortality. The religions of black Africa are typical of those of the phenomenal peoples generally in that they 'do not offer ... a way of "escape", a message of "redemption".'[26] Much the same is true of the native religions of the New World and of Oceania. The afterlife of the soul may nevertheless be important in primitive cultures – for that matter, so is what happens to the corpse. In Chinese religion, respect for one's ancestors and affirming the continuity of family bonds from generation to generation, embodied in the rituals of the misleadingly so-called ancestor worship, are as significant as respect for the corpse of loved ones is to us. The reason for religious preoccupation with the souls of the departed in Africa is perhaps more typical of the phenomenal peoples generally, namely, 'the way in which the dead continue to be involved in *this life* among the living. There is little speculation about "last things" ... for there are no "last things" towards which human life is headed. There is no vision of a culminating "end" to individual lifes or to human history.'[27]

The ontic mind is victimized by absent-mindedness not only when it develops its own institutions of self-definition but also when it studies those created by the phenomenal mind. Many an otherwise observant and expert Western author has fallen into the trap of measuring all religions, and in particular their teachings on death, by the standards that are familiar to all of us. Egyptian religion has been among the most frequently misjudged, though discriminating scholars have fortunately set the record straight: there can be little doubt that 'the body was regarded [by the Egyptians] as the true basis or source of those faculties which made life a reality ... [and that they were] unable to conceive of a *post-mortem* life apart from the physical body; the idea that a disembodied existence could be desirable was obviously beyond [their] comprehension.'[28] More easily recognized has been the fact that 'the basic trait of the Japanese mentality is the absence of the sense of ultimacy';[29] it is, therefore, almost invariably admitted that Japanese religion 'is very much a "*diesseits*", a this-worldly, concern. There is little attention to "the eternal", and hence to the beyond, or to the ethical causality which influences the nature of the future.'[30] Likewise, such Chinese philosophical concepts as *yin* and *yang* may appear to the unwary as dichotomizing reality into 'heavenly and earthly constituents ... Such a dualism, however, was quite alien to the tradition of Chinese thought, for

26 John S. Mbiti, *African Religions and Philosophy* (London, 1969), p. 99.
27 Benjamin C. Ray, *African Religions* (Englewood Cliffs, NJ, 1976), p. 140.
28 Brandon, *Man*, p. 45.
29 Joseph Spae, *Japanese Religiosity* (Tokyo, 1971), p. 32.
30 Ibid., p. 30.

the Chinese saw the universe as a unity, of which man was an integral part.'[31]

I assume I need not explain why the kind of mentality shaped by the concept of reality that depends on apodictic speech should be called 'ontic.' It may be a little equivocal, however, to say that depositional speakers tend to perceive reality 'phenomenally'; one must make clear that the word is being used here in a sense that would have been foreign to the Greek mind, for which *to phainomenon*, 'the apparent,' was not identifiable with 'the real' (i.e., 'what is'), but on the contrary designated that which is interposed between experience and 'what is.'

2. The ontic and the phenomenal concepts of efficient causality

The empirical basis of the concept of efficient causality is the same in all human beings: since consciousness is present to itself, it can attribute its experiencing to itself as its cause; for the act of experiencing consciously is present to itself as such act, or as a 'doing' (of the experiencing), while the corresponding conscious state is present to itself as the experiencing 'done' by the act. This but describes in technical terms a pedestrian, universal experience: no one who is conscious and in his right mind can for a moment suppose that anything or anyone else could do his experiencing for him. The absent-minded, however, come as close to so supposing as may be possible; for, downgrading their own causality to the point where it can be practically ignored, they easily become fascinated – indeed enthralled – by the causal role of objects of experience. In any event, using the term 'responsibility' in abstraction from any moral connotation, we may therefore say that consciousness exhibits to itself its responsibility for bringing itself about. This responsibility is not, of course, for the contents of experience; for the 'otherness' of the object is also given to the experiencer as part of the conscious act.

Informing themselves about themselves, and asserting their self-information by means of concepts that signify it, all human beings develop, therefore, the ability to make thematic assertions in the category of efficient causality. They thus become able to *experience* the efficient causality at work in the world by reference to their own, and not merely to *behave*, as animals do, on the basis of experiencing what in fact are cause-effect relationships. The result is that they become able to *understand* reality causally: by relating a thesis to a theme as cause to effect,

31 Brandon, *Man*, p. 357.

the speaker experiences an 'explanation' of the events because he has reduced the alien to the intimate, the strange to the directly felt. He will be able to interpret even his own observable behaviour (e.g., his manipulation of objects) in terms of cause and effect. And since he understands that other human beings are conscious experiencers like himself, he will also understand that his behaviour has an effect upon them and their experience.

Let us consider a possible objection before we proceed. Few are likely to quarrel with the proposition that the experiencer's organic, physiological activity is a condition of the possibility of consciousness; for almost everyone will grant that inanimate objects do not experience, consciously or otherwise. I have further implied, however, that the act of consciousness is the *sole* efficient cause of consciousness. But is this true? Can reality not be so obtrusive – say, a loud report – as to leave one no choice whether to be conscious of it or not? Loosely speaking, yes. But let us be precise. Since almost invariably we automatically raise to consciousness the experience of anything that may obtrusively inform our senses, the fact that consciousness has the freedom not to do so may not be obvious. Nevertheless, consciousness can actually reject – at its peril, to be sure – the information it receives, if processing it should bring about a conscious state that it cannot or will not tolerate. Consciousness has the capacity to evade reality. In the case of the sense experience of objects this does not happen routinely or often; but the psychotic, the neurotic, and even the hypnotic refusals of the experiencer to become conscious of the reality that informs his senses demonstrate that, even in the case of sensation, human beings are not compelled to experience consciously by the efficient causality of the object. The same explanation accounts for other phenomena. For instance, under certain conditions one may not become conscious of pain even if grave physical injury has been received; one's consciousness may be 'absorbed' by other objects, if experiencing them should be of overwhelming importance. For as we have seen, in an emergency even the most fundamental biological constraints can be made to yield to the unique power conferred on consciousness by its self-presence: the power to manipulate itself preferring its own purposes over those of mere organic life.

At the higher level of thematic consciousness the absence of compulsion results in the evasion of reality much more obviously, easily, and frequently. For example, since every thematic assertion and narrative is at least in part under the control of a consciousness that is self-present, no interpretation of anything ever seems valid except to him who is open to the possibility that it might be so; epicycles are as cheap as plastic spoons, and the tawdriest lace of self-deception is ridiculously simple to weave. Likewise, no human being ever admits to himself, let alone to others, that a certain fact is truly a fact unless he actively allows himself to do so. Thus, objects are the sole efficient cause of the informing effect that they work on the experiencer; but they have no role whatever as efficient causes in the elevation of mere experience to the level of consciousness. What human beings may be said to have 'no choice' about is only *what* to become immediately conscious of;[32] *whether* they become conscious of it depends solely upon themselves.

The differences between the phenomenal and the ontic concepts of efficient causality begin with the point we have just examined. The foregoing objection is the kind that would occur to the ontic mind, for the very reason that the latter is not fully aware of the opposition between the act of consciousness and its object. Just as it is not certain of the source of the assertiveness of its speech, it is not quite clear about where the true responsibility lies for its conscious experience coming into being; the insufficiency of its self-presence inclines it towards attributing to the object the role of efficient cause of the conscious experience. Now, the ontic mind's projection of its efficient causality onto objects of experience will affect in the first place its self-interpretation: the ontic mind mistakes its true function as consciousness – namely, asserting reality experientially – for that of repeating reality inwardly. But having already explored thoroughly this side of the ontic confusion, we should focus instead on its consequences for its interpretation of causal processes in the world.

One of the characteristics of its own causality that the ontic consciousness will experience quite correctly within itself, but which it will unfortunately project onto the world, is that effects take place *necessarily*; for it is true that, the conscious *state* being identical with the conscious *act*, the conscious effect follows necessarily from the conscious act that is its cause. The ontic consciousness assumes, therefore, that any natural process that should exhibit efficient causality must consist not simply in the factually invariable shaping of the consequent by the antecedent, but in the *absolute* invariability of it – that is, in the *necessity* that such shaping take place. Moreover, the conscious act determines the conscious effect not only necessarily, but also *totally* – for the very reason

32 But even this statement should be qualified. Since human beings are aware of their relationship to reality, they are able to rearrange the world so as to ensure, so far as possible, that they shall experience only what they want to experience. For instance, though many things at hand may be enough to satisfy their nutritional requirements, human beings often go to appreciable lengths to rearrange edible ingredients into confections such as strawberry shortcake so that they will then undergo the efficient causality of it upon their taste buds.

that the two are one and the same. The ontic consciousness can, therefore, easily persuade itself that the efficient causality exhibited by worldly
events is the total, as well as the necessary, determination of the effect
by the cause. In other words, the necessary effect will be *reducible* to the
cause that necessitates it. Finally, since the activity of consciousness
determines absolutely and totally every conscious state, the ontic mind
will assume that *every* real entity in the empirical world is either an
efficient cause, or an effect, or rather both cause and effect. Thus, efficacy
and energy are, in effect, synonymous with reality. If *power*, as we shall
see shortly, rules the ontic world, the reason is that efficacy, or energy,
is the stuff out of which the ontic reality is made.

I explained in chapter v why the absent-mindedness of certain non-
thematic speakers would not have prevented either their learning to
conceive efficient causality (albeit deficiently) or their developing thematic speech (of the apodictic type). I call attention, however, to a cultural consequence directly attributable to these handicaps. As apodictic
speakers proceeded to interpret the world and their relationship to it,
their difficulty in recognizing the assertiveness of their speech would
have amounted to their assuming that the efficacy of speech was independent of the speaker. Just as reality was inwardly structured by a
meaning that it asserted towards us, which was the true cause of experience, words enjoyed a causality of their own – namely, their assertiveness. This power – otherwise describable as the capacity of words
for carrying and conveying meaning – was the true cause of communication. To say that words have an inherent efficacy independent of
the speaker, however, is to say that they have a *magical* efficacy. It would
have been a different issue whether the magic of words was absolutely
and aboriginally their own; at some stage in the evolution of at least
some ontic cultures the question would have arisen whether words had
inherent efficacy only because their meaning had been inserted into them
by the primordial Speech, or by whatever ultimate reality had uttered
the world. The consciously developed answers would not have been
uniform.

The foregoing remarks do not imply that only the ontic cultures developed the concept of magic, the idea that rare and wondrous effects
upon animate and inanimate nature can be wrought by means of words.
I do suggest, however, that it is a peculiarity of the magic of the ontic
cultures that words operate magically because they have a causal efficacy
that is independent of the human speaker's assertiveness; their power
resides, immediately, in the words themselves, though ultimately it
resides in the assertiveness of the Speech that utters the world, which
is in turn the cause of our speech. In primitive phenomenal cultures, in

contrast, magic words have efficacy only because they are a means whereby the speaker can bring *his* will to bear upon things; it is an extraordinary technique whereby human beings can attempt to enlist reality in the service of their purposes when ordinary means such as physical manipulation do not avail. Their rationale can be surmised: for all its intangibility, human speech has the ability to affect other human beings and even animals profoundly; why should its influence not extend also to every other reality in the world?

In the phenomenal cultures magic is deemed to work, for instance, because what *the magician* says imitates the way in which animal or inanimate nature works, which evokes sympathy from reality, or the like. Typically, the phenomenal magician coaxes an object, entices it, persuades it, threatens it, or tries to negotiate with it. Events, too, may be wooed, persuaded, or brow-beaten into happening, and the self-respect or the dignity of the *invisibilia*, or of plants and animals, may be appealed to on the grounds of, say, *noblesse oblige*. The foundation of phenomenal magic is, thus, not an objective cosmic power that the speaker merely taps by repeating, through his use of the magic words, what the power itself commands; it is rather the conviction we have already noted: that in the final analysis all things are consubstantial or homogeneous. This consubstantiality is what makes possible the arranging, rearranging, and the quasi-manipulation of reality by the speaker through his use of assertive speech. Observe that this conception of magic, unlike the ontic, is not altogether incorrect; for it is true that speech is inherently powerful, even in relation to inanimate nature. It may not be so in the way that primitive phenomenal cultures simplistically imagine – in this respect, it must be admitted, Francis Bacon's wisdom was superior to the average witch-doctor's – but it is true that whatever power human beings possess has descended to them from their ability to speak.

This cultural consequence of absent-mindedness has not been nearly as well preserved in us as most others; it is not characteristic of recent Western culture to think, without qualification, that words have an inherent aptness for achieving certain effects. Evidently, this means that we are more aware today of our own efficacy as speakers than we were as little as a few centuries ago. But one indication of the limited scope of our progress is the persistence of the feeling that at least *some* words have inherent meaning and independent causal power. For instance, obscene words are sometimes felt to have a polluting effect, whereas equivalent euphemisms feel 'clean.' If we do not believe more commonly than in fact we do that words have magic efficacy, perhaps the influence of several centuries of scientific and other forms of rationalism is part of the reason. But probably yet more effective has been the still more ancient and protracted opposition of Christianity to all forms of unauthorized magic, on the grounds that superstitious beliefs detracted from the power of God. According to Christianity, only the words of sacramental formulae have an inherent efficacy to produce their effects automatically and independently of the dispositions of the speaker – or *ex opere operato*, as the Council of Trent put it. And this is only because God has, quite exceptionally, endowed them with the power to operate in this way. Christianity fostered thus, for its own reasons, the idea that in themselves words are 'only words,' and that, unlike sticks and stones, they will therefore 'never hurt me.' Separated from its original Christian context, this view now rules in Western secular culture, though mixed with remnants of the older, deep-seated primitive IE attitude, which neither Christianity nor Greek philosophy had ever altogether displaced.

The phenomenal mind will ordinarily be unaware of the origin of its concept of efficient causality; like the ontic, it will somehow 'just know' what it means. But it will not assume that its idea of causality is a representation of something called 'causality' that is part of the empirical world; it will assume instead that 'causality' is a way of thinking and speaking about the world that is legitimately applied to the latter whenever, and to the extent that, experience should warrant it and not otherwise. The phenomenal consciousness will thus use its concept of efficient causality much as it would an ordinary concept: to measure things other than those which originally provided the empirical basis of the concept. It will use this category, therefore, without the expectation that the concept is necessarily applicable to all things, and without excluding the possibility that it might be applicable in degrees. It will not confuse unity, totality, and necessity together with causality, as the ontic does.

Therefore, even when effects have invariably followed the cause in the past, the phenomenal consciousness does not think that they have done so necessarily. There is a causal relationship, to be sure, which explains why the effects are such as they are and why they can be expected to follow the cause; but it is a factual relationship, one that depends on the characteristics that agents and patients in fact possess. Nothing is needed to explain the compulsion of the effects, for the simple reason that no compulsion is supposed in the first place. Likewise, the phenomenal mind assumes that efficient causality does not always and necessarily exclude the possibility of novelty in the effect, since it does not assume that effects are necessarily reducible to their causes. In other words, the phenomenal mind spontaneously assumes an idea of causality that, if it were philosophically elaborated, would have to be described in essentially the same terms as the 'emergent causality' that some groups in ontic cultures like ours have only recently discovered – and that we still cannot entertain comfortably or generally agree upon.

Since prehistoric ages, then, our ancestors, like those of the Sumerians, would have perceived the world as a universal system of cause-effect relationships. It would not have been strange if, in time, they should have reasoned that such a system was itself the effect of a First Cause: the ultimate and absolute reality was the ultimate and absolute force that ruled the world. Now, an omnipotent First Cause is, to us today, practically a synonym for God. If we are to judge, however, by the indications that survived into historical times, until the primitive IE cultures received the suggestion from the biblical tradition upon conversion to Christianity, they never conceived the ultimate and absolute cause except in the same way as the Sumerians had. Without exception, they thought of it as an impersonal and abstract principle that determined all that happened in the world – or as a 'natural law,' as we would now say. What seems to have been clear to them from an early date, however, is that the primordial force operates as speech does: assertively. There is an ultimate Power which rules merely by 'saying' what shall happen; it compels the happening of whatever happens simply because its nature is that of absolute Speech.

Accordingly, the religions of all the ontic peoples – there is not a single known exception – have since earliest times held that whatever happens in the world happens because it has been 'fated' to happen. To them this was self-evident: 'what has been spoken' comes to pass without having to be executed, because its happening is identical with the fact that it has been 'spoken' by the transcendent Speech. Some IE cultures have retained this idea with little change; the Buddhist law of 'Karma' (the Sanskrit word for 'causality'), which formulates the way in which the impersonal but ultimate reality operates, illustrates this well. Others have worked and reworked it almost endlessly over centuries and millennia, having been forever dissatisfied with the results. Strikingly different forms have thus been given to the idea of fate, and widely divergent consequences have been drawn from it – though always within the limits of consistency with the presuppositions that generate it. Two examples of such variations are especially important to us, because of the influence they have had in the making of the modern Western mind.

It was a common conviction among the Greeks, reflected in their earliest known mythology, poetry, and popular religion, that there stood 'behind the gods a shadowy reality, a fixed order rather than a power, a divine conscience, at times gathering moral grandeur, at times dreadful and oppressive to man, the reality known as *Moira*[33] or Fate. This impersonal, inscrutable, and abstract, but utterly real, principle was, as we would now say, transcendent, since it determined from somewhere beyond the world and its resident divinities, and with absolute necessity (*anankē*), whatever befell each and everything in the world. Much the same conviction, however, was often expressed by the Greeks in an alternative terminology; they would say, for instance, that the true and decisive cause of whatever happened in the world was that the event had been predetermined *kata physis*, 'in accordance with its birth.' Indeed, Moira was 'almost equivalent to *Physis*.'[34] The thinking behind this metaphor was, of course, that the fate of things had been sealed at birth, or by the very process of their coming into being. Out of this particular version of fate, however, the Greeks eventually developed the idea of rational inquiry into the 'birthness' or 'nature' of things.[35] To do so they had but to make a further supposition concerning the thereto vague and haphazard *location* of the abstract, transcendent principle. The inspiration to which Greek philosophy owes its origin was the daring thought that such transcendent principle might be contained within things themselves. This implied that the fate of the world – which included the way all things operated and all the events they were predetermined to cause – was not administered by the divinities, as *hoi polloi* thought, or otherwise 'allotted' from above. It resulted rather from the operation of the *physis* of each thing, the necessity that structured it from within. The transcendent principle retained thus all its characteristics, but now was immanent in things. The momentous consequence was that, although necessity continued to rule absolutely, the fate of the world (and of man) was no longer inscrutable; its 'laws' were ascertainable by studying the 'nature' of things. Certain and reliable knowledge, or 'science' (*epistēmē*), was the result of reading the cryptic messages written in the book of 'Nature' as a whole.

The biblical belief in predestination is of course a special form of the idea of fate, and is so familiar to most of us that little more need be said about it. I merely call attention to its unusually checkered career; this is as befits its ambiguity, rooted in the paradox that the ultimate and omnipotent reality, who cares for man, is deemed capable of taking into

---

33 William Chase Greene, *Moira: Fate, Good, and Evil in Greek Thought* (Cambridge, MA, 1948), pp. 13–14. It was 'a fixed order rather than a power' in the sense that its effectiveness was not the result of an exertion that overcame contrary forces, but was anterior to any possible exertion of force; however, it was a power in the sense that it was a necessitating force.

34 Ibid., p. 14.

35 The Latin *natura* is, of course, the exact equivalent of the Greek *physis*, 'birth.'

account human desires. It is a not implausible hypothesis, I mention in passing, that this antinomy – the classical theological problem of 'freedom and grace' – has fuelled the inner development of our originally Christian culture, and is responsible for (a) the increasing awareness of the modern Western secular mind of the reality and the value of human freedom, (b) its dwindling belief in fate, and (c) its ever-growing conviction that the outcome of individual and collective human striving rests in human hands. Indeed, perhaps the purest, most atavistic surviving trace in our culture of the ancient IE belief in fate is not found in mainstream biblical religion – fundamentalism is another story – or in the culture's common sense, but in scientific determinism. But even scientific determinism, too, has had its edge blunted a little in recent decades; theoretical physicists have upon occasion made the traditional scientific concept of causality wear a Phrygian cap. However, for the moment at least, and albeit uneasily, determinism retains its triple crown.

It has long been a puzzle to the ontic mind, therefore, how man's immediate experience of himself as causally responsible for his own behaviour is to be reconciled with the law of universal causal determinism. Or rather, belief in fate being a fixed point, the recurrent problem has been how human freedom is to be explained away. The explanations devised by the ontic mind have thus most commonly proposed, in one version or another, that freedom is a delusion. For the Greeks, however, it was more than that; it was also a cruel cosmic jest. The experience of his own freedom tempted man to try to determine for himself what would and would not befall him, instead of accepting his allotted 'portion' (*heimarmenē*). And yet, since in reality man was impotent to change fate, to attempt to rely on oneself was to fall prey to the vain 'self-importance' (*hubris*) that rendered one *deserving* of one's fate. The idea that guilt justifies the fate that overtakes man – because part of his fate is to conspire with fate against himself – and that his freedom is the means through which he himself fulfils his decreed fate, is of course the recurrent theme that defines the dramatic form invented by the Greeks which, not inappropriately, they called the 'poetry of rumination' (*tragoidia*); for meditation upon the tragic situation of man helped him reconcile himself to the irreconcilable, or to digest the indigestible lump of fate. But regardless of the particulars, the usual ontic inclination is to suppose that, if the human will is free, then it is also at bottom an impotent one. For instance, the law of Karma does not prevent anyone from being the author of his own misfortunes; on the contrary, it implies that he is. Christianity maintains that man's freedom is real, yet radically insufficient to enable him to achieve his deepest aspirations; left to itself, human freedom can effectively accomplish only the self-destruction of sin. And the deterministic interpretations of the matter devised by science and still in vogue today are not less rigorous – they are only colder – than those of Judaism, Christianity, Islam, Greek philosophy, Hinduism, and Buddhism. St Augustine seems so much less austere, if one reads B.F. Skinner first.

A necessary part of the ontic *Weltanschauung* is that all reality is questionable. This does not exclude the ultimate reality; indeed, inquiring into it has always been for the ontic cultures the highest form of wisdom. So much follows from the interplay of ideas we have already examined: (a) that understanding is the mind's inner repetition of explanations contained in reality, (b) that reality is synonymous with causal power, and (c) that power or energy explains the processes that make up the world. For this means that the causal power of reality is responsible for bringing about changes not only in the world but also in the mind; it is the power to answer a possible question. Everything in the world is thus like a solution patiently waiting for its problem to be posed – which is why correspondingly, as Aristotle said, the desire to know is natural to man.[36] In this perception of reality we find, then, the immediate cause of the intense curiosity of the ontic mind: it presupposes that reality exists, in part, for the purpose of satisfying the human appetite for understanding, and that the inherent purpose of the latter is to acquire the inexhaustible wealth of intelligibility that reality would fain it reap. It is, to be sure, quite true that the human mind has the ability to question endlessly; this ability is directly implied by its self-presence. But the ontic mind projects such capacity into reality and, therefore, mistakes reality for an infinite ocean of truth, as Newton called it, displaying its ever-receding, beckoning horizons before the human intellect.

This attitude is foreign to the phenomenal mind. The latter will, like the ontic, experience the need to interpret self and world, but it will not proceed to do so assuming that reality is automatically questionable simply because, like Mt Everest, it is *there*. One must have a reason for asking 'why.' Now, one often has such reason – namely, when experience provides it. For only experience can lead anyone to suspect that any given event is an effect, or that it has a cause. Like a Westerner, an Indonesian sees a dented fender and he knows that there must have been an accident. But he knows this only because he is reasonably certain, in the light of experience, that dented fenders are not built into new cars – though there always is a first time for almost anything, is there not? His assumption is that the world is not a closed deterministic system whose processes are predictable in principle and universally.

36 *Metaphysics*, I, 1 (980a22).

True, the world is relatively predictable, as experience demonstrates; though it is not predetermined, many of its events can be reasonably counted upon to repeat themselves. The open-endedness of the world in no way contradicts the possibility of predicting effects from their causes, if the causes are indeed causes – or of ascertaining the causes of effects, if the effects are really effects.

By the same token, since the phenomenal mind does not think that the world runs on power and is steered by necessity, it cannot easily conceive that anything is absolutely impossible; in reality only degrees of possibility are to be found. In Java, for instance, the standard negative reply to the question whether a certain event has happened *in the past* is never a plain 'no,' even when the respondent is fully aware of the fact; it is *belum*, ordinarily translated as 'not yet.' But *belum* is neither negative nor an adverb; it is positive, and an adjective. It describes the condition of that which has not happened, but which may, and of that which may in fact never come to pass, though one has no way of so knowing. Thus, one asks a *kuli* who has neither the means, the wish, nor the intention ever in his life to travel beyond the next village whether he has visited Europe, and his reply will not be *tidak*, as the Westerner would expect, but *belum*. Since this is the same answer that the Indonesian might give if asked whether his *padi* was ready to be harvested, the Westerner is liable to be misled by his assumptions into thinking that the Indonesian hopes to go abroad someday. It will take another question, inquiring whether the Indonesian *would like* to go to Europe, and the latter's negative reply, to verify that no expectation whatever is involved. The Indonesian is simply operating on the assumption that neither necessity nor impossibility is found in the real world.

Indonesians are quite capable of saying the equivalent of 'never [in the past]'; for instance, *belum pernah*, or *sebelumja tahu*. But these actually mean, respectively, 'not-happened [even] once,' and 'the experience [of the event has] not-happened.' And if they cared to make the prediction, they could say that something will 'never' happen in the future – but not in the sense that it was impossible. They might say, for instance, *tidak pernah lagi*, 'not in-the-process-of-happening [even] once,' or most strongly, *sekali-kali tak lagi*, ' not in-the-process-of-happening [even] with-the-repeated-flow [of time].' The idea is that one should not prudently expect it, because one would likely be disappointed. Now, the IE assertion that 'it will never happen' is nothing but a prediction, quite as the Indonesian version is. But the IE speaker is apt to think that his statement is warranted by the supposed impossibility of the event itself. The Indonesian speaker, however, presupposes that a prediction states merely what he thinks will or will not happen, rather than what will be compelled to happen or prevented from happening by the nature of a causal world.[37]

It should not come as a surprise to learn that the concept of fate usually has no place in the mythologies, religions, and philosophies of the phenomenal cultures. If one cannot categorically affirm that it never occurs, it is not because exceptions have in fact been found, but for other reasons. Whereas the ontic cultures have been few, and relatively accessible historically and geographically to modern scholarship, the phenomenal peoples have been far too many and for the most part much too imperfectly studied to permit universal judgments about their fundamental ideas to be confidently made. Moreover, it is not absolutely out of the question that a phenomenal culture should spontaneously develop the concept of fate, since absent-mindedness is possible among them. Above all, problems of interpretation arise. When scholars from an ontic culture such as ours study a phenomenal culture, they cannot always avoid reading the evidence through ontic lenses. For example, they learn that according to Confucius man is subject to *t'ien ming*, usually translated as 'the mandate of heaven,' and it is difficult for some of them not to jump to the conclusion that this indicates belief in fate. It would be unjustified to enter here into the question what this doctrine actually means; for present purposes it should be enough to mention that, according to other Sinologists, when the context is taken into account it is 'quite clear ... that Confucius did not ... rely on destiny nor advise others to do so.'[38] Likewise, the concept of fate (*shay*) is undoubtedly found in Egyptian religion, as many Egyptologists state. But not before the sixteenth century BC[39] – that is, not until the second of the 'two major periods of Egyptian thought,'[40] when Egypt had come

---

37 There are Indonesian expressions translatable as 'impossible' or 'not possible,' but they do not convey the idea of objective prohibition by the nature of reality; they refer either to a prohibition or interdiction by action of a concrete living agent (who may, however, be known or unknown), or else to the unlikelihood of the event in the sense I have described. For instance, *tak mungkin* denies that something is within one's or someone else's capabilities; *tak boleh* conveys that, permission having been previously denied, the matter is not worth pursuing; *bukan-bukan*, literally 'no-no,' similarly assumes a prohibition by a worldly will or agency; *mustahil* applies to that which is so unlikely to happen as to render incredible someone's assertion that it has happened or will happen.

38 Herlee C. Creel, *Confucius and the Chinese Way* (New York, 1960), p. 121. The same point has been made by, among others, Chan Wing-tsit, 'The Individual in Chinese Religions,' in Charles A. Moore, ed., *The Chinese Mind* (Honolulu, 1967), p. 302.

39 Siegfried Morenz, *Egyptian Religion* (Ithaca, NY, 1973), p. 70.

40 H. Frankfort, H.A. Frankfort, John Wilson, and Thorkild Jacobsen, *Before Philosophy: The Intellectual Adventure of Ancient Man* (Baltimore, 1949), p. 104.

under the influence of its ontic neighbours; it is no part of the *original* Egyptian religion developed during the Old Kingdom. In short, the theory here proposed does not imply that it is impossible for the concept of fate to exist outside the ontic religions, but only that this would be most improbable, and that, if there should be exceptions, acculturation is the most likely explanation. The known facts do not, I think, contradict this.

I have explained why the ontic mind, when it conceives causal efficacy, assumes that efficient causality consists in absolute and universal necessitation; I have yet to elucidate why, at the same time, it identifies efficacy with the expenditure of energy, power, or force. Some of the cultural consequences of this are especially important. First I stipulate, however, that in themselves the concepts of force and power are every whit as valid as that of necessitation. They assert the exercise of efficient causality insofar as it is directed to the achievement of a purpose, and are derived from our immediate experience of ourselves as we exercise our efficient causality; for we never exercise it unless for the sake of achieving some goal. The basis of the idea of force is thus the fact, discussed in chapter vi, that efficacy and finality, two different but coupled characteristics of all life, in the case of human organisms become integrated into a single conscious life; this relationship is analogous to the integration of the various organic functional systems – the digestive, the circulatory, the respiratory, and so on – into the single physiological life of the organism. As essential part of their nature, therefore, human beings constantly attempt, with purpose aforethought, to procure the congruence of (a) the effects that can be expected to follow from the conscious exercise of their efficient causality, and (b) the experiences that satisfy the purposes that they have consciously adopted for their own. Of course, this objective may be more or less successfully attained. And the conscious life of human beings can be more or less well integrated. Individuals differ in the degree to which they have developed the ability to govern themselves autonomously – that is, as agents endowed with selfhood and freedom – so as *effectively* to put their efficacy in the service of their inherent as well as their consciously desired ends.

Immediately available to consciousness, then, is not only information concerning its own efficient causality and its purposiveness, but also about the way in which efficacy and finality are related within it; it is possible for human beings to observe that, within the unity of their behaviour, there is some sort of connection between what they do and what they want to experience. What we experience in ourselves as *power*, or as the ability to exert *force, effort*, and the like, is therefore not simply an efficient causality that results (or does not result) in mere effects, but a causality that results (or does not result) in *intended* effects; it is a causality that *achieves* effects or *fails* to do so. For instance, we experience *effort* when we cause a willed muscle contraction, but not when we cause an involuntary one, such as the jerk of a patellar reflex.

In the absence of its being directed to a purpose, however, efficient causality cannot be legitimately described as 'achieving' anything nor as the application of an 'effort' that 'overcomes' a contrary 'force.' For instance, when I push against an inanimate obstacle trying to topple it, the only effort involved is mine; the obstacle does not actually 'defy' my attempt, 'resist' my power, or 'exert' a contrary force. Before it could do so it would have to *care* what happens to it or to others, and so far as we can tell it does neither. In other words, when we apply force to inanimate objects, they do not actually *do* anything at all to hamper or facilitate the achievement of our ends; or rather, they do not do anything they were not doing before. But, to be precise, what they had been 'doing' before was not an action at all: it was simply to have whatever characteristics they had. It is these characteristics that make it difficult *for us* to topple them; for the obstacle, however, it is neither hard nor easy either to be toppled or to remain victoriously upright. Force and power, then, belong exclusively to the realm of life. In the strictest sense they are indeed peculiar to conscious existence, though by analogy they are applicable to infrahuman living agents, whose exercise of efficient causality *is* in fact directed to the achievement of purposes even if it is not *experienced* as such.

Once again, however, though the facts are the same for all, those of us who are absent-minded manage to become perplexed. Our disability makes it easy for us to perceive only confusedly our own experience of exerting force; we may fail to discriminate between the mere efficacy of our behaviour and the effort we experience only because such efficacy is being directed to an end. And once we equate the two, we cannot but think of all efficient causality, even in inanimate agents, as the use of force; we have projected our own power onto reality. Reality must then be thought of as *dynamic* in the literal, etymological sense of the word; to be real and to have power amount to the same thing, and the greater the reality the greater the power. This way of perceiving the world is so deeply ingrained in most of us that we can hardly imagine how anyone could think of efficient causality in any other way. What would a causal process look like, we might well ask ourselves, if it were not the exercise of power or force? Very simple; it would look the same as it does when efficient causality is directed by purposiveness, except for its being directed by purposiveness. And what is left is a cause that works its effects purely factually; it results in effects that have not been compelled, and it operates without using force so as to make something 'do' what it supposedly did not 'want' to do. We first dealt with this when we studied relativistic causality; now we have also seen that this is how the phenomenal cultures think of a cause.

Behind many of the gravest survival disvalues that consciousness can create for itself stands the idea that reality is identical with efficient causality, that causality is compulsion, and that the first law of the universe is that power rules. For these assumptions naturally tend to generate in human beings a life-strategy that in the end is countervailing: the courting, if not indeed the worship, of power, in the hope of turning power to the achievement of human purposes. The worship of power, of course, does not invariably take a liturgical form; for although the rule of power may be given a religious formulation such as the theologically self-evident omnipotence of God, it may also be given a secular one. The awe-inspiring power of technology, scientifically confirmed by the principle of the equivalence of matter and energy, and that of capital, justified by the growing affluence of all the economies that show Mammon due respect, more typically earn our fealty today than does the power of God. But the rite under whose rubrics power is to be worshipped is of relatively little consequence. What matters is whether human beings experience that their reality is somehow inadequately real, whether they are therefore intimidated by their own shadow – their darkly perceived reality – and that of others, and whether they try accordingly to make up for their enraging feelings of impotence by pursuing the accumulation of power in one or else another way. The cultivation of power is not the cause, but the symptom, of a disability whose seat is the defective self-presence that is typical of the ontic mind.

And yet, the evidence of ordinary experience should be enough to cast doubt on the supposition that power rules. This is true not only of an omnipotent, transcendent Power – there is no empirically detectable difference between a world where God intervenes, but always in his customarily mysterious ways, and a world that has been left to its own devices – but even of the finite power supposedly at work in nature. Lao-Tzu derived his inspiration from this observation.[41] Indeed, even within the restricted realm of human affairs (where it should most certainly apply, if anywhere), power is actually not effective of itself. For instance, it is – or should be – obviously false that almost every problem can be solved if enough effort and money are spent on it; some cannot

41 Contrary to what some imagine, he noted, the world is not moved by forces analogous to those that human beings can exert, but by purely qualitative principles; Taoism was built upon the Chinese version of relativistic causality.

be solved except by spending oneself, and many cannot be solved at all. And it is particularly not true that although human conflicts ought to be settled by reason they can in the last analysis be settled by force; for it is an observable historical fact that in they long run they have never been settled, permanently, by this means. If to the unobservant it should seem otherwise, it may be because the use of force tends to hide the conflicts that it fails to resolve. This is one of its dangers: force masks its ultimate lack of success, and therefore the use of force tends to escalate. The history of the world, so far as it has been shaped by the ontic cultures, is thus the history of the escalation of the use of force to solve social, economic, and political problems, both nationally and internationally; for as the ontic mind reasons, if force fails, the explanation must be that not enough has been used. It is difficult for us to believe our senses, but the sensible fact is rather that, of itself, force does not really work.

The impotence of force in human transactions, moreover, extends even to its non-violent, superficially peaceful forms. When reason is used, say, to bludgeon people emotionally or to coerce them into submission – or even to manipulate them subtly – it is in the end quite as countervailing as violence. It may seem to succeed, but it merely diffuses conflict, drives it underground, and spreads it over longer periods of time. For example, the assaults that we in our culture constantly perpetrate upon each other through advertising, salesmanship, and commercial and political PR serve only to compound, and to render chronic, the civilized savagery of our competitive mode of social, political, and economic life. Psychological violence may indeed be worse than brute force. And yet, there is hardly any aspect of our culture that does not institutionalize the use of at least non-violent force. Even the cultivation of understanding often takes the form of a sort of intellectual Darwinism, an adversarial process in which the clash of ideas (competing, presumably, for scarce vital resources such as peer approval and progress through the ranks) is supposed to result in the survival of the fittest truth. But because our belief in the empire of power is a presupposition created in us by the very process that generates our humanity, we cannot easily give it up. We prefer to deny the evidence that, even when it is not naked, power has no clothes.

3. The ontic and the phenomenal concepts
of final causality

The empirical basis of the concept of *final causality* is the fact that every conscious experience is present to itself as having value or disvalue;

invariably, it is either satisfactory or unsatisfactory, more or less welcome or unwelcome (or a mixture of both). To be sure, it can be either (or both) to so small a degree that the value is practically negligible; but it never is perfectly neutral. A conscious experiencer is, therefore, necessarily aware of having likes and dislikes, needs and wants, and of the fact that his experience fulfils, or else denies, his needs and wants. Thus, he not only *has* purposes, and not only *experiences* them, but experiences them *as such*, appreciating their being purposes.

But if someone has become aware not only of his ability to cause his conscious states, but of his purposiveness as well, he cannot but have experienced also his ability to bring about (or at least to attempt to bring about) the satisfaction of needs or desires intentionally; he will realize that he can try to manage events so that the effects he brings about *shall* coincide with his needs and wants. And once he has experienced this aspect of himself, he has conceived his *final causality*, becoming thereby able to measure all things in the world in terms of 'purposes,' 'goals,' 'ends,' ' wants,' 'desires,' 'demands,' 'objectives,' and the like. He can say, for instance, that his pet 'hates' Little Vittles but 'loves' Brand X. Moreover, he would be warranted in so saying by analogy; for even if the animal does not have the conscious experience that we call 'love' or 'hate' in ourselves, it none the less has purposes, and indeed experiences them. Note, however, that it would be unwarranted, except as a poetic figure of dubious art, to say that magnets 'love' iron filings – unless it were true, which I for one doubt, that magnets derive satisfaction from the proximity of the latter and are in some sense unfulfilled in the absence of the metals they yearn for.

Somewhat arbitrarily I propose to reserve the term *final causality* to refer to man's consciously purposive agency, contrasting it with the mere *finality* that infrahuman life exhibits. But whatever the terminology, what matters is that we understand the difference between the two. In animals the exercise of efficient causality is mediated by the experience of purposiveness, but not the experience of purposiveness as such. For instance, a laboratory rat learns to behave appropriately in order to obtain a food pellet; it learns to relate its experiences of manipulating a lever, and of a food pellet becoming available, as a sequence of events whose outcome is the experience of satisfaction. But a behaviouristic explanation is enough to account for all the facts: the rat takes advantage of what in fact is its purposiveness, and of what in fact is a finalistic relationship between its behaviour and the satisfaction of a drive; but there is no need to suppose that the rat experiences them as such, or consciously. The animal creates a value – it satisfies its purpose – but not with forethought. Human beings, however, obtain satisfaction by intentionally causing the coincidence of the proper effects of their behaviour and the desired end. The achievement of the goal is not merely behavioural, but experiential, because it is possible only if efficacy and finality are experienced as such. Thus, human beings not only satisfy their purposes, but do so *on purpose*; they create values *because* they are values. Only in humans does purposiveness itself become, therefore, a *cause* of the satisfaction of purposes. A direct consequence of this is that consciousness may also be described as the ability to determine what one shall actually and effectively want – which is why human beings can, if they so decide, be displeased by pleasure and enjoy pain. *Freedom* is another name for the same facet of conscious life.

An objection should be heard before we continue; it, too, is of absent-minded provenance. Surely, it might be said, it is not true that the conscious experiencer – let alone the animal – creates values. He merely cognizes, and is responsible for selecting, pre-existing values that are part of reality itself. To take the simplest instance, sugar is sweet in itself, and its sweetness is the cause of enjoyment in him who tastes it, who then behaves accordingly to satisfy or deny his want. Therefore, final causality resides not in the agent, but in that which he seeks by reason of its inherent value.

Well, it cannot be disputed that the properties of sugar that account for its tasting sweet belong to the sugar, not to the taste buds. But *what* sugar tastes like is not to the point. What matters is that *whether* the experiencer tastes the sweet depends on what he does *in order to* procure the experience – for instance, on whether he puts sugar rather than salt on his tongue. Moreover, it depends on him only, since the sugar for its part does nothing *to that end*; it seems not to care what tasters experience. Thus, it is not true that we eat strawberry shortcake because we like it; we like it because we eat it. For it is by eating or not eating it – more generally, by managing our efficient causality in accordance with our purposes – that we *alone* bring into being the good or bad of our experience (and of that of others who may share in the consequences of what we do). But to exercise this exclusive responsibility is to convert into a value what otherwise would be a neutral fact: the properties of sugar. Of course, if sugar is unavailable, no amount of striving will enable one to experience sweet; nor is it possible to know, before one tastes them, which substances can be used as a means to produce the goodness of tasting sweets. Nevertheless, the availability of sugar can hardly be the cause of the good quality of the experience. If it were, the avaricious would be right: *having* goods is what counts as value, regardless of whether one can use them or not.

The differences between the ontic and the phenomenal concepts of final causality begin with the ontic mind's confusion on this very point. Absent-mindedness prevents full awareness of the role of purposiveness in the valuing of what is valued – or rather, in its being made valuable. The ontic consciousness projects its final causality onto the objects of want or need; it seems to think of them in somewhat the same way as some males, projecting their unconscious feelings of guilt, characterize 'all women': as provocative trollops and jades who, by flaunting the desirability with which they have been endowed, are the cause of shameful desires. It is, indeed, as if things 'wanted' to be wanted. Clearly, whether a culture makes one of these assumptions rather than the other will have vast consequences for its interpretation of man and world. We shall consider the interpretation of the world first.

Let us suppose, with the ontic thinker, that values inhere in objects. If so, things not only have certain *effects* rather than others, but are also appropriate or inappropriate for inherent *ends*. In other words, since things have values in themselves, they must have purposes of their own, inscribed as it were in their nature. Of course, unless a thing should have the requisite cognitive abilities it would not be aware that it had an inherent purpose; moreover, it might be aware that it had a purpose without being aware of what the purpose was. But in any event, everything exists for a purpose; the world as a whole, too, must have an inherent purpose of its own – as must of course man. We can be certain of this *a priori*, even if we should not have managed to fathom the inherent purpose of any given reality, or of human existence, or of the world.

Throughout history the ontic cultures have always been animated by one or else another version of the purpose – not always deemed benign or fair – that man and world have been preordained to serve. Our own has been no exception; even today many amongst us claim to be privy to the 'divine Plan,' if not in detail at least in general outline. But even those of us who are restrained by our empiricism from going so far nevertheless often suppose that, although we may not have plumbed it, 'there *must* be a reason' why there is something rather than nothing and why each one of us exists. This is perhaps the most common position we in our culture take at present. We may not pretend to have solved the great riddles of 'the meaning of life' and 'the purpose of existence,' but we are convinced that the questions are cogent and that the hopeless, quixotic search for the elusive answers is well conceived and important. Others are yet more modest: the world has no meaning, they say, because it serves no purpose; it is positively refractory to human reason, absurd, and cruelly indifferent to human striving. Therefore, man himself is *de trop*. But they regret exceedingly that this is so, and their despair reveals their contrary expectation. Evidently, they presuppose that reality should have been designed for human consumption, and more's the pity that it was not. And not only 'existentialist' philosophers so assume, as many contemporary English-language works of fiction – for instance, the novels of John Irving – abundantly prove. What we cannot easily do – though the phenomenal peoples do it effortlessly – is to realize that human existence can be meaningful and rewarding even if its purpose is not preordained but created by consciousness for itself by valuing itself.

In respect of their understanding of the moral dimension of human life also, cultures are profoundly affected by whether values are projected onto objects. We should understand the reason, if we considered briefly how morality emerges as part of the evolution of consciousness. We have seen that when animals create pleasure and pain – *factual values*, as I propose to call them – they do so not in contemplation of their being values; whereas intentionally to cause anything to have value for him is proper to man. But if conscious agents are able consciously to direct their efficient causality to the achievement of goals, then they are responsible in a yet higher sense than any we have met so far. A human being is not 'responsible' merely as the efficient cause of what he in fact does, or for creating only the factual values that he and others can experience; he is responsible also as the *consciously* purposive cause of such values. This is what makes him free, not the ability to choose among values; for freedom is not the ability to decide what one shall have, but to decide what one shall want. The difference between this responsibility and that of animals is that the responsibility has now become present to itself. This, however, is a transforming difference. Responsibility for creating factual values because they are values is the kind we call *moral*. Correspondingly, when factual values are created with conscious awareness of the fact that one is causing them to come into being, their creation itself is invested with a yet higher, *moral* value. The factual value as such remains, of course, unaffected by the moral quality of the act that creates it.

Moral values and disvalues are, therefore, not reducible to factual values and disvalues, any more than human purposes are reducible to obtaining pleasure and avoiding pain. But morality emerges in the evolution of the species and of cultures, and in the development of the individual, as a quality of the intentional creation of pleasure and pain. Whether a moral value is positive or negative depends on whether the decision to create any given factual value, be it positive or negative, discharges the agent's moral responsibility for determining the goals he will try to achieve; it depends, therefore, on whether he has exercised his freedom to determine what he shall effectively invest with value. In sum, once human beings have learned to experience themselves as the consciously purposive cause of what they do, consciousness experiences itself not only as will, but also as *conscience* – that is, as responsible for bringing about its own moral good and evil and not only its factual good and bad. The consciously purposive agent thereafter experiences himself with the satisfaction, or else dissatisfaction, that we respectively call moral self-approval and shame.

The good or bad moral quality that a conscious agent can create in himself is thus no more objective – but also no less real – than the goodness of strawberry shortcake and the badness of fast food. But let us remember: though neither whipped cream nor arsenic is good or bad in itself, each has characteristics of its own that do not depend for their nature on their being of value or disvalue to anyone. Likewise, the characteristics of an individual's consciousness are as inalterable by his *fiat* as are the chemical properties of arsenic and butterfat. Moral self-satisfaction or dissatisfaction has a factual basis that any self-assessment must respect before it can be valid, namely, the presence or absence of conscious purposiveness in the discharge of moral responsibility. Of course, it is quite as easy – indeed, easier – for human beings to deceive themselves about the moral value they confer upon themselves than about anything else. With but a little self-manipulation they can make themselves experience no shame even when they have failed to live up to their moral responsibility; they may indeed be positively satisfied with themselves though they have failed to take into account their moral level of existence and to determine for themselves the ends that their behaviour should serve. Since the ability of consciousness to govern itself with consciousness of its moral responsibility may also be described as its *autonomy*, we may also say that the positive or negative moral value that consciousness places upon itself depends on whether its decisions are autonomous. But I stress that whether they are autonomous is a question of fact; wanting that they should be so, or saying that they are, does not make them so.

The empirical facts that add up to morality, however, are conceived somewhat differently – more or less confusedly – by the two forms of consciousness. The ontic mind understands that values are values only in relation to a valuer, but nevertheless assumes that the relationship of 'being valuable for a valuer' inheres in that which is valuable. It experiences moral responsibility, therefore, under the assumption that values – whether factual or moral – are not created, but merely chosen or else rejected, and that conscience merely appraises the objective moral value of prospective behaviour. Accordingly, the moral agent confers moral value upon himself only in the sense that, having the capacity to choose between courses of action, he invests his will with the objective moral character that inheres in the actions that he wills to do. Thus, quite as sugar is factually good (at least in some respects and under certain circumstances), but arsenic factually bad (for instance, as a condiment), moral objects (as they might be called) such as 'stealing' and 'murder' are morally bad in themselves, whereas 'helping the poor' and 'loving one's neighbour' are inherently good.

The implication is that human beings cannot be the original source of either moral good or evil; they merely embrace good or evil, or deliver themselves to it, or take sides with it, acquiring thereby a corresponding moral coloration: moral evil stains the human will and character, whereas morally good conduct lends them a healthy and attractive glow. But, in any case, man is not morally autonomous; if he were, he would be capable of creating right and wrong by legislating what should and should not be done. And this, as the ontic mind self-consistently reasons, would be the denial of morality, since it would imply that right and wrong were not objective values. For this consistency, however, the ontic mind pays a heavy price: it must perceive morality as a requirement, imposed upon it from without, that its behaviour abide by demands imposed upon it from without; man's moral duty does not include the *introduction* into human life of the difference between right and wrong. Morality is, therefore, strictly a matter of *obedience*; it is not a question of *initiative*. By the same token, freedom is merely the ability to arbitrate among the competing bids for man's allegiance issued by various moral objects.

The ontic consciousness could not but wonder why some forms of behaviour are objectively good while others are bad – why some clamour for being selected whereas others, like morally leprous objects, ring out a warning to the conscience of human beings that they are unclean. But here the ontic mind is on much less certain ground; all it knows for sure is that it is not responsible for the existence of good or evil. Numerous hypotheses have therefore been excogitated by the ontic cultures to account for the existence of objective moral values. The most common has been that a transcendent Will, whether literally or metaphorically so called, has commanded that certain moral objects shall be good and others bad. But this theme can be heard in various renditions. It may refer, for instance, to the impersonal, arbitrary, blind, and uncaring cosmic Law that the Sumerians took for granted – but it may also mean the logical and wise, though still impersonal and abstract, 'providence' or 'foresight' of Nature (*pronoia*) supposed by the Stoics. The 'right order' of the early IE religions – both the primitive mythologies and the philosophically elaborate systems such as those of the Vedas and the Upanishads – falls into the same general category. All these should be contrasted with the version that is most familiar to us: right and wrong have been legislated by the personal, wise, and providential, but above all caring and merciful, Will of the biblical God. Compatible with both the biblical and the Greek viewpoints is the idea that the 'natural law' is inscribed in human nature and may be deduced from the essential characteristics of man; but a 'categorical imperative' built into the human mind, issuing commands and creating moral inclinations from within, may also be postulated. A much more recent interpretation, however, is that these inner inclinations are created by organic predispositions to behave in certain ways. Others ascribe them instead to cultural conditioning, and yet others to a mixture of both. The constant is that something other than the moral agent himself – his genes, if all else fails – lays down for him what he should and should not do.

Within the boundaries of the ontic idea of morality variations can also proliferate regarding the objective norms that define man's moral duties. We need not go outside our own culture to sample, by mere allusion, their wide range. We have divergent opinions on what the moral norms prescribe and forbid, on the origin of the norms, on the nature of their authority, on how we ascertain them, on why we should conform to them, and on the consequences of abiding or not abiding by them. But most of us take for granted that, in any case, our moral quality depends on our conformity to antecedent moral norms.[42] Some amongst us, to be sure, deny that there are any authoritative moral norms. Indeed, the ontic mind has been known even to reason that, since the objectivity of moral values cannot be reasonably maintained, then morality is illusory.

42 It would take us unnecessarily far afield to discuss the difference between the deontological and the teleological versions of this idea. I mention only that both types commonly assume that moral demands come to man from without, and that moral responsibility is discharged by conforming to such demands. If, as I suggest, this is not true, it is of little moment whether such demands may be rationally ascertainable from an examination of the factual consequences of human behaviour rather than derived from, say, the belief that a moral Lawgiver has enacted the rules of human conduct. I do not deny, however, the legitimacy of speaking of 'moral duties' as long as we mean the obligation we owe to ourselves because morally good conduct is beneficial to us and moral evil harmful. Nor do I propose that sound moral decisions can be arrived at in abstraction from the factual consequences of our behaviour. Morality must, by its very nature, be in the service of human life, or else it would not have emerged in the course of the evolution of consciousness.

But even this conclusion illustrates, albeit topsy-turvily, the inability of the ontic mind to transcend the supposition that there could be no genuine moral values unless they were objective ones.

The phenomenal idea of morality need not be any more reflexively articulated or philosophically justified than the ontic in order to be effective in the life of individuals and groups. But if a phenomenal culture develops a philosophical tradition, it is likely to assert explicitly its view that right conduct does not consist in obeying objective moral norms, and that man owes it to himself to invent values and to enact rules of conduct that will help him achieve what he truly wants. For instance, according to Confucius, since '[there is] neither may nor may not'[43] (i.e., since there are no objective moral prescriptions and prohibitions), morality does not consist in conformity to norms; even norms that should prescribe socially valuable conduct. Instead, morality requires autonomy; the morally mature person is one who does 'what his heart desires.'[44] That is, what he should do is what he *truly* wants to do, in the sense that it is what he has conscientiously decided to bring about so as to discharge his moral responsibility to himself. The same idea of morality is among the explicitly held convictions of the Japanese tradition. Shinto 'provides no moral code, and relies solely on the promptings of conscience';[45] its ethic 'can be called ... *situational ... contextual ...* [and] relative.'[46]

Denying to man the ability to create moral values is one of the common elements of all the ontic religions, though it is especially evident and uncompromisingly maintained in those which, like Zoroastrianism, espouse moral dualism. Now, the biblical doctrine that man is in no way the original cause of moral *good* is unambiguous; only God is the measure of 'holiness' or moral worth. But since the biblical doctrine quite as rigidly maintains also that God is *not* the source of evil, the problem of the origin and meaning of evil automatically arises in this tradition. Is man, then, the source of evil? The biblical answer is far from clear. In one sense he is; for 'sin' is freely committed by the sinner's will flouting the Will of God. But this is not the end of the matter, since God is responsible for having created the sinner and his rebellious will. Nor is it laid to rest by the explanation that sin entered into human life through the agency of a higher, though created, Evil One; for God created him too. Centuries of theological effort have not succeeded in clearing up the 'mystery' of

---

43 *Analects*, xviii, 8, 4–5.
44 Ibid., ii, 4, 6.
45 W.G. Ashton, *Shinto* (London, 1905), p. 243.
46 Floyd Hiatt Ross, *Shinto: The Way of Japan* (Boston, 1965), pp. 32–3.

evil. One of the most authoritative Catholic solutions finesses the dilemma: moral evil has no first cause.[47] Protestant theology, however, has never been well disposed towards letting man off as lightly as this view does.

If it is true, however, that man is the original source of his own moral value, and if moral rectitude depends on the use of autonomy, it follows that moral evil depends on the failure to exercise it. There is, thus, an explanation for the 'mystery': that human beings can use their capacity for freedom so as to nullify their autonomy. The self-presence of consciousness makes it possible for man freely to make himself unfree, quite as easily as it permits the other forms of self-deception we have previously met. This self-manipulation, however, can be accomplished in many different ways and for various reasons. At one extreme is the relatively crude technique of saying – above all to oneself – that one has 'no choice' but to do as one does. One can then do with a clear conscience what one wanted to do but would have otherwise deemed wrong; self-absolution is the reward of the very self-indulgence that renders one irresponsible. At the other end of the spectrum stand those who, on the contrary, are so self-distrustful, so overwhelmed by the awesome reality of their moral responsibility, that they refuse to bear it. In Erich Fromm's phrase, they 'escape from freedom.' This can be achieved in many different ways, including such simple expedients as abdicating one's conscience in favour of a moral legislative power one deems more legitimately established than one's own. But the fact remains, of course, that it is *one* who so deems it. He who says, for instance, 'Not my will, but Thine be done' has not ceased to will his decisions; he has merely refused to admit the ultimacy of his responsibility for doing what he does. He does not indulge himself, but his fear of himself. Self-righteousness, if he will but collect it, is his well-deserved recompense for having deceived himself about himself.

Regardless of variant, every ontic interpretation should be called a morally irresponsible idea of morality. Like young children innocently playing with fire, the individuals, institutions, and societies who spread it may well be unable and not merely unwilling to overcome their moral myopia; but their innocence does not diminish the evil that they perpetuate. It makes relatively little difference whether they conceive their duty as doing God's will, living in accordance with the demands of human nature, obeying their superior officer, abiding by society's rules, or respecting the ancient ways of their fatherland, state, race, community, or church. They could be an Abraham ready to immolate Isaac

47 See Thomas Aquinas, *Contra Gentiles*, III, 15.

because he was told to do so by someone *he* did not dare or want to gainsay; or an Adolf Eichmann sacrificing more recent descendants of the same patriarch upon a different altar but for the same reason; or the same descendants denying a homeland to others in the name of the very Right that once was invoked to deny a homeland to them; or a Soviet or American statesman patriotically decreeing the death of fellow humans because to defend freedom and truth, of one or else the other kind, was their sacred duty. The point is that, in any case, they do not do as they do because, having faced squarely the reality of what they do, and their responsibility for creating its moral value, they have freely chosen to do it; they do it because they deem their conduct to have been duly *authorized*. Or to put it differently, their morality is irresponsible because they derive too much of their identity from the nation, the society, the religion, the peer group, the work place, or other community to which they literally *belong*, and not enough from their own definition and self-appropriation of themselves. Not illogically, they will trust their community's moral judgment and prize its moral approval more than their own, because such judgment and approval are the only ones that they have learned to call their own. The moral order of society is not threatened by 'individualists' who behave autonomously, but by respectable people whose conduct depends upon their warranting each other and feeling warranted in doing – and who compel each other and feel inwardly compelled to do – nothing but what national, social, or religious consensus defines as morally correct.

Granted, however, that human beings do what is morally right when they behave autonomously, the question may be raised: why should they do what is morally right? In other words, what is morality good for, and what purpose is ill served by moral wrongdoing? Here, too, ontic and phenomenal thinkers tend in opposite directions. The former suppose that morality serves a human purpose only incidentally; as I said earlier, they think not only that what they should do has been objectively prescribed for them, but also that their moral situation – the fact that they have a duty to do whatever may be right – is a demand imposed on them, likewise, from without. For instance, according to the biblical version of this idea, morality exists, like everything else, to serve the purposes of God – though self-denial for the sake of fulfilling God's purposes is most advantageous to man. But the same is true of those secular Western interpretations of morality, such as Freud's, which propose that moral norms are to be observed because the alternative, on balance, would be much worse. It is indeed 'a jungle out there,' and the repressive regulation of behaviour is the least of all evils. This explains why those who do not fear the sanctions of, say, *nemesis*, or of

God, or of some other keeper of the moral fettle of the world, are apt to conclude that, if they should be specially skilled at jungle warfare, not even pragmatic considerations dictate that *they* should do anything but what they please. Their logic is not wanting. If the ontic presuppositions are granted, the reactionaries are right: there is no choice but either the traditional objective moral values (or an equivalent thereof) or else no morality at all.

The phenomenal consciousness assumes, on the contrary, that morality has a strictly human and positive value; it is a necessary means to the adequate management of the human ability to create factual values and disvalues with purpose aforethought. Its contribution to human life is the beneficial regulation (i.e., in the interests of human individual and collective life) of the ability of human beings to please and displease themselves and each other *on purpose*. It enables them to administer prudently – to their ultimate best advantage – their power to determine the value of their life and their selfhood. They can do so, of course, for better or for worse: the quality of life that individuals and societies enjoy or suffer at any given time is the exact measure of what they have managed or not managed to do with themselves. In any event, to the extent that their behaviour is effectively self-regulated, they enact principles of self-guidance that, though very different in superficial manifestation, uniformly tend to facilitate the attainment of fundamentally the same human factual values. For what human beings are satisfied with and frustrated by is, at bottom, fairly constant, since it is determined by their common nature. The reason why human beings should behave autonomously is thus that autonomous behaviour tends to bring about the kind of world that human beings generally find enjoyable, whereas behaviour that is consciously intended yet not autonomous tends to have the opposite effect.[48]

That morality should have emerged in the course of human evolution is therefore eminently intelligible. At all levels of life the inherent purpose of self-regulation is to serve the more fundamental, inherent purposiveness of life. However, since man's final causality, unlike animal

---

48 The clinical experience of psychotherapists supports the view that inner freedom does not promote libertinism or moral anarchy. When human beings are 'genuinely free to choose ... I do not find ... that one person comes to value fraud and murder and thievery, while another values a life of self-sacrifice, and another values only money. Instead there seems to be a deep and underlying thread of commonality. I dare to believe that when the human being is inwardly free ... he tends to value those objects, experiences, and goals which make for his own survival, growth, and development, and for the survival and development of others': Carl R. Rogers, *Person to Person* (New York, 1971), pp. 18–19.

finality, can be used not merely to regulate how the organism's efficient causality is to be directed to its inherent purposes, but also to determine the purposes to which its efficient causality is to be put, morality may be described as the kind of self-regulation that is proper to, and vitally necessary for, conscious life. Deficiency of self-presence, however, cannot but affect the adequacy of the assumptions under which human beings proceed to manage their final causality. Consciousness, I have repeatedly observed, can be dangerous to itself. This is in no wise more direly true than in respect of its ability to understand the nature of the rules that it must write in order to govern itself.

PART FOUR

Epilogue

The evolutionary significance of the emergence of consciousness in variant forms

The hypothesis that speech generates consciousness has enabled us to subsume a number of observable facts under a single theoretical explanation of how the human specificity originated and thereafter continued to evolve. The theory, however, has performed a service that was no part of the burden originally placed upon it: it has alerted us to the fact that the unity of the human species, definable by the universality of thematic speech and of the capacity for self-definition, does not imply uniformity. The human specificity – the human mind – seems to have appeared in variant forms. The question thus arises: what is the evolutionary significance of the racial division of mankind? Some aspects of the answer have already come up in earlier contexts. Somewhat more conclusive reflexions on the subject, however, will be appended at this point.

A theory of evolution is not needed before one can observe that the quantity of efficient causality that human beings can command at any given time bears no necessary correlation with the quality of their lives. The proposed theory, however, enables us to explain why this should be so and, moreover, helps us understand its implications. It means that there are variations in the degree to which human beings can co-ordinate (a) their ability to change reality, and (b) their ability to manage such ability so as to fulfil the inherent purposes of human life. And this is important because, if to fulfil these purposes is to further the self-preservation of conscious life as such (on which is staked not only human welfare but ultimately the health of human organic life), then these differences are the human equivalent of variations in survival value. Defective integration of efficient and final causality may not hinder the ability to master the physical environment, but it interferes with the ability of human beings to adjust to themselves and each other. When this disorder is institutionalized, the result is cultural neurosis. It is, therefore, not merely a harmless bit of homespun moralizing, but a demonstrable conclusion from the nature of human evolution, that if the quantity of power acquired by mankind should increase without a proportionate increase in wisdom – or at very least good sense – the danger to human life would have increased. Consciousness would have succeeded in creating a hazard for itself. In the case of man, the evolutionary challenge comes from within.

I have said that neurotic experience and behaviour need not be confined to the ontic mind. I would now cite an example that proves it, but which at the same time illustrates the difference between a cultural neurosis that is not conditioned by the apodictic form of speech and one that is. The neurotic character of Aztec culture – a phenomenal one, of course, since they were depositional speakers – has often been remarked upon. They were a gloomy people, overwhelmed by the feeling that they carried on their shoulders the ills of the world. Not the least symptomatic of their disability – which did not exclude success in social, economic, agricultural, architectural, artistic, mathematical, astronomical, and many another respect – was their institution of so-called human sacrifice.

This designation, however, inevitably projects onto it the biblical meaning of the term: the offer of a propitiatory victim to a postulated higher power, in the expectation that man's self-abasement will procure the expiation of offence, the placation of wrath, or some other supernatural favour. The Aztec ritual involved no sacrifice in this sense. It presupposed instead a belief that to us may seem fantastic – namely, that the sun fed on human blood – but that is not quite as gratuitous an idea as it may appear at first glance. It is a fact that human beings depend both directly and indirectly upon the sun for health and continued existence – though the dependence, as we know, is unilateral. The Aztec mistake lay in thinking that the sun depended on man quite as man did on the sun. The nature of their mistake, however, reveals a typically phenomenal orientation. Their assumption was that the world is a co-operative commonwealth: if the sun is the food of human life, human life must be the food of the sun. The detailed Aztec knowledge of the apparent irregularities of the celestial motions, moreover, gave colour to their fears that unless the sun were properly nourished it would become enfeebled and, to human detriment, fail to rise. Thus, 'it was not ... an innate tendency to cruelty, but a fanatical belief in man's duty'[1]

1 Walter Krickeberg et al., *Pre-Columbian American Religions* (New York, 1969), p. 50.

and a 'deep-seated idea of man's responsibility'[2] that explain the meaning of the fact. Originally the Aztec victims were drawn from volunteers among their own ranks, though in later times the place of honour was more commonly reserved for prisoners of war; it should not have been difficult to find excellent rationalizations for this development. In either case, however, the Aztecs were animated by a moral motive that we should understand very well and from which they derived, unfortunately, much the same glow of self-respect as we do: patriotism.

Theirs was, to be sure, an exaggerated, abnormal sense of moral obligation; it corresponds to the equally compulsive, equally abnormal moral sensibility that upon not so rare or exclusively ancient occasion has led the ontic cultures cold-bloodedly to kill and cheerfully to die for the sake of God, Freedom, Justice, History, Nation, Race, Honour, and Truth. It is attributable to the inner logic of a phenomenal consciousness that goes to the same insane extremes as we do, though for diametrically opposite reasons: since the phenomenal consciousness experiences itself as the original and sole source of its assertions, it must feel solely and ultimately accountable to itself for whatever it does with itself. It can, therefore, become overwhelmed by its freedom; its responsibility for *originating* the value of its life for better and for worse may be more than it can bear. Thus, *les extrêmes se touchent*. Whereas arrogance and self-righteousness are the favourite excesses of the ontic cultures, and inquisitorial torture and holy war (in either secular or religious variants) its most dangerous ones, self-effacement and self-doubt, sometimes grown to murderous proportions – for example, when Indonesians run *amuk* – are those of the phenomenal mind gone mad. We are not wrong, of course, to recoil with horror from the Aztec practice of human sacrifice. But we are morally blind if we do not recognize comparable, indeed, worse, forms of insanity in ourselves. Of course, part of every insanity consists in having difficulty in recognizing the insanity for what it is. (Another part is to deem abnormal the conduct of the sane.)

We do not lack for non-evolutionary explanations of mankind's cultural neuroses; for instance, it is a widespread notion – available in a gamut of versions ranging from the theological to the sociological – that mismanagement, profound disruptions, self-contradictions, and idiocies are the inevitable price of civilization and progress. Why the nature of civilization and progress should entail these evils, however, is not always made clear. Circular argumentation abounds. Herbert Marcuse was among those who have rather realized that the insanity of cultures has of itself

2 Pierre Grimal, ed., *Larousse World Mythology* (London, 1965), p. 462.

nothing to do with civilization as such – though his explanation of 'repression' as a social rather than as an intrapsychic process is, I think, no more accurate than Freud's.[3] Cultural neurosis, as I have suggested, is rather the contingent though logical outcome of events that were part of human evolution.

I now add, however, that socio-culturally even more than individually mental illness and the self-posed threat to conscious life are contagious. Though the ontic mind's mental disabilities are congenital, it is possible for all human beings and for all cultures to contract them from each other. And in point of fact, cultural insanity seems to have spread; in the record of mankind's cultural evolution we may read the stages of the process. The 5,500-year–long history of human civilization has been characterized by the increasing ascendancy of the ontic cultures over the phenomenal. In recent centuries this trend has accelerated and taken on the particular form known as the cultural homogenization of the species through acculturation to the West. The contemporary situation of mankind illustrates well how the neurotic dispositions of the ontic mind can affect others as well as itself; for the ontic cultures are alone responsible for having originated the sort of peril that today threatens the life of the human species as a whole.

Human evolution, however, practises double-entry bookkeeping, and so far I have discussed only one side of the balance sheet. The proposed theory implies that the same differences between the ontic and the phenomenal forms of consciousness that from the viewpoint of individual cultures amount to differences in mental health and survivability, from the wider perspective of the species as a whole may have a most important evolutionary role. Indeed, for all the dangers that the ontic consciousness poses for the human species, it is most useful for mankind that thematic speech and self-definition appeared in both variant forms. The potential benefit is that exchange of information between the two forms of consciousness could bring about what neither one could produce by itself: awareness of the presuppositions that the form of thematic speech creates in them. And such awareness would promote human self-adaptation – the conscious self-selection of consciousness – and

---

3 But Freud was correct, I believe, in several other respects. He thought that religion, 'perhaps the most important part of the psychical inventory of a culture' (*The Future of an Illusion* [London, 1955], p. 24), was the key to understanding cultural neuroses; and his diagnosis of our own culture's dysfunction as an 'obsessional neurosis' (p. 76) accords very well with the repetition-compulsion *motifs* that are typical of the semantic complex. I think that Freud was wrong, however, when he generalized unwarrantedly from our culture to all mankind and therefore took religion for a 'universal' (p. 76) cultural neurosis.

therefore the welfare and survival of the species. How does the theory support this conclusion?

The mere reproduction of life – an organism's production of an exact duplicate of itself – cannot result in evolution. All evolution depends on the selection of characteristics, and without variations in characteristics there are no 'options' from which selection can take place. At the most primitive levels of life, therefore, when the reproductive power of the organism is no more than its ability to divide itself, evolution is possible only because variations are introduced extraneously into the reproductive process, as 'noise' creeps into the communication of genetic information. When evolution depended exclusively on this sort of reproductive system, it operated negatively and inefficiently. To this may be contrasted the operation of natural selection when it eventually developed sexuality. The sexual mode of reproduction worked for evolution because, almost paradoxically, it served simultaneously to reproduce and to differentiate. As noted earlier, however, sexual reproduction has inherent limitations; it facilitates the perpetuation and accumulation of adaptive improvements only to the extent that they are embedded in the genes. Mankind came into being only because natural selection created speech, a new form of reproduction that was not so limited. But how did this new reproductive mechanism provide for the continued evolution of the consciousness that it generated?

Human evolution does not violate any of the principles of infrahuman evolution. Without individual variations in the quality of consciousness, human nature could not evolve. In itself, however, this is not a problem. Such differences are inherently possible, indeed inevitable, among human individuals – if for no other reason because consciousness is conditioned by organic structures that are subject to genetic variation. But human evolution was faced with the same hurdle that organic evolution once had been: a reproductive system that should have done nothing but reproduce in offspring the consciousness of the parents would have preserved sameness, but would have generated no differences. To the extent that speech served merely to reproduce in the human young the older generation's ability to experience consciously, it suffered from the same limitation, in its own order, that asexual organic reproduction did in its. If human evolution was to have enjoyed an increase in efficiency, rapidity, and positive orientation analogous to that which sexual reproduction had provided for infrahuman evolution, it was necessary that primitive, non-thematic speech develop so that it could do for the evolution of consciousness what sexuality had done for the evolution of infrahuman life. Such development is precisely what the emergence of *thematic* speech represents.

Socio-cultural reproduction, then, overcame the limitations of organic reproduction – but not all at once. The two stages, non-thematic and thematic, of human evolution parallel the two stages, asexual and sexual, through which the evolutionary mechanism had itself progressed before it evolved again in man. Socio-cultural reproduction overcame first the most basic limitation of all organic reproduction, namely, its dependence on the endowment of a structure, the reproductive cell. Non-thematic speech endows the offspring with a purely functional ability – the ability to speak – which the offspring uses to develop its genetically conditioned experiential power into the power to experience consciously. But non-thematic speech reproduces consciousness as invariantly as asexual reproduction does the organism, since it comes in one form only. To be sure, individual non-thematic speakers may differ in assertiveness; but these differences are not transmissible from generation to generation when the 'idea' of speech is transmitted, because there is only one way to speak non-thematically and therefore only one 'idea' of non-thematic speech. Therefore, as long as the evolution of consciousness depended on its reproduction by non-thematic speech alone, variations in the human specificity, however advantageous, died with the individual and were not available to the evolving community. At this stage the self-selective evolutionary mechanism would have operated only to the extent described earlier: it brought about the evolution from non-thematic into thematic speech.

It was only when the latter appeared that the human self-reproductive mechanism *began* to achieve, in respect of the purely functional human characteristics, what sexual reproduction had achieved in respect of organic functional structures. Thematic speech introduced a means to make individual differences in the human specificity available to the self-selective process, because it made consciousness self-defining; and when human beings define themselves by means of thematic assertions, variations in their assertiveness and self-presence are reflected in variations in their self-definitions, which they in turn can transmit by means of thematic speech. In short, variations in the consciousness-generating properties of thematic speech *can* be conveyed from one generation to the next.

A distinction, however, should be made. For thematic speech can make individual differences available for selection in two different ways. I have likened the emergence of thematic speech to the emergence of sexual reproduction, but in the form in which it first began to operate, and in which it has operated so far in human evolution, thematic speech is comparable to sexual reproduction only in part; the more complex form in which it could theoretically work, which is alone fully analogous to sexual reproduction, would have to await further events. We should, therefore, distinguish between the *immediate* and the *ulterior* evolutionary possibilities created by thematicity. The fact that speech emerged in variant forms is irrelevant to the former, but is of crucial importance to the latter. Let us consider why.

Thematic speech made it possible for consciousness to evolve through cultural means only because it furnished consciousness with presuppositions entrenched in the form of thematic speech. These presuppositions vary in accordance with the apodictic or depositional form of speech, but are invariable for each. Since thematic speech is inflexibly transmitted from one generation to the next in its specific variant, variations in the explicit self-definitions communicated through the contents of thematic assertions can obtain, in any given society, only within the limits imposed by the presuppositions created in its members by their specific variant of thematic speech. This limitation could be overcome if speakers became aware of the origin and nature of the presuppositions; for then they could use these critically. They could evaluate the accuracy of their assumptions, and confirm, reject, or modify them accordingly. But how could they become conscious of them?

Even systematic and highly disciplined reflexion, where undertaken – as it was notably in India and Greece – could have revealed at most that self- and world-interpretations depend on certain fundamental concepts. (Both these philosophical traditions discovered accordingly such 'metaphysical principles' as 'being,' 'efficient causality,' and 'final causality.') But reflexion alone could not have revealed to them that the meaning of these seemingly self-evident concepts was questionable, let alone that the concepts were derived neither from our experiencing their counterparts in reality nor from their being implanted innately in the human mind. To learn differently they would have had to discover how the *Vorverständnisse* had instead been generated in their mind by the process of learning to speak. It would seem, then, that the limitation inherent in the form of thematic speech cannot be overcome. For to investigate, think, and reason about one's own experience and speech, one must use one's own speech – and therefore also the presuppositions that one's speech entails. This is true – but it holds only as long as one depends exclusively on one's own culturally conditioned experience of speech. If one should somehow manage to learn that there is an alternative way to speak thematically, and how it differs from one's own, awareness of the presuppositions underlying the two forms of speech would have come within reach. But how could one learn this?

When human beings transmit their self- and world-interpretations to each other within the same culture, or across cultures generated by the same variant of thematic speech, the contents of their assertions reflect, of course, the same consciousness-generating properties of speech; the exchange can only mutually confirm their common presuppositions. (For example, when Christians and Buddhists enter into dialogue, as they have lately, what do they discover but – *mirabile dictu* – that their beliefs are much less incompatible than they had ever suspected?) But when transmitted to a culture shaped by a different variant of thematic speech, the contents implicitly convey one's presuppositions to a culture that does not share them. The opportunity for the latter to become aware of the difference is created by the *incongruence* between the two modes of self-definition. The incongruence would not automatically reveal the source of the difference; but upon arduous reflexion, it could. The presuppositions of both variant forms of consciousness could thus rise to consciousness and be critically appraised; the culture would be able to redefine itself in the light of a more intensive self-presence than either form of culture could achieve by itself. Variations in the form of thematic speech would have become available for conscious self-selection by the human species as a whole.

The self-selection involved at this second stage of human evolution was, therefore, much more complex than that of the first; ultimately it would require an intercultural in addition to an intracultural process. The continued evolution of the self-defining consciousness depended on *cultural miscegenation*, as we may quite properly call it; for such evolution could come about only if the species profited from selecting among variations in the categorical presuppositions of self-definition, and this demanded cultural exchange between the two different forms of consciousness. It is for this reason that most human evolutionary changes since consciousness became self-defining have taken place only in historical times. Exchanges of this kind were understandably few during the early millennia of the second age of mankind, and had to await the prior appearance of settled city life, of articulated systems of self-definition such as primitive mythology and religion, and of sufficient economic development to promote significant volumes of communication among the two kinds of human culture in respect of their self- and world-interpretation. The period between the prehistoric emergence of thematic speech and the dawn of history was only a preparation for the more accelerated evolution of consciousness in more recent times.

Thematic speech contained, thus, the potential for mediating the evolution of the human specificity in the direction of greater adaptation to the inner environment of consciousness – but in two different, successively emerging ways. The *immediate* possibility introduced by thematic speech was that individuals and groups might take advantage of such variations in self-presence as might occur within the limits of their form of speech, consciousness, and culture. But the *ulterior* possibility might bring to the entire species the benefit of the differences between its two races. Although human evolution has not reached the stage at which self-definition proceeds on the basis of conscious, critical awareness of the consciousness-generating properties of speech and of the assumptions that speech creates, it should be possible to interpret the history of human culture as having long and steadily tended in this direction and as having achieved some of the pre-conditions to its attainment. We should appreciate, however, the obstacles in the path of this development; it would enable us to understand why the possibility has not yet been realized – and why it may never be.

The mere communication of self-definition from one culture to another one shaped by a different form of thematic speech does not of itself ensure that the consciousness-generating properties of speech will rise to consciousness. Indeed, the meaning of the incongruity is more likely to remain undeciphered than not. First, the incongruity might not even be acknowledged, if the foreign assertions were filtered through domestic expectations and presuppositions. That is, the differences may be explained away, if the alien culture's ideas are reductively interpreted as a mere approximation to one's own's. This describes what by another name is called *ethnocentricity*. And ethnocentricity may render one unable to perceive even the plainest cultural differences, because it is easy for human beings to hear only what they want to hear, and to want to hear nothing but what they already know. When the differences run as deep as do the *Vorverständnisse* created by thematic speech, the difficulty is multiplied. It is for this reason that cultural exchange among the two forms of consciousness in history has been, for the most part, a *dialogue de sourds*.

The other possibility is the opposite extreme: the incongruity may be overwhelming. Like an individual, for whom 'disconfirmation [of his identity by others] may be ... destructive of self-development,'[4] a culture may accept for its own a self-definition received from an alien culture because it assumes that the discrepancies reveal the falsity of its own self-understanding and the validity of the foreign one. Through acceptance, whether voluntary or coerced, of the contents of another culture's self-definition, an alien culture's presuppositions may come either to supplant the first's or at least to make them recessive, like a gene overshadowed by its dominant counterpart. An alternative route, *acculturation*, leads to the same dead end as ethnocentricity. The culture may

4 Ronald D. Laing, *Self and Others* (Harmondsworth, England, 1971), p. 98.

retain the grammar of its original variant of speech, but it will no longer be shaped – at least, not exclusively – by the properties of its speech. It will be formed, partly or wholly, by cerebrally acquired convictions – transmitted thereafter solely by the contents of thematic assertions – that have displaced its native assumptions.

The acculturation of human groups at this deep level is not an everyday event, but it has occurred; I have cited the historically critical instances of the Hebrews and of the pre-Islamic Arabs. Acculturation can, however, be a question of degree. The steadily increasing ascendancy of the ontic over the phenomenal cultures during the historical period of human evolution has ultimately entailed a certain amount of almost universal – though to be sure, not always profound – acculturation of the phenomenal to the ontic mind. Especially in recent decades, Westernization has more often meant the disruption and demoralization of phenomenal peoples – with their own connivance – than their genuine conversion to our ways of life and thought. But in any event it has, for better *and* for worse, affected most of mankind.

In their extreme form ethnocentricity and acculturation prevent altogether the miscegenation of the human races. If the self-defining consciousness has evolved at all during historical times – and my estimate is that it has, our own culture being the best illustration of it – the reason is that it has reaped the benefit of a few exchanges where the mixing of the two forms of consciousness has created sufficient ambiguity and discomfort to provoke unusually strenuous self-examination and critique. The historically unique condition that characterizes contemporary Western culture – our extraordinarily mixed-up, frustrating, stressful, unhealthy, self-defeating, and in a single, soberly intended word, insane way of life – can be more precisely described as our ever-increasing reluctance to abide by the conclusions that follow from our ontic presuppositions, at the same time that we remain powerless to suppose differently.

I call attention to a telling – though admittedly esoteric – symbol of these processes: the vicissitudes of the concept of efficient causality in our intellectual tradition since the end of the Middle Ages. The history of modern thought is the history of our inner struggles with our assumptions about the nature of causality. In the vanguard of recent scientific and philosophic thought is a concept of emergent causality that excludes determinism – yet deterministic causality continues to be assumed by much philosophy, most science, and all common sense. A more visible token of the same self-contradiction is our typical modern reluctance to conclude that an ultimate reality who created the world exists, at the same time that we continue to think of the empirical world in its totality as having, in effect, the kind of reality that must have come into being as the effect of an anterior cause. Human reason could hardly take a more radically self-defeating form. Nor has the breakdown of the morality of obedience to divine commandments freed us to develop a much more responsible and effective morality than the old; on the contrary, it has simply set many of us morally adrift. In sum, we have largely turned away from our traditional self-definition because our experience contradicted it, but our retention of the assumptions on which such self-definition was erected makes us yearn for its false comforts and, at the same time, forbids our devising satisfactory rational alternatives to it.

Inevitably, the question will bedevil us: is this a net gain or a loss? This is not, however, the right way to ask it. Human evolution continues to be determined by factors that escape conscious control, and most cultural change is an accelerating treadmill; but this takes nothing away from the fact that the determinism of the form of speech has the undiminished potential to generate the level of consciousness that could eventually determine its own evolution without being subject to the determinism of the form of speech. The increasing approximation of mankind to this ulterior possibility, however, does not imply that its realization is increasingly likely. Our presuppositions incline us either towards optimism or else towards pessimism about the future of man, as if the outcome were not to be determined by ourselves but by fate. The pertinent consideration is rather that survival value and disvalue are neither absolute nor possessed by any given characteristic once for all; they are relative to whatever inner- or outer-environmental conditions may exist at any given time. Survivability is thus somewhat like the bankability of film stars, which is never higher than the success of their latest performance. To have survived until today does not of itself ensure survival tomorrow; it only means that one has not been disqualified from the race. But to have survived to the present makes one eligible for future survival with the benefit of whatever advantages past survival may have procured. What changes is, thus, not the probabilities of winning or losing, but the stakes for which the evolutionary game is played.

The ulterior possibility created by the emergence of thematicity in variant forms is perfectly feasible. But to approach it is also to draw nearer the possibility of failing the test. Thus, the only reasonable estimate of the future of the human species we can make is not a prediction, but a factual statement of the alternatives open to mankind today. Either conscious life will evolve in the direction of more highly conscious self-definition – or which is the same, towards greater autonomy than has characterized it in the past – or else conscious life will disappear from the face of the earth.

Appendices

The aptness of communication
for mediating the emergence
of consciousness

A key element of the proposed theory is that speech enables the communicated experience to become self-present only because speech is the kind of communicative behaviour that enables the communicator to experience his reality, efficacy, and finality as such. But before they developed speech, hominids surely exercised many activities, besides communicating, that exhibited reality, efficacy, and finality. Could they not have discovered their own reality, efficacy, and finality as such in any but their communicative guise? No; of all the activities that animals can engage in, communication was the only kind that could have mediated this discovery. It would profit our understanding of human evolution to appreciate why. Let us concentrate on efficient and final causality to begin with.

It is clear, I assume, why hominids could not have proceeded in any event by experiencing the finality and efficacy of natural processes and then recognizing finality and efficacy in *any* of their own activities, not even communicating, as particular instances of finality and efficacy in general. These are categories; they cannot be conceived on the basis of sense information received from the external world. Moreover, prehuman communicators would have been by definition unable to conceive anything; and without conceptualization nothing can be experienced as a particular instance of a general class. When *we*, today, think of the efficacy and finality of our communicative or any other behaviour, we are already conscious and prepossessed of concepts of finality and efficacy acquired as we learned to speak thematically. What we are attempting to determine, however, is what made possible the discovery of finality and efficacy as such even before the appearance of all consciousness and speech. Thus, the problem faced by the species was much like that of the individual child today, who must, before he is conscious, develop an 'idea' of speech, a non-conceptual 'insight' into the possibility of using signs in order to communicate. The difference is that today's child does not have to discover his efficacy and finality entirely on his own; the teachers of speech provide the opportunity for him to imitate not only their communicative behaviour, but also their *managing* their communications and their *intending* to communicate. For instance, they correct his mistakes and approve his successes, and they encourage him to *control* his communications; indeed, they require it of him. In the last analysis the child, too, must discover communicative efficacy and finality within himself; but at least he does not lack for immediate pressure to do so whereas the species had no one – except, of course, natural selection – to teach it to speak.

Both ontogenetically and phylogenetically the communicator's discovery of his communicative efficacy and finality is possible only because the properties of communicative behaviour are inherently apt to permit such discovery. For all communication communicates experience; therefore, any communication can, in principle, be itself experienced as the communication of experience. Thus, if an animal has the abilities (a) to make signals, and (b) to experience his own signals as well as their effect upon a communicand, the possibility thereby exists in principle for the animal to experience the communicative efficacy and finality of its behaviour. If the animal succeeds in doing so, then the activity that, in fact, is an exercise of efficacy and finality can be, moreover, experienced *as such*, despite the fact that the organism is not yet conscious.[1] The possibility of developing consciousness was thus open, in principle, to many animal species. But there were, of course, other requirements, principally a very high level of perceptual ability; this is why only some animals, our hominid ancestors, met with success. Granted, however, that animal communicative behaviour is the sort of efficient and finalistic causal process that is intrinsically related to experience – in the sense that the contents of experience are identical with the contents of the communication of experience – the further question arises: why does the fact that communication communicates experience make communicative behaviour apt to reveal its efficacy and finality to the communicator? The answer is more complex than may first appear; but if we remember the prerequisites of experiencing efficacy and finality as such, it should become plain.

Let us take efficient causality first. To experience it, an experiencer must do two things. One is to discriminate between the events (or the aspects of an event) that are respectively the cause and the effect; the other is to integrate the two as cause and effect. If he did not mentally separate, and indeed, oppose,

---

1 The result would be the *coincidence* of experience with itself, when it is communicated. This is only a pre-condition of consciousness, and as explained earlier is to be distinguished from true self-presence. In the former, the act of experiencing the efficacy and finality of communication is distinct from the act of making the signal; though the communicator has experienced his efficacy and finality as such, the experience of these is only a lived, practical one. Nevertheless, he now experiences not merely what, in fact, are activities involving efficacy and finality; he experiences these as such, though not consciously.

the causal event and the effect, he could hardly experience them as the mutually related cause and effect; and he could not so relate them unless he could experience them as alternative aspects of a single process. Thus, he must be able to look at the same event or events simultaneously, but as if from alternative viewpoints; that is, only he who can consider the cause from the viewpoint of the effect, and the effect from that of the cause, is in a position to identify the cause as the cause of the effect, and the effect as the effect of the cause. But if he can so look at them, and if he further observes the proportion of the characteristics of the cause to the characteristics of the effect, he has experienced efficient causality as such. And this is precisely what communication provides: an opportunity for the communicator to discriminate between, and to relate, the cause (his signalling behaviour) and the effect (the conveyance of meaning to the communicand). If he further perceives, through the process analysed above, the proportion (indeed, the identity) between the effect (the meaning conveyed) and the cause (the meaning of his signalling), he has perceived the efficient causality of his signal-making as such.

The same may be said of final causality. To perceive it as such it is necessary to discriminate between, yet relate, the ability to bring about certain effects and the ability to want to bring them about. For final causality is not simply the ability to bring about effects that, in fact, satisfy wants, but the ability to do so *because* they satisfy such wants; that is, it is the ability to procure (or at least attempt to procure) the coincidence of the effects of one's behaviour and the satisfaction of one's purposes. And this is precisely what communication provides: an opportunity for the communicator to differentiate between, yet to relate, the efficient communicative cause (namely, his signalling behaviour), and its antecedent final cause (namely, his purpose of conveying a meaning to a communicand).

But granted that communication is inherently apt to allow the communicator to experience his efficacy and finality as such, the next question may be raised whether communication is not only one among other activities that might offer a similar opportunity. For instance, a hominid chipping flint to make a tool is exercising his efficient causality to satisfy a certain want. Why could this and other forms of behaviour not have provided the opportunity for him to experience his own efficacy and finality as such? Let us compare communicating and flint-chipping from this viewpoint in order to see why not. Again, we shall consider efficacy and finality in turn.

The relevant difference between signalling and chipping flint is that in the latter form of behaviour the agent exercises efficient causality upon another, whereas in the former he exercises it upon himself. This is important; in order to experience efficient causality prior to having the ability to conceive it, prehumans had to learn to experience the effect as the converse of the cause, and vice versa; the causal agent could have experienced the efficacy of his own behaviour only if he could have empathized with the effect. But though the flint-chipper communicates (e.g., a shape) to his material, he does not communicate *with* it. He cannot empathize with it, because the effect as such – that is, as causally related to his behaviour – remains altogether foreign to his experience. He can, of course, observe the changes in the flint as he works on it; but this is hardly the same as to perceive the flint's *undergoing* the chipping, its passively *being chipped*, as the *effect* of his activity. In other words, prior to conceiving efficient causality, the flint-chipper cannot *share* the flint's 'experience' of being chipped. And if he cannot envisage his causal activity from the viewpoint of the effect, an essential element of experiencing efficient causality as such is missing. Of course, if he were already conscious and had developed a concept of efficient causality, it would be enough that he perceive his own activity for him to perceive the flint's being chipped as the effect of his activity; if *we*, today, undertake an activity like flint-chipping, we require no empathy with the effect to perceive the effects as effects. To empathize with the communicand's experience, however, is precisely what a communicating agent can, in principle, do. He can relate the effect of his communicative behaviour upon a communicand, to himself as its cause, because it is possible for him to identify what the communicand hears and what he hears, and what he hears and the sounds he makes.

The same is true of finality. To experience the finality of an efficient cause directed to the achievement of an end, one has to experience the ends-means relationship that the finalistic agent superimposes upon the mere efficient cause-effect relationship. And the same sort of simultaneous integration and differentiation is required to perceive the former as the latter. For the experiencer must perceive not simply the wanting that moves him to act; he must also perceive the want as capable of being satisfied by the exercise of efficient causality – that is, by the use of means which cause the sort of effect that satisfies the want. Now, the prehuman flint-chipper could certainly have not only *had* wants, but also *experienced* them (though, lacking consciousness, he could not have experienced them *as wants*). And he could have learned to behave appropriately, in the light of his non-conscious experience, in order to satisfy its wants; laboratory rats are most proficient at this. What only prehumans managed to accomplish was to identify as means-to-ends the efficient causality that they had, in fact, long used as means to their ends. Therefore, only they managed to envisage their goals as *intended* effects of their exercise of efficient causality.

As with efficacy, the difficulty may not be readily apparent to us today, who, being conscious, can easily perceive *any* efficient cause as a possible means to the satisfaction of our wants. In the absence of consciousness, however, the aptness of efficient causes for serving as means to ends had to be demonstrated. A mere flint-chipper could have gone on chipping flint forever, adequately achieving his purposes and experiencing satisfaction through the exercise of his efficacy, but never having had the occasion to experience his efficacy as a means to achieve his purposes – and therefore, without ever having been afforded the opportunity to experience his purposes as such. The use of communicative efficacy, however, allows the communicator to experience his signalling as means to an end, and his communicative intent as a want that the signalling can satisfy. For once he has perceived his communicative causality as such, he can perceive his own behaviour simultaneously from the viewpoint of his *doing* the signalling and from that of his *wanting* to do it, since the two coincide in the one action of making the signs. The inherent aptness of communication for revealing its own efficacy to the communicator is the basis of its aptness for revealing also that efficient causes can be used as means to ends.

We may conclude that the efficacy and finality of communicative behaviour are inherently and uniquely apt to become present to themselves experientially, even before the agent is conscious. In its properties we find the explanation of what otherwise would have been impossible: that efficacy and finality could have become experienced *as such*, and therefore become inchoatively self-present – that is, self-coincident – before consciousness had appeared, and indeed as the crucial condition of the possibility of its emergence.

Finally, the same must be said of the experience of reality as such. *Any* animal able to experience its own organism and its own activities experiences what in fact is its own reality – a chimpanzee's intelligence and a full-length mirror are scarcely necessary. But this is not enough for it to experience its reality *as real*. Moreover, any communicating animal able to perceive its signal-making experiences what, in fact, is its reality as a communicator. But even this is not enough, because the animal does not thereby perceive that its behaviour is communicative. Other aspects of animal life, however, cannot provide the ground upon which the experience of reality as such can grow, whereas communication can. For communication is inherently apt to become present to itself as such behaviour – or to develop assertiveness. It is, therefore, inherently apt also to permit the interaction between experience and the communication of experience that, by another name, is the generation of consciousness by speech.

Table of the
principal linguistic families
of the world

Family	Sub-family	Sub-sub-family	Example
I. Indo-European	[See Appendix 3]		
II. Ural-Altaic	1. Finno-Ugric		Magyar (Hungarian) Lapp Suomi (Finnish) Karelian Estonian
	2. Altaic	a. Turkic	Turkish Uzbek Kirghiz Chuvash
		b. Mongolian	Mogul Daghur Ordos Buryat
		c. Manchu-Tungus	Manchu Lamut Evenki Nanay
	3. [?]		Japanese [?]

		4. [?]	Korean [?]
III.	Caucasian	1. Kartvelian	Georgian
			Laz
			Svan
		2. Abkhazo-Adyghian	Circassian
			Abkhaz
			Adyghian
		3. Nakho-Dagestanian	Avar
			Chechen
			Dargwa
IV.	Hamito-Semitic	1. Semitic	Arabic
			Hebrew
			Aramaic
			Maltese
			Phoenician
			Moabite
			Ugaritic
			Akkadian
		2. Cushitic	Galla
			(Ethiopian)
			Somali
			Afar
		3. Berber	Tuareg
		4. Egyptian-Coptic	Egyptian
		5. Chad	Hausa
V.	Nilo-Saharan	1. Eastern Sudanic	Teso
			Luo
			Lango
		2. Central Sudanic	Sara
			Lugbara
		3. Saharan	Kanuri

VI. Congo-Kordofanian	1. Bantu	Swahili Rwanda Sotho Xhosa Zulu
	2. Mande	Bambara Vai
	3. Gur	Mossi
	4. West Atlantic	Fulani
	5. Adamawa	Sango
	6. Kwa	Twi Yoruba Ibo
VII. Khoisian		Hottentot Nama Sandawe
VIII. Dravidian		Tamil Kannada Telugu Gondi Tulu
IX. Malayo-Polynesian	1. Indonesian	Malay, Indonesian Javanese Tagalog Sundanese
	2. Polynesian	Maori Hawaiian Tongan Tahitian
	3. Melanesian-Micronesian	Fijian Gilbertese

x. Sino-Tibetan	1. Chinese		Mandarin
			Wu
			Cantonese
			Hsiang
	2. Thai-Kadai		Thai
			Lao
			Yuan
			Shan
	3. Miao-Yao		Miao
			Mien
			Laka
	4. Austro-Asiatic		Vietnamese
			Khmer (Cambodian)
			Mon
			Muong
	5. Tibeto-Burmese	a. Tibetic	Central Tibetan
			Western Tibetan
		b. Burmic	Burmese
			Lisu
			Pyen
xi. Eskimo-Aleut			Innuit (Eskimo)
			Aleut
xii. Athabascan			Navaho
			Apache
			Haida
xiii. Algonkian			Cree
			Ojibwa
			Micmac
			Cheyenne
			Shawnee

XIV. Macro-Siouan		Sioux
		Dakotan
		Crow
		Winnebago
		Cherokee
		Mohawk
XV. Hokan		Yuma
XVI. Penutian		Maya
		Quiche
XVII. Aztec-Tanoan	1. Kiowa-Tanoan	Taos
		Kiowa
	2. Uto-Aztecan	Nahuatl (Aztec)
		Hopi
		Shoshoni
XVIII. Oto-Manguean		Zapotec
		Otomi
XIX. Andean-Equatorial	1. Arawakan	Siboney
		Taino
		Guajiro
	2. Tupian	Tupi
		Guarani
	3. Quechumaran	Quechua
		Aymaran
XX. Ge-Pano-Cariban	1. Cariban	Choco
		Macusi
	2. Macro-Ge	Bororo
		Otuke
	3. Macro-Pano	Pano

xxi. Macro-Chibchan

Cuna
Guaimi

xxii. Tucanoan

Tucanoan

Table of the principal Indo-European languages

Division	Sub-family	Branch	Sub-branch	Example Ancient	Modern
1. Eastern	A. Indo-Iranian	1. Iranian	a. Western Iranian	Old Persian	Modern Persian Kurdish Baluchi
			b. Eastern Iranian	Avestan Sogdian	Pashto (Afghaɪ
		2. Indic	a. Dard		Kashmiri
			b. Sanskritic	Sanskrit Pali Prakrits	Hindi, Uɪ Nepali Panjabi Rajasthaɪ Bengali Sinhalese
	B. Balto-Slavic	1. Baltic		Old Prussian	Lithuaniaɪ Latvian
		2. Slavic	a. Southern	Old Church Slavonic	Slovene Serbian Croatian Macedoni Bulgarian

				b. Western	Old Czech	Czech
						Slovak
						Polish

			b. Western	Old Czech	Czech
					Slovak
					Polish
			c. Eastern	Old Russian	Russian
					Ukrainian
					Byelo-russian
	c. Anatolian			Hittite	
				Luwian	
				Lydian	
				Lycian	
	d. Thracian			Thracian	
				Phrygian	
				Illyrian	
				Ligurian	
	e. Armenian			Old Armenian	Armenian
	f. Albanian				Albanian
	g. Tocharian			Torfanian (Tocharian A)	
				Kuchean (Tocharian B)	
Western	A. Hellenic			Ionic	Modern Greek
				Attic	
				Doric	
				Aeolic	
	B. Italic	1. Osco-Umbrian	Oscan	Umbrian	
				Sabellian	
		2. Latinian		Latin	Spanish
				Old Provençal	French
					Italian

		Old French	Portug‹
		Langue d'Oc	Catalan
		Langue d'Oïl	Roman‹
		Venetic	Proven‹
			Roman‹
			Ladino
			Haitian
c. Celtic	1. Continental	Gaulish	
	2. Brythonic		Welsh
			Cornish
			Breton
	3. Goidelic		Irish Gaeli‹
			Scottish Gaeli‹
			Manx
D. Teutonic	1. Eastern		Gothic
	2. Nordic	Old Norse	Icelandi‹
			Swedish
			Danish
			Norweg‹
			Faröese
	3. Western	Old High German	English
		Old Saxon	German‹
		Anglo-Saxon (Old English)	Dutch
			Afrikaa‹
			Flemish
			Yiddish

Index of Names

Index of Subjects

279–80; distortion of experience of, by absent-mindedness, 281–2; experience of the passage of, 34; linguistic manifestations of differences in the concept and experience of, 282–3, 290–2, 279–80; nature of the experience of, 279–80; origin of the category of, 279; similarities and differences between the Indo-European and the Sumerian experiences of, 297–8. *See also* Space, concept of, as simultaneous

Truth: semantic interpretation of the nature of, 153–4; syntactic interpretation of the nature of, 152–4

Understanding: as mediate conscious experience, 78–80; distinction between sense consciousness and, 117–18; emergence of, 221–58; misinterpretation of, as faculty distinct from sensation; 135–48; nature of, 117–29. *See also* Self-definition

Value(s): concept of, 343–5; creation of, 343–5; distinction between factual and moral, 346; moral, human responsibility for creating both good and evil, 348–53; ontic projection of, into all reality, 345–9

Verbal predication. *See* Speech, thematic, apodictic variant of

Vorverständnisse. *See* Categories; Cultural neurosis; Fundamental assumptions

Will. *See* Self-determination, human

World, Hebrew concept of the, 316–17

World religions. *See* Religion(s), in general, world

Writing, differences between ideogrammatic and phonetic, 299–300